de Gruyter Studies on North America 3

Economic and Strategic Issues in U.S. Foreign Policy

de Gruyter Studies on North America

Politics, Government, Society, Economy, and History

Economic and Strategic Issues in U.S. Foreign Policy

Edited by

Carl-Ludwig Holtfrerich

Walter de Gruyter · Berlin · New York 1989

Carl-Ludwig Holtfrerich
Professor of Economics
John F. Kennedy-Institut
für Nordamerikastudien
Freie Universität Berlin

Printed on acid free paper

Library of Congress Cataloging-in-Publication Data

Economic and strategic issues in U.S. foreign policy.

(De Gruyter studies on North America ; 3)
Bibliography: p.
1. United States – Foreign economic relations. 2. United States – Commercial policy. 3. Competition, International. I. Holtfrerich, Carl-Ludwig. II. Series.
HF1455.E315 1988 337.73 88-30957
ISBN 0-89925-535-3 (U.S.)

CIP-Titelaufnahme der Deutschen Bibliothek

Economic and strategic issues in US foreign policy / ed. by Carl-Ludwig Holtfrerich. – Berlin ; New York : de Gruyter, 1989
(De Gruyter studies on North America ; 3)
ISBN 3-11-011793-2
NE: Holtfrerich, Carl-Ludwig [Hrsg.]; GT

 – Typesetting and Printing: Arthur Collignon, Berlin. – Binding: Dieter Mikolai, Berlin. – Cover Design: Hans-Bernd Lindemann, Berlin. – Printed in Germany.

Contents

Introduction

Carl-Ludwig Holtfrerich

This book aims at contributing to the discussion of current issues in American foreign economic and security policies. It addresses questions such as the following:

Do the large U.S. foreign trade deficits of the 1980s primarily reflect global macroeconomic imbalances or the loss of international competitiveness by U.S. industries (McCulloch, Scherrer, Destler)? Will the U.S. be able to continue to afford its traditional role and commitments in NATO (Calleo)? Does the U.S. national interest require restricting or expanding sales of high-tech products to communist countries (Jacobsen)? Has the Reagan administration's defense build-up, along with its supply-side oriented economic policies, restored American strength and leadership in the Western world (Haftendorn)? Did trade legislation during the Reagan administration signal the end of the era in which the White House had assumed active responsibility for the formulation of trade rules and thus had appeased the more protectionist forces in Congress (Fuerst)? To what extent did neoconservative anticommunism shape U.S. foreign trade policies during the 1980s (Beckmann/Minkenberg)? Is the Canada – U.S. Free Trade Agreement of 1988 the continuation of a long-term trend toward North American economic and military integration, following such earlier steps as the 1959 Defence Production Sharing Agreement and the 1965 Auto Pact (Avery, Wiesner)? What can we learn from domestic and foreign economic policy choices the U.S. exercised for economic reconstruction after 1945 and vis-à-vis communist countries (Sylvers, Janković, Gwiazda)?

The papers contained in this volume were first discussed during a symposium at the John F. Kennedy Institute of the Free University of Berlin on July 3 and 4, 1987. The meeting was sponsored by the Volkswagen Foundation as the final part of a three-year program that provided for the funding of research by scholars from all over Europe at the Kennedy Institute, with its excellent library for North American studies. The diversity of the participants – prominent American scholars, senior and junior faculty from Berlin and East and West European universities as well as experienced researchers and doctoral students from West Germany – produced very stimulating and fruitful discussions. While the younger scholars revealed a comparative advantage when it came to asking fresh questions, the more experienced and advanced participants shared their knowledge in a generous and intelligible way. I would like to take the occasion to thank all participants and the Volkswagen Foundation for their respective contributions to the success of the conference.

In planning the meeting and its program, a central theme emerged that I proposed to the contributors as a starting point for their respective papers: the tension between established U.S. foreign policy aims and military commitments, on the one hand, and the relative weakening of the American economic base for worldwide leadership aspirations, on the other. Scholars have observed and demonstrated many times that worldwide influence and military power is preconditioned by superior economic resources. If these fall behind or are even weakened by the very worldwide political and military engagement, dominant powers fall (most recently on this, see Kennedy 1988). Can this outcome for the U.S. be prevented by measures of adjustment in the organization of the international economy or by revitalizing the domestic economy through such measures as were initiated by President Reagan in his *America's New Beginning. A Program for Economic Recovery* shortly after his inauguration in 1981? Let's take a look at the history of the problem.

The U.S. emerged from the Second World War with a more preponderant economic position and with greater political influence in the world than ever before. In 1950 the American economy produced about 50 percent of total world GNP excluding the socialist economies (Petersen 1971: 4). This economic potential had already been decisive in tipping the scales in favor of the Allies during the War. It equipped the U.S. government with the political leverage necessary for establishing the *Pax Americana* in the Western world after 1945.

In the economic sphere the U.S. dollar was internationally accepted as the key reserve, transaction, and intervention currency in the Bretton Woods Agreement on principally fixed exchange rates. Robert Gilpin (1987: 6) has taken the view that the international role of the dollar "has been the foundation of American hegemony." It allowed the U.S. to place part of the burden of its extensive military and political engagements abroad in a hidden way onto the shoulders of foreign citizens instead of American taxpayers. In addition to uniting the Western world under the dollar standard after 1945, the then industrially and financially most competitive U.S. succeeded in winning the cooperation of its allies in liberalizing world trade in manufactured products within the GATT and in opening national frontiers to the free flow of capital with the return to currency convertibility in the later 1950s.

In strategic matters American predominance asserted itself in forming a number of military alliances against the communist world when the Cold War broke out in the late 1940s. In particular, Berlin and Germany, both divided

Table 1. Gross domestic incomes per capita, in percent of the U.S. gross domestic income per capita (Kravis et al. 1982: 15)

	1950	1960	1970	1975	1979
France	48.2	59.2	71.9	81.9	81.8
West Germany	40.8	68.0	76.5	83.0	85.9
Italy	27.5	38.5	48.0	53.8	52.2
Japan	17.1	29.8	58.5	68.4	70.9
Korea	7.6	8.2	11.8	20.7	24.8

between East and West, have been clear examples of how strategic choices can limit the range of economic options and vice versa. As a result of Soviet strategy the East was denied the benefit of the Marshall Plan. Due to generous American economic assistance the majority of the citizens of the Western parts of Germany and Berlin saw no future in real socialism and were attracted to the economic and political standards of the U.S. The *Pax Americana* was an attractive offer to most of the war-torn industrialized countries in Europe and Asia except those under communist rule.

Surely, the promotion of liberal market principles in the organization of the non-communist world economy suited well the national interest of the U.S. by opening outlets for its abundant capital and production resources. But at the same time the worldwide adoption of liberal principles in international relations contributed to the dynamics of economic growth. Thus, not only the U.S. was able to enjoy a constantly larger piece of the economic pie, but also every nation that cooperated within or with the liberal world economic community.

Some industrial countries in Europe, especially within the European Community, and in Asia, especially Japan and the newly industrializing countries (NICs), profited economically even more from the liberal world system than did the U.S., the hegemonic partner who had shaped and promoted the rules of the game. Their economic growth turned out to be much faster. Kravis et al. (1982) have made intercountry comparisons of national accounts meaningful, as shown in Table 1, by converting the local-currency estimates into a common currency through purchasing power parity relations instead of the official exchange rates.

Table 2 shows the changes in percentage shares of world exports for the U.S. and some other countries from 1950 to 1986.

The first dangerous symptom of America's weakening hegemonic role appeared around 1960, when Robert Triffin pointed out the U.S. dollar's untenable position in the world monetary system in the longer run (Triffin 1958). Charles Kindleberger noted at the time and later repeated with respect

Table 2. Percentage shares in total world exports (UNCTAD 1988: 2)

	1950	1960	1970	1975	1980	1986
France	5.0	5.3	5.7	6.0	5.6	5.7
West Germany	3.3	8.8	10.9	10.3	9.6	11.5
Italy	2.0	2.8	4.2	4.0	3.9	4.6
Japan	1.4	3.1	6.1	6.4	6.5	9.9
U.S.A.	16.7	15.8	13.7	12.3	11.0	10.3

to that period "that the United States could no longer dictate to other countries what needed to be done in the field of economic foreign policy; it was obliged at that time to ask, not to tell them. Dominance was giving way to leadership" (Kindleberger 1981: 243; cf. also Kindleberger 1961). Robert Keohane placed the beginning of the end of U.S. dominance in the world political economy in the mid-1960s (Keohane 1984: 9). From then on the U.S. had lost the power to impose the terms of "international regimes" (Krasner 1983), that is, the rules of the game in international relations, on other Western countries. The stability of the international system began to be dependent on U.S. foreign economic policymakers assuming responsibility not only for their own national welfare, but also for international needs and requirements, that is, on assuming an international leadership role. As Kindleberger (1981: 243) put it: "Leadership may be thought of at first blush as persuading others to follow a given course of action which might not be in the follower's short run interest if it were truly independent ... it has strong elements of both arm-twisting and bribery." Such leadership contrasts with dominance, which is characterized by a situation where other countries are strongly affected by and must take account of what the dominant country (the "hegemon") does, but not vice versa.

A serious loss of international competitiveness of the American economy during the period of the Vietnam War was evidenced by growing strains on the U.S. balance of payments (Calleo 1982: 45–61). The U.S. found itself drawing heavily on the real resources of its allies in Europe and Asia. It had thus reversed the foreign economic relationship of the Marshall Plan days. The very system of fixed exchange rates with the dollar at the center left the U.S. with no autonomous policy tool when the exchange rate needed correction in order to defend the international competitiveness of American industries. The Nixon shock of August 1971 – cutting the link between the dollar and thus the world monetary system, on the one hand, and gold, on the other – not only marked the end of the Bretton Woods international regime, but also indicated the realization on the part of the U.S. government that the system had given other economically strong countries more and more opportunities to make use of its rules for a "free ride" to enjoy the benefits without sharing the burdens of the *Pax Americana*. The U.S. revolted against shouldering the burden of leadership responsibilities alone in what had become a highly interdependent world with a number of strong economic players.

The 1970s turned out to be a decade of international relations characterized by extraordinary international imbalances. Large fluctuations in exchange rates, the worldwide slowdown of productivity and economic growth, increasing unemployment and high inflation were regarded as symptoms of a situation in which the U.S. no longer fully carried the responsibilities of economic leadership and other countries were unable or unwilling to take up the role or to share adequately in it (Kindleberger 1980: 77). The worldwide adoption of a flexible exchange rate system in 1973 and strong tendencies since then to undermine the liberal world trading system by neoprotectionist policies have somewhat reversed the achievements of the *Pax Americana* in the international economic field. Up to the present, nation-states tend to assert domestic priorities over international commitments or norms. The market as an organizing principle of international trade relations is in retreat. Government interventionism, while politically under attack in domestic affairs in the past ten years, has reached new dimensions in international economic relations (Gilpin 1987: 407). A regionalization of trade and monetary relations has taken place. Since 1982 the U.S. itself has been pursuing a policy of creating free trade zones; agreements with Israel and Canada have been reached, others with Mexico, Caribbean states, or even Japan and other Pacific states may follow. Bilateralism or "minilateralism" has replaced "the postwar ideal of a multilateral liberal system" (Gilpin 1987: 407 – 8) and sectoral protectionisms for specific industries regarded as nationally important (e. g., textiles, steel, semiconductors, etc.) have been spreading. "The return of the reciprocitarians" (Bhagwati/Irwin 1987) has allowed for protectionist demands to be disguised as efforts to promote a fair and open world trading system.

In the field of financial relations the U.S. has turned from the world's number-one creditor to the largest debtor within a period of just a few years during the 1980s. Instead of exporting capital for economic development abroad, it has soaked up savings not only from other industrialized, but also from third-world countries. Most economists agree that this was the result of basic divergences in macroeconomic policy orientation in the U.S., on the one hand, and in the European countries and Japan, on the other. While the latter pursued policies of public-sector deficit reduction in the 1980s, the U.S. developed large federal budget deficits which led to high real interest rates, which in turn attracted savings from abroad (Marris 1985: 5 – 13). The U.S. has been "running a raid on the world's savings," as the *Financial Times* observed (cf. Goldstein 1986: 121 – 122). The growing trade deficit was a reflection of these capital movements. The external deficit problem was exacerbated by the failure of the Reagan administration to raise the savings rate of private households in America. Instead, this savings rate fell further from 7.5 percent of personal disposable income in 1981 to 5.1 percent in 1985 and below 4 percent in 1987. A solution to the U.S. external deficit problem also requires a reversal of this trend (Feldstein 1988: 2–3).

But even if the American economy should keep growing satisfactorily and a major adjustment crisis should be avoided, there is no chance that it could recapture the dominant position it once enjoyed immediately after the Second World War. The economic backlog caused by war and destruction in Europe and Japan not only was a constituent part of American dominance at the time, but created an essential condition for the spectacular fast-track economic growth process well into the 1960s, in which the European and Japanese economies narrowed the gap in productive power vis-à-vis the U.S. Meanwhile, the American economy has lost its competitive edge in even a number of its traditionally strong branches, such as the machine tool and portions of the high-tech industries.

The conclusion seems clear. As economic power relationships will not shift back to the early postwar pattern, the structure of political leadership and military commitment in the world will have to be adjusted to the current distribution of economic resources. In America there has been strong agreement "that the country needed a better balance between security and purpose, between commitments and means, and between national imperatives and imperial needs" (Serfaty 1987: 4). The shouldering of increased political and military responsibilities on a global scale by Europe and Japan is required as the U.S. further reduces its foreign engagements to a size more suitable to its relative economic potential.

References

Bhagwati, Jagdish N. and Douglas A. Irwin (1987): The Return of the Reciprocitarians: U.S. Trade Policy Today. *World Economy* 10: 109 – 130.

Calleo, David P. (1982): *The Imperious Economy*. Cambridge, Mass.: Harvard University Press.

Feldstein, Martin (ed.) (1988): *The United States in the World Economy*. Chicago – London: University of Chicago Press.

Gilpin, Robert (1987): *The Political Economy of International Relations*. Princeton, N. J.: Princeton University Press.

Goldstein, Walter (1986): The Foreign Economic Policy of the Reagan Administration. In W. Goldstein (ed.) *Reagan's Leadership and the Atlantic Alliance. Views from Europe and America*. Washington D. C.: Pergamon-Brassey's.

Keohane, Robert O. (1984): *After Hegemony. Cooperation and Discord in the World Political Economy*. Princeton, N. J.: Princeton University Press.

Kennedy, Paul (1988): *The Rise and Fall of the Great Powers. Economic Change and Military Conflict from 1500 – 2000*. London: Unwin Hyman.

Kindleberger, Charles P. (1961): La fin du rôle dominant des Etats-Unis et l'avenir d'une politique économique mondiale. *Cahiers de l'Institut de Science Economique Appliquée, Série P 5* (May): 91 – 105.

Kindleberger, Charles P. (1980): The Rise and Fall of the United States in the World Economy. In *The Business Cycle and Public Policy, 1929 – 80*. A Compendium of Papers Submitted to the Joint Economic Committee, Congress of the U.S. Washington D. C.: U.S. Government Printing Office: 67 – 79.

Kindleberger, Charles P. (1981): Dominance and Leadership in the International Economy. *International Studies Quarterly* 25: 242 – 254.

Krasner, Stephen D. (ed.) (1983): *International Regimes*. Ithaca – London: Cornell University Press.

Kravis, Irving B., Alan Heston and Robert Summers (1982): *World Product and Income. International Comparisons of Real Gross Product*. Produced by the Statistical Office of the U.N. and the World Bank. Baltimore – London: Johns Hopkins University Press.

Marris, Stephen (1985): *Deficits and the Dollar: The World Economy at Risk*. Washington D. C.: Institute for International Economics.

Peterson, Peter G. (1971): *The United States in the Changing World Economy*, vol. 2. Washington D. C.: U.S. Government Printing Office.

Serfaty, Simon (1987): Lost Illusions. *Foreign Policy* 66: 3 – 19.

Triffin, Robert (1958): *Gold and the Dollar Crisis*. New Haven, Conn.: Yale University Press.

UNCTAD (1988): *Handbook of International Trade and Development Statistics*. Supplement 1987. New York: United Nations.

Part I
International Competitiveness

U.S. International Competitiveness in a Changing Global Economy

Rachel McCulloch

During the final years of the Reagan administration, the United States reached a major turning point in its economic relations with other industrial powers. In an emphatic departure from earlier policies, administration officials moved aggressively against Japan, imposing punitive tariffs on some Japanese products while demanding further concessions on bilateral trade. U.S. officials pressed export-oriented developing nations to open their own markets to American products. Under the flag of "macroeconomic coordination," the United States repeatedly urged Japan and Germany to stimulate their domestic economies – but lagged in making good on its own commitment to reduce the huge federal budget deficit.

Meanwhile, the U.S. Congress placed high priority on passage of a major new trade bill. The new law passed in August 1988 toughens U.S. trade rules, further increasing the ability of U.S. firms to gain temporary relief from foreign competition at home and abroad. Earlier versions of the legislation also incorporated the controversial "reciprocity" measures advocated by Representative Richard Gephardt of Missouri, a Democratic contender for the U.S. presidency. The reciprocity approach would make foreign access to U.S. markets explicitly conditional on satisfactory access abroad for U.S. goods and services, with bilateral balance the likely yardstick of fair U.S. access. Although Congressional zeal for reciprocity seemed to wane following the October 1987 stock market crash – amid dire warnings that new trade restrictions might, like the Smoot-Hawley tariff of 1930, transform a drop in U.S. stock prices into a worldwide depression – the perceived need to "get tough on trade" remained strong both in Washington and in the U. S. business community.

The U.S. initiatives on trade reflected the nation's continuing concern about the long-term erosion of U.S. international performance. To many, the problem was evidenced most strikingly by the huge U.S. merchandise trade deficit, a staggering $ 166 billion in 1986 and $ 171 billion in 1987. However, slow productivity growth, stagnant real wages, low national saving, unemployment, and "deindustrialization" were related long-term developments that cast their own shadows on America's economic future.

These developments threatened not only the rising standard of living to which Americans have become accustomed in the years since World War II, but also the U.S. national security and the nation's central role in the Western Alliance. Some question how much longer the United States can maintain its leadership role in global institutions. Competitors abroad, understandably proud of their recent gains at the expense of a once-invincible economic rival, are at the same time uneasy about the broader implications for future international stability.

Has the United States indeed entered a period of irreversible economic decline? Or has the prolonged period of post-World War II recovery and investment simply boosted other industrial countries to near-parity with the United States? In either case, what are the implications for global relations in the years ahead? What options are open to U.S. policymakers?

In this chapter, I review evidence on the changing position of the United States in the world economy, returning at the end to these questions. Section 1 considers alternative definitions of "international competitiveness," focusing on the relationship between competitiveness and national well-being. Section 2 interprets selected evidence on the recent economic performance of the United States. Section 3 analyzes the macroeconomic roots of the huge U.S. trade deficit, the "smoking gun" of U.S. competitive decline. Section 4 evaluates implications of declining U.S. hegemony for global relations and sums up U.S. prospects and options.

1 What Do We Mean by Competitiveness?

Despite a growing consensus that the United States is "losing its international competitiveness," the precise meaning of this assessment is rarely spelled out. In fact, loss of competitiveness clearly means different things to different people. For most Americans, the decline in U.S. competitiveness simply refers to the nation's huge and persistent deficit on merchandise trade.

However, most economists believe the aggregate trade imbalance has little to do with the frequently mentioned failures of U.S. innovation, management, or marketing, nor with unfair trade policies or industrial targeting abroad. Rather, the root of the trade imbalance is the large federal deficit and a resulting excess of total domestic spending over total domestic production. That excess has been met by a corresponding excess of U.S. imports over exports, financed by foreign borrowing. From this perspective, the trade deficit indicates a problem, but the problem is primarily one of national macroeconomic management rather than of relative economic performance at the industry level.

Others see the loss of competitiveness in terms of declining U.S. market shares – shares of domestic or foreign markets, across the board or in specific industries, especially certain basic industries (e.g., automobiles, steel) or the high-technology industries in which U.S. firms so recently enjoyed a commanding lead over rivals abroad (e.g., computers, aircraft). As this perspective suggests, an important aspect of the national concern about competitiveness is the uneasiness with which many Americans regard the shifting composition of U.S. output and employment. Yet there is no consensus about the "right" composition of economic activity in a modern industrial economy. Where some see and deplore deindustrialization, others celebrate the dawn of a new "information economy" in which knowledge and skills will displace metals and fuels as the key primary inputs to industrial production.

Still another view of international competitiveness is in terms of the growth of U.S. employment, wages, or productivity relative to that abroad. Such definitions tie success in international competition, basically a means rather than an end in itself, to one ultimate objective of national policy: a rising standard of living for American citizens.

The President's Commission on Industrial Competitiveness, appointed by President Reagan in 1983, adopted its own definition combining several of these elements:

> Competitiveness is the degree to which a nation can, under free and fair market conditions, produce goods and services that meet the test of international markets while at the same time maintaining or expanding the real incomes of its citizens (President's Commission on Industrial Competitiveness 1985: 6).

The Commission's task was to assess the state of U.S. international competitiveness and to recommend ways to restore the nation's preeminence in world markets. Although greatly concerned about the nation's growing trade deficit, members of the Commission sought by their choice of definition implicitly to rule out corrective prescriptions based mainly on wage cuts, devaluation, or protectionism.[1] Instead, the Commission's recommendations emphasized measures to spur U.S. productivity growth, including increased incentives for research and development and for capital formation, improved education at all levels, and better labor-management relations.

But while measures to spur productivity growth can be desirable elements of public policy, they are not necessarily effective means of reducing the trade deficit. Among the Commission's specific proposals were some that would surely aid the efficient functioning of the U.S. economy. However, most such proposals would be equally worth implementing in an economy closed to international competition. Moreover, because productivity-enhancing measures affect primarily microeconomic efficiency rather than macroeconomic relationships, the impact of their successful implementation on the nation's aggregate trade deficit could be negligible – or even perverse.[2]

2 Indicators of U.S. Economic Performance

These alternative definitions suggest that "international competitiveness" has many dimensions, and that any objective measure is likely to give at best an incomplete assessment for even a single dimension. However, the definitions do provide a useful framework for weighing evidence on recent trends in U.S. performance, relative both to the nation's own past history and to the current performance of major industrial competitors.

2.1 Aggregate Trade Balances

By far the most dramatic indicator of lagging U.S. performance was the rapid deterioration of the nation's balance on merchandise trade. The United States experienced its first merchandise trade deficit of the postwar period in 1971. That deficit, just over $ 2 billion, looks insignificant in comparison to recent figures, yet to some it was a clear sign that U.S. producers could no longer ignore the challenge from competitors abroad. In fact, the United States showed a merchandise trade surplus in only two of the subsequent seventeen years.

A broader measure of U.S. international performance is the balance on "goods and services" trade, including travel, transportation, and other "invisible" transactions along with trade in tangible goods. Here for a time U.S. prospects seemed brighter; a rising surplus on service transactions offset the usually negative net figure for merchandise trade.

With the vast majority of U.S. workers employed in service industries, some interpreted the growing surplus on services as evidence that U.S. international comparative advantage was shifting from goods to services. In contrast to the sharp deterioration of U.S. merchandise trade performance during the first half of the 1980s, services continued to make a significant positive contribution. As recently as 1982, the U.S. surplus on service transactions was large enough to reverse a sizable deficit on merchandise trade, so that the United States still showed a global surplus on trade in goods and services.

The optimistic assessment that growth in service exports could compensate for declining U.S. performance on merchandise trade was, however, at odds with the facts. The healthy growth in the U.S. surplus on service trade was due mainly to increases in net earnings on foreign investments at a time of unusually high interest rates. Interest rates worldwide fell dramatically in the mid-1980s, although there was evidence by 1987 of a return to somewhat higher rates. But in the meantime the U.S. net investment position has been reversed, with the United States emerging as the leading borrower in international capital markets. Accordingly, the contribution of investment income to U.S. current-account performance has shrunk and even become negative during some periods.

In contrast, some U.S. service exports do have the potential for rapid expansion. The sectors most likely to expand international sales in the near future are knowledge-based business services such as insurance, banking, and telecommunications. However, these sectors currently account for a very minor portion of U.S. earnings from service exports. Thus, even highly favorable global conditions for these industries can be expected to have only a modest effect on the nations's overall trade position.[3]

While aggregate trade balances are the data used most often to "document" the extent of the deterioration in U.S. competitiveness, they are a relatively poor indicator of the nation's overall economic performance.[4] Aggregate trade imbalances are viewed by economists as a reflection of basic macroeconomic relationships, specifically the relationship of overall national spending to overall national production. While a large and growing trade imbalance is indeed a problem and deserves national attention, it is not primarily a problem of productive efficiency. The macroeconomic roots of the trade deficit and the merits of alternative macroeconomic remedies available to the United States are analyzed in greater detail in section 3.

2.2 Technology and Trade

Until the end of the 1960s, the technology gap between the United States and other industrial nations appeared to provide a permanent advantage to U.S. firms over competitors abroad, especially for the high-technology industries. Massive public and private expenditures on research and development (R & D) created a steady stream of new products and processes. Early access to these innovations allowed American manufacturing to remain internationally competitive despite labor compensation far higher than that abroad.

That a technological edge was essential to U.S. trade performance can be seen from two diverging trends: in high-technology industries (defined in terms of their proportion of "professional, technical, and kindred" employment or by R & D as a fraction of sales), the trade surplus continued to increase, while in the rest of manufacturing there was a rising deficit. As late as 1980 the U.S. trade position in high-technology manufacturing was still rising almost every year; net trade in other manufacturing followed an opposite trend.

But even while experts remained busy theorizing about the economic and social forces that would prevent other nations from catching up to the United States, the technology gap began to vanish with a speed few had anticipated. And with the closing of the technology gap came an even more rapid erosion of postwar trade and investment relationships based on U.S. technological superiority.

The decline of U.S. technological preeminence reflected several major changes in the global economic environment. Some were new developments, but equally significant was the recovery in Europe and Asia from wartime destruction and dislocations. In retrospect, any modern-day technology gap is better interpreted as a temporary disequilibrium rather than a permanent feature of the world order. Under normal conditions, new knowledge, no matter where created, quickly becomes available to other potential users around the globe.

Of the many channels by which new knowledge is disseminated internationally, most important is the movement of people. Prior to World War II, many American scientists went abroad to complete their education. In the 1930s and 1940s, the U.S. scientific establishment was boosted by a rapid influx of distinguished European scientists. Even today, immigrant scientists constitute a large fraction of U.S. researchers. They in turn contribute to knowledge flows from the United States to other nations through research publications, teaching, personal communication with foreign scholars, and temporary or permanent return to their native lands.

The worldwide dissemination of new scientific and technical knowledge has been reinforced by national policies abroad. Impressed by U.S. gains from technology-driven growth, other industrial nations have stepped up their own R & D expenditures. A number of developing countries have done likewise. Although some of these R & D funds have supported basic research, a large part has been used specifically to speed the acquisition and adaptation of technology from abroad, especially from the United States. Dramatic improvements in communications and transportation have also helped to further internationalize education, research, and production activities.

The growth of U.S. multinational corporations served as a major vehicle for the international transfer of new commercial technology, first to postwar Europe and later to a number of developing nations. Multinationals provided not only access to proprietary technological information but also to the know-how and financial capital needed to implement the new technologies. The technology-disseminating activities of multinationals, although profit-motivated, were in many case actively encouraged by host countries' policies toward direct investment and technology transfer.

While the postwar scientific and technological advances in Europe and Asia were undeniably impressive, these gains were made possible in large part by the existence of a technology gap between the United States and other industrial nations. Even in those cases where considerations of national security prompted the United States to limit foreign access to its advanced technology, scientists abroad were often able to duplicate U.S. results at a small fraction of the original cost. But as other nations achieve parity with the United States in scientific and technological endeavors, global patterns of innovation and dissemination will undergo corresponding changes.

Like other nations, the United States has always derived substantial benefits from imported scientific and technological knowledge. In the postwar period, however, the significant U.S. lead in most areas meant that this source of advance was of only secondary importance. While catch-up abroad entails painful adjustments for the U.S. economy, it also means a potential increase in U.S. gains from technological imports. Although the specter of other nations closing the technology gap is evidently distasteful to some nationalistic Americans, over the long term it offers the opportunity for mutual gains through expanded two-way trade in new knowledge. Other consequences include greater U.S. participation in international cooperative research projects and commercial joint ventures, trends already well underway.

2.3 Investments in Science and Technology

Comparisons of aggregate spending for R & D are often used as indicators of future trends in national performance in science and technology. However, evaluations based on these statistics are complicated by at least four factors: the huge size of the United States economy, the importance of defense-related expenditures in the U.S. total, differences in types of support used by the United States and its major rivals, and the growing R & D activities of U.S. companies abroad.

Critics of U.S. policy argue that the United States has "fallen behind" in research and development, relative both to other major nations today and to its own past efforts. This assessment is based largely on comparisons of R & D spending as a share of gross national product (GNP), a measure that shows other nations catching up or even surpassing the United States. Yet the United States still spends far more in total than any other OECD nation, a reflection of the nation's much larger size. (The Soviet Union, not an OECD member, is estimated to allocate an amount comparable to that of the United States.)

R & D spending as a fraction of GNP varies little across the major industrial nations, but there are significant differences in the allocation of funds among alternative uses. In relation to its major commercial rivals, the United States skews its R & D resources toward defense projects and basic research. Among the major nations, West Germany and Japan devote the highest proportion of GNP to nondefense R & D spending. In addition, the United States is alone among major nations in its almost negligible direct support of commercial R & D projects. These funding patterns help to explain why the United States has been able to maintain its lead in most areas of military technology and basic science but has lost ground to other nations, especially Japan, in translating U.S. scientific advances into commercial gains.

Moreover, a significant share of "foreign" R & D is actually performed by subsidiaries abroad of U.S. firms. An important recent example is the breakthrough in superconductivity research that earned the Nobel prize for two IBM scientists working in the firm's Swiss laboratories. A similar phenomenon exists for European and Japanese firms operating in the United States. As more foreign companies establish U.S. subsidiaries, these firms are also increasing their local R & D activities.

In the past, multinationals typically centralized most research activities in a single domestic location, undertaking R & D at locations abroad primarily to tailor products and processes to local needs. The recent increase in research undertaken abroad stems in part from cost considerations, especially labor costs. However, tax and incentive policies of host governments have become an increasingly important factor in determining the location of corporate research activities.

2.4 U.S. Shares in Global Markets

In 1950, the United States accounted for more than 40 percent of total world output and about 17 percent of world exports. By 1980, the U.S. share in global output had dwindled to 22 percent and its exports to 11 percent. These data are used by Bhagwati and Irwin (1987) to establish a striking parallel between the postwar decline in U.S. global dominance and the relative decline of Britain in the nineteenth century.

However, the use of 1950 as a base year for the comparison may exaggerate the decline in relative economic strength of the United States. As Baldwin (1984) points out, the period immediately after World War II was itself atypical. The United States had emerged from the war with greatly expanded productive capacity, while its erstwhile adversaries and allies alike had sustained extensive losses of capital and manpower. Every U.S. manufacturing industry was able to show a trade surplus, a situation that masked the relative weakness of some. U.S. shares of world activity just after the war were significantly above the corresponding measures for the period just before the war. The U.S. share of total exports of the ten most important industrial countries was 35 percent as late as 1952, while it had been only 26 percent in 1938 and 28 percent in 1928.

Even for the postwar period, the usual indicators of U.S. market losses may overstate the extent of the nation's decline as an economic power. For world manufactured exports, the U.S. share fell from over 17 percent in 1966 to less than 14 percent by 1983. However, the share of U.S. multinational firms remained unchanged over almost two decades, with gains in exports of majority-owned foreign affiliates compensating for declines in exports from parents (Lipsey and Kravis 1986). Thus, while it is true that U.S. manufactured exports are losing their share of world markets, to a great degree they are losing it not to foreign competitors but to themselves, i.e., to foreign subsidiaries of U.S. companies.

This evidence suggests that much of the current discussion of declining U.S. competitiveness does not fit the facts. In particular, analyses that focus on failings of U.S. management and innovation are inconsistent with the sustained market shares of U.S. firms. Rather, the data suggest that the United States has lost ground as a locus of production. Presumably cost differences underlie the shift abroad by multinational corporations of production activities. Policies to improve the competitiveness of the United states as a site for industrial production must, therefore, address the determinants of these costs. The most important is relative wages.

2.5 Wage Trends

As long as new products and processes were available in the United States but not abroad, U.S. producers could remain internationally competitive even with U.S. wages significantly in excess of those paid elsewhere. The closing of the technology gap between the United States and its commercial rivals has meant increased competition on other dimensions of cost, especially wages. As a consequence of global diffusion of new technologies, labor productivity and earnings rose rapidly abroad, while the growth of U.S. earnings slowed. In some U.S. manufacturing industries real earnings actually fell for the first time in the postwar period as U.S. producers attempted to remain internationally competitive.

These trends were reinforced by demographic changes. The recent bulge in new entrants to the U.S. labor force was absorbed in large part through expansion in the service sector, with slow or negative growth of compensation. With fewer new entrants to the labor force (as in Japan), or with greater downward rigidity of wages and employee benefits (as in the European Community), a smaller number of new jobs would have been created, while the higher cost of employing additional workers would have induced employers to adopt more capital-intensive (i.e., more "productive") technologies. Thus, national and sectoral patterns of productivity growth and earnings reflect not only the rate of technological advance but also labor-market developments and tax policy, both of which help to shape firms' capital-spending decisions.

2.6 Trends in Growth

Long-term studies of U.S. growth indicate a prolonged slowdown since 1973. U.S. gross domestic product rose at an annual rate of only 2.3 percent from 1973 to 1984, in comparison to a rate of 3.2 percent from 1965 to 1973 (World Bank 1986: Table 2). Other growth indicators show a similar downturn after 1973. Output per employed person rose just 0.06 percent annually from 1973 to 1982, compared to a rate of 2.16 percent from 1948 to 1973 (Denison 1985).

While the reasons for lower U.S. growth in the recent period are complex and poorly understood, the post-1973 slowdown was a global phenomenon affecting every industrial country and virtually every less-developed country. Most European countries grew even more slowly than the United States. Even Japan, which grew at the astonishing annual rate of 9.8 percent from 1965 to 1973, slowed down to "only" 4.3 in the later period. Similar declines were recorded by many of the "newly industrializing countries" (NICs), both oil-exporting and oil-importing.

Whatever the underlying causes of the post-1973 slowdown in economic growth, it is clear that low growth rates threaten to make an ever-rising standard of living a thing of the past. Moreover, slower economic gains in the United States and other industrial countries may promote protectionism and a return to mercantilistic policies – "solutions" that will almost surely add to current problems and exert an additional downward pull on productivity.

2.7 Growth of Service Employment

One possible contributor to lower measured growth rates is the long-term shift in employment into the service sector, which appears to experience lower average rates of productivity increase than does manufacturing.[5] In the United States, fewer than one worker in four is now employed by the sectors that create tangible products – manufacturing, agriculture, mining, and construction. While import competition has contributed to declining employment in these sectors, by far the major force is rising productivity. Thus, it is U.S. *employment* that is "deindustrializing"; industrial *output* has remained almost constant as a share of national income (Lawrence 1984: 6).

The emergence of a "service economy" is not, however, a recent phenomenon. Indeed, the growth of service jobs as a fraction of total employment goes back at least a century in the United States. Neither is the trend unique to the United States; in the postwar period service jobs have grown as a share of total employment in every industrial and many developing countries.

In the United States some have viewed the expansion of service-sector employment as a positive development, offering potential replacement for secularly declining employment opportunities in manufacturing. However, proponents of this view tend to ignore important links between manufacturing and the service sector. Many U.S. service jobs are tied to manufacturing production; demand for these would disappear if the underlying manufacturing activities moved abroad. Also, part of the observed growth of service employment is actually a change in the structure of industries and in the relationships between workers and employers rather than in the tasks performed. Secretaries, computer programmers, or maintenance workers are counted as service-sector employees rather than manufacturing workers when contractors take over jobs previously performed "in house."

Even if newly created service jobs can replace jobs lost in manufacturing, the prospect is itself controversial. The optimists focus on a relatively narrow set of knowledge-based service activities, including ones closely linked to high-technology manufacturing. While some of these sectors have indeed enjoyed rapid growth in recent years, their size relative to the broad aggregate of services is quite small, both in the domestic market and in international transactions. And as noted, further decline in the size of the U.S. manufacturing sector is likely to slow or even reverse the growth of associated service activities as well. U.S. labor unions, which are concentrated in manufacturing industries, point ominously to the low average earnings in many types of service employment and to the lower average rate of productivity increase in services relative to that in goods-producing sectors.[6]

3 Macroeconomic Roots of the U.S. Trade Deficit

Like an economic Sputnik, the rapid growth of the U.S. trade imbalance in the early 1980s galvanized the American public. To many Americans, the steady escalation of the U.S. trade deficit was simply tangible and dramatic evidence of the nation's declining industrial competitiveness, in turn reflecting erosion of the commanding lead in science and technology the United States once enjoyed. Other popular explanations focused on trade-distorting practices abroad, export disincentives at home, and allegedly poor management practices of U.S. companies. Likewise, the seemingly ever-increasing surpluses of U.S. trading partners (and especially Japan) were seen as evidence of bad faith in complying with agreements to open their markets to U.S. goods, or as proof of the superiority of public policies and management practices abroad relative to their American counterparts.

3.1 The Role of the U.S. Deficit

An alternative analysis offers a completely different assessment of the forces underlying rapid escalation of the U.S. trade deficit. According to this view, promoted as early as 1982 by the U.S. Council of Economic Advisers, the growth of the trade deficit was the largely predictable result of a single important macroeconomic development in the United States: a major increase in the size of the federal budget deficit. The corresponding prescription for restoration of U.S. competitiveness: cut the budget deficit.

The Council's macroeconomic explanation was initially greeted by disbelief and even ridicule. However, it gained broad acceptance as the continued tandem rise of the "twin deficits" offered further circumstantial evidence in support of a linkage. The basic insight was, at least after the fact, a rather simple one. The large increase in the federal deficit translated into a comparable drop in the nation's total saving, pushing up U.S. interest rates. Drawn in by higher rates, foreign funds filled the gap. The foreign demand for U.S. assets also drove up the value of the dollar, pricing U.S. goods out of many markets at home and abroad. Thus, rather than "crowding out" domestic capital formation, as some had initially feared, the larger federal deficit crowded out domestic production of tradable goods.

But like most single-factor explanations, this one ignored other forces of comparable importance. The analysis emphasized U.S. demand for foreign funds, but gave little attention to factors influencing the supply of those funds to the U.S. market. While the enlarged federal deficit alone would have put upward pressure on domestic interest rates and promoted U.S. capital inflows, the actual size of the inflows was also determined by important "supply" factors in international capital markets.[7]

3.2 Supply of Foreign Funds

If growth in the federal budget deficit explained the greatly increased U.S. appetite for foreign funds, it was only one of many reasons why foreign lenders stood ready to satisfy that appetite. Other factors influencing the supply of foreign funds to U.S. capital markets can be grouped into three categories. Of these, two apply to lenders generally (including U.S. lenders, who cut back their own foreign loans in favor of domestic alternatives), while the third is specific to the most important foreign lender, Japan:

1. Increased attractiveness of U.S. investments, reflecting, among others, enhanced tax incentives for capital formation, financial and industrial deregulation, repeal of the withholding tax on earnings of U.S. assets held by foreigners, and successful anti-inflationary macroecononomic policies
2. Reduced attractiveness of lending abroad, due to economic stagnation in much of Europe and the debt problems and capital flight affecting many less-developed countries
3. Increased capital outflows from Japan, resulting from liberalization of restrictions on capital outflows (accelerated at the request of the United States as part of the 1984 dollar-yen agreement[8]) and lower Japanese budget deficits.

Even without the large increase in the U.S. federal deficit, these factors would have tended to push the U.S. capital account toward surplus, putting upward pressure on the international value of the dollar and downward pressure on U.S. merchandise trade performance.

3.3 Stock Adjustments and Continuing Flows

A further complication in the link between the U.S. budget deficit and U.S. borrowing from abroad is that the rise in the deficit created an ongoing demand for foreign capital, while the inflows from abroad have reflected both one-time readjustments of asset holdings in response to new market conditions and ongoing supply effects. In the specific case of capital inflows from Japan, the liberalization of capital outflows resulted in sizable shifts of accumulated Japanese assets. But the surplus of Japanese private savings over domestic absorption of those savings (into domestic capital formation and government deficit spending) translates into an ongoing supply influence that can be expected to push new capital into world markets year after year.

Over time, the resulting increases in foreign holdings of U.S. assets and in U.S. holdings of foreign assets have direct implications for the composition of the current account and for the relative value of the dollar. A rising net-debtor position for the United States should mean rising net outflows of interest and profits, pushing the U.S. services account toward deficit. For a given level of capital inflow, this means a shrinking deficit on merchandise trade and less upward pressure on the value of the dollar. This compositional effect would tend to reinforce sluggish adjustment of trade flows to the lower value of the dollar.

3.4 Correcting the Aggregate Imbalance

Given the full set of contributing macroeconomic conditions, what can be said about the outcomes of alternative corrective policies? The U.S. external imbalance reflects an excess of total "absorption" – spending (public plus private) for both consumption and investment purposes – over production in the United States, and a corresponding shortfall of absorption relative to production abroad. Measures to reduce the imbalance can seek to reduce the U.S. spending excess or to reduce the foreign shortfall.

The most obvious choices for direct U.S. action have become the bread and butter of national policy debate: raise taxes, cut government spending, or both. A third alternative for bringing total U.S. spending into line is to reduce domestic capital formation. This option, seldom explicitly considered, has obvious negative implications for the future growth of U.S. productive capacity. However, it may be chosen by default if policymakers are unable to cut total public and private spending for other purposes, or if new taxes enacted to reduce the deficit also reduce incentives for domestic investment.

Moreover, even a successful effort to reduce the budget deficit need not produce a comparable reduction in the nation's demand for capital imports. Although customarily described in terms of the increased federal deficit, the root of the nation's increased appetite for foreign funds (or, equivalently, of its increased deficit on current account) is actually increased *spending* – specifically, the increase in total domestic absorption of goods and services. Because changes in the federal government's plans for taxing and spending usually have important effects on decisions of state and local governments and of the private sector, merely reducing the federal deficit does not necessarily have a comparable effect on total absorption; major offsets are possible.

As a practical matter, progress on deficit reduction has been slow in coming. In 1988, conflicts between President Reagan and the Democratically-controlled U.S. Congress were exacerbated by election-year politics. Meanwhile, Treasury Secretary James Baker prodded U.S. trading partners, especially West Germany and Japan, to assume more responsibility for effecting the desired adjustment by stimulating their own economies and thus increasing absorption at home.

An alternative to increasing foreign domestic absorption is redirecting foreign funds toward other nations, especially less-developed nations. If the United States does not want capital from abroad, other nations surely do. This redirection could be achieved via increases in bilateral official development assistance or contributions to multilateral agencies, or via increases in portfolio and direct investment.

Increased European and Japanese spending for foreign aid could prove a mixed blessing for U.S. exporters. Informal arrangements tend to link aid flows to recipient expenditures for donor exports of goods and services. While little aid is explicitly tied, aid is rarely committed without specific project plans; potential borrowers rely on the donor-country firms or agencies for expert advice in formulating the plans, which typically call for imports of donor-country capital equipment and other products. Mixed-credit financing is a related problem.

Commercial lending and direct foreign investments in developing countries are an alternative means by which Japanese and European surplus savings could be "recycled." Given the ongoing debt problems of many developing nations, this route currently looks hazardous to both potential lenders and potential borrowers. In the longer term, however, it is likely that "normal" capital-flow relations between rich and poor nations will be reestablished, with funds from Japan and Europe playing an important role.

3.5 Taxing Capital Imports

Given the greatly increased federal deficit, only the net inflow of capital from abroad has kept U.S. interest rates from going through the roof. Instead, the U.S. trade deficit has gone through the roof. Until U.S. domestic absorption can be cut, the nation will continue to face the same two choices. Over time, the exact terms of the trade-off will depend on investors' preferences, but the United States can influence that choice by taxing capital imports.[9]

Controlling U.S. capital imports would shift a greater part of the adjustment to higher deficits onto U.S. borrowers and lenders, rather than allowing much of the "crowding out" to be exported. From the U.S. perspective, the effect is similar to what would be obtained via expansion abroad. However, there are two potentially important differences. First, without specific expansionary policies in place abroad, U.S. capital controls could push the rest of the world into a deflationary spiral. Second, and perhaps key for some U.S. officials, capital controls would reverse recent U.S. gains in penetrating foreign (especially Japanese) markets for financial services.

4 Looking Ahead

The evidence on recent U.S. performance is mixed. Some alleged U.S. problems simply reflect the postwar recovery and technological catch-up of other nations, i. e., a return to normal conditions from highly atypical ones. Others are indeed problems, like the slowdown of productivity growth, but are global rather than national problems.

I have argued that the rapidly growing U.S. trade imbalance was produced by macroeconomic conditions, not by trade or industrial policies at home or abroad. In this sense, the imbalance can be viewed as a "temporary" factor rather than a long-term development signifying a profound defect in the U.S. private sector.[10] Even so, elimination of the imbalance without serious damage to the U.S. economy and those of its trading partners may be difficult to achieve. Should investors turn away from U.S. financial markets before the United States is able to reduce domestic absorption, U.S. interest rates will be forced upward with potentially disastrous consequences for the economy.

But if the nation's competitiveness problems have been exaggerated, it is nonetheless clear that the era of unquestioned U.S. economic hegemony is over. Today, Japan and the European Community rival the United States in important dimensions of economic achievement.[11] Yet the United States remains the acknowledged leader of the Western Alliance in both economic and security matters. One possible reason is the apparent reluctance of other economically powerful nations, specifically Japan and West Germany, to assume the burdens and costs of an active leadership role. That reluctance may be another legacy of the unique circumstances that propelled the United States into its postwar hegemonic role.

Given that relative economic circumstances are now dramatically changed, a shift in global leadership seems overdue. However, we understand relatively little about how and when such changes occur. Historical evidence suggests that the period of transition is likely to be turbulent. At a minimum, it seems probable that major world institutions, including the General Agreement on Tariffs and Trade, the International Monetary Fund, and the World Bank, will be reshaped when new powers with different economic and political outlooks choose to assume a leadership role. The extent of that reshaping will depend on whether a new leader actually displaces the United States or merely enters an explicit or implicit arrangement of shared hegemony.

Of course, there will be changes not only in the institutions themselves but also in the problems confronting those institutions. In terms of required economic adjustments, the relationship between the United States and its major trading partners may well be entering a new phase. As these nations grow more similar in terms of technology base, abundance of capital and skilled labor, as well as per capita income, intra-industry trade is likely to grow. In particular, two-way trade in technology and in technology-based services should become increasingly important as other nations move from adaptation into innovation. In the mature industries and even some that are now considered "high-technology" sectors, all the industrial market economies will be faced with increasing competition from a new tier of competitors in Asia and elsewhere.

Likewise, for all the industrial economies, problems of sectoral adjustment will continue to generate strong pressures for import protection and other forms of assistance to industries losing ground to newcomers. Sectoral trade conflict between the United States and other developed nations will be concentrated on the two ends of the industrial spectrum in terms of technological sophistication, with issues raised by contrasting approaches to the phasing out of industries losing their comparative advantage (e. g., steel, autos) and to the nurturing of new industries (e. g., aircraft, superconductors).

Still, many Americans are reluctant to accept a future in which the United States is but one of several economic leaders. By redoubling its efforts, could the United States return to its one-time position of unquestioned technological preeminence? Even with vastly increased resources allocated to research and development, this kind of advantage probably can no longer be sustained – by the United States or any other country – in a world that has become highly interdependent. The commercial advantage of being first in innovation has been undermined by the greatly increased speed with which new technical knowledge becomes available to potential competitors all over the globe. This does not mean that research and development has become less important. On the contrary, technological improvements will continue to provide the basis for a rising standard of living both in the United States and abroad. However, the benefits of R & D efforts can no longer be counted mainly in terms of the advantages conferred to one nation's industries over competitors elsewhere.

Notes

1 The Commission's definition does not, however, entail continued growth in real earnings for any group, and could be satisfied even with the nation's future economic gains accruing primarily to those already at the high end of the income distribution scale.

2 The latter possibility arises if productivity-enhancing policies cause the United States to become more attractive to investors. Any net improvement in the nation's capital-account balance must be matched by an equal deterioration in the current account.

3 Even if the aggregate effect is not large, favorable market conditions abroad would provide substantial benefits to some U.S. firms in the relevant sectors. Much of the private-sector lobbying in support of a U.S. initiative to liberalize international competition in services has come from the insurance industry.

4 The trade deficit is often interpreted as an indicator of U.S. jobs lost as a result of foreign competition. Yet the national unemployment rate continued along a steady downward course while the U.S. trade deficit climbed to new record levels.

5 Some analysts believe that differences in reported rates of productivity increase are mainly a statistical illusion. Due to the intangible nature of the product, it is more difficult to measure changes in the output of service industries. In some cases, input is used as a measure of output, so that productivity is stagnant by definition.

6 Based on an analysis of recent job creation in the United States, the Industrial Union Department of the AFL-CIO concluded that service occupations "experiencing the largest net growth in the number of jobs demand little skill, are only weakly organized into unions, and usually offer little pay – ranging from building custodians to fast food workers... prospects for upward mobility out of these lower rung jobs... are slight" (AFL-CIO 1984: 11 – 12). However, other researchers view growing service-sector employment in a much more favorable light. For example, see Lawrence (1984) and Urquhart (1984).

7 In addition to its neglect of factors influencing the supply of funds to U.S. borrowers, the conventional wisdom implied that the appreciation of the dollar was a necessary consequence of the inflow of foreign funds. In fact, the theoretical consequences of a financial transfer for the exchange rate are ambiguous, depending crucially on spending patterns at home and abroad. The more similar those spending patterns and the larger the proportion of total expenditure devoted to tradable goods, the less the exchange rate would have to move to "effect" the transfer of current purchasing power to the United States. This helps to explain how the dollar could fall so much with capital inflows still rising. The prolonged period of a very strong dollar caused permanent changes in consumer information and in producer costs of serving the U.S. market. Specifically, at a *given* exchange rate, more U.S. consumers would choose foreign products over their domestic counterparts when priced comparably in dollars, while foreign producers would be able to set higher dollar prices for goods aimed at the U.S. market.

8 See Frankel (1984) for a review of this agreement. The agreement was promoted as a means to raise the value of the yen by increasing its role as a reserve currency. However, the predictable short-run result, borne out by subsequent events, was just the opposite.

9 This has been proposed in recent years by James Tobin and Rudiger Dornbusch, among others; see Dornbusch and Frankel (1987).

10 Some argue that the fecderal deficit itself may indicate a deeper problem in the U.S. economy. Certainly it is an indication that federal revenues have grown more slowly than the cost of the government-provided goods and services Americans have come to expect. So perhaps the twin deficits do really attest to inadequate economic growth in the United States. My personal belief is that low productivity growth should be a concern of policymakers, but it is not the primary force behind the U.S. trade deficit. The large deficit emerged quickly, long after the slowdown in U.S. productivity gains but on the heels of a major tax cut and other important macroeconomic and regulatory policy changes at home and abroad.

11 At the January 1988 dollar/yen exchange rate, Japan has actually surpassed the United States in GNP per capita and other measures of economic success.

References

AFL-CIO, Industrial Union Department (1984): *Deindustrialization and the Two Tier Society: Challenges for an Industrial Policy*. Washington, D.C.: Industrial Union Department, AFL-CIO.

Baldwin, Robert E. (1984): U.S. Trade Policy since World War II. In Robert E. Baldwin and Anne O. Krueger (eds.), *The Structure and Evolution of Recent U.S. Trade Policy*. Chicago: University of Chicago Press, 3 – 27.

Bhagwati, Jagdish N. and Douglas A. Irwin (1987): The Return of the Reciprocitarians: US Trade Policy Today. *The World Economy* 10: 109 – 130.

Denison, Edward E. (1985): *Trends in American Economic Growth. 1929 – 1982*. Washington, D.C.: Brookings Institution.

Dornbusch, Rudiger and Jeffrey A. Frankel (1987): Macroeconomics and Protection. In Robert M. Stern (ed.), *U.S. Trade Policies in a Changing World Economy*. Cambridge, Mass.: MIT Press, 77 – 130.

Frankel, Jeffrey A. (1984): *The Dollar/Yen Agreement: Liberalizing Japanese Capital Markets*. Washington, D.C.: Institute for International Economics, December.

Lawrence, Robert Z. (1984): *Can America Compete?* Washington., D.C.: Brookings Institution.

Lipsey, Robert E. and Irving B. Kravis (1985): The Competitive Position of U.S. Manufacturing Firms. *Banca Nazionale del Lavoro Quarterly Review* 153: 127 – 154.

Lipsey, Robert E. and Irving B. Kravis (1986): The Competitiveness and Comparative Advantage of U.S. Multinationals, 1957 – 1983. National Bureau of Economic Research Working Paper No. 2051, October.

President's Commission on Industrial Competitiveness (1985): *Global Competition: The New Reality*. Washington, D.C.: U.S. Government Printing Office.

Urquhart, Michael (1984): The Employment Shift to Services: Where Did It Come From? *Monthly Labor Review* 107: 15 – 22.

World Bank (1986): *World Development Report 1986*. New York: Oxford University Press.

Structural Impediments to International Competitiveness of U.S. Manufacturing

Christoph Scherrer

The mounting trade deficit of recent years notwithstanding, a number of respected economists are of the opinion that "it would be extremely difficult to conclude that the United States faces any fundamental problem of international competitiveness" (Bergsten 1983: 314; see also Branson 1981; Lawrence 1984; CEA 1985: 99 – 110; and Galbraith 1987). In their view the trade deficit is a well-understood macro-economic phenomenon, a result of "the strong dollar, reduced U.S. exports to heavily indebted developing countries, and faster growth in the United States compared with its industrialized trading partners" (CEA 1985: 102). Thus, the competitiveness debate has been seen as an ephemeral fad bound to disappear into obscurity once the exchange-rate policies would be reversed. However, only after three years of dramatic devaluation of the U.S. dollar against most major currencies, the trade deficit has shown the first signs of reversal.

In tandem with the "unwillingness" of the deficit to wither away, more "pessimistic" viewpoints on the international competitiveness of U.S. industry have gained currency in the public debate, to the point where Congress is drafting strong protectionist measures. Within the many different arguments put forth in the industrial-policy debate (for an overview see Norton 1986: Appendix) three causes for the apparent deficiencies of U.S. manufacturing receive repeated mention. These are: (a) lack of capital (e.g., Young 1985); (b) short-term planning (e.g., Hayes and Abernathy 1980); and (c) incoherent government policies (e.g., Walters 1985). While these arguments can claim explanatory validity for particular instances, they do not seem to illuminate the overall issue of the changing competitive position of U.S. industry. For one, in light of these arguments it becomes difficult to understand the past record of industrial success. Furthermore, the case of General Motors (GM), for instance, provides an illustrative counter-example on two accounts: despite a sophisticated long-term strategy and billions spent on retooling, GM was not able to halt the erosion of its competitive position (Hampton and Norman 1987).

In an attempt to overcome some of the shortcomings of conventional explanations I want to consider the structural causes for the erosion of U.S. industrial strength. It is my thesis that many of the competitive problems of U.S. industry result from the legacy left by institutions and practices that were part of what I call the *domestic market growth model.* With the advance of a fully integrated global economy many aspects of this growth model have become dysfunctional and, ergo, represent major obstacles for the success of U.S.-based and U.S.-owned companies in both their home and international markets.

In developing my arguments, I will part company with those who have argued that practices more conducive to international competitiveness could have been adopted at an earlier point in time (Lawrence and Dyer 1983; Salter et al. 1985). Instead, it will become evident that a change of strategy in favor of a more flexible response to foreign competition is only possible in the context of the internationalization process.

Furthermore, while the attempt to highlight institutional rigidities may express a certain kinship to Olson's theory of institutional sclerosis (1982), the two approaches are quite different. Contrary to Olson's line of argument, institutional deviations from the neo-classical ideal of unrestrained markets are not viewed as counter-productive to economic development at all times, but are analyzed in their specific historical context.

Accordingly, I will start with a brief description of the domestic market growth model as it developed in the United States, its features, its workings, and its inherent contradictions. In a second step, I will analyze in what ways some aspects of this model become counter-productive once foreign companies can offer products below the price levels prevailing in the United States. Finally, I will examine a few attempts to change the traditional structures and practices.

1 Contours of the Domestic Market Growth Path

Although U.S. industry dominated the world market in the postwar years, it produced primarily for the domestic market. In 1965 manufacturing exports represented only 5.1% of U.S. shipments. They rose to 10.7% by 1980 (Eckstein et al. 1984: 17). The great bulk of the exported goods were produced by a very select number of industries (Scott 1985: 28). By comparison, most West German manufacturers were engaged in foreign trade and together they exported 18.7% of their production in 1967 (Altvater 1980: 156). Instead, U.S. companies served foreign markets increasingly through subsidiaries. Direct investments in foreign countries rose dramatically from $ 11.8 billion in 1950 to $ 49.2 billion in 1965, and accelerated to $ 133.1 billion in 1975 (Krasner 1978: 70). The domestic outlook of U.S. industry also became manifest in the organizational separation between domestic and foreign business either within companies or between companies, e. g., while AT&T exclusively served the domestic telephone market, ITT was active only abroad (Wiley 1980).

By the same token import penetration was very low in the United States. In 1965 4.3% of available goods were imported; thereafter the figure rose steadily reaching 13.5% in 1980 (Eckstein et al. 1984: 16). Geographic factors and the very gradual reduction of tariffs contributed to this isolation of the U.S. economy in the first postwar decades (being selectively applied, until the late 1950s tariffs had appreciable effect only on very few selected imports; Pincus 1980: 446). However, U.S. corporations were primarily shielded against foreign competition by their leadership in productivity. Until the mid-1970s, per-hour output in manufacturing in Japan, West Germany, and the U.K. remained well below the U.S. level. According to the PCIC study, these countries reached 50% of the U.S. level only in 1970 (1985: 166). This average, however, masks the fact that some Japanese and West German companies had already matched their U.S. counterparts (Scherrer 1983: 129).

The origin of this impressive lead in productivity seems to rest in the early development of what I call a domestic market growth strategy and what others have called a mass production economy (Piore and Sabel 1984), or a regime of intensive accumulation – in short, "Fordism" (Aglietta 1979). The predominant features of this growth model are the institutional circuits that connect mass production and mass consumption: oligopolization of major markets, contractualization of labor, rise in indirect wages, credit money as legal tender, and Keynesian economic policies (Lipietz 1984: 86).

Some brief theoretical thoughts on productivity may be of help in understanding the workings of this model. The basic means of increasing productivity consist of implementing labor-saving machinery and fully exploiting its economies of scale. Aside from the technological revolution which reduced the costs of production equipment, productivity gains resulted predominantly from the use of larger machinery with ever-increasing economies of scale. The latter, however, can only be fully exploited if markets grow. This can be achieved through lower prices, which allow growth at the expense of competitors, as well as the creation of new markets. If, however, markets expand more slowly than do the possibilities for cost reductions, then the result will be under-utilization of capacity. In that case the invested capital will not earn its expected return.

What could cause such disequilibrium? At least three causes can be identified: (a) the indivisibility and durability of plant and equipment which make it difficult to expand capacity step by step as markets grow (Steindl 1976: 10); (b) the lumpiness of products, especially consumer durables, which cannot be bought out of current income (Aglietta 1979: 159); and (c) the possibility that labor-saving techniques reduce the quantity of predistributed income (Lipietz 1985: 63). When any of these obstacles prevent the expansion of demand in accordance with production capabilities, producers historically have engaged in price wars. The resultant destruction of capital and work places, usually hastened by a financial panic, led to a cumulative shortfall in effective demand. Although these crises proved to be "creative" in the long run, they nevertheless severely disrupted any steady progress in productivity.

What mechanisms have been available to avoid possible discrepancies between productivity gains and market growth? With the rise of capital-intensive industry around the turn of the century, the predominant strategy was to externalize the problem by vigorous export promotion. This imperialist solution had its obvious limits. Another strategy was slow in being "discovered" in the United States. The early expansion of mass production was greatly facilitated by affluent small landowners and a burgeoning middle class (Piore and Sabel 1984: 41). However, the ensuing tremendous growth came to an abrupt end when the demand capacity of the middle classes as consumers was exhausted by the mid-1920s (Aglietta 1979: 95). With the New Deal the principal structures for a domestic solution emerged: stabilization of the economy through a rise in distributed purchasing power that anticipated gains in productivity (Lipietz 1985: 66). In other words, a growth model was found that would guarantee producers domestic markets for their own ever-increasing output volumes. As already indicated, this model rests on four basic institutional practices, which will be briefly mentioned below.

A. *Collective bargaining* primarily limits the consequences of capitalist insecurity on employment and the formation of individual wages. It thereby enables workers to meet the financial commitments contracted with the acquisition of consumer durables (Aglietta 1979: 159). The satisfaction of working-class consumer demand with industrially manufactured goods also reduces the costs of the recuperation of labor power (e.g., household appliances that save domestic labor). If, in addition, union contracts link real wages to productivity gains, then demand for consumer products will grow more or less in accordance with production capabilities. Productivity-oriented wage policies, furthermore, help to legitimize the continuous introduction of new machinery.

B. *Monopolistic competition* allows corporations to make prices insensitive to contingent disturbances in demand and thereby to avoid price wars. This control over prices in turn enables corporations to renew their fixed capital on a regular basis. (The control over prices is of course restrained by the ability of other capitals to enter this industry.) The permanent depreciation of capital can be anticipated and compensated for by a financial flow which is incorporated a priori into cost prices (Aglietta 1979: 313). Monopolistic competition also facilitates collective bargaining, since competitiveness is not based on low wages.

C. *Central bank money* unifies all private bank money and thus overcomes the restrictions of a gold currency. Liquidity crises become manageable as central banks, in their capacity as lenders of last resort, substitute for settlement in gold. Thus, financial panics can be avoided. Furthermore, the unrestricted social acceptance of central bank money constitutes an essential precondition for the regular participation of wage-earners in the consumption of commodities, since their wages are not secured in kind (Aglietta 1979: 341 – 347).

D. The *social security state* safeguards workers against the loss of purchasing power due to illness, old age, and unemployment. It thereby performs the vital function of preventing a cumulative shortfall in effective demand once a business contraction sets in. This social insurance allows, on the one hand, the intensification of work and, on the other, the reconstitution of labor power by capitalist means (Hirsch 1980).

2 Sources of Crisis

By the end of the 1960s, the dynamics of the domestic market growth model had been exhausted. The annual rate of productivity growth slowed from 3.2% for 1948 – 1965 to 2.3% for 1965 – 1972, to 1.1% for 1972 – 1977 (Thurow 1980: 85; for a comparison of different productivity studies, see Wolff 1985). At the same time, the rise in real wages became sluggish and even turned negative; the annual rate of increase in average weekly gross earnings in manufacturing declined from 2.5% for 1950 – 1959 to 1.5% for 1960 – 1969, to –0.3% for 1970 – 1979 (Szymanski 1984: 314).

The dynamic interplay of three basic developments appears to account for the economic slowdown: (a) the socio-technical limits of the Taylorist production paradigm; (b) the increasing costs of collective consumption; and (c) the rise of foreign competition.

A. Increases in productivity became increasingly difficult to realize on the basis of an ever-deeper fragmentation of tasks and implementation of special-purpose machinery. Barriers were partly technical and partly social in nature. For example, imbalances on the assembly line became more frequent as individual tasks became more specialized (Nobel 1984). Facilitated by favorable labor-market conditions, the increasing mental and physical exhaustion of workers led to different kinds of workers' protest (Naples 1986). The effect was that increases in capital expenditures no longer yielded equivalent productivity gains (Lipietz 1986). Producers reacted with a restraint on capital formation (Eckstein and Tannenwald 1981).

B. While direct wages were linked to productivity increases, payments for social benefits as expressed both in indirect wages and taxation rose disproportionately. After-tax earnings of U.S. nonfarm workers peaked in 1972 and declined to the 1959 level in 1981 (Scott 1985: 36). At the same time public expenditures on social insurance programs as percent of GNP increased from 5.06 in 1970 to 7.3 in 1980 (based on Wolfe et al. 1984: 612). In the steel industry the share of indirect wages of total employment cost rose from 19% in 1970 to 30.1% in 1980 (based on AISI 1981: 22).

This tendency reflected, on the one hand, an increasing demand for social consumption, which was fueled by the progressive erosion of tradition means of reproduction (family). On the other hand, a number of important collective services such as health service could not be subjected to labor-saving mass-production techniques (Thurow 1985: 79). The resulting low productivity increases made these services relatively expensive compared with industrially manufactured goods. National health-care expenditures as proportion of GNP rose from 4.4% in 1950 to 7.6% in 1970 and to 10.6% in 1984 (Meyer and Kern 1986: 196).

This unbalanced development caused a twofold effect: although indirect wages rose faster than productivity (and thus reduced profits), they did not provide for additional market outlets for manufactured goods.

C. The emergence of foreign competitors has to be understood in terms of the respective country's position vis-à-vis the United States. The latter's contribution to the European and Japanese "economic miracles" was based not primarily on the much-lauded "Marshall Fund," but on the inauguration of a new system of international relations which created the necessary stability for an orderly growth in trade. Furthermore, while keeping the dollar overvalued after the mid-1950s, the U.S.A. stimulated capital exports and commodity imports from the emergent countries. The capital exports facilitated the diffusion of superior U.S. management and production techniques. With these favorable external stimuli, it became possible for a number of economies to develop their own domestic markets (especially for automobiles), which allowed them to match the economies-of-scale levels of U.S. producers (Aglietta 1982; Altvater et al. 1980). Supported by lower wage bills and newer equipment, these countries were able to compete successfully with the United States.

Theoretically, these three developments reinforce each other in the following way: A slowdown in productivity growth will lead to rising prices, if levels of investment and wages increase at the traditional rate. Higher prices, however, will stimulate the entrance of foreign competition. U.S. producers then face the choice of either letting market shares slip or engaging in price competition. If they choose the first alternative, they are threatened by a cumulative decline in capacity utilization with detrimental effects on productivity. (This effect can be avoided, if the industry closes down its inefficient plant and keeps the other plants running at a higher rate of capacity utilization. For various reasons, however, many U.S. industries seem to have postponed the reduction of capacity for too long. Consider the example of the steel industry discussed in Crandall 1981.) If they meet the foreign competition head on, they will suffer lower profit margins, which in turn will reduce their ability to invest in new machinery. A third alternative, the restoration of their profitability through a reduction of wages, will also result in negative repercussions. Any reduction of purchasing power limits overall market growth, unless counterbalanced by the expansion of consumer credits. The latter, of course, cannot continue indefinitely. Furthermore, cuts in wages do not lead necessarily to a smaller total wage bill. Collective consumption may display a different dynamic. In sum, once these three developments assert themselves, the domestic market growth model loses its impetus. In fact, U.S. industry was caught enmeshed in the contradictions between these alternatives.

3 Structural Impediments to Adaptation

Having explained the general mechanisms of the domestic market growth model, I want to discuss a number of U.S. post-war institutional arrangements or practices which seem no longer to be adequate for international competitiveness. I will proceed by first showing how the respective practices fitted into – or were at least not dysfunctional for – the domestic growth strategy. Then I will try to elucidate in what ways these practices may have become an obstacle to further economic growth. This inquiry will be rather brief and therefore will not cover the subject exhaustively. The order of presentation will follow in a very loose manner the descent from the macro to the micro level. However, it will become evident during the course of the presentation that the macro and micro levels are quite interrelated.

3.1 Keynesian Demand Management

As already stated, government intervention plays a key role in the domestic market growth model. Demand management smooths out the business cycle and therefore prevents the development of any major imbalances.

In an open economy, however, demand stimulated by government expenditures will not automatically be satisfied by domestic production. If the domestic industry is not internationally competitive, consumers will also spend some of their income on foreign products. Any portion of the newly created demand spent on these products will not activate the Keynesian multiplier unless the increased demand for foreign products induces these foreigners to raise in turn their demand for other products of that country. Thus, once a country experiences a trade deficit, demand stimulation will lose some of its effectiveness. Increasing trade deficits will therefore require ever-growing government expenditures. The U.S. experience confirms this dynamic: The mounting deficit in the merchandise trade balance has been accompanied by a similar rise of the federal budget deficit.

The effects of demand management are also dependent on (a) the way it is carried out and (b) the profile of a nation's industrial strength. If, for example, a country does not produce manufactured goods for low-income groups but stimulates demand mainly through transfer payments to lower income groups, then it will basically subsidize other foreign countries. A case in point may be the deficiencies of U.S. producers in the area of consumer electronic products and small cars; the same happens when income is transferred to the rich and they spend it on, say, Porsches and French champagne. Military Keynesianism avoids this problem, since military procurement orders are basically closed to foreigners.

Furthermore, once transfer payments have only a limited impact on the utilization of a nation's capacities, they are no longer economically beneficial and appear only as additional costs. A higher tax burden impedes international competitiveness.

However, even if demand management succeeds in stimulating demand, negative long-run consequences for international competitiveness cannot be ruled out. The success may lead to the preservation of "inefficient" capacity. Postponing the adjustment process may aggravate the pain of adaptation in the future. The negative impact will be even greater, if demand stimulation only works at the expense of an ever-increasing budget deficit. The inflationary impulse of the deficit will further erode the competitive position (Altvater et al. 1983: 155).

Besides fiscal stimulus, Keynesian macro-economic management also included interest-rate policies. Within a closed economy, the lowering of the interest rate was an appropriate method for inducing additional investments. However, in an open economy with well-developed international capital markets, interest-rate politics may be counter-balanced by capital movements. Instead of stimulating new investments, low interest rates may prompt capital to look for higher interest rates abroad. In sum, Keynesian politics do not seem to work well in internationally competitive markets.[1]

3.2 Savings Habits

Average net savings as percent of GNP for 1960 – 1980 were 8.3 in the U.S.A. versus 15.7 in West Germany and 21.4 in Japan (Wellons 1985: 362). Thus, by international comparison, the U.S. economy displays a rather low savings rate. Personal savings is especially low, in 1982 being 6% in the U.S.A., 14% in West Germany, and 18% in Japan (Thurow 1985: 208). This low savings rate reflects the widespread use of consumer credit; the U.S. ratio of consumer credit to disposable income is, at 20 percent, twice the Japanese ratio (Hoadley 1984: 180). Furthermore, a substantial part of these household savings were locked into home-building (Caspersen 1981: 144).

Although some fairly fundamental aspects of societal arrangements account for most of the differences in national savings rates, certain aspects of government policy have clearly promoted U.S. consumer spending over saving. These include: (a) unlimited tax deductions for consumer debt and mortgages (Wellons 1985: 364); (b) interest ceilings on bank deposits, which has meant that small savers were offered rates of return far below the rate of inflation (Baumol and McLennan 1985: 208); and (c) tax-law biases favoring investment in housing.[2]

For a closed economy a low savings rate does not necessarily pose a problem, since the indispensable investment funds can be created by forced savings through higher prices. In a domestic market growth model increased savings may even lead to lower investments via reduced aggregate demand and investors' expectations. In an open economy, however, marginal increases in consumer spending may not find their way back into domestic industry, but may be spent on foreign products. Forced saving is thus ruled out. As a result, a low personal savings rate may lead to a scarcity of domestic funds and consequently to higher capital costs (Wellons 1985: 360) – it would be wrong, however, to assume that a higher savings rate will lead automatically to higher investment levels, for during a recession increased savings would only lead to more monetary liquidity. Companies become dependent on cyclically vulnerable retained corporate earnings and on open capital markets that show large price fluctuations caused by variations in foreign and domestic capital movements (Eckstein et al. 1984: 35). In fact, a number of studies have shown that the costs of capital are highest in the U.S.A. However, it appears doubtful whether U.S. consumerism is the sole contributing factor (Wellons 1985; see below "financial system").

3.3 Education

The quality of U.S. education has become the subject of heated debates and alarming studies (see, e.g., National Commission on Excellence in Education 1983). While the debates have focused primarily on the poor quality of secondary education (see Long 1984), from the standpoint of international competitiveness, the state of technical, engineering, and science programs is of greatest importance. Factory automation, small-batch production, and quality competitiveness require a well-skilled labor force.

The problem in engineering and science seems to date to be more of a quantitative nature. According to Brooks:

> Among students in higher education, the fraction in engineering and science programs has been only 1.6% in the U.S. compared with 4.2% in Japan.... As long as participation in higher education was much higher in the U.S. than in the rest of the world, the lower fraction in engineering and science was of little consequence. But... the rest of the world has dramatically expanded access to higher education (1985: 349).

Technical training in the U.S.A. appears to be both quantitatively and qualitatively insufficient. Apprenticeship programs exist only for a limited number of skills. For reasons of labor-market control, the unions, which are usually in charge of such programs, practice only a very restrictive enrollment policy. Thus, these programs play a very minor role, e.g., fewer than 300,000 young workers were enrolled in 1980 (Krekeler 1981: 159). Most vocational training takes place in high schools and community colleges. However, a majority of these schools offer training in only a very limited number of skills, suffer from a lack of new equipment, and lack a clear sense of the needs of the labor market. Furthermore, a disproportionate amount of the federal fiscal support goes into home economics and related courses (1981: 174).

The dominant procedure for acquisition of skills is on-the-job training where know-how is casually passed on from worker to worker. This method is highly sensitive to the business cyle. Due to the seniority system, during recessions half-trained workers are either the first to be laid off or are bumped back down the job queue to less-skilled jobs. This failure to train skilled workers during a recession leads to skilled-labor shortages in subsequent phases of expansion. Employers react by raiding each other for skilled labor (Thurow 1985: 201). Not surprisingly, the resulting employee mobility further discourages companies to invest in formal training (PCIC 1985: 148).

Such deficiencies in technical training were less apparent in the absence of foreign competition. On the one hand, the U.S.A. was able to draw on foreign-trained workers. From the mid-1960s on this source of skilled labor, however, has been fading away as rising wages in other industrialized nations (especially West Germany) have removed the incentive to migrate (Thurow 1985: 203). On the other hand, the very success of Taylorism itself drastically reduced the demand for skilled labor. In the 1890s the National Association of Manufacturers, alarmed by Germany's rapid rise as an industrial power, called for state-assisted vocational training to match the German system of vocational schools (Kantor 1982: 26). By the mid-1920s the then-successful vocational reformers were confronted with the fact that the demand for skilled labor was no longer growing (Kett 1982: 94). By the time Taylorism had increased productivity to such an extent that foreign competition was no longer a threat, it had de-skilled the labor process.

3.4 Anti-Trust Laws

While the strong anti-trust rhetoric in U.S. politics did not prevent capital concentration and centralization, the anti-trust laws were at least useful in averting the most offending practices of monopoly power (Scherer 1981: 307). Since the logic of the domestic market growth model restricted the forces of competition, political intervention in the form of anti-trust legislation played at least to a small extent the role of a corrective for gross discrepancies between the rate of return within and among different industries.

The return to conditions of competition seems to make anti-trust rules superfluous nowadays. Vigorous import competition in many industries polices pricing and quality, although industries such as steel have continued their traditional practices at the risk of losing further market-shares for many years (Scherer 1981: 307 – 309). Thus, anti-trust regulation may not just be redundant but in fact even dysfunctional in the context of global competition. On the one hand, the traditional merger guidelines did not take account of the fact that success in international competition requires in certain industries higher levels of capital centralization (Bower and Rheman 1985; Williamson 1986). On the other hand, traditional anti-trust restrictions on anti-competitive behavior placed serious constraints on cooperative efforts in the vital area of research and development (Alpert and Holt 1980; see below "inter-industry cooperation"). One more example in this context is the situation whereby the prohibition of exclusive franchise agreements, which bind a dealer to a particular make of car, paved the way for the establishment of dealership networks of foreign automobile producers (Altshuler et al. 1984: 173).

3.5 Financial System

At the turn of the century a few financial magnates directed the formation of giant trusts in almost every major industry (Chandler 1977). New Deal banking laws and the general stabilization of the economy led to a decentralization of the financial system, while the practice of mark-up pricing provided corporations with growing internal funds. Capital markets have become the central means for external finance. Decision-making rests mainly with the corporations themselves (Zysman 1984: 269).[3]

According to Zysman (1984: 63), the dominance of capital markets fosters arm's-length relations between financial institutions and companies, with an emphasis on short-term lending. Here again, anti-trust laws served the purpose of installing some measure of competition in an otherwise oligopolized economy.

With the advent of international competition, the fragmented nature of its financial system becomes a liability for U.S. industry. In its adjustment process to international competition, industry cannot count on strategic long-term support from the financial community. Instead, the arm's-length relationship reinforces the pursuit of quarterly profit increases. The resultant "paper entrepreneurialism" has been well documented (Reich 1983).

According to Wellons (1985), the decentralized nature of the financial system also contributes to higher capital costs by generating higher risk premiums. The risks of loan defaults are increased by the large amount of financial intermediates (some 14,000 commercial banks) which impedes negotiated solutions for companies in crisis. Furthermore, without equity interests, the banks may lack intimate knowledge of their debtors' situation and hence be tempted to place the burden of loss on the shareholders (1985: 368 – 371).

Finally, Zysman claims that the fractured financial system limits the government's capacity for direct industrial intervention (1984: 269).

3.6 Economic Regulation

State regulation of industries, which started with the railroads in the 1880s, was extended to more and more industries during the New Deal (Schwartz 1973). By 1965, industries that together contributed about 10% of the GNP were subjected to economic regulation, i. e., a state agency controlled one or more aspects of private-enterprise operations, such as market entry or exit; rate, price, and profit structures; and service standards (Scherer 1970: 519). These industries can be classified as follows: (a) those with long capital turnover times, such as the public utilities and telephone companies; (b) those for whom competition may be destructive (e. g., air-traffic and trucking); and (c) those whose irresponsible actions might affect the entire economy (e. g., banking and insurance).

Regulation of these industries constituted an integral part of the domestic growth strategy. While the guaranteed return on fixed assets promoted the continuous implementation of labor-saving equipment (Capron 1971: 10 – 12), the control of entry facilitated the broad unionization of those sectors which stimulated aggregate demand (see the lucid account of the teamster organizing technique, by James and James 1965). Users are protected against predatory pricing and benefited from greater stability and reliability (Thayer 1984; Kleinsteuber 1977: 56).

The fight against regulation became a crusade for economists during the 1970s. An ever-growing body of literature has extensively expounded on the deficiencies of economic regulation. These can be briefly summarized by noting that high rents (trucking), excessive service levels (airlines), and overcapitalization (AT&T) are all examples of economic inefficiencies fostering inflation (see Kahn 1970; Phillips 1975; and Breyer 1982).

However, these negative aspects of regulation only gained significance once the user industries lost their ability to pass higher prices on to the consumer. Furthermore, the institutional set-up of regulation is not well suited for the promotion of international competitiveness. In contrast to public enterprises, the regulatory agencies do not allow the state to influence directly the investment decisions of particular firms (Mitnick 1980: 396 – 415).[4]

3.7 Job-Control Unionism

The specific form of the industrial relations in the major manufacturing industries can be characterized as job-control unionism (Piore 1982). In the voluntarist tradition of American industrial relations, the state regulates only marginally the content of the collective bargaining agreements. The low level of social security provided by the state, furthermore, enlarges the scope of possible bargaining issues between the union and the employer. Although management is free to make basic entrepreneurial and managerial decisions, its discretionary power over the allocation of labor and the conditions of employment has been severely restricted by the three pillars of job-control unionism, i. e., legalistic conflict resolution, detailed job classifications, and a comprehensive seniority system (Katz 1985). In other words, most aspects of labor relations in unionized manufacturing plants have been governed by the collective-bargaining agreement.

The system of job classifications specifies in quite some detail the individual tasks within the production process, and, e. g., a large assembly plant may have 50 to 100 nonskilled job-titles (Parker 1985: 28). Under this system a qualitative change in the workload requires the approval of the local union (Dohse et al. 1984: 12 ff).

The better-known seniority system, which regulates the lines of succession in regard to hiring, firing, and internal promotions according to the length of service, further limits management's allocative powers. On the other hand, the use of the seniority principle allows the smooth adaptation of manning levels to changes in business volume, since the criteria for the selection of those to be laid off are accepted by all sides (see Doeringer and Piore 1971; Medoff 1979; 380 ff; and Köhler and Sengenberger 1983).

Through the legalistic enforcement of these rules by means of the grievance procedure, management has been further locked into the rigidities of these practices. In the past, when all suppliers of the U.S. market faced similar restrictions and long production runs were common, job-control unionism did not represent a major threat to the economic prosperity of domestic manufacturers. It had proven itself to be a workable mechanism for coordinating the different interests of capital and labor (Freeman and Medoff 1984). Nevertheless, already by the mid-1960s, the rigidities of these practices were impeding further productivity increases. In the new open environment these limits became obvious: U.S. companies now face foreign competitors who enjoy much more flexibility in assigning workers to different jobs. The savings gained by integrating certain maintenance and quality-control functions in the job assignments of production workers, for example, have been quite substantial.[5]

Furthermore, since job positions are not allocated according to merit or performance, workers have no incentive to compete for job opportunities. Without the possibility of rewarding quality-conscious workers with tangible benefits, management faces severe difficulties in motivating the work force to deliver on quality – while of course management's past inattentiveness concerning quality issues certainly has not helped to motivate workers in this regard either (Abernathy et al. 1982: 100).

3.8 Supplier-Assembler Relations

In the postwar period most manufacturing industries were characterized by a high level of vertical integration (Scherer 1980). The degree of vertical integration was usually positively correlated with the market share of a company.[6]

Relations to supliers have been at arm's length. Contracts were awarded semiannually or annually and without exact specification of the amounts to be delivered. This competitive bidding procedure left prices as the major influence in the buying decision. Although one can assume that most contracts were renewed repeatedly, the practice of multiple sourcing, i. e., plant managers kept two or more supliers for the delivery of identical parts, guaranteed competition (White 1971: 85).

The advantages of a high degree of vertical integration were numerous. It allowed for a balanced growth between the production capacities for intermediate and final products (Aglietta 1979: 117), it raised the barriers of entry (Lamoreaux 1985), and it reduced the risk of falling behind in the technological development of parts. Monteverde and Teece (1981) have argued that – given the costs of transferring the knowledge of real-life persons between separate companies – the development of new technologies is strongly encouraged by vertical integration.

The practices of annual bidding, multiple sourcing, and tapered vertical integration (meaning reliance on both in-house production and outside sources for the same parts) reflected the concern that major assemblers had of becoming strategically dependent on one supplier. Today, for example, the possibility of international sourcing reduces the automakers' exposure to the "opportunism" (Williamson 1985) of their domestic suppliers. This process of internationalization has also forced U.S. management to rethink its traditional approach to parts sourcing. On the one hand, U.S. manufacturers now face the competition of Japanese producers who excel in operating their production processes at a high level of product output over extended periods of time (Abernathy et al. 1982). The higher yield is said to be primarily the result of a superior materials control system which is embedded in the "Shitauke" system of dependent-parts suppliers. The close collaboration between assembler and parts suppliers allows for "just-in-time" (JIT) production[7] and mutual problem-solving. Furthermore, the considerable wage differentials within the "Shitauke" system provide for additional benefits (Nomura 1985: 11 – 16). On the other hand, due to the vagaries of competition, flexibility has become essential. Vertical integration, however, converts variable costs into fixed costs. The high costs of product development and special-purpose machinery make the integrated companies captives of their own designs – i.e., vertical integration impedes the adoption of the latest innovations (Hayes and Abernathy 1980: 72).

Implementation of the JIT principles also presupposes cooperative industrial relations. A strike, even at a small supplier, has the potential of shutting down an entire assembly plant. The postwar decentralization of assembly plants in the U.S. auto industry was, however, according to Philip Caldwell, former chairman of Ford, a deliberate strategy to keep the newly unionized workers as much dispersed as possible (*Business Week*, June 21, 1982, p. 62).

4 Fragility of the Efforts for Change

4.1 Demise of Job-Control Unionism

Beginning in the early 1970s, some manufacturers, especially in the auto industry, started to experiment with "quality circles" and team-work approaches. The crisis of 1981/1982 led to an intensification of efforts to redefine industrial relations, but so far a complete overhaul of the traditional system has yet to be achieved (Cole 1985).

The major problems faced by this transformation towards more flexible and participatory industrial relations seem to stem from (a) a general resistance to change, (b) the lack of institutionalization within the political system under which American unions suffer (Erd and Scherrer 1984: 83 – 87), and (c) the combination of both cooperative and distributive modifications (Altshuler et al. 1984: 281).

A. What has proven to be successful in the past will not easily be changed. Resistance to more effective work practices can also be observed at non-union plants. In general, unwillingness to change is correlated with the age of a plant (McKersie and Klein 1985: 146). The low investment levels of U.S. manufacturing companies, therefore, reinforce uncompetitive labor relations.

B. Unions have only been rudimentarily institutionalized within the political system because of the pronounced resistance of American capital to macroeconomic conceptions – e.g., the recognition that unions play a socially useful role – as well as the liberal, anti-interventionist tradition of the state and the union's own voluntarist tradition. From this it follows that the labor bureaucracy cannot compensate for changed labor-market conditions with its own political influence (Piore 1983). In fact, American unions seem to enjoy only minimal legal protection against attempts by employers to exploit the new balance of power in the marketplace by, e.g., unilaterally canceling collective-bargaining agreements. Under these conditions organized labor in the U.S.A. lacks the ability to influence the restructuring of a particular industry through the state, as is the case with its European counterparts (Ross and Gourevitch 1984).

Since unions are heavily dependent on their shopfloor control for both their power and legitimacy, changes in shopfloor relations bear the risk of endangering survival of the organization itself. If, for example, a union agrees to the broadening of job classifications and to a less-rigid enforcement of the lines of demarcation, its members might no longer feel protected by its apparatus. If, then, the workers' complaints are handled by company or jointly selected "team leaders," shop stewards might become dispensable in the eyes of the union members. In the absence of legally mandated codetermination structures, the unions face the risk that once cooperation has undermined their legitimacy, management will try to get rid of unions altogether (Mroczkowski 1984: 56). In fact, current U.S. labor law is not supportive of any cooperative efforts (Schlossberg and Fetter 1986).

C. Forced to act quickly as a result of the severe recession of 1981/1982, the automakers tried to combine the introduction of more flexibility into human-resource allocation with a reduction in wage levels. Obviously the strategy of taking dollars from workers' pockets contradicts any attempts to elicit their cooperation for a more efficient design of the labor process. This "strategic confusion" (Katz and Sabel 1985) generally led to giving priority to temporary wage reductions at the expense of institutional changes in labor relations.

Usually, management initiated changes in labor relations at plants whose work force was in a weak bargaining position either because a plant shutdown loomed in the near future due to low levels of demand, or because plans for out-sourcing existed. However, the fact that these changes are usually achieved only at "gunpoint," clouds their prospects if conditions change. It is not surprising that workers at GM's Flint (Michigan) plant stopped participating in a two-year-old quality program to protest the planned layoff of 1350 workers (*International Herald Tribune*, November 9, 1983, p. 7; for more such examples, see Parker 1985: 63–67). Furthermore, the implementation of quality circles does not automatically end the traditional adversary relationship between labor and management (Katz et al. 1983: 15). Without a corresponding new comprehensive industrial-relations model, a quality circle is an "unstable organizational structure that is likely to self-destruct" (Lawler and Mohrman 1985: 64).

4.2 Intra-Industry Cooperation

The semiconductor industry is an additional example of an attempt to adjust structurally to foreign competition. U.S. semiconductor companies were once the envy of the world for their innovativeness and dynamism. But in the last several years, Japanese manufacturers have taken the lead in many areas of semiconductor technology (*New York Times*, January 7, 1987, p. D7). Some of the problems of the U.S. semiconductor industry can be traced to the crisis in the traditional manufacturing industries. Its domestic market has become smaller with the exodus of the U.S. entertainment electronics industry and the decline of other important users of microchips, such as the machine-tool and automobile industries (Schulze 1986).

Nevertheless, many of the causes of the dire conditions of the U.S. semiconductor business are internal to the industry. For one, companies neglected quality manufacturing, although they were not subject to restrictive union practices.[8] Second, the much-praised "venture-capital" structure appears to be no longer adequate for the more mature state of the industry. Especially merchant suppliers – companies that sell to outsiders – lack the financial might to keep up research during economic downturns. In contrast, Japanese manufacturers are integrated into large electronic combines which provide them with a captive market and financial staying power. As a result, Japanese chipmakers have kept up investment levels even during phases of declining demand (Uttal 1987: 57).

The industry responded with anti-dumping charges against the Japanese, which culminated in the U.S.-Japan semiconductor trade agreement of 1986, and the industry has embarked on new ways to spread R & D costs among its members. The first cooperative reserach venture, the Semiconductor Research Cooperative (SRC), was established in 1982 by the Semiconductor Industry Association. Its purpose was to fund basic research at U.S. universities. Earlier hopes in having an annual budget exceeding $ 30 million by 1985 (Finan and LaMond 1985: 163) have not materialized. Annual budgets have amounted to $ 18 million (*New York Times*, September 30, 1986, p. D1).

With the strong support of the Department of Defense, which also has committed $ 1.1 million to SRC, the industry is now lobbying for the establishment of a Semiconductor Manufacturing Technology Institute, called Sematech. This $ 1 billion cooperative manufacturing venture is supposed to be funded jointly by government and industry (*New York Times*, January 6, 1987, p. D1). While most merchant suppliers envisioned Sematech to be huge and to sell chips on the open market, anti-trust rules, which prohibit competitors from cooperating in the manufacture of products, allow only a small pilot manufacturing project that would develop new technology which could be used by member companies (Kehoe 1987 a,b). Besides anti-trust restrictions, Sematech faces numerous other obstacles. Member companies are expected not to lend their best engineers and to guard their know-how tightly. IBM has not committed any technology as yet (Uttal 1987: 58). A national cooperative effort has also been called into question by the increasing numbers of joint ventures with Japanese manufacturers. For example, the semiconductor production equipment and materials industries, which also supply Japanese producers, have been reluctant to take sides in the U.S.-Japanese chip dispute (Kehoe 1987 b). Another obstacle will be the budget restraints of the federal government (*New York Times*, January 6, 1987, p. D7). Since, in terms of the budget, reliance on trade sanctions is least costly and thus the favorite mode for Washington's lawmakers, the future of Sematech and the U.S. semiconductor industry remains clouded.

4.3 Southern Trends

The description of the domestic growth of the U.S. economy has so far largely focused on institutions of the northern part of the United States. Regional diversity, however, is a prominent feature of U.S. society. Traditionally, a great divide has run between the north and the south. Lacking a tradition of mass-production industries, the south has been governed by a set of social regulation that differed markedly from those in the north. As a result of the federal structure of the U.S. and an implicit understanding with northern industrialists (Domhoff 1972), southern politicians were able to exempt their states from many social provisions of the New Deal legacy, e. g., social security rolls were closed to blacks, local autonomy in administering relief programs led to persistently lower levels of welfare payments in the south than in the northeast, and the passage of right-to-work laws in the wake of the Taft-Hartley Act in 1947 undercut previously enacted pro-labor legislation such as the Wagner Act (Piven and Cloward 1971).

The resulting availability of a large and docile labor pool, a low level of taxation, and high responsiveness to infrastructural requirements made the south attractive for northern capital in the 1960s (Bluestone and Harrison 1982; Cobb 1984). As has already been explained, the rise of southern manufacturing aggravated the problems of the industries in the north (see Scherrer 1987 for the impact of the north/south dynamic on the steel industry). While acknowledging the painful aspects of this shift, Norton (1986) has emphasized the therapeutic value of this U.S. regional diversity. In a process of "creative destruction" more jobs were created within the manufacturing sector of the south in the 1970s than were destroyed in the north (1986: 14). Can one agree with Norton? Is regional heterogeneity a source of renewal which will spare the U.S.A. the kind of institutional sclerosis that is apparently bedeviling Britain? Does the south work as an incubator for a model of international competitiveness which will succeed the domestic market growth model?

While it is indisputable that the south has provided U.S. capital with profitable outlets (e.g., the city-building dynamic) as well as with leverage over organized labor, a number of arguments raise doubts with regard to the future viability of the southern model.

First, many of the above-described institutional impediments to international competitiveness also apply to the south. For example, the south has traditionally neglected education. McKersie and Klein argue that advantages like lower absenteeism or the absence of work rules "are not enough to offset the human capital disadvantages of a very transient work force that is not highly trained" (1985: 144; see also Weinstain et al. 1985).

Second, a strategy based on low wages and a non-union environment runs the risk of losing industrial jobs to even more "favorable" environments abroad (Bluestone and Harrison 1982).

Finally, the southern economic model seems to possess only a limited capacity to reproduce itself. Since it rules out the linkage of wages to productivity increases, reproduction depends on outside markets. Thus, once the possibilities for substituting the northern industries are exhausted, southern manufacturing will be confronted by demand constraints unless it succeeds in replacing foreign products. In light of the educational deficiencies of the southern work force, this industrial leadership position does not seem to be likely – at least not for a broad spectrum of products.

5 Conclusion

Throughout the postwar period the relative ability of the United States to shape the scope and direction of rule change in the international economy may have reduced the perceived need for structural adaptation (Ilgen 1985). Acting on an earlier awareness of the necessity for structural change, however, would certainly have been a truly Herculean task. Strongly interrelated, the institutions of the domestic market growth model are remarkably resistant to change. Some institutions, such as the education system, may take a generation to reorganize.

Nevertheless, some serious efforts are under way to adapt past practices to today's competitive environment. The examples I have presented of these efforts have been primarily concerned with forming closer and more cooperative links within industry. The mechanisms to elicit this cooperation seem to be rooted in the same processes that make these changes necessary: the possibility to "source" globally, the potentialities of new technology, and the eventuality of economic disaster if the necessary changes are not made.

Interestingly, this "cooperation in the context of competition" is organized in the main independently of the political system. In the absence of government legislation to institutionalize or support a mechanism of flexible adaptation, voluntary programs are likely to be subjected to the vagaries of shifting opportunities. Although Keynesian demand management has been proven inadequate for the new competitive environment, a shift to supply-side policies may not be sufficient. What seems to be required, is a new quality of state intervention which links macro with micro policies.

Even should the United States succeed in regaining its industrial leadership position, the success might turn out to be bitter-sweet. Reduction of the current trade deficit will result in a massive redirection of trade flows with devastating consequences for other nations, unless it is accompanied by a worldwide growth dynamic. In view of the current efforts directed mainly at wage and employment reduction, chances are high that the basis for long-term economic growth, i.e., the distribution of income in anticipation of productivity gains, is going to be eroded worldwide.

Notes

1 This statement has to be qualified for certain countries, such as Sweden, which occupy a favorable position in the international division of labor and where Keynesian demand management is complemented by active supply-side policies.

2 "There are five provisions in the federal income tax code that favor investment in the housing sector: (1) exclusion of net imputed rent for owner-occupied homes, (2) deductibility of mortgage interest, (3) deferral of capital gains on home sales, (4) one-time exclusion of up to $ 125,000 in capital gains from home sales for those fifty-five years and older, and (5) exclusion of interest from tax-exempt mortgage bonds" (Baumol and McLennan 1985: 210).

3 Although studies on corporate interlocks have indicated a dominating influence of some financial groups in the U.S.A. (Fitch and Oppenheimer 1970; Kotz 1978), the control that U.S. banks have over industry is not comparable to the German "Universalbankensystem."

4 The West-German postal system, however, seems to display the capability for adaptation (Lüthje 1986).

5 In Japan apparently only 1.8 hours of inspection and repair personnel are required per automobile produced, compared with about 4.1 hours in the U.S. (Dohse et al. 1984: 19).

6 General motors, for example, has historically bought only 10 to 15 percent of standard components outside (Hunker 1983: 31), while for Chrysler this figure is about 70 percent (Stundza 1985: 31).

7 The primary goal of JIT production is to reduce inventory stocks through tight delivery schedules. Materials, parts, and components are scheduled to arrive at the point of assembly just before they are needed. The resulting smaller buffer stocks save on inventory carrying costs, plant-size requirements, and materials handling personnel. For a detailed description of the JIT system in Japan, see Monden (1981) and Sugimori et al. (1977).

8 Japanese manufacturers enjoy much higher process yields, 38% versus 23% in the U.S.A. (Finan and LaMond 1985: 156).

References

Abernathy, William J. (Chairman) (1982): *The Competitive Status of the U.S. Auto Industry: A Study of the Influences of Technology in Determining International Industrial Competitive Advantage*, Washington D.C.: National Academy Press.

Aglietta, Michel (1982): World Capitalism in the Eighties. *New Left Review* 136, (November – December): 5 – 41.

Aglietta, Michel (1979): *A Theory of Capitalist Regulation. The US Experience.* New York: NLB.

AISI, American Iron and Steel Institute (1981): *Annual Report*. Washington D.C.: AISI.

Alpert, Norman and Eugene L. Holt (1980): Inter-Industry Cooperative Research and the Government: Two Case Studies. In D. H. Ginsburg and W. J. Abernathy (eds.), *Government, Technology, and the Future of the Automobile.* New York: McGraw-Hill, 334 – 342.

Altshuler, Alan, et al. (1984): *The Future of the Automobile. The Report of MIT's International Automobile Program.* Cambridge, Mass.: MIT Press.

Altvater, Elmar, Jürgen Hoffmann and Willi Semmler (1980): *Vom Wirtschaftswunder zur Wirtschaftskrise.* Berlin: Olle and Walter, 2 vols.

Altvater, Elmar, Kurt Hübner and Michael Stanger (1983): *Alternative Wirtschaftspolitik jenseits des Keynesianismus.* Opladen: Westdeutscher Verlag.

Baumol, William J. and Kenneth McLennan (1985): Toward an Effective Productivity Program. In William J. Baumol and Kenneth McLennan (eds.), *Productivity Growth and U.S. Competitiveness. A Supplementary Paper of the Committee for Economic Development.* New York: Oxford University Press, 187 – 224.

Bergsten, C. Fred (1983): The International Dimension. In G. W. Miller (ed.), *Regrowing the American Economy.* Englewood Cliffs, N.J.: Prentice-Hall, 151 – 168.

Bluestone, Barry and Bennett Harrison (1982): *The Deindustrialization of America.* Washington, D.C.: Basic Books.

Bower, Joseph L. and Eric A. Rheman (1985): Benevolent Cartels. *Harvard Business Review*, (July/August): 124–132.

Branson, William H. (1982): Industrial Policy and U.S. International Trade. In Michael Wachter and Susan Wachter (eds.), *Toward a New U.S. Industrial Policy?* Philadelphia: University of Pennsylvania Press, 378–408.

Breyer, Stephen (1982): *Regulation and Its Reform*. Cambridge, Mass.: Harvard University Press.

Brooks, Harvey (1985): Technology as a Factor in U.S. Competitiveness. In Bruce R. Scott and G. C. Lodge (eds.), *US Competitiveness in the World Economy*. Boston: Harvard Business School Press, 328–356.

Business Week, June 21, 1982, 59–63.

Capron, William M. (ed.) (1971): *Technological Change in Regulated Industries*. Washintgon D.C.: The Brookings Institution.

Caspersen, Finn M. W. (1981): Contribution as a discussant to "Capital Formation." In Michael Wachter and Susan Wachter (eds.), *Toward a New U.S. Industrial Policy?* Philadelphia: University of Pennsylvania Press, 143–145.

CEA, Council of Economic Advisers (1985): *Annual Report*. Washington D.C.: Government Printing Office.

Chandler, Alfred D. (1977): *The Visible Hand: The Managerial Revolution in American Business*. Cambridge, Mass.: Belknap Press.

Cobb, James C. (1984): *Industrialization and Southern Society 1877–1984*. Lexington, Ky.: University of Kentucky Press.

Cole, Robert E. (1985): Target Information for Competitive Performance. *Harvard Business Review*, (May–June): 100–109.

Crandall, Robert W. (1981): *The U.S. Steel Industry in Recurrent Crisis: Policy Options in a Competitive World*. Washington D.C.: Brookings Institution.

Doeringer, Peter B. and Michael J. Piore (1971): *Internal Labor Markets and Manpower Analysis*. Lexington/Mass.: Lexington Books.

Dohse, Knuth, Ulrich Jürgens, and Thomas Malsch (1984): *Reorganisation der Arbeit in der Automobilindustrie – Konzepte, Regelungen, Veränderungstendenzen in den USA, Großbritannien und der Bundesrepublik Deutschland – Ein Materialbericht*. Berlin: International Institute for Comparative Social Research, Labor Policy, Wissenschaftszentrum Berlin, IIVG discussion paper 84-220.

Domhoff, G. William (1972): *Fat Cats and Democrats: The Role of the Big Rich in the Party of the Common Man*. Englewood Cliffs, N.J.: Prentice-Hall.

Eckstein, Otto and Robert Tannenwald (1981): Productivity and Capital Formation. In Michael Wachter and Susan Wachter (eds.), *Toward a New U.S. Industrial Policy?* Philadelphia: University of Pennsylvania Press, 95–127.

Eckstein, Otto, Ch. Canton, R. Brinner, and P. Duprey (1984): *The DRI Report on US Manufacturing Industries*. New York: McGraw.

Erd, Rainer and Christoph Scherrer (1984): Amerikanische Gewerkschaften – Opfer des Weltmarkts. *Prokla* 54: 78–96.

Finan, William F. and Annette M. LaMond (1985): Sustaining U.S. Competitiveness in Microelectronics: The Challenge to U.S. Policy. In Bruce R. Scott and George C. Lodge (eds.), *U.S. Competitiveness in the World Economy*. Boston: Harvard Business School Press, 144–175.

Fitch, Robert and Mary Oppenheimer (1970): Who Rules the Corporation? *Socialist Revolution* 1(4–6): 33–94.

Freeman, Richard and James Medoff (1984): *What Do Unions Do?* New York: Basic Books.

Galbraith, James K. (1987): The Case for Shock Treatment. *Challenge*, (July–August): 4–10.

Hampton, William J. and James R. Norman (1987): General Motors: What Went Wrong. *Business Week*, March 16: 44–51.

Hayes, Robert and William Abernathy (1980): Managing Our Way to Economic Decline. *Harvard Business Review*, (July): 67–78.

Hirsch, Joachim (1980): *Der Sicherheitsstaat. Das „Modell Deutschland", seine Krisen und die „neuen sozialen Bewegungen"*. Frankfurt: Suhrkamp.

Hoadley, Walter E. (1984): Banking and Finance: The Cost of Capital in Japan and the United States. In Chalmers Johnson (ed.), *The Industrial Policy Debate*. San Francisco: Institute for Contemporary Studies, 173–194.

Hunker, Jeffrey Allen (1983): *Structural Change and the U.S. Automobile Industry*. Lexington, Mass.: Lexington Books.

Ilgen, Thomas L. (1985): *Economy and Interdependence. U.S.-Western European Monetary and Trade Relations, 1958–1984*. Towota, N.J.: Rowman and Allanheld.

International Herald Tribune, November 9, 1983, 7.

James, Ralph and Estelle James (1965): *Hoffa and the Teamsters*. Princeton, N.J.: Princeton University Press.

Kahn, Alfred E. (1970): *The Economics of Regulation: Principles and Institutions*, 2 vols. New York: Wiley.

Kantor, Harvey (1982): Vocationalism in American Education: The Economic and Political Context, 1880–1930. In Harvey Kantor and David B. Tyack (eds.), *Work, Youth, and Schooling. Historical Perspectives on Vocationalism in American Education*. Stanford: Stanford University Press, 14–44.

Katz, Harry C. (1985): *Shifting Gears: Changing Labor Relations in the U.S. Automobile Industry*. Cambridge, Mass.: MIT Press.

Katz, Harry C. and Charles Sabel (1985): Industrial Relations and Industrial Adjustment in the Car Industry. *Industrial Relations* 24(3): 295–315.

Katz, Harry C., Thomas A. Kochan, and Kenneth R. Gobeille (1983): Industrial Relations Performance, Economic Performance, and QWL Programs: An Interplant Analysis. *Industrial and Labor Relations Review* 37(1): 3–17.

Kehoe, Louise (1987 a): Chip Makers Ask Congress for Help. *Financial Times*, March 5: 4.

Kehoe, Louise (1987 b): Bid to Make U.S. World Leader in Semiconductor Technology. *Financial Times*, May 14: 6.

Kett, Joseph F. (1982): The Adolescence of Vocational Education. In Harvey Kantor and David B. Tyack (eds.), *Work, Youth, and Schooling. Historical Perspectives on Vocationalism in American Education*. Stanford: Stanford University Press, 79–109.

Kleinsteuber, Hans J. (1977): *Staatsintervention und Verkehrspolitik in den USA: Die Interstate Commerce Commission. Ein Beitrag zur politischen Ökonomie der Vereinigten Staaten*. Stuttgart: Metzler.

Köhler, Christoph and Werner Sengenberger (1983): *Konjunktur und Personalanpassung, Betriebliche Beschäftigungspolitik in der deutschen und amerikanischen Automobilindustrie*. Frankfurt: Campus.

Kotz, David (1978): *Bank Control of Large Corporations in the United States*. Berkeley: University of California Press.

Krasner, Stephen D. (1978): United States Commercial and Monetary Policy: Unravelling the Paradox of External Strength and Internal Weakness. In Peter J. Katzenstein (ed.), *Between Power and Plenty: Foreign Economic Policies of Advanced Industrial States*. Madison: University of Wisconsin Press, 51 – 87.

Krekeler, Nobert (1981): Berufliche Bildung – die Zukunft der Bildung in den USA? In Rüdiger Ahrens (ed.), *Amerikanische Bildungswirklichkeit heute*. Hildesheim: Georg Olms, 157 – 188.

Lamoreaux, Naomi R. (1985): *The Great Merger Movement in American Business*. Cambridge, England: Cambridge University Press.

Lawler, Edward E. III and Susan A. Mohrman (1985): Quality Circles After the Fad. *Harvard Business Review*, (January/February): 64 – 71.

Lawrence, Paul R. and Davis Dyer (1983): *Renewing American Industry*. New York: Free Press.

Lawrence, Robert Z. (1984): *Can America Compete?* Washington: Brookings Institution.

Lipietz, Alain (1984): Imperialism or the Beast of the Apocalypse. *Capital and Class* 22: 81 – 110.

Lipietz, Alain (1985): *The Enchanted World, Inflation, Credit and the World Crisis*. London: Verso Books.

Lipietz, Alain (1986): Behind the Crisis: The Exhaustion of a Regime of Accumulation. A "Regulation School" Perspective on some French Empirical Works. *Review of Radical Political Economics* 18(1 & 2): 13 – 32.

Long, Robert Emmet (ed.) (1984): *American Education*. New York: H. W. Wilson.

Lüthje, Boy (1986): Regulierungskrise im Telekommunikationssektor in der BRD. *Prokla* 64(3): 64 – 84.

McKersie, Robert B. and Janice A. Klein (1985): Productivity: The Industrial Relations Connection. In William J. Baumol and Kenneth McLennan (eds.), *Productivity Growth and U.S. Competitiveness. A Supplementary Paper of the Committee for Economic Development*. New York: Oxford University Press, 119 – 159.

Medoff, James L. (1979): Layoffs and Alternatives under Trade Unions in U.S. Manufacturing. *American Economic Review* 69(3): 380 – 395.

Meyer, Jack A. and Rosemary Gibson Kern (1985): The Changing Structure of the Health Care System. In Phillip Cagan (ed.), *The Impact of the Reagan Program, Essays in Contemporary Economic Problems, 1986*. Washintgon D.C.: American Enterprise Institute, 191 – 222.

Mitnick, Barry M. (1980): *The Political Economy of Regulation*. New York: Columbia University Press.

Monden, Yasushiro (1981): What makes the Toyota Production System Really Tick? *Industrial Engineering*, January, 36 – 40.

Monteverde, Kirk and David J. Teece (1981): *Contractual Incompleteness, Human Capital and the Vertical Integration of Production: Some Evidence from the U.S. Automobile Industry*. Stanford University: Graduate School of Business.

Mroczkowski, Tomasz (1984): Is the American Labour-Management Relationship Changing? *British Journal of Industrial Relations* 22(1): 47 – 62.

Naples, Michele I. (1986): The Unraveling of the Union-Capital Truce and the U.S. Industrial Productivity Crisis. *Review of Radical Political Economics* 18(1 & 2): 110 – 131.

National Commission on Excellence in Education (1983): *A Nation at Risk: The Imperative for Educational Reform*. Report to the Nation and the Secretary of Education, April. Washington D.C.: U.S. Department of Education.

New York Times, September 30, 1986, D1.

New York Times, January 6, 1987, D1, 7.

New York Times, January 7, 1987, D7.

Noble, David (1984): *Forces of Production. A Social History of Industrial Automation*. New York: Knopf.

Nomura, Masami (1985): *"Model Japan"? Characteristics of Industrial Relations in the Japanese Automobile Industry*. Berlin: International Institute for Comparative Social Research, Labor Policy, Wissenschaftszentrum Berlin, IIVG discussion paper 85-207.

Norton, R. D. (1986): Industrial Policy and and American Renewal. *Journal of Economic Literature* 24(1): 1 – 40.

Olson, Mancur (1982): *The Rise and Decline of Nations. Economic Growth, Stagflation and Social Rigidities*. New Haven, Conn.: Yale University Press.

Parker, Mike (1985): *Inside the Circle: A Union Guide to QWL*. Boston: South End Press.

PCIC, Report of the President's Commission on Industrial Competitiveness (1985): *Global Competition: The New Reality*, 3 vols. Washintgon D.C.: Government Printing Office.

Phillips, Almarin (1975): Introduction. Almarin Phillips (ed.), *Promoting Competition in Regulated Markets*. Washington D.C.: Brookings, F 3 – 26.

Pincus, J. J. (1980): Tariffs. In Glenn Porter (ed.), *Encyclopedia of American History*. New York: Scribner's, 439 – 450.

Piore, Michael J. (1982): American Labor and the Industrial Crisis. *Challenge*, (March/April): 5 – 11.

Piore, Michael J. (1983): *Fissure and Discontinuity in U.S. Labor Management Relations*. Presentation to Conference on Labor Markets, Industrial Policy and Economic Growth, Stressa, Italy, July 4 – 10.

Piore, Michael J. and Charles Sable (1984): *The Second Industrial Divide*. New York: Basic Books.

Piven, Frances Fox and Richard Cloward (1971): *Regulating the Poor*. New York: Random House.

Reich, Robert B. (1983): The Next American Frontier. *The Atlantic Monthly*, (April): 97 – 108.

Ross, G. and P. Gourevitch (1984): Conclusion. In P. Gourevitch et al., *Unions and Economic Crisis: Britain, West Germany, and Sweden*. London: George, Allen and Unwin, 360 – 386.

Salter, Malcolm S., Alan M. Webber and Davis Dyer (1985): U.S. Competitiveness in Global Industries: Lessons from the Auto Industry. In B. R. Scott and G. C. Lodge (eds.), *An International Political Economy*. Boulder, Colo., Westview, 185 – 229.

Scherer, Frederic M. (1970/80): *Industrial Market Structure and Economic Performance*, 1st/2nd ed., Boston: Houghton Mifflin.

Scherer, Frederic M. (1981): Regulatory Dynamics and Economic Growth. In Michael Wachter and Susan Wachter (eds.), *Toward a New U.S. Industrial Policy?* Philadelphia: University of Pennsylvania Press, 289 – 320.

Scherrer, Christoph (1987): *Mini-mills – A New Growth Path for the U.S. Steel Industry?* Freie University Berlin, John F.-Kennedy-Institut, Working Paper No. 7.

Scherrer, Christoph (1983): *Kritische Würdigung des konservativen Beitrages zur U.S. Reindustrialisierungsdebatte. Das Beispiel der U.S. Stahlindustrie.* Unpublished Diplomarbeit, Frankfurt: J. W. Goethe University.

Schlossberg, Stephen I. and Steven M. Fetter (1986): Analysis of U.S. Labor Law and Future of Labor-Management Cooperation. *Daily Labor Report*, June 17, D 1 – D 13.

Schulze, Peter W. (1986): Der Kampf um die Märkte der Zukunft: Internationaler Wettbewerb und Technologieentwicklung. *WSI-Mitteilungen* 39(6): 415 – 422.

Schwartz, Bernard (ed.) (1973): *The Economic Regulation of Business and Industry. A Legislative History of U.S. Regulatory Agencies*, 5 vols. New York: Chelsea House.

Scott, Bruce (1985): U.S. Competitiveness: Concepts, Performance, and Implications. In Bruce R. Scott and G. C. Lodge (eds.), *US Competitiveness in the World Economy*. Boston: Harvard Business School Press, 13 – 70.

Steindl, Josef (1976): *Maturity and Stagnation in American Capitalism*. New York: Monthly Review Press.

Stundza, Tom (1985): New Supplier System at Chrysler. *Purchasing* 99, July 25: 42 – 9.

Sugimori, Y., K. Kusunoki, F. Cho, and S. Uchikawa (1977): Toyota Production System and Kanban System: Materialization of Just-In-Time and Respect for Humans System. *International Journal of Production Research* 15(6): 553 – 561.

Szymanski, Al (1984): Productivity Growth and Capitalist Stagnation. *Science and Society* 48: 295 – 322.

Thayer, Frederick (1984): *Rebuilding America: The Case for Economic Regulation*. New York: Praeger.

Thurow, Lester (1980): The Zero-Sum Society. New York: Basic Books.

Thurow, Lester (1985): *The Zero-Sum Solution*. New York: Simon and Schuster.

Uttal, Bro (1987): How Chipmakers Can Survive. *Fortune*, April 13, 57 – 58.

Walters, Robert S. (1985): Industrial Crises and U.S. Public Policy. In W. Ladd Hollist and F. LaMond Tullis (eds.), *International Political Economy Yearbook*. Boulder, Colo., Westview.

Weinstein, Bernard, Harold T. Gross, and John Rees (1985): *Regional Growth and Decline in the United States*, 2nd ed. New York: Praeger.

Wellons, Phillip A. (1985): Competitiveness in the World Economy: The Role of the U.S. Financial System. In Bruce R. Scott and George C. Lodge (eds.), *U.S. Competitiveness in the World Economy*. Boston: Harvard Business School Press, 185 – 229.

White, Lawrence J. (1971): *The Automobile Industry Since 1945*. Cambridge: Harvard University Press.

Wiley, R. E. (1980): Competition and Deregulation in Telecommunications: The American Experience. In Ernst-Joachim Mestmäcker (ed.), *1980: Kommunikation ohne Monopole*. Baden-Baden: Nomos.

Williamson, Oliver E. (1985): *The Economic Institutions of Capitalism*. New York: Free Press.

Williamson, Oliver E. (1986): Transforming Merger Policy: The Pound of New Perspectives. *The American Economic Review*, (May): 114 – 119.

Wolfe, Barbara L., Philip De Jong, Robert Haveman, Victor Halberstadt, and Kees Goudswaard (1984): Income Transfers and Work Effort: The Netherlands and the United States in the 1970s. *Kyklos* 37(4): 609 – 637.

Wolff, Edward N. (1985): The Magnitude and Causes of the Recent Productivity Slowdown in the United States: A Survey of Recent Studies. In William J. Baumol and Kenneth McLennan (eds.), *Productivity Growth and U.S. Competitiveness. A Supplementary Paper of the Committee for Economic Development*. New York: Oxford University Press, 29 – 57.

Young, John A. (1985): Global Competition: The New Reality. *California Management Review* 27(3): 11 – 25.

Zysman, John (1984): *Governments, Markets, and Growth: Financial Systems and the Politics of Industrial Change*. Ithaca: Cornell University Press.

Japan-U.S. Relations: The 1980s and Beyond

I. M. Destler

Japan's economic expansion, and the U.S.-Japanese alliance, have been among "the most remarkable and least expected success stories of the past thirty years." So concluded four American and Japanese scholars, myself among them, in a Brookings study published twelve years ago (Destler, Sato, Clapp & Fukui 1976: 1). Had we known then what the next twelve years would bring, we could only have been more impressed by the strength and durability of the relationship. For nothwithstanding the return of Okinawa to Japanese sovereignty, few would have foreseen the extent of military and security cooperation that has developed over the past decade. Still less would many have predicted that economic relations could remain tolerable – if not exactly harmonious – with a bilateral trade imbalance exceeding $ 50 billion. The peak as of 1975, after all, had been $ 4 billion.

Yet the mid-1980s have seen mounting U.S.-Japan economic tensions, reaching a level unprecedented in the postwar period, culminating in the Reagan administration's trade sanctions over semiconductors in March 1987, and another retaliatory restriction – this one against Japanese construction firms – imposed by the United States Congress the following December. Both actions were products, in important part, of the huge trade imbalance to which the policies of *both* countries had contributed so much.

As Americans face the future of this relationship, moreover, they are significantly divided on how best to conceive of Japan: as economic ally and partner, or as prime adversary and industrial "threat." This chapter will explore first the recent past – how it is that two advanced nations committed to strong, cooperative relations *created* an egregious trade imbalance that undermined this goal. It will then address the question of how Americans view the current relationship and our options for managing it in the future.

1 1981 – 1987: Creating a Crisis

When historians write their analyses of the world economy of the 1980s, of what went wrong and why, they are likely to be very harsh in their judgments of both the Japanese and American governments. (They will probably be harsh on European governments, too, and particularly the German government, but that is beyond the scope of this essay.) The reason for this is simple. Trade imbalances are, as Rachel McCulloch argues elsewhere in this volume, overwhelmingly the product of macroeconomic forces. And at the beginning of this decade, both the United States and Japanese governments changed macroeconomic policy in directions bound to increase the trade imbalance between them, and each nation's imbalance with the world.

The Reagan administration won approval, beginning in 1981, of major income tax cuts and defense spending increases, driving the U.S. budget deficit to an annual average of $ 209 billion in fiscal years 1983 through 1986. The Japanese government pursued a policy of "administrative reform" aimed at reducing that nation's public borrowing – as a result, Japan's structural budget deficit dropped from 4.1% of GNP in 1980 to 1.3% in 1984 (Bergsten and Cline 1985: 27; Marris 1985: chap. 2). For the United States, a huge and growing public deficit meant, given low private savings, an enormous new need to borrow money from abroad. In Japan, such sharp deficit reduction meant, given high private savings, a enormous surplus in investment funds ready to move abroad.

As elementary macroeconomics teaches us, international flows of capital on this scale would inevitably be offset by flows of goods – out of Japan, and into the United States. Between 1983 and 1986, this logic played itself out through the ballooning of trade imbalances. Bilaterally, the gap rose from $ 19 to $ 34 to $ 46 to $ 59 billion, using the more conservative (f. a. s.) U.S. measurement which excludes shipping costs. The global U.S. current account deficit shot up from $ 46 to $ 106 to $ 118 to $ 141 billion, while the global Japanese current account surplus increased from $ 21 to $ 35 to $ 49 to $ 86 billion.

For the United States, imports from all other countries (conservatively measured) reached 1.67 times exports in 1986. Before the 1980s, no major peacetime industrial nation had *ever* run such an imbalance. Japan's trade pattern was a mirror-image: her exports in 1986 were 1.65 times imports (with imports here measured c. i. f., to include shipping costs).

Trade frictions predictably increased through this period. Yet the two nations persisted in their policies, notwithstanding the commitment of both President Ronald Reagan and Prime Minister Yasuhiro Nakasone to strong bilateral ties. The United States kept running record budget deficits, digging itself an ever-deeper financial hole. Japan kept targeting its government borrowing, notwithstanding growing international economic spillover – in the form of increased surpluses and upward pressure on the yen – and growing political spillover, "Japan-bashing" not just from across the Pacific, but from European and Asian nations as well.

The obvious question is *why*. Why did the two governments behave in such a counterproductive, crisis-creating way? It is not a comforting question. The failure of policy in Washington and Tokyo has triggered wrenching economic changes in both countries: first an unprecedented rise in U.S. import volume, now "yen shock" in Japan. These real changes, and the incredible trade numbers which reflect them, have produced the most serious jolts to bilateral relations since President Eisenhower had to cancel his planned 1960 visit to Tokyo. It remains uncertain at this writing, in the wake of the October 1987 stock market plunge and amidst the continued sinking of the dollar, whether the advanced industrial nations can extract themselves from the current mess without a very severe recession or something even worse.

Why have both governments allowed this to happen? Why, even today, have the two governments only begun to reverse their disastrous economic policy courses?

One possible explanation is that politicians and bureaucrats may not have been able to know, in advance, the trade impact of their economic policies. And it is true, of course, that the exact *magnitude* of the imbalances could not easily be predicted – Japan's surplus widened significantly in 1986, for example, as a result of the sudden plunge in the world price of oil. But the *direction* of the impact of American and Japanese policies was foreseeable, and foreseen, both outside and inside government.

C. Fred Bergsten wrote in the fall of 1981 that the combination of loose fiscal and tight monetary policy in the United States was resulting in "overvaluation of the dollar [which] will produce huge U.S. trade deficits" (1981: 25). The President's Council of Economic Advisers (CEA) reported in February 1983, "As the effects of the strong dollar are increasingly reflected in U.S. trade, the trade deficit will widen.... If large budget deficits are allowed to continue to depress the U.S. national saving rate ... the trade deficit could remain high for several years." And in a message to would-be American protectionists, the CEA concluded, "The main sources of the U.S. trade deficit are to be found not in Paris or in Tokyo, but in Washington" (U.S. Council of Economic Advisers. 1983: 67).

Concerning, Japan, Secretary of State George Shultz noted in the spring of 1985: "Japan must deal with its saving-investment imbalance if its chronic imbalance of trade is to be corrected" (Shultz 1985: 29). An advisory group to Japan's Ministry for International Trade and Industry (MITI) offered the same basic analysis that June. And beginning in 1986, the Maekawa Commission began recommending far-reaching shifts in Japanese economic policy to move it away from trade surpluses to domestically driven growth.

Yet through the mid-1980s national leaders have seemed to ignore the macroeconomic connection. Nakasone came to office at the end of 1982. Over his first two years, and through the first Reagan term, negotiations between the two nations addressed not the broad economic policy imbalance but specific product issues like the Japanese market for American-made baseball bats. Such micro matters could hardly affect a growing macro imbalance, and the deficit increased. In the spring of 1985 the United States Senate exploded, passing by a 92-0 vote a resolution lambasting the "bilateral trade imbalance" which was "costing the United States hundreds of thousands of jobs every year." Representative of the accompanying rhetoric was the declaration of Finance Committee Chairman Bob Packwood, a trade moderate, that he had reached "the limits of my patience with the Japanese.... I am going to do everything I can to retaliate in kind to any of their products that come to this country" (1985: S3558).

As a close observer of U.S.-Japan trade conflicts, I recall asking Japanese officials in that contentious spring: Isn't your government setting itself up? Why sound the trumpets about packages of small "market-opening measures" in a year when the total value of Japan's imports is expected, for macroeconomic reasons, to decline? Why put forward these offerings which will be seen as failures, or worse, as examples of Japanese perfidy? Why persist in a "domestic" economic policy which creates burgeoning surpluses which the world is bound to interpret as being caused by Japanese trade policy, thereby bringing political attack down on Japan?

To Americans, I would pose a very different set of questions. Why pretend our trade problem is with Japan when our trade balance has deteriorated with virtually every nation? Why not recognize that the American trade deficit is basically "made in U.S.A.?" Let us stop Japan-bashing and start getting our own policy house in order. One sophisticated aide to a senior Republican senator, to whom I made this argument that spring, replied: "You don't understand. The target isn't the Japanese; it's the White House." The point here was that leaders of both parties felt that the Reagan administration's policies were significantly at fault, but that the way to get the admainistration to listen was to demonstrate the costs of inaction to the U.S. relationship with Japan.

In that spring, neither the Reagan administration nor the Nakasone government seemed to be listening. They kept acting as if the trade balance problem was a trade policy problem, that negotiation on import barriers could address it. They showed considerable sophistication in the management of these specific issues – the Market Oriented Sector-Specific (MOSS) talks of 1985, for example, led to significant liberalization of Japanese regulatory policies on telecommunications. But they still avoided, until the fall of 1985, serious action on the macroeconomic matters that were at the root of the trade imbalance and the resulting crisis in bilateral relations.

Finally, of course, the pressure on the Reagan administration became too great to avoid action. At the September 22, 1985, meeting of the group of five finance ministers at the Hotel Plaza in New York City, Secretary of the Treasury James Baker III led an effort to bring the dollar's value down – first through making this an official goal, then through coordinated exchange market intervention. The Bank of Japan was particularly cooperative in this effort, and if one measures the actions by what followed in the exchange market, the effort was clearly successful. Within a year, Japanese were saying it was too successful, as their currency rose in value from roughly 240 to the dollar in September 1985 to around 160 by summer 1986. It would rise further – to 125 by the end of 1987!

The exchange rate adjustment clearly affected the flow of goods – the volume of Japan's exports stopped increasing in 1985. And in volume terms, the U.S. balance began improving significantly in 1986. But the dollar-measured imbalances continued to grow, in part because of the inevitable lags in the impact of exchange rate change (the J-curve effect), and in part because neither government accompanied the exchange rate effort by serious changes in fiscal policy. With the deficit huge and growing, the Reagan administration and the Congress spent 1986 enacting, of all things, a "revenue-neutral" tax bill! With an urgent need across the Pacific to encourage domestic demand, the Japanese prime minister staked his reputation, in early 1987, on enactment of a *consumption tax* by the Diet! (It failed.)

Japan continued to *tighten* her central government budget until the spring of 1987, when a Y6 trillion stimulus package appeared to signal a shift, at long last, in the direction of domestically driven growth. By December 1987, as its government prepared an expansionist budget for the next fiscal year, Japan could claim to be the *only* major industrial nation to have made serious fiscal policy adjustments in the needed direction.

The United States had failed to deal effectively with its budget deficit, notwithstanding the enactment of the Gramm-Rudman-Hollings legislation in 1985 which ostensibly required regular deficit cuts, and notwithstanding a one-shot improvement of $ 70 billion in fiscal year 1987 due to the phasing in of tax reform. The stock market plunge of October 1987 brought the Reagan administration and Congressional leaders together for new budget negotiations, but the results were, according to the consensus of leading economists, "grossly inadequate," since "the agreed 'cuts' would leave the structural deficit in FY 1989 no lower than its present level" (Institute for International Economics 1987: 7).

As each nation delayed addressing its fundamental policy need, rhetoric in each inclined toward scapegoating the other. Americans blamed Japanese for trade problems that were clearly global; Japanese sometimes seemed to regard the rising yen, an inevitable result of running huge current account surpluses, as an affliction visited on them from Washington.

We are still left, however, with the question of why each nation failed to address the economic policy roots of the trade problem. The basic answer, it appears, is a simple one: each government undertook a major policy change – Reaganomics in Washington, "administrative reform" in Tokyo – for overridingly domestic reasons. Thereafter, strong domestic political commitments by key actors made reversing the policy extraordinarily difficult, international spillover notwithstanding.

For the United States, the overriding political commitment was that of one man, Ronald Reagan. As David Stockman put it in the final paragraph of his book: "The American economy and government have literally been taken hostage by the awesome stubbornness of the nation's fortieth President" (1986: 458). There were many players in the 1981 actions which started the nation on the path toward $ 200 billion deficits; no party or institution was blameless. But the failure to take sufficient remedial action in the years thereafter was due primarily to Presidential resistance.

The elements of a deficit-reduction bargaining have long been clear in Washington, and other actors – like Senate Republican leaders in 1985 – have been bold enough to put them on the table from time to time. The President should agree to tax increases, an issue where he holds Democrats hostage; the Democrats in turn would agree to reduce the growth of social security (retirement) payments, the issue on which Republicans are most vulnerable. Defense and other spending would be further pruned, with the balance again reflecting a compromise between the two parties. There has existed, for several years, a "Bipartisan Budget Coalition" headed by Peter G. Peterson making the case for just such a compromise, and suggesting what its components might be.

But for such a package to work, in the American system, the White House must take the lead – Congressional leaders are simply not strong enough to get very far out in front on such an issue. Many have conspired, repeatedly, with members of the administration to win some spending reductions and tax increases. But for major change, they need the protection of doing it *with* the President. And this protection Ronald Reagan has consistently, persistently, failed to provide. His acceptance of modest revenue increases in November 1987 was a modest tactical adjustment, but it did not signal any fundamental change in his "awesome stubbornness" on the fiscal issue.

It is disturbing, to say the least, that notwithstanding a strong elite consensus about the budget deficit, the United States has been unable to act in a sufficient and timely manner. But at least there has been consensus about need to shift policy in the direction which would attack the international imbalance and hence the roots of the U.S.-Japan conflict. There has even been a growing appreciation of the broad economic relationships, especially the budget/trade deficit linkage. If there had not been this appreciation, there would surely have been far worse trade legislation than that which Congress is now considering.

In Japan, there also seems to have been an elite consensus; one has the sense of a national leadership – the Prime Minister, the business community, the Finance Ministry – in determined accord on budget policy for nearly a decade. But whereas in the United States the Presidentially-frustrated consensus has been in the direction of redressing imbalance, in Japan the Prime Ministerially-supported consensus was in support of policies which made the international situation worse, policies which delayed and impeded Japan's adjustment to her new world position.

There were, of course, some counter-pressures; by spring 1987 Diet members were conspiring with Foreign Ministry officials to use international summit conferences as vehicles to propose a reversal of the budget-tightening, "administrative reform" approach. And the Prime Minister was, at long last, modifying his stance. But the counter-coalition was long in forming, and it remains of uncertain strength.

One is left with a sense of remarkable collective insensitivity, or Japanese insularity, or worse. But an American should not be too critical, because our nation's economic policies have been at least equally insular and insensitive to international economic realities.

2 Looking Ahead: Three Perspectives on U.S.-Japan Relations

The imbalance of the 1980s has by no means played itself out. Enormous further adjustments will be required of both Japan and the United States. There can be no assurance that such adjustments can occur without a serious, global economic recession, even conceivably a cataclysm.

Still, it seems a fair bet that, sometime in the early 1990s, the United States and Japan will emerge with their trade and current accounts rebalanced, while still being:

Political-strategic allies
Economic competitors, and
The two most productive national economies in the world

The United States will be poorer, relatively and (probably for a while) absolutely as Americans grow re-accustomed to living within their means.

Japan will be richer, yet her firms will be forced by the super-strong yen to move much labor-intensive manufacturing offshore, and her home-based economy will become dependent for its growth on home demand.

The United States is likely to remain the "leader" of the alliance, the initiative-taker: both sides seem to want this. But whether America will play this role effectively – and whether indeed it will seek to play it – will be a function, to some degree, of the view American leaders take of the bilateral relationship and what its management requires. How is the United States to conceive of and deal with a nation which is, simultaneously, its most formidable economic challenger and most amenable security ally?

Polls indicate that the American people have a quite favorable overall attitude toward their Pacific partner – notwithstanding concerns about trade competition, Americans respect and admire Japan and the Japanese, and they see the relationship as a positive, mutually beneficial one. Among those who deal directly with the Japanese, however, attitudes are often mixed. And among specialists, Japan's success has generated significant differences in perspective. Most analysts fall within one of three broad groupings. The first are the *liberals*, who see economic competition among Japanese and American *firms* as the source of enormous gain to citizens of both nations. They have been challenged over the past decade by the *neo-mercantilists*, who posit a clash between *nations* which will determine both relative living standards and the world geopolitical power structure. Last but hopefully not least are the *conflict managers*, who are optimistic about the bilateral relationship *if* specific conflicts can be kept within bounds. (The labels are mine, as is the placement of individual authors and works under each category.)

For *liberals*, the postwar U.S.-Japan relationship has been an overwhelming success, within an even-greater worldwide success – that of the expanding, relatively open global economy that has emerged since 1945. The trade explosion – emphatically including Japan's sales to America – has been a boon, because trade is a positive-sum game. The principle of "comparative advantage" insures that each national economy is better off buying and selling internationally than it would be foregoing the gains from trade. We benefit from imports as well as exports; productivity gains in Japan tend to bring better lives for Americans, as the prevalence of VCRs can attest. There are, liberals recognize, competing U.S.-Japan interests, mainly in the distribution of trade gains. But to them, common interests dwarf competing interests.

Liberals would not claim, of course, that "free trade" exists in an absolute sense – they recognize and deplore many specific import barriers and other trade-distorting practices, visible and invisible. But these are seen as the reflection of strong specific interests *within* national economies –

Japanese rice farmers, American textile manufacturers. These protectionist interests may be reinforced by an erroneous belief that import barriers for competing products benefit the nation as a whole. But in fact, according to liberals, trade barriers in each nation *harm* both nations, and most of all the nation that imposes them. Japan may be more restrictive, in practice, than America, but that reflects the legacy of the past.

Why then is there a bilateral trade imbalance? Liberals point first to "triangular trade," the tendency of nations with differing factor endowments to run offsetting imbalances with different countries and regions. Hence the United States ran a $ 16 billion trade deficit with Japan in 1981, even though both nations' global accounts were in balance. But if a nation's bilateral imbalances are not offsetting, if it runs a substantial global surplus (or deficit), that is the product of macroeconomic factors: a savings surplus (or deficit); weak (or strong) domestic demand; a strengthening (or weakening) government fiscal position; and/or a weak (or strong) currency.

From these diagnoses flow standard policy prescriptions, some of them set forth earlier in this chapter. Attack global imbalance by adjusting macroeconomic policy. Persist in opening markets and reducing trade barriers, preferably on a multilateral basis. The GATT principle of generalized, or diffuse, reciprocity is the best route to trade liberalization, because it offers the broadest scope for negotiated gains. If goods and services and investment capital are able to flow freely across national borders, then interdependence will grow and production will become globalized. Already such phenomena are making nation-state-based trade statistics obsolete. IBM has long been a major exporter of "made in Japan" computers; Honda has become America's most efficient automaker. Once global imbalances have been redressed, liberals tend to believe, political pressures for protection will recede, opening the way for expanding trade and still-greater overall welfare. (For examples of this view, see Bergsten and Cline 1985; Krugman 1986; Patrick and Rosovsky 1976; and works by Gary Saxonhouse, Philip Trezise, and Edward Lincoln. Note that these authors are all economists.)

A very different perspective is offered by the *neo-mercantilists*. They begin with what liberals tend to dismiss – the competition among national economies for wealth and power. They stress that the *relative growth* of nations is what determines, over time, the distribution of national power. For them, the key U.S. trade problem is not the recently burgeoning imbalance of imports and exports but what they see as a longer-term but continuing erosion of the nation's competitive position.

In explaining this erosion, they center on a phenomenon not well addresed by classical economics: changes in nations' comparative advantages over time, and the influence of government on these changes. If policymakers can so structure domestic incentives and international transactions as to move a nation's producers progressively into high-technology, higher-value-added products, then not only will that nation's absolute living standards rise markedly, but it will gain relative position – as Japan and Korea, for example, have gained.

Neo-mercantilist analysts stress the rivalry in U.S.-Japan relations. They point to Japan's departures from liberal policies and her apparent gains from such departures; sheltering domestic auto and semiconductor producers, for example, until they were strong enough to take on the world. They contrast a purposive Japan – the "developmental state," in Chalmers Johnson's phrase – with a disorganized United States, which has been, by virtue of its reigning position, Japan's primary target. They call for the United States to respond to Japanese targeting – by halting it, emulating it, or retaliating, or some combination of the three.

Neo-mercantilists find it necessary, therefore, to confront Japan diplomatically and economically. In specific trade conflicts, they opt for "specific" or "sectoral" reciprocity, a strategy of tit-for-tat bargaining within particular product areas featuring actual or threatened retaliation. If Japanese sell semiconductors freely in the United States but resist buying those made in the U.S.A., neo-mercantilists see this as a direct threat to a key U.S. industry and argue for meeting this treat directly. (Liberals would tend, by contrast, to say that while we should of course seek market-opening for semiconductors, we should not place inordinate value on product-by-product measures of trade equity.)

But neo-mercantilists also have, like liberals, a key domestic prescription, and that is to improve industrial productivity. They see macroeconomic policy changes as necessary but insufficient, appropriate to the short-run problem of the trade imbalance. To address the more important problem, American decline, requires a comeback by U.S. firms and workers, a resurgence of competitiveness. "Manufacturing matters," they argue. Only through significant changes in industrial practice, facilitated by government policy, can the United States expect to hold its own in the 21st century. (For variants of this view, see Cohen and Zysman 1987; Johnson 1982; Krasner 1987; Morse 1987–88; Prestowitz 1988; and Vogel 1979 and 1985. Note that these authors are primarily political scientists.)

A third perspective, perhaps less prevalent in the policy literature, is that of *conflict management*. This begins, like neo-mercantilism, with politics rather than economics. But its point of departure is the U.S.-Japan alliance relationship: its centrality to American foreign policy; the need to maintain it and strengthen it in order to buttress international security and manage economic interdependence.

Conflict managers share much with liberals: a belief in the overriding compatibility of Japanese and American interests; the view that "U.S.-Japan" economic conflicts are generated, by and large, by subnational interests. Such conflicts are inevitable in two large, leading-edge, intertwined economies; they are complicated, in the U.S.-Japan case, by contrasting cultures. There is a constant need, therefore, to manage conflicts, to broker them, to find compromise resolutions which maintain the political base for harmonious relations within *both* countries.

Unlike pure liberals, conflict managers will sometimes favor trade restrictions if the alternative is intense, continuing economic conflict: examples are the textile clash of 1969–1971, or the auto export restraints of 1981. They will also sometimes favor specific reciprocity, but as a means to contain conflict, to keep it from spilling over beyond affected producers and/or escalating to the level of national leaders. In 1979, for example, a dispute over the purchasing practices of Nippon Telephone and Telegraph (NTT) threatened to poison a summit conference between President Jimmy Carter and Prime Minister Masayoshi Ohira. But the United States backed off and resorted instead to tit-for-tat bargaining: unless NTT opened its contracts to foreign bidders, the U.S. would deny Japanese bidders the benefits of American adherence to the new GATT code internationalizing government procurement.

Conflict managers stresss that old modes of bargaining may reflect the now-departed era of American dominance. All too often, both Americans and Japanese expect that the former will do the demanding, exert the political pressure, and that the latter will adjust to that pressure. But with Japan's rise that pattern no longer makes sense for either country: it exaggerates American power, it denies Japan's emerging coresponsibility, and its fuels resentments on both sides.

Perhaps the key factor distinguishing conflict manangers from the other two groupings is that they tend to see the *substance* of most trade conflicts as marginal. Most are battles for minor advantage by firms of middling importance. Very few are worth risking serious strains in the alliance, but unles the interests involved are appeased to some degree, such strains are likely to be the result (see Frost 1987; Destler et al. 1976, 1979; Destler and Sato 1982; Report of the Japan-United States Economic Relations Group 1981; and, for a related perspective, Calder 1985).

Traditionally, U.S. officials have blended the first and the third approaches – only when driven by strong pressure, as over semiconductors in 1985–1987, have they adopted aspects of the second. Unless the American economy can hold its own in industrial productivity, however, the appeal of the neo-mercantilist perspective will increase. Conversely, a United States confident that "American can compete" is the one most likely to be able to work toward further opening of the global economy, and cooperative management of the economic disputes that will assuredly remain.

References

Bergsten, C. Fred (1981): The Costs of Reaganomics. *Foreign Policy*, (Fall): 24–36.

Bergsten, C. Fred and William R. Cline (1985): *The United States-Japan Economic Problem*. Washington, D.C.: Institute for International Economics, Policy Analysis No. 13, October.

Calder, Kent E. (1985): The Emerging Politics of the Trans-Pacific Economy. *World Policy*, (Fall), 593–623.

Cohen, Stephen S. and John Zysman (1987): *Manufacturing Matters: The Myth of the Post-Industrial Economy*. New York: Basic Books (for the Council on Foreign Relations).

Destler, I. M. and Hideo Sato (eds.) (1982): *Coping With U.S.-Japanese Economic Conflicts*. Lexington, Mass.: Lexington Books.

Destler, I. M., Haruhiro Fukui, and Hideo Sato (1979): *The Textile Wrangle: Conflict in Japanese-American Relations 1969–1971*. Ithaca, N.Y.: Cornell University Press.

Destler, I. M., Hideo Sato, Priscilla Clapp, and Haruhiro Fukui (1976): *Managing an Alliance: The Politics of U.S.-Japanese Relations*. Washington, D.C.: Brookings Institution.

Institute for International Economics (1987): Resolving the Global Economic Crisis: After Wall Street. A statement by Thirty-three Economists from Thirteen Countries, Institute for International Economics, Special Report No. 6, December. Washington, D.C.: Institute for International Economics.

Johnson, Chalmers (1982): *MITI and the Japanese Miracle: The Growth of Industrial Policy 1925–1975*. Stanford, Calif.: Stanford University Press.

Krasner, Stephen D. (1987): *Asymmetries in Japanese-American Trade: The Case for Specific Reciprocity*. University of California at Berkeley, Institute of International Studies, Policy Papers in International Affairs, No. 32.

Krugman, Paul (1986): Is the Japan Problem Over? Cambridge, Mass.: National Bureau of Economic Research, Working Paper No. 1962, June.

Marris, Stephen (1985): *Deficits and the Dollar: The World Economy At Risk*. Washington: Institute for International Economics, Policy Analysis No. 14, December.

Morse, Ronald (1987–88): Japan's Rise to Pre-eminence. *Foreign Policy*, (Winter): 3–21.

Packwood, R. (1985): *Congressional Record*, Daily Edition, March 28, S3558.

Patrick, High and Henry Rosovsky (eds.) (1976): *Asia's New Giant: How the Japanese Economy Works*. Washington: Brookings Institution.

Prestowitz, Clyde V., Jr. (1988): *Trading Places: How We Allowed Japan to Take the Lead*. New York: Basic Books.

Report of the Japan-United States Economic Relations Group (1981): Prepared for the President of the United States and the Prime Minister of Japan, January.

Scott, Bruce R. and George C. Lodge (eds.) (1985): *U.S. Competitiveness in the World Economy*. New York: Harper and Row.

Shultz, George P. (1985): National Policies and Global Prosperity. Address prepared for delivery at the Woodrow Wilson School of Public and International Affairs, Princeton University, April 11. *Department of State Bulletin*, June 1985, 27–30.

Stockman, David (1986): *The Triumph of Politics: The Inside Story of the Reagan Revolution*. New York: Harper and Row.

Vogel, Ezra (1979): *Japan as Number One: Lessons for Americans*. Cambridge, Mass.: Harvard University Press.

Vogel, Ezra (1985): *Comeback Case by Case: Building the Resurgence of American Business*. New York: Simon and Schuster.

U.S. Council of Economic Advisers (1983): *Economic Report of the President*, February. Washington, D.C.: Government Printing Office.

Part II
The Shaping of Foreign Trade Policy

The "Interaction Mechanism" Between Congress and the President in Making U.S. Foreign Trade Policy

Andreas Fürst

The line of responsibility drawn between Congress and the President in making foreign policy has been described as an "invitation for struggle" (Corwin 1940: 200). The same can be said about the making of foreign trade policy. The Constitution grants Congress the power "to regulate Commerce with foreign Nations" and to levy duties and tariffs (Article 1, section 8). The President, on the other hand, has the constitutional powers for conducting foreign relations (Article 2, section 2).

In creating foreign trade policy, there also exist tensions between the President and Congress in terms of protectionism versus free trade. Because it is more entangled with domestic special interests, Congress usually adopts a more protective trade policy. The executive branch, however, views international trade more as a part of its foreign policy and works to promote greater liberalization of the world economy.

To explain this "double-track" struggle between the President and Congress, Robert Pastor has introduced a model of interbranch politics. He points out that the interaction between the executive and legislative branches is characterized by three variables: (a) Presidential leadership; (b) congressional self-discipline; and (c) a legislative-executive process based on trust and responsiveness (Pastor 1980: 57).

This chapter will argue that in this interbranch politics a certain pattern has developed since the 1930s which will be called the "interaction mechanism." The functioning of this mechanism can be characterized as follows:

1. Under pressure from special interests and frustrated with presidential "nonaction," Congress demands more protectionism and initiates measures (i e., bills, amendments, resolutions) working in this direction.
2. The President responds and initiates new rounds of bilateral or multilateral negotiations.

3. The President receives negotiating authority after the executive and legislative branches had hammered out a new trade act. The President, backed with the trade act, goes to the negotiating table. Any agreement reached there is sent back to Congress for approval. In this third step, both branches compromise: the executive, by its responsiveness to protectionist demands, and Congress, by exercising self-restraint, and quickly pushing through the legislation in a "fast-track approval process."

A historical overview will show that since the 1930s Congress has been the whistle-blower for unfair trade practices and an advocate of more protectionism. Traditionally, the executive branch has responded to legislative pressures for trade restrictions by calling for a new round of international trade negotiations as an instrument to build public support for free trade policies. This executive responsiveness to signals from Congress and presidential leadership in the process of creating a new trade act have been key to the functioning of the interaction mechanism. The interaction mechanism has proven successful in protecting Congress as well as the President from domestic pressures. For Congress, pressures from special-interest groups have been relieved by granting the President negotiating authority for new trade acts, and by establishing remedies for injured industries. The President, on the other hand, has been exempted from protectionist pressures while he has been negotiating or implementing international trade commitments. Also, international commitments have usually prevented trade issues from becoming subject to domestic politics.

This interaction mechanism continued to function into the 1970s even as three developments working against trade liberalization appeared. These were: (a) the decline of U.S. hegemony in international trade; (b) the souring of domestic support for free trade; and (c) structural changes in Congress. These three factors played a major role in changing the development of U.S. foreign policy. U.S. trade policymaking, however, did not change because both the executive and legislative branches continued to deal with each other using the interaction mechanism.

In the mid-1980s, however, this mechanism seems to be breaking down. After congressional demands failed to bring about an executive response, both houses of Congress introduced comprehensive trade bills of their own. The Reagan administration refused to get involved and take the lead in brokering the outcome of these initiatives.

It will be argued here that whenever a U.S. President chooses to reduce his leadership role in foreign trade policy, Congress will step in and take the initiative. The agenda will be set by congressional actions, with the President being relegated to a defensive position.

1 The Development of the "Interaction Mechanism"

Since the time that the Smoot-Hawley Act was identified as one of the causes of the Great Depression in the 1930s, Congress and the President have been expected to work together to lower tariffs and trade barriers. In the course of this process the interaction mechanism developed.

1.1 The Legacy of Smoot-Hawley: A Warning for Decades to Come

Until the mid-twentieth century, Congress exercised its foreign commerce authority mostly with regard to a few bilateral agreements and tariffs. The last comprehensive exercise in direct tariff setting was the Smoot-Hawley Act of 1930. After a prolonged period of prosperity, this tariff act was formulated between 1928 and 1930. Although President Hoover initiated the process, he refused to take the lead in formulating the policy and leading it through the legislative process. This resulted in congressional excesses of logrolling and horse trading which contributed to almost every individual duty rate. In the Senate alone, 1253 amendments were attached to the House bill (Pastor 1983: 162). Without the protection and backing of the President, Congress was pressured by interest groups on which their members were dependent for a variety of reasons (for example, campaign contributions). Decisions were made more for reasons of private interests than economic need.

The economic results were a series of retaliatory measures taken by other countries which caused a decline of world trade from $ 34 billion in 1929 to $ 12 billion in 1933 (Pastor 1983: 162). The political result, however, was that "for present purposes, Smoot-Hawley's most lasting legacy has been a lingering public impression, fostered by the president, that near-total congressional control of international trade is synonymous with protectionism" (Koh 1986: 1194).

1.2 Bilateralism and Reciprocity: 1934 – 1945

The consensus of the time was that protectionism and the resulting trade retaliation by other countries exacerbated the Great Depression. To overcome the depressed economy it was seen as necessary to spur economic growth which could only be done by fostering increased trade rather than protecting domestic industries. One of the strongest believers in this task was President Roosevelt's Secretary of State Cordell Hull. He recognized not only the necessity of free trade as a prerequisite for a prosperous economy but also the importance of international trade as part of foreign policy. And as in foreign policy, Congress and the President could legitimately argue about the general outlines, while the details had to be left to the negotiators.

This new trade regime could therefore work only with a President who initiated trade policy and at the same time protected and insulated Congress from special-interest pressures. Congress, on the other hand, had to restrain its influence in formulating trade policy and to follow rules which make it easier for the President to conduct his trade policy.

The Reciprocal Trade Agreements Act of 1934 was the testing ground for this new interbranch politics. It not only worked but also set the standards for the trade acts to come. President Roosevelt took the lead in all steps of the legislative process. He stayed in close contact with the congressional leaders and took into account their demands while pursuing his policy. As a buffer for interest groups he established an Executive Committee on Reciprocity to which individual firms could address their concerns and introduce relief measures from tariff concessions. With this procedure individual protection for domestic producers was taken out from the trade acts and was granted only when injury could be proven. Protectionist legislation became the exception, rather than the principle.

The Trade Act of 1934 also included, however, congressional authorization for the President to negotiate and conclude reciprocal tariff-cutting agreements with individual foreign nations. While the President was given a broad advance authority for negotiation, Congress preserved its influence by setting up "sunset provisions" which could terminate the President's negotiating authority. These provisions gave Congress the ability to monitor the executive actions and to request changes from the President before renewal of the negotiating authority. The Reciprocal Trade Agreements Act was then extended by Congress routinely every three years (Koh 1986: 1195). The result was encouraging. By 1945 twenty-eight agreements with U.S. trading partners were conducted and tariffs fell from an average of 59.3% in 1932 to 28.2% in 1945 (Pastor 1983: 164).

1.3 The Hegemonic Period: 1945 – 1962

After World War II the U.S. was at the peak of its political, military, and economic power. All of a sudden it was the indispensable leader in any movement to reestablish an international economic order. This position brought new support for an open trading system in the U.S.A. International trade was viewed as an integral part of foreign policy. In order to establish a global political and economic order conducive to U.S. interests, trade agreements had to be conducted on a multilateral, rather than a bilateral basis.

Congress gave President Truman the authority to conduct multilateral trade negotiations and in 1946 the U.S. and twenty-two other countries began the first round of the General Agreement on Trade and Tariffs (GATT) negotiations on reducing tariffs on a reciprocal and nondiscriminatorial basis. Five other large-scale tariff negotiations followed between 1947 and 1956 drastically reducing the world's tariff levels.

Although the postwar climate in the U.S.A. was very good for liberalization of foreign trade, Congress was careful to circumscribe the presidential power to alter U.S. tariff rates. As in the bilateral trade acts of preceding years, the authority to negotiate was limited to only a few years, and the President was given no authority to negotiate the reduction of nontariff trade barriers. In addition, Congress also insisted on a "peril point reporting requirement" and an "escape clause." Under this clause Congress authorized the Tariff Commission (now the International Trade Commission) to recommend to the President import relief to domestic producers injured by tariff reductions or unfair trade practices. Amid concerns that the executive was ignoring the Tariff Commission's recommendations, Congress in 1958 provided for itself a right to override a presidential decision by a two-thirds vote.

1.4 The Kennedy Round: 1962 – 1967

The main reason for the concern of U.S. producers in the early 1960s was the changing world economy. The change in the United States from an inward-looking to an open international trading regime after World War II was made possible only under its economic leadership. As the hegemonic world economic power it could not only afford to reduce tariffs and open its markets to other nations, but it also had the power to force smaller members of the GATT regime to practice reciprocity. This GATT regime was based on the commitment of open markets and nondiscriminatory treatment among its members.

This commitment, however, underwent some critical changes in the United States with the decline of American predominance in world trade. Between 1950 and 1960 U.S. exports dropped from 50% to 25% of the exports of all advanced industrialized countries. The European Economic Community and Japan were emerging as powerful economic units, and the U.S. dollar was no longer quite as impregnable as it had been in the years immediately following World War II (Vernon 1982: 490).

Congress reacted to this new situation when President Kennedy requested negotiating authority to deal primarily with the emerging Common Market. The Trade Expansion Act of 1962 that resulted was therefore a mixed bag. This new trade act authorized the President to reduce duties by 50% of the 1962 level, and for the first time it allowed negotiations about the reduction of nontariff barriers. At the same time Congress gave the President greater negotiating discretion, it also widened its control over the outcome of such negotiations. It required, however, that the final trade agreements be brought back to Congress for subsequent approval. In order to follow the negotiations Congress put into the law a provision that gave its representatives the status of observers in the U.S. trade delegation. In the same act Congress also removed the responsibility for trade negotiations from the State Department because of the concern that it was more interested in maintaining good foreign relations than in pursuing U.S. trading interests. The negotiations were transferred to a Trade Representative to be situated in the White House. The intention was to establish an "executive broker" between domestic interests and foreign governments, between the executive branch and the Congress, and among the governmental agencies (Destler 1986a: 89). This can be seen as an indication of the shifted emphasis of international trade from a means of foreign policy to one furthering domestic economic interests.

Congress, being very sensitive to its constituencies, also believed that the executive was ignoring most of the requests by industries injured by tariff reductions and unfair trade practices. In 1962 it revised the statute for the escape clause permitting the President's decision to be overridden by a simple instead of a two-thirds majority. Especially favored by the AFL-CIO, a trade adjustment assistance concept was included in the Trade Act by Congress. It encompassed readjustment allowances for business firms which had been injured by tariff cuts.

The General Agreement of 1967 was approved by Congress and signed by forty-five other nations, thus concluding the Kennedy Round. The average duty for the industrialized countries was brought down to about 9% (Pastor 1983: 166). After the early postwar GATT negotiations, the Kennedy Round marked the second period in U.S. efforts to liberalize the world's trading system.

1.5 The "Interaction Mechanism" at the End of the Kennedy Round

With the end of the Kennedy Round the relationship between Congress and the President in shaping foreign trade policy had achieved a working balance. While the President was the driving force in establishing open markets by multilateral trade negotiations, Congress was more concerned about the effects of free trade on domestic producers. Congress recognized, however, that the subject was too complicated and delicate for it to play a direct role in it, and therefore granted the President negotiating authority, while reserving the power for subsequent approval or disapproval of any agreements the President concluded.

The delegation to the President of authority to reduce trade barriers was also one of the principal devices Congress employed to insulate itself from interest-group pressures to which it was much more exposed than the President. Other protective mechanisms were procedures outside the legislative process through which trading firms could obtain import relief by proving injuries to the International Trade Commission or the Department of Commerce. The U.S. Trade Representative was created to function as a mediator between the competing international and special interests, and Congress pressured the President to arrange "voluntary export restraints" to be enforced by the seller country. Destler has pointed out that "the system allowed members so inclined to advocate, even threaten, trade restrictions, while nicely relieving them of the need to deliver on their threats" (Destler 1986b: 98).

But these mechanisms were not automatic. They could work only as long as the President took the lead in setting the agenda for foreign trade policy, adjusting it to the new economic situation, and balancing it with the special interests, which pressured Congress. In adapting the bicycle theory (Destler 1986a: 15), it can be said that the trade system needed to be moved forward by comprehensive multilateral free trade agendas and negotiations or else it would fall down. While the President had to set the direction, Congress performed like a braker on the back seat, which only let the brake loose when the bicycle stayed on a smooth trail. But before we follow driver and braker on their bicycle tour in the 1970s and 1980s we will examine the changes inside Congress and how these changes affected the legislative-executive relationship.

2 Interlude: Changes in the 1970s

In the 1970s three developments working against trade liberalization appeared. These were the further decline of U.S. hegemony in international trade, the souring of domestic support for free trade, and changes within Congress. Here, the changes in Congress will be examined more closely.

There are basically four developments in Congress which changed the legislative process and the congressional structure in the 1970s: Change of the membership, procedural reforms, enhancement of congressional support systems, and greater interdependence with the public.

First, the membership of Congress has changed. Over half of the House of Representatives and the Senate has been newly elected since 1972. These new members brought not only the average age of legislators down, but they also represented a new generation of politicians. They were usually strong individualists with loose party ties and little personal loyalty to the President. Many of them ran for Congress on "anti-Washington" platforms expressing their skepticism toward the political establishment. They were the driving force to abolish seniority in the committee system and were no longer content to serve the expected apprenticeship under powerful chairpersons. They also knew how to use the media and expressed their viewpoints forcefully on policy questions in public.

Second, major procedural reforms changed the power structure within Congress. The traditional committee system in which the chairpersons had all the power came under repeated attack. Increasing the numbers of committees and subcommittees and decreasing the power of the chairpersons resulted in a dispersion of power in Congress. This trend toward decentralization gave individual congressmen and senators a more influential role in the legislative process and new opportunities to start their own initiatives.

Third, the enhancement of congressional information capabilities resulted from the increase in congressional personal staff, the establishment of new legislative support systems, and the growth of external information sources. Since 1945 committee staffs had increased almost eightfold and personal staffs had increased fivefold (Malbin 1980: 4). This rapid growth gave the members of Congress greater independence from the executive branch in gathering information and provided them with a capability to make their own impact on issues of importance. The results were more information, more expertise, a greater workload, more bills, and more votes, and less time for the legislators to deliberate with each other about policy. "The result is that the new staff bureaucracy and the workload it helps create threaten to bury Congress under its own paperwork" (Malbin 1980: 7). In addition to the increase of personal staff, the Office of Technology Assessment and the Congressional Budget Office were established in the 1970s and the Congressional Research Service and General Accounting Office were enlarged.

Fourth, greater access to the legislative process for the public also began in the 1970s when committee hearings and markup sessions became open, roll-call votes were recorded, and television was allowed first in the House of Representatives and subsequently in the Senate. This greater access to Congress and the greater attention to political events that resulted from the Vietnam War and Watergate, made the public aware of the interdependence between congressional actions and everyday life. But this opening up resulted also in the increasing activity of pressure groups mobilizing constituents in pursuing special interests. These groups are highly sophisticated, prepared and equipped to attract a member's attention on specific policy issues and to promote special legislation on their behalf. Because of the new campaign style of running as a political entrepreneur without help from party organizations, the members also became increasingly dependent on interest groups successful in mobilizing voters or raising money.

In short, Congress has become a more individualistic, democratic, informed, and open institution. Its members are better prepared to start their own initiatives but also more responsive and vulnerable to various social, political, and economic interests. By exercising more independence this "new Congress" has abolished the "imperial presidency" and created a more balanced relationship between the governmental branches.

Foreign policy used to be an area where the President had the dominant decision-making role. However, the new executive-legislative relationship in the 1970s produced a congressional control-mechanism for executive actions which were at times so severe that some even viewed them as "obstructionist" (Oppenheimer 1981). In a series of legislative initiatives the formerly almost unrestricted power of the President in making foreign policy was contained by Congress. Some of these were:

- The War Powers Resolution of 1973, which imposed restraints on the presidential power to commit U.S. combat troops abroad, compelling him so seek congressional approval within 60 days of any such action
- The Jackson-Vanik Amendment of 1974, which tied the most-favored-nation status to freedom of emigration from the Soviet Bloc
- The Hughes-Ryan Amendment of 1974 and the Clark Amendment of 1976, which increased congressional overseeing of the CIA's covert activities
- The Nuclear Non-Proliferation Act of 1978, which put conditions on export of nuclear equipment and fuel to countries which do not accept safeguards on all their nuclear facilities
- The fact that the SALT II Treaty was never brought before the Senate because of its strong opposition to certain provisions

The foregoing discussion gives rise to the following questions: How did these changes in the 1970s influence the making of U.S. foreign trade policy? Did the interaction mechanism also work in a period of dramatic decline in U.S. trade hegemony, significant shifts in political attitudes towards trade liberalization, and within a "new Congress"? And finally, how was this mechanism implemented?

3 The "Interaction Mechanism" in the 1970s

New trade laws were enacted in 1974 and in 1979. They brought a further reduction of tariff and nontariff barriers. They also proved that the legislative-executive relationship concerning foreign trade policy remained stable and effective. This can be explained by the fact that this relationship was embedded in the interaction mechanism, which has been developed and strengthened over time because, unlike in other policy areas, Congress has always been involved in shaping international trade policy.

3.1 The Trade Act of 1974

At the peak of the "imperial presidency" in the early 1970s the executive was continuously trying to break out of the "interaction mechanism." But it was forced to realize that these attempts only had the effect of setting the mechanism into motion through congressional whistle-blowing activities.

When the President went on to accept a comprehensive Antidumping Code, over congressional objection, Congress reacted by refusing to approve the repeal of the American Selling Price method, which the executive had also negotiated without congressional approval (Koh 1986: 1199). Congress also did not pass two bills in 1969 and 1970 which would have extended the presidential negotiating authority for four years. Finally, Representative James A. Burke and Senator Vance Hartke introduced a trade and investment bill which declared free trade to be the cause of unemployment and proposed a series of protectionist measures. The bill also signaled the desertion of the labor unions from free trade and "was to many the most persuasive sign that the trading system was in peril" (Pastor 1983: 175).

The Nixon administration received these signs and in 1973 requested broad trade policy authority from Congress in order to conduct a new round of multilateral trade negotiations. After the House and the Senate passed their own trade bills in 1973 and 1974 a compromise version of both bills and the presidential proposal was finally adopted at the end of 1974.

The Trade Act of 1974 pursued two objectives. First, it hoped to bolster the executive branch's negotiating credibility which had become more and more weakened after the Kennedy Round. Second, it sought to impose greater congressional control on presidential discretion. To meet these two objectives a new legislative mechanism was created, commonly known as the "fast-track procedure." This device required the President to consult with any congressional committee whose jurisdiction would be affected by a trade agreement and notify the House of Representatives and the Senate 90 days before entering an agreement. In exchange the act delegated to the President broad advance authority to negotiate tariff and nontariff reducing agreements. As a measure of congressional self-discipline the act established legislative procedures which provided that a pending trade bill be automatically discharged from committee consideration after 45 days, limited floor debate to 20 hours, and required that the bill be voted upon within 15 days, with no amendments allowed.

In exchange for the broad negotiating authority granted to the President and the "fast-track approval process," Congress curtailed presidential initiative in trade matters in a number of ways. As in the 1962 Trade Expansion Act, any negotiated agreement was made subject to a "sunset" provision. As another new control method, Congress attached a legislative veto on six provisions to constrain executive discretion. An additional innovation was the status of ten members of Congress as official advisers on the U.S. negotiating team, and a range of requirements for formal certifications and postnegotiating reports.

In an effort to channel protectionist pressures, Congress established the "judicialization" of trade remedies "to enhance indirect third party leverage on executive action" (Koh 1986: 1191). The most important provisions were Sections 201 and 301 of the Trade Act. Section 201 regulates import relief in order to prevent or to remedy serious injury to domestic producers resulting from increased imports associated with tariff reductions. For the first time private individuals were empowered to initiate proceedings directly against foreign industries at the U.S. International Trade Commission (ITC). The ITC determines the existence of injury and, when appropriate, sends a recommendation to the President for remedial actions. These could be tariffs, quotas, or negotiated export restraints. Congress reserved the power to disapprove the presidential action or nonaction within 90 legislative days. Section 301 of the 1974 Trade Act is an unfair trade practices statute. It is designed to ensure fair and equitable access of U.S. products in foreign markets. Under this statute a private individual can file complaints with the U.S. Trade Representative who is required to investigate petitions and make recommendations for the President to take action "(1) to enforce U.S. rights under trade agreements, or (2) with respect to conduct of another country that 'is unjustifiable, unreasonable, or discriminatory and burdens or restricts' U.S. commerce" (Kassinger 1983: 222). As a concession to the labor unions the Trade Act made it much easier to obtain adjustment assistance to workers, firms, and communities adversely affected by import competition.

What we can see in the Trade Act of 1974 is that even in the early 1970s when "congressional-executive clashes in trade matters had become increasingly commonplace" (Koh 1986: 1191) the interaction mechanism worked. This is even more astonishing given the poor executive-legislative relations of this period. But as long as there was responsiveness on both sides the mechanism functioned effectively.

The interaction mechanism was triggered again as the opinion grew in Congress that the President took too much freedom in dealing with international trade. It started to blow the whistle by rejecting two trade bills and introducing the Burke-Hartke Bill. The President responded in an act of good will with the extension of multilateral arrangements on textiles, negotiation of voluntary export restraints with Japanese and European steel producers, and abolition of the fixed exchange rate system in 1971 (Baldwin 1984: 14). These were important factors to start the debate to the 1974 Trade Act. The act itself gave the President a broad advance negotiating authority and a "fast-track procedure," while giving Congress greater control over executive discretion and unprecedented participation in the upcoming multilateral negotiations.

3.2 The Trade Act of 1979

The Trade Act of 1974 was a prime example of how differing interests can be harmonized by adequate reactions and formal devices. On the other hand, the trade politics of the Carter years showed how personal trust and mutual responsiveness can also be very powerful in keeping U.S. trade policy constructive.

Robert Strauss, President Carter's special Trade Representative, espoused this type of politics. Through close consultations with key players in Congress he succeeded in pushing international trade towards liberalization while keeping special interests and Congress at bay. The Trade Act of 1979 reflected the combination of Strauss' skillful, informal, and trusting relationship with Congress and his tactical use of the "fast-track procedure." At the end of the Tokyo Round, Strauss used the provision to consult Congress 90 days before entering a multilateral agreement to involve the Ways and Means and Finance Committees in drafting the implementing bill. In closed "non-markup sessions" and a "non-conference," Strauss together with the committee members, hammered out a draft which reconciled the goals of the administration with congressional demands. The bill was thus already accepted before it was formally submitted at the initiative of the President, and the subsequent legislative process of approval was completed within only five weeks.

The principal actor in this "success story" (Destler 1980) was without doubt Trade Representative Strauss. He took a clear lead in guiding the bill through "non-sessions and non-conferences" where he took a "centrist, politically sustainable substantive position against import restrictions in principle but [he was] flexible in cases of genuine injury to industry or important political pressure" (Destler 1981: 355). While protectionist forces such as the AFL-CIO were divided on the bill, Strauss succeeded in mollifying key elements of a potential opposition coalition. "In the minds of many trade experts the process was less a matter of building a winning coalition than avoiding the formation of a losing one" (Thompson 1984: 87). Another reason for this "success story" was the "fast-track procedure" which allowed "the new Congress... to operate as the old Congress had operated: in closed sessions with executive branch officials included but the public excluded with the functional equivalent of the closed rule once their deliberations were complete" (Destler 1981: 357).

4 The Reagan Administration

The "changing of the guards" in 1981 from the administration of President Carter to that of President Reagan brought a new style of presidential politics. This new style can be characterized by showing strength rather than exercising leadership and by a laissez-faire approach rather than a constructive engagement.

In the area of economic policy this new style had its substantive equivalent in the implementation of supply-side economics. By cutting taxes and reducing restrictions on investment this policy was strictly consumption oriented. It showed some impressive short-term domestic successes in promoting economic growth and creating new jobs. Its effect on international trade policy, however, was devastating. Through the trigger mechanism of the increasing budget deficit, higher real interest rates, and the overvalued dollar, the trade deficit shot up from $ 36.2 billion in 1980 to $ 148.5 billion in 1985 (Holliday 1986: 2) and $ 156.2 billion in 1986 (*Washington Post*, August 12, 1987: F5).

Pursuing its laissez-faire approach to economic management, the Reagan administration refused to acknowledge the rapidly increasing trade deficit and its internal causes. President Reagan even praised the strong dollar as a reflection of American strength in the world economy (Destler 1986b: 102). This lack of presidential leadership in dealing with the unprecedented high trade deficit placed Congress under great pressure from domestic producers and spurred its members to take an increasingly active role in U.S. trade policymaking. This greater congressional involvement has been manifested by:

- Involvement in the drafting of the Trade Act of 1984
- Introduction of a series of "reciprocity bills" based on a new concept of mutual accountability
- Forcing the administration to act in response to various legislative proposals
- Passing a new Omnibus Trade Bill

4.1 The Trade Act of 1984

Despite the climate of growing protectionism since the beginning of the 1980s, it was again the personal engagement and skill of a Trade Representative which made it possible to block off most protectionist proposals and to negotiate with Congress a trade bill which was acceptable to both Congress and the President.

Reagan's first Trade Representative, Bill Brock, a former Senator from Tennessee was not only experienced in manuevering the 1984 Trade Bill through the legislative process but he also used his floor privileges to take part in the debates. Congress, however, played a most decisive role in drafting the bill only precedented by formulating the Trade Bill of 1979. The Trade Act of 1984 granted the President authority to renew the trade preferences for developing countries (GSP) and to enter negotiations for a comprehensive bilateral free trade agreement with Israel. On the other hand, it enhanced congressional control of the presidential authority to negotiate bilateral or multilateral trade agreements and proposed statutory limits on the presidential discretion to deny import relief to affected domestic industries.

The Trade Act of 1984 modified the "fast-track procedure" by extending the period in which the President must notify Congress about his intentions to enter into free trade negotiations. In addition to the 90-days notice, it required a 60-days prenegotiation consultation with the Ways and Means and the Finance Committees. A "fast-track procedure" for the subsequently negotiated agreement could be accepted only if neither committee disapproved the negotiations during the 60 days consultation period. A committee disapproval would dramatically reduce the chances for a negotiated agreement to survive an unexpedited legislative process. This provision gave Congress more time to bring in its demands plus the option to extract concessions from the President as a condition for granting his proposal a "fast-track procedure."

In additon to these changes in procedures, the Trade Act also limited the President's discretion to deny import relief to affected industries through the establishment of new escape clause provisions, amendments to the antidumping and countervailing duty provision, and additional consultation and reporting requirements.

The Trade Act of 1984 was a success because of Trade Representative Brock's skill and engagement in leading the bill through Congress and the large-scale compromises that were required. This active approach in trade matters, however, has been more an exception rather than a principle in the Reagan administration. This became clear when Brock, soon after his success with the 1984 Trade Act, was moved to the Department of Labor and the position of Trade Representative was left vacant for three months.

The low priority afforded to trade issues by the Reagan administration brought about increased congressional activities sending messages to the executive in the form of protectionist bills. One of the strongest of these was the so-called Jenkins Bill in 1985 which would have severely restricted imports of textiles, apparel, and shoes. The bill passed the House of Representatives as well as the Senate but was vetoed by President Reagan. The two-thirds required to override the veto were missed by only eight votes in the House. This bill was a clear sign of the congressional frustration over the lack of presidential attention to trade and the huge trade deficit. The declared goal of many supporters of the bill was to send a message to the President rather than to make it law. Representative Matsui stated: "You don't want this thing to become law.... It is really just to send a signal to both the President and to our foreign competition" (cited in Koh 1986: 1223n).

4.2 Reciprocity Bills

Another set of warning signals took the form of a series of "reciprocity bills" beginning in 1982. The focus of these bills shifted the concept of reciprocity away "from the traditional concern with equality of concessions exchanged in negotiations to concerns with the equality of the remaining restrictions and their impact upon trade" (Gadbaw 1982: 694). This shift was based on the congressional perception that imports received a better treatment in the United States than U.S. exports did in other markets. The emphasis of the reciprocity trade initiatives was therefore on increasing the opportunities for U.S. exports in other countries. In pursuing this goal congressional concerns also moved beyond tariff and nontariff barriers to investment restrictions, government-controlled industrial policies, and trade in the service sector. As products of special interests, the reciprocity bills dealt almost exclusively with special trade problems. Often contradicting GATT formulas for settling international trade disputes, the proposals contained mostly bilateral, sectorial, and product-specific measures.

In Congress there has always been a tendency to pursue unilateral standards of reciprocity, discrimination, and the threat of retaliations. This approach, however, has usually been neutralized by presidential interactions. Having been more concerned and engaged with overall economic interests and the U.S. global commitment, the executive in the past solved trade problems within the multilateral, and nondiscriminatory framework of international agreements.

President Reagan in exercising his laissez-faire politics gave up this approach and refused to play his role in trade matters. The growth of the trade deficit to unprecedented levels, however, created such strong pressures for action that the administration could no longer remain inactive and was forced to respond. But lacking an overall trade policy the administration was not able to deal with emerging trade problems on an international scale but only on a case-to-case basis. The result was the establishment of a number of unilateral and sectorial trade barriers. Although a staunch supporter of free trade, President Reagan became the "most protectionist president in decades." In an editorial, entitled "Talking Tough," Michael Kinsley pointed out that "in 1980 only one eighth of American imports entered this country under some restrictive policy. Today it's close to a quarter" (1987: A23).

These executive actions resulted less from original presidential initiatives rather than from the President's realization that he would have to take action to prevent more congressional protectionism. With executive activities solely reacting to legislative pressures, the agenda-setting in foreign trade policy shifted partly from the President to Congress.

Nevertheless, the administration continued exercising its policy of "muddling through" from case to case instead of taking the lead by introducing new multilateral initiatives. The Reagan administration's mistrust of multilateralism also prompted its querulous conduct towards GATT. Instead of pushing hard for the recently inaugurated "Uruguay Round" and making it the center of its trade policy, the administration has undertaken a variety of bilateral trade initiatives such as the Caribbean Basin Initiative, the U.S.-Israeli Free Trade Agreement, and the free trade negotiations with Canada.

Refusing to stress multilateral trade agreements and negotiations, the administration stripped itself of a very effective shield against congressional pressures. The executive-legislative relationship turned upside down. Congress took over the agenda-setting and was successful in shifting the balance of power in dealing with international trade to its advantage. The President ended up in a defensive position toward congressional pressures. This represented a departure from a working relationship between President and Congress whereby the interaction mechanism could go into effect.

4.3 Outlook: The Trade Act of 1988

Lacking a comprehensive trade initiative from the executive, Congress has not only sent a series of minor warning signals but has also introduced a trade bill of its own. At the close of the 99th Congress, the House passed a trade bill (H.R. 4800), while the Senate had several trade bills under consideration (among them S. 1860 and S. 1837). Immediately after the 100th Congress had convened, these bills were packaged into the Omnibus Trade Bill of 1987 (H.R. 3). This bill passed the House and the Senate in the spring of 1988 and became law in the summer of 1988.

The Trade Act of 1988 extends the President's negotiation authority for tariff agreements, which expired 1980, and nontariff agreements which is due to expire in 1988. On the other hand, it excludes the reduction of tariffs on certain import-sensitive items and also sets new prerequisites for "fast-track" considerations of final trade agreements. It is interesting to note, that the section on trade-negotiating authority for the President is one of the shortest parts of the law. The majority of this new act contains protectionist provisions. This has been a common practice with past trade acts. However, the difference was in the size of the new act. In comparison to its 1000 pages, the Trade Act of 1979 with its 173 pages was small. Senator Daniel Moynihan (D.-N.Y.) has already complained: "It does not take a foot of legislation... to give the president the power to proceed with the Uruguay Round" (1987: F3).

The content of the act reflects the perception in Congress that there is a need to set up new standards for international trade. The belief is that the current GATT rules are no longer effective in today's economic situation. It also reflects congressional mistrust of President Reagan's willingness to represent domestic interests against unfair trade practices. Among some of its major provisions, the Act

- Limits the President's power to avoid taking retaliatory action in trade cases involving products traded fairly and unfairly
- Eases export-control loans to help U.S. high-technology industries
- Orders the government to increase its efforts to promote export
- Broadens the definition of what constitutes unfairness
- Allows the imposition of a tax on imported oil

Although the Trade Act of 1988 does not restrict imports directly, it, in some parts, contradicts international rules by singling out countries with trade surpluses and by unilaterally setting new standards for defining fair and unfair trade.

Instead of jumping into the debate surrounding the Omnibus Trade Bill as soon as it emerged, the administration has continually refused to become active and has given Congress no signs of cooperation. The only reactions from the executive branch were the labeling of some provisions as "protectionist" and threats to veto the bill. On the eve of the start of the Senate's debate, the Reagan administration "warned... that major sections of the bill would hurt the economy, cost Americans jobs, and provoke retaliation." The White House also released a 34-page analysis of the 1000-page trade bill (*Washington Post*, June 25, 1987: F1).

According to Susan Schwab, legislative director of Sen. John Danforth and a key drafter of the bill, the Trade Act of 1988 was "the first major trade law drafted in the Congress – rather than by the Administration – since the early 1930s" (cited in Nicolaides 1988: 119). As a result it contains more protectionist measures than any other law since that time. This was probably also the reason for President Reagan's veto in May 1988. Officially, however, he vetoed the bill because of the attached Plant Closure Amendment. The amendment was therefore taken out and the Omnibus Trade Bill was approved in the House as well as in the Senate with more than two-thirds of the votes. This left President Reagan with no other choice than to sign the bill into law.

Gone seems to be the day when Trade Representatives together with committee members hammered out a draft for a trade bill. What is also missing are the three decisive components of the interaction mechanism: responsiveness, trust, and cooperation between the President and Congress. Presently, Congress seems to be left alone to pass a trade bill which the President in turn threatens to veto. Instead of working together to protect each other from pressures of special interests, this emerging polarization of the executive and legislative branches exposes the international trade issues to domestic politics. Some observers believe that certain members of Congress tried to capitalize on the trade bill debate. One of the scenarios, explained by Representative Thomas Foley (D.-Wash.), saw the Democrats not pursuing the passage of the bill or hoping for its veto by the President in order to generate "a popular and effective central issue in the 1988 election" (1987: A17).

The liberalization of international trade since the 1930s was successful only because the politicization of foreign trade could be avoided by working within the interaction mechanism. This mechanism functioned on the basis of mutual responsiveness, trust, and cooperation, not by polarization and politicization. From Congress, this required self-restraint, and from the President, leadership and constructive engagement.

President Reagan started his presidency under the slogan "the less government the better." According to this premise he has been generally inactive in international trade policy. As a result Congress has taken over the agenda-setting, and power between the executive and legislative branches in the management of international trade has shifted in its favor. The interaction mechanism, however, requires a balance of power in trade matters, which can be achieved only when the President and Congress respond to each other's demands and take the necessary steps to reconcile their differing interests. It is unfortunate that the signs point to an administration whose actions and "nonactions" threaten to destroy the interaction mechanism which has developed and worked effectively for half a century.

References

Baldwin, Robert E. (1984): The Changing Nature of U.S. Trade Policy Since World War II. In Robert E. Baldwin and Anne O. Krueger (eds.), *The Structure and Evolution of Recent U.S. Trade Policy*. Chicago: University of Chicago Press.

Corwin, Edward S. (1940): *The President, Office and Powers, 1787–1957; History and Analysis of Practice and Opinion*. New York: New York University Press.

Destler, I. M. (1980): United States Congress and the Tokyo Round: Lessons of a Success Story. *World Economy* 3: 53–70.

Destler, I. M. (1981): Trade Consensus, SALT Stalement: Congress and Foreign Policy in the 1970s. In Thomas E. Mann and Norman J. Ornstein (eds.), *The New Congress*. Washington, D.C.: American Enterprise Institute for Public Policy Research.

Destler, I. M. (1986a): *American Trade Politics: System Under Stress*. Washington, D.C.: Institute for International Economics.

Destler, I. M. (1986b): Protecting Congress or Protecting Trade? *Foreign Policy* 62: 96–107.

Foley, Thomas (1987): *Washington Post*, April 20, A17.

Gadbaw, R. Michael (1982): Reciprocity and Its Implications for U.S. Trade Policy. *Law and Policy in International Business* 14: 691–746.

Holliday, George (1986): Trade. *Congressional Research Service*, Issue brief 87003.

Kassinger, Theodore W. (1983): The Trade Agenda of the 98th Congress. *Federal Bar News and Journal* 30: 219–225.

Kinsley, Michael (1987): Editorial. *Washington Post*, March 25, A23.

Koh, Harold H. (1986): Congressional Controls on Presidential Trade Policymaking After I.N.S. versus CHADHA. *New York University Journal of International Law and Politics* 18: 1191–1233.

Malbin, Michael J. (1980): *Unelected Representatives. Congressional Staff and the Future of Representative Government*. New York: Basic Books.

Moynihan, D. (1987): *Washington Post*, June 26, F3.

Nicolaides, Phedon (1988): Trade Warfare: The Quest for Fair Trade. *World Today* 44: 119–123.

Oppenheimer, Bruce I. (1981): Congress and the New Obstructionism: Developing an Energy Program. In Lawrence C. Dodd and Bruce I. Oppenheimer (eds.), *Congress Reconsidered*. Washington, D.C.: Congressional Quarterly Press.

Pastor, Robert A. (1980): *Congress and the Politics of U.S. Foreign Economic Policy, 1929–1976*. Berkeley: University of California Press.

Pastor, Robert A. (1983): The Cry-and-Sigh Syndrome: Congress and Trade Policy. In Allen Schick (ed.), *Making Economic Policy in Congress*. Washington, D.C.: American Enterprise Institute for Public Policy Research.

Thompson, Margaret (1984): *Trade*: U.S. Policy Since 1945. Washington, D.C.: Congressional Quarterly.

Vernon, Raymond (1982): International Trade Policy in the 1980s: Prospects and Problems. *International Studies Quarterly* 26: 483–510.

Washington Post (1987) August 12, F5.

Washington Post (1987) June 25, F1.

Neoconservatism and U.S. Foreign Policy: The Case of Foreign Trade

Petra Beckmann and *Michael Minkenberg*

It is a striking paradox that one of the most pragmatic people is quite ideological when it comes to foreign policy (Schlesinger 1983: 1 f). Among the various reasons for the paradoxical character of American foreign policy with regard to its domestic settings, the "newness" of the nation (Lipset 1967), its limited experience with foreign affairs and lack of traditional (European) diplomacy (Almond 1965: 69), and the primordial occupation of Americans with private values and economic interests (Almond 1965: 29 ff) are often referred to. As a result, according to some of the theories, Americans did not accomplish a balanced foreign policy in a way which adequately and continuously serves the interest of the country in a realistic fashion. Rather, American foreign policy fluctuates between different moods which conflict with American interests and produce ideologies which sometimes diverge extremely from a realistic approach.

However, there seems to be enough evidence that the emergence of neoconservatism in American foreign policy signals a new wave of ideological foreign policy orientation in the U.S.A.: From the early intellectual criticism of American foreign policy during the Nixon/Kissinger era it has risen to the dominant "mood" in the late 1970s and became the foreign policy platform of Ronald Reagan, who finally took it into the White House in 1981.[1]

In our chapter, we want to elaborate the neoconservative foreign policy agenda with particular emphasis on foreign trade issues in the context of American foreign policy traditions and ideologies. The foreign trade issue area seems to be particularly interesting since in this field the tension between ideological purity (international free trade with the Western world and trade controls with the Communist world) and economic interests (the rising tide of protectionism and loopholes in the trade with Communist countries) becomes most apparent.

The underlying question of this essay is to what degree do major foreign policy traditions in the U.S.A., as reflected in the premise of the neoconservative foreign policy views, shape and condition their foreign trade positions, and do our sources allow us to speak of a coherent neoconservative foreign policy "platform" or do they suggest a mere harmony of concepts in the field of foreign trade? These questions point at the general focus of our contribution. The intention is to illustrate the orientation of a certain elite group in the context of American political culture and not to try to evidence the translation of this level to the level of political action and behavior on behalf of foreign policy makers.

The first part of our essay concentrates on the major foreign policy traditions of the U.S.A. and their link to political culture. Then, we proceed to illustrate the emergence of neoconservatism as a new ideological grouping in the United States and its foreign policy views. These will be interpreted in relation to the general framework of American political culture and foreign policy traditions. The second part focuses on several sources which provide insights into the neoconservative views on foreign trade. Since this group is composed of neoconservative intellectuals, on the one hand, and New Right activists and organizations on the other, which have very different political backgrounds, the question of the coherency of their positions becomes particularly relevant. Our sources include publications by the Harvard history professor Richard Pipes (1984a, b), who has been published in journals like *Foreign Affairs* and *Commentary*. Whereas the former certainly does not represent a liberal mouthpiece but can be regarded as an organ of the mainstream establishment, *Commentary* has "fostered the growth of the 'neoconservative' movement... responding to the 'soft' position liberal Democrats were taking toward world communism" (Wolfe 1987: 190). Further, we analyzed "Tariffs: The Preferred Tax of Masochists," an article in a Christian newsletter, written by Gary North (1987); a Congressional background paper by Daphne Miller (1987), entitled *Competitiveness or Protectionism: Which works Best?* and published in Washington D.C. by the Republican Study Committee (a New Right Congressional research organization and clearinghouse); the article "How America Is Being Taken In Trade" by Robert W. Lee (1986) published in (one of)the leading New Right journals, *Conservative Digest*; and the booklet *A Strategy for Peace Through Strength*, edited by the American Security Council Foundation (1984) in Boston. Among this foundation's "Strategy Board" members are such prominent New Right and neoconservative names as Edwin Feulner, president of the Heritage Foundation, John M. Fisher, president of the American Security Council, and Dr. Richard Pipes. The list of Coalition for Peace through Strength National Organizations includes all well-known New Right and neoconservative political action committees, lobbying organizations, think tanks, and associations. Finally, we also analyzed the Heritage Foundation's *Mandate for Leadership*, first and second volumes, which was designed at the end of President Carter's term in order to provide a detailed conservative guideline for the next administration which was expected to be Republican conservative. Both volumes of *Mandate* contain policy analysis combined with detailed policy advice and are among the most comprehensive publications of the New Right with regard to public policy issues. We have chosen as a time frame the period from 1980 to the present which is marked by the election of Ronald Reagan as president with close ties to the neoconservative and New Right network and the recent congressional election in 1986 which put an end to the Republican majority in the Senate from 1980 on – a period in which, for the first time since the New Deal realignment, a Republican President enjoyed a Republican majority in the Senate over several terms.

1 American Foreign Policy and the Rise of Neoconservatism

1.1 Patterns of U.S. Foreign Policy

Our general approach to American foreign policy follows from its already mentioned characteristic: its strong dependence on internal sources. An effort to systematically define all sources of foreign policy is provided by James Rosenau who distinguishes between individual, role, governmental, societal, and systemic sets of variables which determine foreign policy and who suggests that in an open society with a developed economy like the U.S.A., societal variables like major value orientations, the extent of industrialization, etc. play a major role in foreign policy.[2] With regard to the formulation of foreign policy options (as distinguished from the execution of foreign policy) we may go a step further and assume that in the U.S.A., which lacks the tradition of long-range participation in international affairs and, thus, experience in traditional diplomacy and interest politics, political culture, understood as the "subjective dimension of politics" in terms of long-lasting political values and patterned orientation towards the political system, its inputs and outputs, and the role of the individual,[3] is a crucial factor in providing the cues for shaping foreign policy agendas. Major value orientations and the "American character" may be seen as the long-range cultural forces, whereas shifts in "moods" and attitudes are the rather short-term factors. Together with the environment of foreign policy, the long-term and short-term internal forces provide the context within which foreign policy operates (Almond 1965: 9f; Schlesinger 1983; Hughes 1978; Kegley and Wittkopf 1982: 237–312). With this basic framework in mind we want to have a closer look at the political-culture background of American foreign policy.

Among the cultural forces which constitute the context for the ideologies and traditions of American foreign policy, two seem to be the most outstanding: liberalism and Puritanism. The American liberal tradition (Hartz 1955) rests on the principles of John Locke's political philosophy, in particular the idea of inalienable individual rights of life, liberty, and property.[4] The stress on individualism and property were important contributions to the belief that free enterprise was the economic equivalent to the design of the American political system. Empirical analyses have shown that still in the 1970s "Lockean liberal values evidently represent much of the political culture of the United States" (Devine 1972: 366f). The Puritan heritage in the American political culture contrasts with the liberal tradition in that it defines a religiously inspired sense of purpose for the American people which goes beyond the mere pursuit of individual interest and the rationalistic approach of liberalism. With Lockean liberalism, these principles merged into the doctrines of fundamental moral law, of the free individual, of the philosophy of progress, of American constitutionalism, and of the mission of American democracy to save the world, thus constituting the basics of the American "civil religion"[5] and of the American "democratic faith."[6] However, the civil religion is not equally shared across ethnic, class, and regional lines but its ambiguities and contradictions (moral universalism vs. moral relativism, individual interests and free enterprise vs. moral order and common purpose) have invited different emphasis on and ideological instrumentalizing of the various doctrines (Shell 1986: 22).

The tensions between the two poles of American political culture are carried over to the two poles of American foreign policy: Moralism and the sense of a global mission of the U.S.A. favor an ideological approach in foreign policy, whereas liberalism and the pursuit of mainly economic private interests require a more realistic interest-based foreign policy. With this dichotomization we do not mean that interest and ideology are mutually exclusive concepts – ideologies may legitimize and/or mask real interests, interest politics may serve ideologies. But in a fundamental sense we believe that a major emphasis on either ideology or interests in politics has quite different consequences. While an ideological approach serves to legitimize one's own interests (however defined) and delegitimizes the interests of others, thereby reflecting a rather simplistic and moralistic worldview, it justifies different means in politics than an interest-based approach which concedes a certain legitimacy of the political opponent's interests and reflects a more complex and realistic worldview.[7]

It is exactly this meaning of ideology which characterizes American foreign policy orientations and agendas at most points in American history and caused it to be seen as a history of American foreign policy doctrines which all have significant ideological and even religious connotations (Crabb 1982: 375–386) or in terms of fluctuating moods of extroversion and introversion (Holmes 1985). Both internationalism and isolationism were justified in terms of the American mission to the world, but they were different interpretations of how the mission should be carried out. Already the founding fathers were afraid of American intervention in other countries' affairs and preferred to let America redeem the world by example, yet they had a sense of power politics and national interest which led them to oppose the destruction of the European balance of power through Napoleon (Schlesinger 1983: 2 f; Holmes 1985: 28 f). The culmination of this phase of internationalist orientation and interest-based politics was the Monroe doctrine. Afterwards, America became introverted in its foreign affairs and chose to perfect its own institutions, thus maintaining its superiority and example function.[8] The moralistic rejection of European power politics competed with a realistic appreciation of it when America massively reentered the international arena in the latest phases of internationalism, first in the beginning of the twentieth century (culminating in Wilson's creation of the League of Nations), next during World War II (Klingberg 1979: 38; Holmes 1985: 20–37). The last change from isolationism to internationalism, however, was accompanied by major changes which deeply affected the parameters of American foreign policy and would make it difficult to withdraw again. In the words of Arthur Schlesinger:

> The competition between realism and ideology was complicated, however, by two developments: by the fact that the United States in the twentieth century became a great power; and by the fact that the balance of power in the twentieth century faced the gravest possible threats.... These threats demanded U.S. intervention abroad and brought the tradition of isolationism to a permanent end. But the growth of American power also confirmed the messianism of those who believed in America's divine appointment (1983: 4 f).

The proposition that in the aftermath of the Second World War the tradition of isolationism was brought to a permanent end does not mean that its existence ceased completely, but that it would not be likely to become a dominant mood again.

While during the 1930s the majority among the elites and mass public opposed American involvement in international conflicts, particularly participation in a European war (Jonas 1966: 15), Roosevelt's decision to enter World War II revived and added a foreign policy cleavage to the already existing cleavage between supporters of his New Deal liberalism and its opponents.[9] Active involvement of the U.S.A. in the war and in postwar international politics was supported mainly by anglophile Democrats of the East Coast and the South (which had its own tradition of internationalism since the founding of the United States). The isolationist opposition of Roosevelt's foreign policy was largely found among conservative Republicans, particularly Midwestern Protestants (often of German and Scandinavian descent) and fundamentalists, who since the end of World War I had rejected U.S. involvement in European power politics and had favored a Pacific orientation of the U.S.A. and a unilateral "America First" position, and who were afraid of the concentration of executive power in Washington D.C. which was necessitated by the war and could be used for further egalitarian changes of the American system once the war was over (Miles 1980: 47–51; Shell 1986: 56–62).

This cleavage and with it the isolationist position lost its salience and relevance to the degree that the United States became continuously involved in the East-West conflict as the opponent of the Soviet Union (Link 1980). Already in the 1920s, Americans experienced a "Red scare," but not anti-communism which in the U.S.A. has a global as well as domestic dimension and this has contributed to a rise of internationalism and a reorientation of the party system with regard to foreign policy issues. Both at the elite and the mass public level, anti-communist internationalism united Democrats and Republicans from the late 1940s on (Maggiotto and Wittkopf 1981; Wittkopf and Maggiotto 1983). A major change took place within the Republican party in which anti-communist internationalism collided with its pre-war isolationist position and contributed to a conversion of Republicans towards higher military expenses, a stronger air force, and nuclear armament on the nationalist wing of Senator Taft, as well as aggressive messianism which propagated a roll-back of the victory over the Soviet Union on the right wing with the position of "moral leadership" of the U.S.A. as the unifying theme for the various party wings (Miles 1980: 84–89; Shell 1986: 78). For the problem of domestic anti-communism, which cannot be discussed here, see Miles (1980: 123–148; Shell 1986: 84–93; also Lipset and Raab 1978: 209–247). With the nomination of Barry Goldwater as presidential candidate in 1964, the militant conservative wing of the Republican party dominated within the party which now challenged the Democratic foreign policy from a perspective of right-wing internationalism. But only four years later, a Republican took over the White House and continued the non-militant foreign policy of conciliation and tokenism towards the Soviet Union which had been started by the Democrats during the 1960s (Kegley and Wittkopf 1982: 58, especially Fig. 3.1).

Although Nixon and Kissinger did not give up the idea of containing the Soviet Union,[10] they executed foreign policy in a rather European sense of conservative power politics with a complex worldview and a Realpolitik approach which was in striking contrast to the ideologically simplistic tradition of American foreign policy discussed above (Hoffmann 1984: chaps. 2 and 3). While Nixon and Kissinger tried to reduce tensions and increase accommodation between the two superpowers based on the linkage theory, they continued to fight the war in Vietnam, even escalated by invading Cambodia, in order to achieve "peace with honor," and initiated political relations with Communist China, thus upsetting the Taiwanese ally. This approach to foreign policy (not some of the single policies like détente) was criticized by the

Democrats who practically forced their President to resign in 1968 over the Vietnam issue, while also not finding unanimous support among Republicans, some of whom were strong enough to push President Ford to a position of military strength as a prerequisite of arms control negotiations.[11] In the meantime, Democratic foreign policy orientations had moved away from Roosevelt's and Truman's balance of power oriented interventionism and, influenced by the Vietnam war, shifted towards limited international engagement and continuance of détente with the Soviet Union. Under Jimmy Carter, the human rights issue became an ideological focus of the trilateral approach to international affairs which tried to improve political and military relations with both the Western world and developing nations in order to avoid political isolationism in the world community (Kegley and Wittkopf 1982: 66 f). The human rights issue and the decreased emphasis on the East-West conflict in favor of the North-South conflict marked a clear departure from the Soviet-centered Realpolitik approach of Kissinger, but it did not mean a lasting substitute for the option of militant containment.[12]

1.2 The Coming of the Neoconservative Foreign Policy Agenda

The Vietnam war undoubtedly contributed to the mobilization of a "protest generation" which, after having been raised in an era of relative well-being and security in economic and military terms, were able to develop "post-materialist" value priorities and unconventional forms of political participation (Inglehart 1977; Barnes et al. 1979). The rise of the post-materialist New Left and its participation in Democratic party reform politics (Shafer 1983) as well as the controversy around the Vietnam war in the context of a fundamental change of the American society towards a phase of "post-industrialism" (Touraine 1969; Bell 1973; for a review of literature see Lipset 1981: 506 f) have provoked a new conservative response. If conservatism is understood in terms of a "situational ideology" (as belief system; see Huntington 1957) reaction, even in anticipation, to the threat of status and privileges by fundamental changes of social differentiation and new demands of emancipation and participation in the context of bourgeois capitalist society,[13] then neoconservatism in general is bourgeois modernism becoming conservative in the face of the latest radical attack (Dubiel 1985). It is the response of traditional conservatives and liberals both at the elite and at the mass level to a fundamental change in culture and values which does not any longer reflect the old cleavage as expressed in class and partisan lines but a new cleavage based on value change and which sees its political opponent on the New Left of post-materialist oriented strata and the related political agenda (Minkenberg and Inglehart, in press). Neoconservatism is not simply a revival of conservatism but a new coalition of forces which see their common enemy in the post-materialist oriented strata of the New Left and their new political agenda. Neoconservatism includes parts of the working class-based Old Left who felt challenged by the New Left and traditional conservative groups. This reaction is expressed by a heightened concern with sociocultural values and issues (nationalism, law and order, family, religion, and bourgeois morality) which are translated into policy issues like opposition to the Equal Rights Amendment, to the Supreme Court's decision on abortion and school prayer, etc., but support for the values of industrial capitalism, particularly the idea of progress, and by a general acceptance of the basic welfare state accomplishments. Whereas the Old Right defined itself as the adversary of welfare statism, defended an elitist concept of "limited democracy" against egalitarian views of "popular democracy," and was based socially in the business world and upscale groups who felt their feeling of superiority being taken away by the modern welfare state (Goldmann 1977: 289), neoconservatism has lower class support and a more egalitarian bent. Furthermore, whereas the Old Right was identified politically with the Northeastern wing of the Republican party, neoconservatism includes Democrats and Republicans as well (Minkenberg and Inglehart, in press).

Regarding the context of our presentation we define neoconservatism in American foreign policy as the moralist-ideological version of anti-communist internationalism with an offensive or even aggressive sense of "global mission" of the U.S.A. At the elite level, the neoconservative foreign policy agenda is mainly formulated by neoconservative intellectuals or New Right leaders who, despite their differences in background as well as political involvement and sophistication, moved ever closer to each other in their basic policy options, particularly in foreign policy, during the second half of the 1970s. This agenda became part of the foreign policy agenda of Reagan-as-candidate and entered, to a considerable degree, the Republican party platforms in 1976 and 1980. Empirical research on public opinion with regard to foreign policy orientations at the mass and at the elite level has produced evidence that along with the above-mentioned fundamental social and cultural changes and events the single internationalist/isolationist dimension in foreign policy ceased in the 1970s and the internationalist consensus fractured into different groups (Wittkopf and Maggiotto 1983: 307 f). In an analysis of 1974 and 1975 data, Mandelbaum and Schneider suggest a liberal/conservative dimension cutting across the traditional internationalist/isolationist dimension: While the latter is defined in terms of *whether* the U.S.A. should play an active role in world affairs, the former is defined in terms of *what kind* of role it should play. These authors find that 57% of the 1975 sample were internationalist with 42% of them favoring internationalism but rejecting militaristic and interventionist positions (liberal internationalists) and 58% favoring both, thus representing the Cold War internationalist consensus (conservative internationalists; Mandelbaum and Schneider 1979: 41 f., also for the following). While conservative internationalists tended to be less well educated and more concentrated in the South than their liberal counterparts, they were only slightly more Republican than the liberals and had the same proportion of Democrats (42%) as the liberal internationalists. They reject détente and favor an aggressive American leadership of the Western alliance as the best means to obtaining national security, while their liberal counterparts, far from being neo-isolationist like parts of the far left, think of international problems more than usual in economic terms and define American national security not through a hegemonic role but through economic and humanitarian involvement. Although they see the world quite differently, they agree on a crucial point: Each demands that Amercian foreign policy have a moral basis, something that both regard as conspicuously missing from Henry Kissinger's diplomacy (Mandelbaum and Schneider 1979: 65). These findings are mainly confirmed by a leader and mass sample comparison of 1974 data done by Maggiotto and Wittkopf, who provide evidence that the two cross-cutting dimensions apply equally to leaders and masses, with slight differences in the frequency distributions (as shown for each subgroup in Fig. 1). A fading minority of the leaders are either isolationists or hardliners (fearing communism and willing to use troops abroad), almost all of them support cooperative involvement, but they are evenly split on the issue of militant involvement (Wittkopf and Maggiotto 1983: 317; Oldendick and Bardes 1982). The mass public splits into four almost equally strong quarters in each category. The leadership surveys done by Holsti and Rosenau (1984) again support the Mandelbaum and Schneider findings that isolationism is contrasted with two versions of internationalism (thus making a "three-headed eagle" of the American leadership). Whereas military officers, business executives, and public officials (in that order) were strongest on cold war internationalist positions, educators and media leaders were weakest (Holsti and Rosenau 1984: 170 f). Comparisons over time reveal a relative stability of the foreign policy beliefs between 1976 and 1980. However, a comparison of mass public beliefs between 1974 and 1978 made by William Schneider showed that conservative internationalism gained in public support but only with regard to "symbols" such as the military, anti-communism, the CIA, business, and U.S. power. Schneider concludes: "Foreign policy attitudes between 1974 and 1978 shifted in the direction of greater conservatism and less internationalism" (Schneider 1983: 45; see also Russett and Deluca 1981).

While these changes in mass public attitudes may reflect an increase in ideological internationalism (as defined above), they do not by themselves indicate that the American public has acquired a conservative internationalist ideology (as belief system).[14] At the level of intellectual elites and political leadership, however, the neoconservative foreign policy agenda has increas-

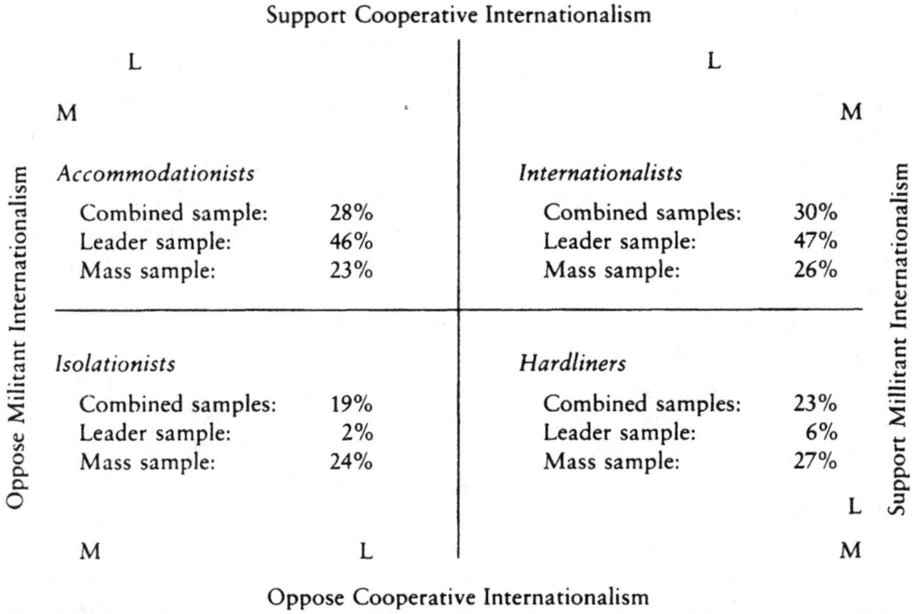

L refers to the leader sample: M to the mass sample. Each point represents the average factor score for each group within the opinion category based on the combined sample

Figure 1: The Distribution of Leaders and Masses among Four Categories of Opinion Holders

Source: Wittkopf and Maggiotto (1983: 322)

ingly gained importance in the 1970s. The neoconservative intellectuals are former (New Deal) liberals or even radicals with cold war internationalist positions during the 1950s who became disenchanted with the Great Society liberalism through their own participation in social planning and frustration about the limits and (perceived) failures of the modern welfare state (Ashford 1981; Moynihan 1975: 8; for a comprehensive overview see Steinfels 1979; Schissler 1983; and Peele 1984). As members of the academic community, they turned to the defense of American values and institutions, particularly in the field of higher education, in the face of the student protests, thus siding with political conservatives who shared their interest in the stability of the social order (Moynihan 1975: 188). As members of the Jewish community, most of them were sensitive to the demands of the civil rights movement and the New Left and the government's and courts' positive response with regard to quotas and school busing (Bell 1972). Irving Kristol, the "godfather of neoconservatism" (*Esquire*) offers a canon of eight neoconservative principles which include "the belief that a predominantly market economy... is a necessary if not sufficient precondition for a liberal society..., the belief in the importance of economic growth... as indispensable for social and economic stability," the belief in a "conservative welfare state" (à la Bismarck) and "family and religion as indispensable pillars of a decent society (Kristol 1983: 75–77). For the neoconservative view on the intrinsic relationship between liberal democracy and capitalism see (Novak 1983).

In contrast to the East Coast, Democratic background of the neoconservative intellectuals, the New Right leaders have a predominantly Republican past and Midwestern and Southern populist roots.[15] As with the disillusionment of the neoconservatives with the liberal establishment, the New Right leaders were mobilized through disillusionment with the conservative, Republican establishment. According to Richard Viguerie, one of their most influential leaders, they organized themselves in the aftermath of Ford's selection of the liberal Nelson Rockefeller as Vice-President in 1974 in order to get their message across without the help of the Republican party (1981: 50). The rise of the New Right was conditioned and facilitated by the anti-East Coast mood after Watergate, the new campaign finance laws passed by Congress in 1974, the resurgence of anti-modern religion which, in turn, was closely related to an increasing awareness of the decay of the family and traditional moral and religious values (Phillips 1983; Liebman and Wuthnow 1983). During the 1970s, the leaders of the New Right established a close network of fund-raising organizations (e.g., the Richard Viguerie Company), grassroots mobilization, leadership training, and lobbying groups (e.g., the Conservative Caucus), political action committees (e.g., NCPAC), and think tanks (e.g., the Heritage Foundation); see Crawford (1979) and Saloma (1984). They have helped to build up conservative religious organizations like Moral Majority led by Jerry Falwell.[16] The ideology of the New Right is a cluster of social, moral, economic, and foreign policy issues which are unified by the definition of the common enemy of the various political and religious groups: "secular humanism."[17] They stand for social traditionalism and family issues, and oppose women's liberation, the E.R.A., homosexuality, evolution theory, sex education, and the ban on prayer in public schools; while they support economic libertarianism, free enterprise on Main Street, they oppose labor unions, big business, and the modern welfare state.[18]

Whereas neoconservative intellectuals still differ from new Right leaders with regard to welfare state issues, their emphasis on religion and political strategies (reflecting their different partisan and intellectual background), they have come to see themselves as a "working alliance" [19] and share most of their positions in foreign policy. They are equally critical of Kissinger's conservative Realpolitik which did not center around a general moral purpose of foreign policy and of Carter's human rights concern which, in their eyes, did not discriminate enough between communist and non-communist dictatorships. Based on the conviction that the United States has a global mission to redeem the world from the communist threat and to spread the values of democratic capitalism and that American foreign policy has to reflect basic moral values of the U.S.A., the morally justified fight against communism in general and the Soviet Union in particular and the restoration of American economic and military superiority as a means to that end (and as an end in itself: as example to others) become the primary concerns of the neoconservative foreign policy agenda (Kristol 1975: 54; Podhoretz 1980: 37 ff; Falwell 1981: 213; Viguerie 1981: 110; for an overview see Dippel 1983). The relations to the Soviet Union are seen as a moral duopoly which leaves little chance to consider the legitimate interests of the other side.

From this simplistic view, the conviction that the complex worldview of the Johnson and Nixon administrations and the New left were a "failure of nerve,"[20] follow various consequences in foreign policy options. First, détente and arms control negotiatons with the Soviet Union had to be abandoned since they would precipitate American inferiority in certain nuclear weapon systems and should be resumed only after the restoration of U.S. military strength and superiority – hence the opposition to SALT II (Schissler 1983: 90 f). This meant the farewell to the Kissinger approach which linked American concessions to "good behavior" on the part of the Soviet Union. Instead, the whole quality of U.S.-Soviet relations depends upon non-interference of the Soviet Union with other countries' affairs – not only in Third World countries but even in countries within the Soviet sphere of influence.[21] Since the dichotomy Free World vs. Communist World overshadows all international conflicts in this perspective, U.S. relations with all other countries have to be seen in the light of the East-West conflict. This perspective, for example, shapes also the role of Israel in the neoconservative worldview. Besides the traditional support of the Jewish community for the American commitment to Israel, neoconservatives see Israel as a basic strategic outpost against Soviet influence in the Middle East and a stabilizing force in the region which helps to secure the oil supply (for example Tucker 1977; see also Dippel 1983: 129 – 135).[22]

For the United States' dealing with dictatorships, Jeane Kirkpatrick proposed "double standards" (thus winning the sympathy of Ronald Reagan just in time as he became President). She demands a "morally and strategically acceptable and politically realistic program for dealing with non-democratic governments who are threatened by Soviet sponsored subversion" (Kirkpatrick 1979: 34). The U.S.A. should distinguish between authoritarian regimes (traditional, right-wing autocracies) which are friendly to America and totalitarian regimes (revolutionary, left-wing autocracies) which are unfriendly to the United States because of their extremist persuasion – after all, "traditional authoritarian regimes are less repressing than revolutionary autocracies"[23] and from this U.S. foreign policy can draw a minimum of moral legitimation in preferring right-wing regimes to left-wing regimes when looking for bulwarks against the Soviet threat. On the whole, the neoconservative positions on foreign policy can be summarized into four key issues: the battles against détente, moralism, globalism, and militarization, while the neoconservative terminology resembles the "vocabulary of the apocalypse, not the language of rational analysis" (Dippel 1983: 148, our translation).

The political relevance of neoconservatism in foreign policy was demonstrated long before Ronald Reagan came to power. One of the staunchest critics of the Nixon/Kissinger détente policy was Democratic Senator Henry Jackson, who with neoconservative intellectuals (like Ben Wattenberg and Jeane Kirkpatrick) and labor leaders founded the Coalition for a Democratic Majority in 1972/1973. This group was organized in reaction to the rise of the New Left within the Democratic party which culminated in the nomination of the outsider George McGovern as Democratic presidential candidate in 1972 (Schissler 1983: 54f) and was seen as a major reason for the disastrous defeat of the party in the general election. Senator Jackson became the leading figure in the fight of the neoconservative coalition of Republicans and Southern Democrats on Capitol Hill against détente in general and Kissinger in particular. In 1974 his efforts to block détente with the Soviet Union succeeded when the Senate approved a compromise version of his amendment to the Trade Act with the Soviet Union, originally designed by the Nixon administration in order to further an opening of the American economy for trade with the Soviet bloc. The amendment linked loans and most preferential treatment, which the Trade Act wanted to allow in trade with communist countries, to a liberalization of these countries with regard to their policies permitting emigration of minorities (in particular Soviet Jews). When the Stevenson amendment to the Trade Act introduced a ceiling of $ 300 million for loans to these countries, the Soviet Union called off the contract. Ironically, the Trade Act which was controversial between free traders and protectionists was helped in passing through Congress by the Jackson amendment: the quarrel between Eastern trade and human rights supporters overpowered the one between free traders and protectionists.[24]

Since this controversy, neoconservatives have continuously contributed to shaping foreign policy debates and platforms. In 1976 and 1980, large parts of the emerging neoconservative foreign policy agenda could be identified in the Republican party platforms basically shaped by the Reagan wing of the Republican party. Already in 1976, President Ford, who sought his first nomination by his party, dropped the word détente and favored a "position of strength" as prerequisite to arms limitation agreements and an "essential increase" of the defense budget (Ford 1976). However, he did not give up his stand in strategic arms limitation talks, thus being suspicious to the anti-communist Reagan camp. At the convention, Reagan supporters and Senator Jesse Helms pressed for tougher language in the party platform and succeeded in preparing a minority report which became known as the "morality in foreign policy" plank of the platform. It began with the statement, "The goal of Republican foreign policy is the achievement of liberty under law and a just and lasting peace in the world" (the American mission), and led to the principle of national defense, "military strength is the path to peace," which required an increased defense budget, "realistic assessment of the Communist challenge in the world" and a limited role of arms limitation agreements. The language of the Panama Canal plank was less strong than the conservatives expected and read that the 1903 treaty with Panama gave the U.S.A. rights to the canal zone "as if it were sovereign" (Weinberg 1976). On foreign trade issues, the platform pledged for removing barriers to an open economic system and opposing new restrictions to trade, thereby subscribing to the principle of "fair trade." In case of foreign competition negatively affecting industries and jobs, some adjustment assistance under the 1974 Trade Act is available.

Four years later, when Ronald Regan was nominated, the Republican platform read even more conservative. Senator Helms helped to introduce the language of "military and technological superiority" over the Soviet Union and an "immediate increase in defense spending" was asked for, favored by 84% of the delegates (Farah 1983: 274 f). The harsh language of the Soviet challenge was reflected by the majority of the delegates: 59% believed it was a big mistake to try too hard, to get along with the U.S.S.R. (Democratic delegates in 1980, 15%; Farah 1983: 274 f). The foreign trade plank advocated a "policy of free trade" insisting on the principles of reciprocity and equity with the U.S. trading partners in order to protect American jobs. Furthermore, "our international economic policy will be harmonized with our foreign and defense policies... [hence] Republicans oppose the transfer of high technology to the Soviet Union and its Eastern European satellites ...."

2 Interest and Ideology: Neoconservative Foreign Trade Positions

2.1 General Outlook

Neoconservative foreign trade positions are determined by the basic economic principle of free trade with regard to trade with the Western countries and the East-West conflict regarding trade with communist countries. Because of their commitment to capitalism as the economic order in congruence with basic American values such as individual freedom, the pursuit of happiness, competition, and a liberal, pluralist democracy, neoconservatives see unlimited trade as the best way to secure the leading position of the American economy, thus being in line with the Republican party on this issue. Moreover, in the U.S.A. this principle traditionally has been regarded as the premise for the maximization of mutual economic welfare which fitted well into the American self-image as the "patron of international freedom" (Calleo and Rowland 1973: 33, 35).

Free trade calls for free trading partners. Thus, this principle refers to trade relations with partners of the capitalist world only and excludes U.S.-Soviet relations. From a strict neoconservative viewpoint, East-West trade should fulfill aims other than mutual economic welfare, namely it should make a contribution to the transformation of the Soviet system (American Security Council Foundation 1984: 137, 144). This falls in line with the overall view of neoconservatives and New Right leaders on U.S.-Soviet relations: not to simply favor a containment of Soviet influence but to link the fight against communism to the expectation that through deterrence and arms build-up the Soviet empire might "come to reason" and be forced to liberalize from within (Butler et al. 1984: 292–299).

An operational justification for separating the trade areas between the Western world and the Soviet bloc can easily be derived from the overall goal of strengthening the wealth of the United States through efficient trade relations:

> In order to reverse the trend of limiting exports, an export should be reexamined in terms of point of destination, rather than placing primary reliance on the nature of the product to be exported. The major division should be between Soviet bloc trade and all other trade (Heatherly 1981: 36).

Moreover, the logic of this general statement falls in line with the basic neoconservative premises on how to evaluate international relations. Since all international relations are permeated by the East-West conflict, the logic of separating Soviet bloc trade from trade with other nations is the same as the one in Kirkpatrick's argumentation that the criterion of left-wing Marxist ideology should decide over classifying "bad guys" from "good guys."

2.2 East-West Trade

In the neoconservative opinion, communist governments are identical with the category "bad guys." According to the perception of the aggressive hegemonial character of such countries and the feeling of a military threat from the East in general, in the area of trade relations neoconservatives anticipate the permanent danger that the communist world might draw advantages from trade with the U.S.A. or her allies and use them against the West. Therefore, they demand that Soviet bloc trade should be subject to strict export controls.

The function of East-West trade – to help transform the Soviet system – should be pursued in a twofold perspective: On the one hand, the "economic arm of freedom" should be instrumentalized to shatter the U.S.S.R.'s power structure from within, i. e., especially to cause dissatisfaction with the limited possibilities of consumption that the Soviet economy itself offers. On the other hand, it is intended to handicap Soviet capabilities for intervening in its satellites' affairs by deepening problem aspects of their relationship (Pipes 1984a: 14; American Security Council Foundation 1984: 137, 142, 144). In concrete terms, the latter strategy could imply (controlled) exports of American goods which the Soviet Union cannot provide or can rarely provide its allies in order to contribute to an alienation within the Soviet bloc.

The strategic imprint which emerges here is reinforced by the environment of East-West trade and military reactions: In the case of Soviet interventions, neoconservatives agree upon economic sanctions as an adequate answer from the West but differ as far as implications are concerned. In Pipes' opinion (1984b: 270–272), economic sanctions represent a direct response to the aggressor. He places them between a military reaction, on the one hand, and acquiescence, on the other. But *Mandate for Leadership*, however, regarding sanctions as symbols to achieve political reactions on the side of adversaries and/or to set signposts in world politics (Heatherly 1981: 40; Butler 1984: 306), does not go as far as to put them next to military action.

Often, authors seem to equate East-West trade with Soviet-bloc trade (American Security Council Foundation 1984; Pipes 1984a, b). This stems primarily from the feeling of a military threat coming from the U.S.S.R. as being the dominant antagonist to the U.S.A. But neoconservative ideas and demands concerning trade relations with the East apply to the communist world in general. This is shown, for example, in Lee's (1986) illustration of the similarities in the development of U.S.-Soviet trade relations and trade relations between America and the People's Republic of China. He argues that U.S. technology exports to the Soviet Union helped her to intervene in foreign countries and explains the role and the influene of "Moscow's trade lobby" in the U.S.A., but he also warns that trade relations with Red China seem to go a similar way because U.S. exports, made possible by the characterization of the People's Republic as a "friendly, non-allied country... assigned to 'Country Group V' along with the NATO countries, Japan, Australia, New Zealand, and other authentically friendly nations," also include sensitive goods such as computers, machine tools, semiconductors, etc. (Lee 1986): 61 f.). His argumentation consists of two strains: First, he denies legitimacy of technology exports to any communist country grounded upon anti-communist conviction, and, second, he points to the danger of a growing accommodation between the U.S.S.R. and the People's Republic which could become a vital threat to the Western world when supplied with electronic equipment (Lee 1986: 63).

The whole neoconservative concept of foreign trade with communist countries strongly contrasts with the Nixon/Kissinger linkage theory which – apart from its (perceived) failure[25] – was seen as the voluntary subordination of America as guardian of the free world being the dictatorship of the U.S.S.R. This interpretation represents a logical consequence of the neoconservative understanding of the East-West conflict, which was initiated and "kept alive" by the Soviet Union. Thus, every step toward the antagonist is regarded as pure suicide. Accordingly, the issue of technology transfer is seen as the most volatile element in East-West trade, accompanied by the call for a strict supervision of Western technology exports in order to prevent Soviet aggression. The urgency of this demand is not only justified by current examples such as Soviet soldiers having invaded Afghanistan with the help of American trucks built at the Kama River plant but also with reference to resources which enabled the Soviet Union in the 1920s/1930s, then relying heavily on Western help (Pipes 1984a: 27; 1984b: 259 ff), to start their industrialization. A control of technology transfer might range from the complete exclusion of technology export from U.S.-Soviet relations to the instrumentalization as a "reward" or "punishment" of Soviet political behavior; if it does not help the Soviets to use it against the Western interests (Dippel 1983: 146 f).

The dilemma of a coherent justification of the problem of technology transfer is a twofold one: First, nearly all technology could always be used for military purposes ("dual-use technology and equipment"). This aspect is reinforced by the thesis that the Soviet economy is a permanent war economy because of the strong overlap and interdependence of military and civilian competences.[26] Second, even grain sales to the Soviet Union might be strategically important in the sense that they allow the Soviet Union to redirect its resources from the agricultural area to military research, development, and build-up.[27]

Trade relations with the Soviet Union and its allies are seen as an attempt "to undertake customary transactions with an entity which has no enduring stake in the maintenance of the global economic system" (American Security Council Foundation 1984: 142).

Under the premise that East-West trade is regarded as an "important element in the national security equation" (Butler et al. 1984: 277) or even a "mandate to wage economic warfare" (American Security Council Foundation 1984: 138) against the Soviet bloc, its redefinition and strict limitation is further enforced in the call for the creation of an Office of Strategic Trade. This independent agency should represent an advisory body to the National Security Council. The idea is to reorganize and centralize the export control system by delegating to this office the Commerce Department's current licensing responsibilities as well as the responsibilities of the State Department's Office of East-West Trade under the Arms Control Act (Butler et al 1984: 277, 279). The intended effect lies in enhanced national security and financial savings in defense costs as a consequence of the acceleration of the decision-making process in "denying or delaying Soviet bloc acquisition" (Butler et al. 1984: 277, 279).

The American Security Council Foundation goes beyond this defensive approach. In the context of a comprehensive non-military offensive, the Office of Strategic Trade should search for the economic vulnerabilities of the Soviet bloc and exploit them as well as develop strategies to complicate and disorganize the Soviet economy (American Security Council Foundation 1984: 138). In particular, it should, for example, help prevent incidents such as the Soviet "grain robbery"[28] by establishing national marketing agencies which could execute large-scale negotiations with the Soviet Union. The effect of an enhanced U.S. negotiating position would make up for the administrative preparations, namely an exemption from U.S. antitrust legislation.[29] Another function of the Office of Strategic Trade would be the elaboration of "economic sanctions contingency plans." In order to secure their effect, these plans should be developed in collaboration with the allies. Because critics claim that sanctions hurt one's own economy more than they achieve political purposes, it is proposed to

> ... devise potential sanctions with fully researched analysis of the effects on individual industries and economic sectors, for contingency use, thereby allowing for development of offsetting financial measures ahead of crises (American Security Council Foundation 1984: 140).

Interestingly, in the case of the Office of Strategic Trade, neoconservatives support the establishment of a new administrative agency, although in general they strongly oppose "big government" which they take as a synonym for a monstrous bureaucracy and a huge amount of basically unnecessary expense. But this is contradictory only at first glance. In our opinion, it again underlines the deep anti-communist sentiment of the neoconservatives which leads them to place national security and ideology before economic principles. Besides, it is argued that costs that might arise would be more than offset by the reduction in defense expenditures made possible through the perfection of export controls (Lee 1986: 59). Related to this approach are measures such as the limitation or reduction of Soviet hard currency wherever possible or the realization of transactions exclusively on a cash basis (Butler et al. 1984: 279; Pipes 1984b: 272 f; American Security Council Foundation 1984: 137) meant to significantly reduce Soviet chances of purchasing sensitive goods and technology by bringing them to an inferior position on the world market. In order to reinforce the intended effects, some neoconservatives suggest trying to persuade other capitalist countries to follow these proposals and to support the U.S. in its Soviet-bloc trade policy on a bilateral level or through adequate organizations like the Coordinating Committee for the Multilateral Control of Exports – COCOM.[30] Although from the organizational aspect, COCOM is regarded as the most relevant agency, neoconservatives are quite skeptical about its current effectiveness. In their view, the international export control system is handled too laxly. In 1972 alone, the Pentagon was overruled by COCOM decisions to relax trade standards in 59 cases (Lee 1986: 59). The COCOM control on high technology and licenses should be tightened and quests for exemptions in order to export sensitive goods being subject to the COCOM list should be refused. Finally, the elimination of the unanimity rule in the decision-making would give concerned members a better chance to protect newly developed technologies against leakage by other members (American Security Council Foundation 1984: 138 f.).

Although Soviet bloc trade in general is determined by national security considerations and ideology, trade with countries like Poland is also subject to the human rights situation. Because of the imposition of martial law it was recommended to continue limiting trade with Poland through existing sanctions (Butler et al. 1984: 301, 306 f). However, imposing export limitations on the grounds of human rights policy, as is the case with South Africa, is viewed as being a "counterproductive failure" (Heatherly 1981: 42). For neoconservatives, differing recommendations about the treatment of nations whose governments violate human rights do not imply a contradiction, since Poland falls into the category "totalitarian regime with Marxist persuasion," whereas South Africa has an "authoritarian government friendly to the U.S." This is another example of how the neoconservative foreign trade position is under cross-pressure between the East-West conflict and domestic economic interests and principles.

Neoconservative views on Soviet-bloc trade merge into a harmony of ideas and concepts which almost could be labeled a platform comprised of the various policy options of the different organizations. While our sources do not reveal any substantive differences on central points, such as the idea of an Office of Strategic Trade or the need for tightening COCOM's export control system, they do differ in the rhetoric as well as the intended effects; i.e., more offensive (American Security Council Foundation 1984; Pipes 1984a, b) vs. more defensive (Heatherly 1981; Butler et al. 1984; Lee 1986).

This gives the impression that some neoconservative recommendations are more moderate than others which, however, is misleading since the all embracing anti-communism of the various groups and authors mentioned goes beyond a simple containment policy and seeks a liberalization and transformation of the Soviet empire. These considerations perhaps suggest a compatible bundle of ideas bound together by the same shared principles, but they do not permit us to assume the existence of a coherent neoconservative platform with regard to foreign trade issues.

2.3 Trade with Western Nations

With regard to trade relations with capitalistic nations neoconservatives display a sensitivity to protectionist concerns in relation to the domestic market, while still adhering to the free trade principle. Basically, free trade is regarded as the underlying principle supporting international competition among equal partners sharing "equal opportunity." But the feeling that fair trade and reciprocity have been violated calls for measures to protect the American market, jobs, and industries from foreign exploitation.

Mandate (Heatherly 1981) tries to find a way that will both prevent unfair trade in the interests of the U.S. economy and at the same time uphold the principle of free trade against protectionist pressures. With regard to the perspective that "a realistic import policy should seek to accommodate political realities without abandoning the free trade premise," two explanations are represented to justify import restrictions. For one, they could support internal U.S. market demands and thereby ease "social transitions in failing industries" (Heatherly 1981: 48). But more important, import restrictions could be imposed in order to force reductions in non-tariff barriers to U.S. exports maintained by OECD trading partners, and thus help reduce the trade deficit: "It is recommended that we use the U.S. internal demands for protectionism to buttress our negotiating position for demanding the lowering of non-tariff entry barriers by our OECD trading partners" (Heatherly 1981: 48). *Mandate* itself demands that the Japanese should be the first and foremost target of this strategy.[31]

Although the argumentation for protectionist measures seems to be based in equal parts on internal necessities and the demand for lowering trade barriers, it becomes obvious that import restrictions in the first place are regarded as an adequate means to improve U.S. export rates. In contrast to the internal demands of the American market – which are not specified at all – the (perceived) advantages for Japan and disadvantages for the U.S.A. of Japanese trade barriers for U.S. goods, especially agricultural products, are discussed in detail.

Interestingly, a military argument serves as an important additional justification for American import restrictions in the sense that since the U.S.A. provides advantages for Japan's security being disproportional to Japan's own military spending, it should be punished by U.S. trade barriers (Heatherly 1981: 48). However, it is not ultimately clear how concrete and far-reaching *Mandate*'s recommendations are for imposing trade barriers against Japan. Indeed, considering that free trade is fully congruent with free enterprise and competition, the *Mandate* position does not fit with the idea that the principles of capitalism are a bulwark of the neoconservative stand.

A Republican Study Committee paper (Miller 1987) explains why import restrictions, meant to protect industries at home while being a retaliation against countries using "unfair trade practices," will not help to reduce the trade deficit and at the same time insure fair trade. The overall argument is that "protectionist measures are anti-competitive, and that is anti-consumer" (Miller 1987: 3). Protectionist quotas on Japanese cars, for example, mean that the U.S. auto industry has less need to keep prices down to compete with Japanese import prices. This does not serve the American consumer, since price increases are accompanied by diminished choices. Neither does it help American industry, because only competition makes a company do better and be more productive (Miller 1987: 3). In addition, since competitiveness is the very essence of an economy which depends on world trade, curbing competition means hurting the economy itself. Approximately 20% of U.S. exports are industrial goods and at least 70% of the production competes with foreign merchandise (Miller 1987: 9). This competitiveness- and consumer-oriented argument falls in line with the neoconservative idea that trade promotes mutual welfare.

North (1987), also arguing on a consumer-oriented level against protectionist measures, morally justifies free trade with "God's own will." Since the Bible teaches that every man is to work out his own salvation (or damnation) with fear and trembling (Phil. 2:12), people have to be left free to do anything they choose unless it is immoral. In North's opinion, this also applies to trade: selling and buying is not immoral unless the item or the service is immoral. "Trade should therefore be either completely free or completely prohibited; tariffs and quotas have no role to play in improving economic morality" (North 1987: 2). The Christian newsletter in which this appears also argues on a mere economic basis which stresses the need for ailing American industries to adjust to the standards of those who have taken away their market shares. This reveals a double-track justification of free trade which helps the issue to be accepted by religious conservatives and non-religious libertarians alike, thus reflecting the conglomerate of religious and economic positions in the New Right ideology.

3 Conclusions

This review of the literature has shown that neoconservatives and the New Right share a common approach to foreign trade which is related to their general foreign policy premises. However, foreign trade with Western countries is hardly an issue for neoconservative intellectuals since they are basically preoccupied with the domestic market situation and theoretical rather than policy-oriented considerations (cf. Irving Kristol's fascination with supply-side economics). Because of the emphasis in these publications on the value of the free enterprise system and capitalism, the virtues of individual freedom and competition, and their adherence to a limited variant of the interventionist state, we can assume that they do not stand in opposition to the Western trade options as promoted by New Right leaders and organizations but that they agree with the underlying premises. As has been demonstrated, a major concern of both neoconservative intellectuals and New Right activists is the role of East-West trade as a functional part of their anti-communist foreign policy approach. If the United States has the global mission to redeem the world from communism, then there is no room left for considering East-West trade as an economic matter. But the ideological purity which would demand cutting off the Soviet bloc from all benefits it might derive from even minimal trade with the West is watered down by the economic interests of the U.S.A. to sell at least non-strategic goods and profit from the deficiencies of the Soviet economy. More than that, the position to use East-West trade as a weapon to spread the values of American democracy into the Soviet sphere, which is justified on ideological as well as practical grounds by virtually all neoconservatives, also runs counter to the pure ideological position of not dealing with the enemy (Soviet system) at all and trying to isolate it economically. As the Jackson-Vanick Amendment and its support among neoconservatives suggest, neoconservatives are willing to let the Soviet Union benefit from the standard of the Western economy if they in turn are ready to pay a price in terms of human rights and gradual inner liberalization. On just how far the Soviet Union might profit from this version of East-West trade, neoconservatives cannot agree. This essay has shown that their positions range from a mere exclusion of strictly "sensitive" goods and technology from East-West trade to implementing sanctions on a broader scale whenever deemed necessary (cf. *Mandate*'s embargo propositions). On the whole, the ideological foreign policy orientation, which does not concede a legitimacy to the interests of the political opponent, prevents neoconservatives from seeing East-West trade as being able both to serve U.S. and Soviet economic interests in the long run, while at the same time primarily promoting American economic superiority and transforming the Soviet system.

The degree to which neoconservatives agree on East-West trade as being a weapon in a global struggle with the Soviet Union, if not the whole communist world, is not matched by their agreement on how far the principle of free trade with Western countries should be upheld against rising domestic pressures to protect American industries and jobs against foreign competition. The review of the literature has revealed that several strains of justification are used to support the free trade principle. They range from moral reasons, which refer to the authority of the Bible, to economic reasons, which require that in the ultimate interests of the U.S. economy it must adjust to the standards of foreign producers and compete with them on the American market without politically based restrictions – free trade is seen to be in keeping with the basic American values of individual competition and free enterprise and, which reject government regulating trade through tariffs. However, while the Christian newsletter argues in favor of abolishing all trade restrictions, other neoconservatives generally add that the principle of free trade is threatened by the "unfair" trading practices of Western trading partners, notably Japan. This points to the basic understanding of neoconservatives that competitiveness cannot be unrestrained but has to follow some "rules of the game," that is, the standards of fairness. But while they do not spell out who is to determine the rules of the game, they seem to interpret the decline of some American industries themselves as a sign of a violation of fair trade by the trading partners. Therein lies a striking paradox: American competitiveness, once seen as evidence of American moral superiority in line with the Puritan tradition, now has ceased to speak for itself and must be protected with the help of moral arguments.

In conclusion, we find that neoconservative foreign trade positions, swinging between economic and foreign policy rules, clearly follow the latter as far as Soviet-bloc trade is concerned, which represents a logical consequence of their anti-communist conviction. With regard to trade relations with the capitalist world, neoconservatives are seemingly split over the question whether protectionist measures should be imposed in order to improve their own economic situation, although in theory they identify with free trade principles without deviation. Similarly, concrete policy proposals are offered for Soviet-bloc trade which give shape to political intentions – differing slightly from organization to organization. The pro-protectionist *Mandate* study does not spell out elaborate measures against Japan, while the anti-protectionists present competitiveness and consumer arguments without referring to different backgrounds (moralist-religious vs. economic).

Overall, the neoconservative foreign trade positions, though not constituting a coherent platform, are clearly constructed along the lines of the primordial emphasis on the East-West conflict, not only in strategic but also in moral terms, and by the effort to reconcile the free trade principle with the domestic market situation. On this level, the neoconservative position not only contributed to the public debate on American foreign economic policy in the 1970s, but was also adopted by the Republican party under the dominance of the radical Reagan wing in 1976 and 1980. This is demonstrated by the issue positions taken in the Republican party platforms through these years. However, with Reagan as President, neoconservatives have been increasingly disappointed – beginning with the lifting of the grain embargo in 1981 and continuing with his recent proposal to share SDI technology with the Soviet Union. Also, Reagan's position on free trade, constantly held up against rising pressures for protectionist measures in Congress and throughout the country, had to be watered down in the Republican platform of 1984 which responded to these pressures by promising protection of American jobs in endangered industries.

> We will not tolerate the loss of American jobs to nationalized, subsidized, protected foreign industries, particularly in steel, automobiles, mining, footwear, textiles, and other basic industries (Republican Party Platform 1984: 8).

With Reagan leaving office in early 1989, neoconservatives are going to have a hard time finding a candidate who suits them as well as Reagan-as-candidate did before 1980. With the Reagan experience in mind, however, they might come to the conclusion that they have to turn to "the people" again and try to make their way through Congress rather than hoping for the White House. But with a protectionist sentiment in the country and on Capitol Hill, and the prospects for a president less conservative than Reagan and a cooperative Soviet leader, neoconservatives may be obliged to either revise their positions fundamentally and cease as a group or stiffen into ever more radical opposition to these developments.

Acknowledgment: We would like to thank Dr. Jakob Schissler for his time and energy in providing us with helpful advice on this subject.

Notes

1 We do not have to emphasize the metamorphosis of party platforms once presidential candidates enter the White House. However, party platforms are more than mere "electioneering documents" (Key 1964: 421), as empirical analyses show; see Pomper and Lederman 1980.

2 See Rosenau's "Pre-Theories and Theories of Foreign Policy" (1971: 95 – 149, particularly pp. 107 – 109 and Table V on p. 149); also Kegley and Wittkopf (1982). For a similar approach which provides the model of a grid of international relations which contrasts sharply with the Morgenthau school, see Czempiel (1981).

3 This, of course, is the classic definition by Almond and Verba (1965: 13 f), which is only one way of defining the concept and has been criticized widely. It would lead too far to discuss the value of the concept in this paper; for major criticism, see Almond and Verba (1980); for an overview of all concepts of political culture as used early in the U.S.A. and until now in West Germany, see Iwand (1985).

4 In the Declaration of Independence, Thomas Jefferson named "life, liberty, and the pursuit of happiness" as the "inalienable rights"; see John Locke (1965: 309–344).

5 For an overview of the consensual aspects of the political system and culture see Bluhm (1974); Shell (1975), Merkl and Raabe (1977); and Schissler (1983).

6 See Gabriel (1965: 37 f.), who examines the parallels among these five doctrines and doctrines of Protestant Christianity. For the Protestant-religious background of the founding period, see Marty (1970: 14–23, 35–45). A recent and more general overview is provided by Reichley (1985).

7 The concept of ideology is widely and differently used in social science. We do not want to open a debate on the merits and flaws of the concept in this paper; however, we do want to acknowledge the source of the concept as we have introduced it above. We understand ideology in the above context in the sense Mannheim developed it in his *Ideology and Utopia* (1978: 49–94); see also Lieber (1985). Ideology as a "belief system" is a descriptive concept developed by Converse (1964) and may be used differently in the discussion below.

The interest/ideology dichotomy can also be expressed in different terms like empirical/dogmatic, or realist/moralist, etc.; see Schlesinger (1983: 4). See also the elaborate work of the interest/ideology dualism in the foreign policy beliefs of American businessmen, e. g., Russett and Hanson (1975: particularly chap. 4).

8 Almond holds that since "Americans typically overreact in their self-evaluations" (Almond 1965: 63), they are torn between the feelings of superiority and inferiority which affects their readiness to withdraw or intervene in external affairs.

9 With the New Deal, an intense ideological debate occurred in which the terms "liberal" and "conservative" found their definite reinterpretation in the American context. The liberalism of the New Deal, its main constituents being among as diverse population groups as Southern Whites, Catholics, Blacks, Jews, lower-income groups, and workers, did not only mean socioeconomic governmental intervention, but also national integration, in part through a strong central government and the participation in the Second World War. See Beer (1966) and Ladd and Hadley (1978; chap. 1).

10 According to Kissinger himself, détente was an effort to devise "new means to the old end of containment," quoted in Kegley and Wittkopf (1982: 65).

11 At the Republican Convention in 1976, 85% of the delegates were in favor of increased military defense spending, while 26% wanted to try to get along with the Soviet Union (see Farah 1983: 274 f).

12 At the 1976 Democratic Convention more than half of the delegates still favored détente with the Soviet Union and a third supported increased military spending (see Farah 1983: 274 f).

13 Our definition of conservatism is basically derived from Mannheim (1927); see also Greiffenhagen (1971) and Grebing (1971).

14 For the difference in "issue constraints" among leaders and the mass public in general, see the seminal work by Converse (1964). There are some indications, however, that since the 1950s the American public has become more ideological in terms of issue consistency; see Nie et al. (1976).

15 See Crawford (1979). For a comparison of neoconservatives and the New Right leaders in the eyes of a self-confessed "neo-Marxian populist conservative," see Phillips (1979: D4).

16 Moral majority has now been renamed Liberty Federation because of increasing public rejection of the old name.

17 New Right preachers like Tim LaHaye have introduced the term "secular humanism" as a man-centered, atheist-rationalistic movement which has endangered Christianity as the national creed; see Flake (1984: 38 f) and Falwell (1981: 199).

18 The New Right's attachment to capitalism has religious roots, since the Bible is believed to teach the free enterprise system; see Falwell 1981: 207; Webber 1981: 23 – 27.

19 Jeane Kirkpatrick in a personal interview in May 1986.

20 This is the title of Kristol's contribution to a *Commentary* symposium in 1975 (see Schissler 1983: 84).

21 See the reaction to the suppression of Solidarnosc in Butler et al. (1984: 296).

22 Another reason for the particular New Right support for Israel is related to the facts that fundamentalists are avid readers of the Old Testament and that the state of Israel plays a crucial role in the scenarios of the Second coming of Christ (see Flake 1984: 22).

23 Kirkpatrick (1979: 34). Norman Podhoretz puts it even more extremely: "To this day it is hard to find a single Communist regime that permits the people living under it as much as even the worst non-Communist dictatorship the world has known since the death of Hitler," (1980: 40). See also "Human Rights and American Foreign Policy – A Symposium" in *Commentary* (Nov. 1981: 38).

24 See Rode (1986: 162), who points out that among the staffers of Jackson during the quarrel with the Nixon and Ford administrations was Richard Perle (1986: 154).

25 Kissinger in the *New Republic* (June 2, 1985: 15): "Soviet behavior in recent years has given the lie to the argument that trade and credits by themselves will bring about benign evolution of the Soviet system" (quoted in Pipes 1984b: 269). Jeane Kirkpatrick (1979) comes to a similar conclusion in her analysis of Carter's foreign policy.

26 See Pipes (1984a: 29); additionally, the author argues that because of technology exports the U.S.A. has to spend larger sums in defense in order to match the improvements in the Soviet military.

27 As Jakob Schissler explained to the authors, the "Klopapier dilemma" consists in the physical relief achieved by Western toilet paper which in turn sets free physical and mental resources that can be used against the West.

28 In 1972, the Soviet Union having been a monopoly buyer brought the American grain market in quite a difficult situation by buying up nearly the entire American grain surplus which in turn increased grain prices immensely and contributed to the destabilization of the world grain market in 1972/1973; for the context see Rode (1986: 117 f).

29 See American Security Council Foundation (1984: 140); Pipes expresses a similar view (1984a: 270 f).

30 COCOM is a Paris-based agency consisting of the NATO members minus Iceland plus Japan.

31 See the development of "managed trade" in Destler (1986: 166 – 173) and the history of Japanese-U.S. trade relations in Hunsberger (1968: 267 – 282).

References

Almond, Gabriel A. (1965): *The American People and Foreign Policy*. New York: Praeger.

Almond, Gabriel A. and Sidney Verba (1965): *The Civic Culture*. Boston: Little, Brown.

Almond, Gabriel A. and Sidney Verba (eds.) (1980): *The Civic Culture Revisited*. Boston: Little, Brown.

American Security Council Foundation (1984): *A Strategy for Peace Through Strength*. Boston: The American Security Council Foundation.

Anthony, Dick and Thomas Robbins (1983): Spiritual Innovation and the Crisis of American Civil Religion. In Mary Douglas and Steven Tipton (eds.), *Religion and America. Spiritual Life in a Secular Age*. Boston: Beacon Press, 229 – 248.

Ashford, Nigel (1981): The Neo-Conservatives. *Governments and Opposition* 16: 353 – 369.

Barnes, Samuel et al. (1979): *Political Action*. Beverly Hills: Sage.

Beer, Samuel (1966): Liberalism and the National Idea. *The Public Interest 5: 70 – 82.*

Bell, Daniel (1972): On Meritocracy and Equality. *The Public Interest 29: 29 – 68.*

Bell, Daniel (1973): *The Coming of the Post-Industrial Society*. New York: Basic Books.

Bellah, Robert N. (1967): Civil Religion in America. *Daedalus* 96: 1 – 21.

Bluhm, William T. (1974): *Ideology and Attitudes: Modern Political Culture*. Englewood Cliffs: Prentice-Hall.

Butler, Stuart M. et al. (eds.) (1984): *Mandate for Leadership: Continuing the Conservative Revolution*. Washington D.C.: Heritage Foundation.

Calleo, David P. and Benjamin M. Rowland (1973): *America and the World Political Economy. Atlantic Dreams and National Realities*. Bloomington: Indiana University Press.

Congressional Quarterly Almanac (1981 – 1985) Washintgon, D.C.: C.Q. Press.

Converse, Phil E. (1964): The Nature of Beliefs Systems in Mass Publics. In David Apter (ed.), *Ideology and Discontent*. New York: Free Press of Glencoe, 206 – 261.

Crabb, Cecil V. jr. (1982): *The Doctrines of American Foreign Policy*. Baton Rouge: Louisiana State University Press.

Crawford, Alan (1979): *Thunder on the Right. The "New Right" and the Politics of Resentment*. New York: Pantheon Books.

Czempiel, Ernst-Otto (1981): *Internationale Politik. Ein Konfliktmodell*, Paderborn: Schöningh UTB.

Dahl, Robert A. (1964): *Congress and Foreign Policy*. New York: Norton.

Destler, I. M. (1986): *American Trade Politics: System Under Stress.* Washintgon D.C.: Institute for International Economics.
Devine, Donald J. (1972): *The Political Culture of the United States.* Boston: Little, Brown.
Dippel, Horst (1983): Heroismus zu später Stunde? Die außenpolitischen Vorstellungen der Neokonservativen. In Jakob Schissler (ed.), *Neokonservatismus in den USA.* Opladen: Westdeutscher Verlag, 11 – 150.
Dubiel, Helmut (1985): *Was ist Neokonservatismus?* Frankfurt: Suhrkamp.
Falwell, Jerry (ed.) (1981): *The Fundamentalist Phenomenon.* Garden City: Doubleday.
Farah, Barbara et al. (1983): Convention Delegates in the post Reform Era. In James Lengle and Byron Shafer (eds.), *Presidential Politics.* New York: St. Martin's Press, 264 – 274.
Flake, Carol (1984): *Redemptorama. Culture, Politics, and the New Evangelicalism.* Garden City: Anchor Press.
Ford, Gerald (1976): State of the Union Address. *Congressional Quarterly*, January 24, pp. 144 – 148.
Franck, Thomas M. and Edward Weisband (1979): *Foreign Policy by Congress.* New York: Oxford University Press.
Gabriel, Ralph H. (1965): *The Course of American Democratic Thought.* New York: Ronald Press.
Goldman, Eric (1977): *Rendez-vous with Destiny.* New York: Vintage Books.
Grebing, Helga (1971): *Konservative gegen die Demokratie.* Frankfurt: Europäische Verlagsanstalt.
Greiffenhagen, Martin (1971): *Das Dilemma des Konservatismus in Deutschland.* München: Piper.
Hartz, Louis (1955): *The Liberal Tradition in America.* New York: Harcourt, Brace.
Heatherly, Charles L. (ed.) (1981): *Mandate for Leadership: Policy Management in a Conservative Administration.* Washington D.C.: Heritage Foundation.
Hoffmann, Stanley (1984): *Dead Ends. American Foreign Policy in the New Cold War.* Cambridge, Mass.: Ballinger.
Holmes, Jack E. (1985): *The Mood/Interest Theory of American Foreign Policy.* Lexington, Ky.: University Press of Kentucky.
Holsti, Ole R. and James N. Rosenau (1984): *American Leadership in World Affairs: Vietnam and the Breakdown of Consensus.* London: Allen and Unwin.
Hughes, Barry B. (1978): *The Domestic Context of American Foreign Policy.* San Francisco: Freeman.
Human Rights and American Foreign Policy – A Symposium (1981): *Commentary* 72: 25 – 63.
Hunsberger, Warren (1968): United States Foreign Policy and Japan. In Benjamin Cohen (ed.), *American Foreign Economic Policy. Essays and Comments.* New York: Harper and Row, 267 – 282.
Huntington, Samuel P. (1957): Conservatism as an Ideology. *American Political Science Review* 51: 45 – 473.
Inglehart, Ronald (1977): *The Silent Revolution. Changing Values and Political Styles Among Western Publics.* Princeton, N.J.: Princeton University Press.
Iwand, Wolf Michael (1985): *Paradigma Politische Kultur.* Opladen: Leske and Budrich.

Jonas, Manfred (1966): *Isolationism in America, 1935–1941.* Ithaca, N.Y.: Cornell University Press.

Kegley, Charles W. jr. and Eugene R. Wittkopf (1982): *American Foreign Policy – Patterns and Process.* New York: St. Martin's Press.

Key, Valdimer O. (1964): *Politics, Parties, and Pressure Groups.* New York: Crowell.

Kirkpatrick, Jeane (1979): Dictatorships and Double Standards. *Commentary* 65: 34–45.

Klingberg, Frank L. (1979): Cyclical Trends in American Foreign Policy Moods and their Policy Implications. In Charles W. Kegley jr. and Patrick J. McGrowan (eds.) *Challenge to America: United States Foreign Policy in the 1980s.* Beverly Hills/London: Sage Publ., 37–55.

Kristol, Irving (1975): America Now: A Failure of Nerve? *Commentary* (July): 54.

Kristol, Irving (1983): *Reflections of a Neoconservative.* New York: Basic Books.

Ladd, Everett C. jr. and Charles D. Hadley (1978): *Transformations of the American Party System.* New York: Norton.

Lee, Robert W. (1986): How America Is Being Taken in Trade. *Conservative Digest* (June): 57–64.

Lieber, Hans-Joachim (1985): *Ideologie. Eine historisch-systematische Einführung.* Paderborn: Schöningh UTB.

Liebman, Robert C. and Robert Wuthnow (eds.) (1983): *The New Christian Right: Mobilization and Legitimation.* New York: Aldine.

Link, Werner (1980): *Der Ost-West Konflikt.* Stuttgart: Kohlhammer.

Lipset, Seymour M. (1967): *The First New Nation.* Garden City, N.Y.: Anchor.

Lipset, Seymour M. (1981): *Political Man. The Social Basis of Politics.* Sec. expanded edn. Baltimore, Md.: Johns Hopkins University Press.

Lipset, Seymour M. and Earl Raab (1978): *The Politics of Unreason. Right-Wing Extremism in America 1790–1977.* Chicago: University of Chicago Press.

Locke, John (1965): *Two Treatises of Government.* New York: Mentor.

Maggiotto, Michael A. and Eugene R. Wittkopf (1981): American Public Attitudes Toward Foreign Policy. *International Studies Quarterly* 25: 601–631.

Mandelbaum, Michael and William Schneider (1979): The New Internationalism. In Kenneth Oye et al. (eds.), *Eagle Entangled.* New York: Longman.

Mannheim, Karl (1927): Das konservative Denken. *Archiv für Sozialwissenschaften und Sozialpolitik* 57: 68–142, 470–495.

Mannheim, Karl (1978): *Ideologie und Utopie.* Frankfurt: Schulte-Bulmke.

Marty, Martin E. (1970): *Righteous Empire. The Protestant Experience in America.* New York: Dial Press.

Merkl, Peter H. and Dieter Raabe (1977): *Politische Soziologie der USA. Die konservative Demokratie.* Wiesbaden: Akademische Verlagsanstalt.

Miles, Michael W. (1980): *The Odyssey of the American Right.* New York: Oxford University Press.

Miller, Daphne (1987): *Competitiveness or Protectionism: Which Works Best?* Washington D.C.: Republican Study Committee.

Minkenberg, Michael and Ronald Inglehart (1988): Neoconservatism and Value Change in the USA. Tendencies in the Mass Public of a Post-Industial Society. In John R.

Gibbins (ed.), *Politics and Contemporary Culture: New and Old Politics*. Beverly Hills/London: Sage (in press).
Moynihan, Daniel P. (1975): *Coping. On the Practice of Government*. New York: Vintage Books.
Nie, Norman H., Sidney Verby, and John R. Petrocik (1976): *The Changing American Voter*. Cambridge, Mass: Harvard University Press.
North, Gary (1987): Tariffs: The Preferred Tax of Masochists. *Biblical Economics Today* 10(2): 1–4.
Novak, Michael (1983): *The Spirit of Democratic Capitalism*. New York: Touchstone.
Oldendick, Robert W. and Barbara A. Bardes (1982): Mass and Elite Foreign Policy Opinions. *Public Opinion Quarterly* 46: 368–382.
Peele, Gillian (1984): *Revival and Reaction: The Right in Contemporary America*. New York: Oxford University Press.
Phillips, Kevin (1979): The Neoconservatives: Chiefs without Indians. *Washington Post*, August 26: D4.
Phillips, Kevin (1983): *Post-Conservative America*. New York: Vintage Books.
Pipes, Richard (1984a): How To Cope With The Soviet Threat. A Long-Term Strategy For The West. *Commentary* 78(2): 13–30.
Pipes, Richard (1984b): *Survival Is not Enough. Soviet Realities and America's Future*. New York: Simon and Schuster.
Podhoretz, Norman (1980): The Present Danger. *Commentary* (March): 27–40.
Podhoretz, Norman (1981): The Future Danger. *Commentary* 71: 29–47.
Pomper, Gerald M. and Susan S. Lederman (1980): *Elections in America: Control and Influence in Democratic Politics*. New York: Dodd, Mead.
Reichley, James A. (1985): *Religion in American Public Life*. Washington D.C.: Brookings Institution.
Republican National Committee (1976, 1980, 1984). *Republican Party Platforms*. Washington D.C.
Rode, Reinhard (1986): *Sicherheit vs. Geschäft. Die Osthandelspolitik von Nixon bis Carter*. Frankfurt: Campus.
Rosenau, James N. (1971): *The Scientific Study of Foreign Policy*. New York: Free Press.
Russett, Bruce M. and Donald R. Deluca (1981): Don't Tread On Me: Public Opinion and Foreign Policy in the Eighties. *Political Science Quarterly* 96: 381–399.
Russett, Bruce M. and Elisabeth C. Hanson (1975): *Interest and Ideology. The Foreign Policy Beliefs of American Businessmen*. San Francisco: W. H. Freeman.
Saloma, John S. III (1984): *Ominous Politics. The New Conservative Labyrinth*. New York: Hill and Wang.
Schissler, Jakob (ed.) (1983): *Neokonservatismus in den USA*. Opladen: Westdeutscher Verlag.
Schissler, Jakob (1984): Human Rights, Détente and Neoconservatism in American Foreign Policy. In Rob Kroes (ed.), *Neoconservatism. Its Emergence in the USA and Europe*. Amsterdem: VU Uitgeveri: 81–99.
Schlesinger, Arthur jr. (1983): Foreign Policy and the American Character. *Foreign Affairs* 62: 1–16.

Schneider, William (1983): Conservatism, Not Interventionism: Trends in Foreign Policy Options, 1974–1982. In Kenneth Oye et al. (eds.), *Eagle Defiant*. Boston: Little, Brown, 33–64.

Shafer, Byron E. (1983): *Quiet Revolution. The Struggle for the Democratic Party and the Shaping of Post-Reform Politics*. New York: Russell Sage.

Shell, Kurt L. (1975): *Das politische System der USA*. Stuttgart: Kohlhammer.

Shell, Kurt L. (1986): *Der amerikanische Konservatismus*. Stuttgart: Kohlhammer.

Steinfels, Peter (1979): *The Neoconservatives*. New York: Simon and Schuster.

Touraine, Alain (1969): *La Société Post-Industrielle*. Paris: Denoël.

Tucker, Robert (1977): Oil and American Power. Three Years Later. *Commentary* 63: 32–45.

Viguerie, Richard A. (1981): *The New Right: We'Re Ready to Lead*. Falls Church, Va.: Viguerie.

Webber, Robert E. (1981): *The Moral Majority: Right or Wrong*. Westchester, Ill.: Cornerstone Books.

Weinberg, C. (1976): *Congressional Quarterly*, August 14, p. 2181.

Wittkopf, Eugene R. and Michael A. Maggiotto (1983): Elites and Masses: A Comparative Analysis of Attitudes Toward America's World Rule. *Journal of Politics* 45: 303–334.

Wolfe, Gregory (1987): *Right Minds. A Sourcebook of American Conservative Thought*. Chicago: Regnery Books.

Part III
U.S.-Canadian Relations

Canadian Defence Policy and Economic Relations with the United States, 1939–1988: An Overview

Donald Avery

In 1988 Canada faces a major test in its long and often difficult relationship with the United States. After two years of intense negotiations the Canadian government of Brian Mulroney and the Reagan administration have signed a sweeping trade agreement which promises to chart "a new course for the largest and most important trading relationship in the world." Under the terms of the December 10, 1987 pact, tariffs between the two countries would be eliminated, some immediately and others over ten years. The Free Trade Agreement (FTA) would also remove export duties on agricultural products, end Canadian restrictions on the import of U.S. auto parts, and do away with taxes and duties on energy exports. In addition, joint Canadian and American arbitration will be established with the purpose of settling trade disputes. In a number of public statements both national governments have declared their complete satisfaction with the deal, and predicted that their respective economies "will grow and prosper" (FTA 1987: 1).

The Canadian-U.S. Free Trade Agreement must, however, be ratified by an increasingly protectionist American Senate and a suspicious Canadian Parliament. In Ottawa the battle lines are now drawn, and there is serious talk of a federal election on the issue. The Conservatives have indicated that their future electoral position will focus on the principles stated in the preamble of the Agreement:

> Once in force.... It will add significantly to economic growth, incomes and employment in Canada. Canadian business will become more competitive in the Canadian market and world markets. Canada will become a stronger and more confident country in the world trading community. It will mean a richer Canada, a Canada which can afford to maintain and enhance the quality of life through, and for, Canadian cultural endeavors. A richer Canada will allow governments to stimulate economic development in Canada's poorer regions and maintain a safety net of social programs for all Canadians (FTA 1987:1).

Opponents of the Free Trade Agreement – most notably the federal Liberal and New Democratic parties, and the provincial governments of Ontario, Manitoba, and Prince Edward Island – have rejected this lofty vision. Instead, they have predicted that all sectors of the Canadian economy will be adversely affected by this particular trade arrangement. Concern has also been expressed about the future of Canada's social programs and cultural industries within an integrated continental economic system.[1]

At the same time that Canadians are engaged in an emotional national debate over the merits of free trade with the United States, the American Air Force is testing their Cruise missiles in the Canadian north. Under a 1981 secret agreement between the two countries – Canada's international peace role notwithstanding – this ominous nuclear weapon has now been tested ten times at the Canadian Forces Base, Cold Lake, Alberta (Regehr 1987: 121). Meanwhile guidance systems for these same cruise missiles are being assembled at the Litton Systems of Canada plant in Rexdale, Ontario under the auspices of the Defence Production Sharing Agreement and the Canada-U.S. Defence Development Sharing Program. Indeed, the Canadian weapons industry has rapidly expanded during the last decade. In 1985, for example, Canadian military goods sold to the United States exceeded $ 1.6 billion; in return, Canada purchased roughly the same amount from the United States in dollar terms, but with a higher technological component (Rosenblum 1985: 130–152). In reality North America has already become a unified military production entity.[2]

What are the connections between continental free trade and North American defence integration? Does the Canadian experience in dealing with the United States in the joint production and trade of military goods provide an encouraging model for those defending the 1988 Free Trade Agreement? And, finally, what are the most important historical factors in Canada's military and economic relationship with the United State since the Second World War?

1 Historical Background, 1945–1984

1.1 Military and Economic Cooperation, 1939–1950

One of the most important aspects of the Second World War for Canada was its involvement in defence research, development, and production with Britain and the United States. In the early stages of the war it was primarily the British connection that made Canada a partner in this form of alliance warfare (Kevles 1979: 300–328; Eggleston 1950: 5–67). One reason for this phenomena was the impact of the British decision to shift some of their research facilities to Canada in 1940 because of their desperate military situation and their need to obtain more effective access to American technological and economic resources. Both the chemical warfare operation at Ottawa and Suffield, Alberta and the establishment of the Montreal atomic research laboratory in 1943 are important examples of this trend. Canadian scientists, many of whom had been seconded to the National Research Council and to various defence agencies, were thus able to gain access to highly confidential scientific data through the medium of joint British and Canadian military research projects. Equally important was the extent to which the British connection made it possible for Canadian scientists to become involved in sophisticated American military projects, especially after the British scientific and technical mission under Sir Henry Tizard arrived in North America in August of 1940 (Eggleston 1978: 116 – 186; Clark 1965: 2 – 200).

Yet being consulted did not mean being equal, and Canadian scientists and military officials quickly discovered that theirs was a subordinate status. The junior partner role was institutionalized with the formation of the British-American Combined Chiefs of Staff in January of 1942, which functioned as the supreme high command of the Anglo-American global military effort. There was, however, no formal Canadian representative. What was particularly troubling from a Canadian point of view was exclusion from the important Combined Munitions Assignment Board which had the task "of coordinating the assignment of weapons and equipment to various theatres in accordance with the needs of strategy" (Dziuban 1959: 15 – 58; Stacey 1970: 485 – 528). Fortunately, some of the organizations established under the Ogdensburg Agreement of 1940 and the Hyde Park Declaration of 1941 facilitated direct military, economic, and scientific interaction with the United States. Of particular importance was the Permanent Joint Board of Defence and economic bodies such as the Material Co-Ordination Committee and the Joint War Production Committee which provided "for the coordination and rational integration of the war industries of Canada and the United States" (Dziuban 1959: 58 – 109).

Canadian involvement in the development of all the major weapon systems – including the Manhattan Project – was through the medium of joint planning agencies. The most important of these was the Combined Policy Committee which was created after the 1943 Quebec Conference in order to coordinate "In the field of scientific research and development... full and effective interchange of information..." (Eggleston 1978: 200 – 345; Sherwin 1977: 44 – 47). For Canada's military and scientific establishment the war years were an exciting and challenging experience, a chance to play in the military technology "big leagues." Yet information of this type of research also meant that Canada, for the first time, had to function within rules and procedures which sought to protect scientific secrets from enemy agents, and even from its wartime ally, the U.S.S.R. (Villa 1981; Jockel 1983: 352 – 358).

By the end of the war it was the United States, because of the scale of its military research, who determined what secrets would be shared. Britain, and even more so Canada, became supplicants, dependent on the good will of the Truman administration, Congress, and the American Joint Chiefs of Staff for access to top secret information. The situation further deteriorated in 1946 with the Gouzenko espionage disclosures, which revealed that British scientists and Canadian citizens had been implicated in the spy scandal, and these revelations "fatally weakened Attlee and King's argument for future cooperation with the United States on atomic energy, and ultimately guaranteed an even stricter policy of exclusion" (Herken 1982: 116). This situation prevailed until the mid-1950s when the United States arrived at a new *modus vivendi* with its two closest military allies (Gowing 1974: 55 – 120).

The Second World War also provided great opportunities for the Canadian economy. In these years Canada adopted what one author has called socialism, capitalist style. Federal economic planning was parallelled by massive levels of government expenditures. By 1944 federal spending had reached $ 4.5 billion, or 44% of the gross national expenditure. Under the tax rental agreement of 1941, Ottawa collected 90% of all taxes, a trend which was perpetuated until the mid-1950s. The Bank of Canada (established in 1934), and the Department of Finance also assumed a crucial role in financing the war effort, and in managing the nation's money markets. But above all, it was the role which the federal government assumed in the production of war material; by 1945 Canada was the fourth largest of the Allied Powers. Munitions, tanks, warships, and planes rolled off the production lines as Canadian industry, labor, and government joined together in a common commitment to win the war. Of particular importance were the links between the federal government and the corporate sector. The Minister of Munitions and Supply, C. D. Howe was largely responsible for the war economy, and he was remarkably successful in luring to Ottawa an outstanding collection of "dollar a year" executives. These men directed the many economic planning boards, as well as the 28 crown corporations which were created to meet specific wartime needs. There was also a dramatic increase in the size, function, and expertise of the federal civil service. Having successfully directed Canada's war effort and postwar reconstruction, these high-ranking government experts now turned their attention to other aspects of Canada's economic future, and to the role the country should play in the international arena. Above, all they welcomed closer ties with the United States (Owram 1986: 287 – 334).

This pro-American outlook was very pronounced during the free trade negotiations of 1947 – 1948. At this time Canada was facing rather serious economic problems, most notably an enormous trade deficit with the United States and a drastic shortage of American dollars. As a result, some leading civil servants and politicians in the departments of Finance, Trade and Commerce and External Affairs began free trade talks with the American State Department, and a tentative agreement was drafted which called for the immediate removal of all duties by both countries and the elimination of all trade preferences granted to Great Britain. In return, the scheme gave virtually free access to the American market for most Canadian goods, and it allowed Canadian manufacturers five years to prepare for free trade. Yet despite the apparent economic advantages, the Canadian government decided not to proceed any further with the negotiations. Adverse public opinion had reinforced the suspicions of William Lyon Mackenzie King, Canada's aging Prime Minister, that this was not just a free trade agreement, but rather a very menacing customs union which would threaten Canadian independence (Cuff and Granatstein 1978: 64 – 82).

Ironically, at the same time that the King government was rejecting closer trade relations with the United States, the military interaction between the two countries was rapidly expanding. In planning for the joint defence of North America, the Permanent Joint Board of Defence (1940) continued to assume an important role, but now its activities were complemented by other binational agencies such as the Military Cooperation Committee (1946), the Joint United States-Canada Industrial Mobilization Committee (1949), and the Joint United States-Canadian Civil Defence Committee (1951; Willoughby 1979: 109 – 135).

1.2 Canada-U.S. Military and Economic Relations, 1950 – 1984: Cooperation and Conflict

The Korean War greatly enhanced the opportunities for Canadian companies to gain access to the rapidly expanding market for military goods and services. In Canada defence spending soared to a record $ 3 billion or about 35% of total government expenditures; the rearmament program was coordinated by the newly established Department of Defence Production. Another important development was the level of American military procurement in Canada, which reached $ 127 million in 1953, and there was the prospect of even higher spending in the future. "Astronomical defence budgets, the arms race, arms sales, and a permanent military-industrial complex all became characteristic of the post-Korean institutional setting.... [T]hey underscored the utility for Canada of securing a continuing and cooperative economic relationship with the United States" (Cuff and Granatstein 1978: 230).

Many of the companies involved in the arms business in Canada were either subsidiaries of large Canadian companies or branch plants of large corporations based in the United States. The war years had witnessed the creation and expansion of integrated corporations and conglomerates in both countries. But in many ways Canada was the more secure place for the business giants to operate, largely because Canadian anti-combine laws did not even begin to seriously threaten corporate concentration or its hold over the national economy. In 1973, for example, the 25 largest non-financial corporations accounted for 24% of corporate assets. Within the manufacturing sector the 100 largest companies accounted for 48% of sales, and even within this category the tendency was towards oligopoly with the "big three" automakers, the "big three" steelmakers, and the "big five" integrated petroleum companies dominating their respective sectors. Even more controversial were the activities of the major conglomerates with Canadian Pacific Enterprises, Argus Corporation, and Power Corporation being the primary focus of social critics (Green 1980: 3 – 45; Bliss 1987: 578 – 582). Many of the major Canadian companies also functioned as multinationals with a significant portion of their sales and assets outside the country. In 1976 the business publication *Fortune* listed 39 Canadian-based companies among the 500 largest non-U.S. industrial corporations operating in the global economy, with Massey Ferguson, Alcan (Aluminum Company of Canada), Seagrams, and INCO (International Nickel Company) having overseas assets of more than $ 1 billion each. However, only 22 of these 39 companies were Canadian-owned (Niosi 1981: 34 – 78).

The issue of foreign ownership of Canadian companies was a source of considerable controversy throughout the 1960s and 1970s. Actually, the opening salvo came from a most unlikely quarter – a federal royal commission. In 1957 the Royal Commission on Canada's Economic Prospects (the Gordon Commission) expressed concern about the scale of American direct investment, and recommended that the federal government guarantee Canadians access to jobs, reserach opportunities, and shareholdings in foreign-owned businesses. The fact that about 80% of these companies were based in the United States meant that debate on the issue was inexorably linked with the growing unpopularity of many of the domestic and foreign policies of the United States. This was particularly pronounced after the Suez Crisis of 1956, when the Eisenhower administration appeared to go out of its way to humiliate Great Britain. Subsequent examples of extra-territoriality, sometimes linked with the American anti-communist crusade, also created a great deal of bitterness in the country. Ironically – at least when considering the 1988 situation – anti-Americanism became associated with the meteoric career of John D. Diefenbaker and his federal Conservative Party (Granatstein 1986: 26 – 31; Bothwell et al. 1981: 140 – 151).

During the Diefenbaker administration, 1957 – 1963, defence issues became of paramount importance in Canadian-American relations. What caused the greatest controversy were the implications of the 1957 North American Air Defence Agreement (NORAD). In large part, NORAD was an extension of the wartime and the immediate postwar cooperation between the armed forces of the two countries, most notably between the Royal Canadian Air Force (RCAF) and the United States Air Force. Indeed, throughout the late 1940s there had been proposals for a massive air defence scheme even before there was any credible threat from the Soviet Union. Joint planning for North American defence was greatly expanded during the Korean War, with the threat of long-range Soviet bombers armed with nuclear weapons: "The Americans looked to Canadians as friends but saw them as essentially unprepared.... If the Canadians would not defend their own air space and the route to the United States, then Americans would" (Granatstein 1986: 101 – 138). Not surprisingly, therefore, it was the Pentagon which pushed for an air defence system which would combine operational integration and centralization of authority. Although Canadian autonomy was theoretically guaranteed, through an elaborate consultative procedure, the real decision making remained with the United States Air Force.

It was soon evident that the Diefenbaker government had not fully appreciated the extent to which involvement in NORAD would alter Canadian defence policy. Instead of a comprehensive analysis of the Agreement, the Prime Minister and Cabinet had relied almost exclusively on the advice of the Canadian Chiefs of Staff, a decision they would soon regret. The Cuban Missile Crisis of October, 1962 was NORAD's first serious test. From Ottawa's perspective the results were disappointing. Not only was the consultation inadequate, but even more serious was the fact that the Kennedy administration had expected immediate compliance with their military strategy. The hesitation in the Canadian response created a serious rift between the two governments, and undermined the authority of Prime Minister Diefenbaker. As one government official put it, "the main lesson to be drawn from all this [the crisis]... is that when the U.S. President chooses to psychologically mobilize the American people on the occasion of a serious threat to them, the Canadian people will be drawn up in the process also" (Granatstein 1986: 136 – 138).

Many Canadians also sided with Washington during the nuclear weapons controversy of 1963. Again, it was Canada's participation in NORAD which was at the heart of the matter. From the American viewpoint Canada had agreed to accept and operate nuclear-armed Bomarc missiles as part of its contribution to North American defence. In addition, the Pentagon insisted that Canadian Armed Forces in Europe be equipped with nuclear weapons in order to carry out their NATO commitments. Yet at this juncture the Diefenbaker government was seriously reassessing whether the country should become a member of the nuclear weapons "club," and the Cabinet was seriously divided on the issue with the Minister of External Affairs, Howard Green, opposed to further nuclear proliferation, while the Minister of Defence, Douglas Harkness, demanded that Canadian soldiers should have the best possible weapons. Ultimately, the Prime Minister sided with the doves, despite immense pressure from Washington and from influential groups within his own party.

The rapid conversion of Liberal leader Lester B. Pearson to the nuclear weapons camp meant that the subsequent 1963 election would highlight the issue. It also meant that American interference in Canadian domestic politics became a major campaign theme of a beleaguered John Diefenbaker. The narrow Liberal victory was hailed by the Kennedy administration as a return to normal Canadian-American relations, and the American ambassador in Ottawa confidently informed his superiors that the ineffectiveness of Diefenbaker's anti-American appeal would have "salutary lessons which will not be overlooked by future aspirants to political office in Canada" (Granatstein 1986: 136 – 138).

Another important development of these years was the extent to which Canada became an integral part of the American military-industrial complex. In the United States the value of military contracts soared during the postwar years. By 1960, out of a total of $ 77.23 billion for government expenditures, the Department of National Defence accounted for $ 43.7 billion. Over $ 14 billion of this amount went for procurement of military hardware, most of which was secured from a relatively small number of large corporations – DuPont, General Dynamics, McDonnell Douglas, Boeing, and General Motors being the most important. The involvement of retired generals and admirals in the defence industries reinforced the lines of communication between the Pentagon and corporate boardrooms (Polenberg 1972: 154 – 183; Francis 1970: 1 – 58).

In Canada the scale and influence of defence contractors was relatively insignificant, at least compared with the American situation. Nevertheless, a Canadian arms industry did develop, particularly after the Korean War, which greatly escalated government expenditures on defence. One of the most ambitious undertakings of this decade was the Arvo CF-105 (Arrow), a highly sophisticated supersonic, all-weather jet interceptor. Both the company, A. V. Roe of Canada, and the federal government assumed that the Arrow's technological prowess would be enough to penetrate the American military market. This naive assumption was soon dashed. American defence contractors were not about to lose lucrative contracts to foreign companies, and the Pentagon was not prepared to take chances with military security. Nor could the RCAF afford to pay almost $ 12 million a plane, which a limited production would entail. Nevertheless, the February, 1959 decision by the Diefenbaker government to terminate the Arrow project brought a howl of protest, not only from the company and its 14,000 workers, but also from Canadian nationalists. And an Arrow mythology emerged which was to affect future high-technology ventures: "The world's greatest fighter plane cruelly and mistakenly brought down by Canadians' lack of enterprise and vision." It was also the last major attempt by Canadian companies to export an integrated defence system to the United States (Bliss 1987: 474 – 477).

With the Canadian government's acceptance of American Voodoo Jets and the NORAD Agreement, Washington became more amenable to share defence contracts. In 1959 the two countries signed the Defence Production Sharing Agreement (DPSA), a kind of Auto Pact of the arms industry, which allowed Canadian companies to bid for American military contracts. Both Washington and Ottawa justified this Agreement on military and economic grounds and predicted that it would provide "the armed forces of our countries with the best equipment at the lowest cost, at the right time." In 1963 there was an important amendment to the DPSA, which stipulated that there should be a "rough balance provision" whereby Canada was committed to buy as many military commodities in the United States as Canadian companies sold in the United States. During the Vietnam War the American government did not apply the balance provision, and between 1964 and 1966 military sales to the United States doubled, reaching $ 317.1 million (Regehr 1987: 8, 60 – 68).

In the early 1970s, however, the Nixon administration, as part of their get-tough policy with their trading partners, decided to demand that the 1963 amendment of the DPSA be applied. "The result was that Canada would have to do things: first, it would have to increase Canadian military spending and second, much of the increased spending would have to take place in the United States if Canadian industry was to recapture access to the American market." Throughout the 1970s and early 1980s a wide range of negotiations were conducted between Ottawa and Washington for the purchase of enormously expensive equipment for the Canadian Armed Forces. In order to cushion the cost somewhat, Canadian negotiators sought guarantees that some of the production would occur in Canada, and that prime contractors such as the Lockheed Corporation would undertake "offset" purchasing in this country. In most cases, however, what this meant was that Canadian-based companies were producing parts for weapons systems designed and developed in the United States, with a substantial amount of the technology and even the components being imported. Also, most of the firms involved in this activity were subsidiaries of the large American aerospace and electronics companies which had traditionally received the bulk of the Pentagon contracts (Regehr 1987: 60 – 75, 204 – 207); see Table 1).

The most famous example of this economic link is Litton Systems (Canada) Ltd. of Rexdale, Ontario – a subsidiary of General Dynamics – which describes itself as the "world's leading producer of inertial navigational systems for military aircraft." During the 1980s it gained notoriety because of its extensive contracts to build elements of the Cruise missile's navigational system. Because of the controversy over the testing of the Cruise missile in

Table 1. Canadian military exports by industry sector: total 1959 – 1985 ($ million)

	U.S.	Other	Total	% of Total
Aerospace	4,203.5	2,221.0	6,424.5	42
Armaments	799.9	239.9	1,039.8	7
Electrical/electronics	3,668.8	1,310.3	4,979.1	33
General purchasing	268.6	45.4	314.0	2
Shipbuilding	971.6	112.6	1,084.6	7
Vehicles	1,349.7	104.7	1,454.4	9
Total	11,262.1	4,033.9	15,296.0	100

Source: Tabulated from the annual reports of the Department of External Affairs

Canada, the economic activities of Litton Industries came under intense scrutiny. Peace groups condemned the company for its part in producing this menacing new weapon, and thereby escalating the arms race. Canadian nationalists denounced the extent to which American branch plants were being supported by Canadian tax dollars. Both groups agreed that the level of DIPP grants, which by 1983 had soared to $ 169.2 million, was excessive and unwarranted. Particular emphasis was placed on the fact that DIPP grants represented almost 20 cents on every dollar of Canadian military export to the United States, and that under the DPSA the Department of National Defence must import one dollar of completed American weapons for every dollar of parts exported to the United States. According to one estimate, Canada spent $ 1.6 billion more than it earned through the DPSA program between 1971 and 1984 (Rosenblum 1985: 147 – 151).

During the 1960s and 1970s Canada's military relationship with the United States, and American economic control of Canadian industry became closely related subjects in the debate over Canadian sovereignty. And in these years Canadians were very much divided on these issues. For some protectionism was an outdated principle, and they readily supported the arguments of market-place economists such as Harry Johnson:

> ...it is hard to see how a nation can be made more independent by lowering its citizens' standard of living and forcing them to earn a living in occupations at which they are inefficient. If the public is to be taxed for the privilege of having a national identity – which is what the protectionists ar really arguing for – there are far more worthy monuments of national independence than a second-rate manufacturing sector... (1963: 127).

In contrast, there were an increasing number of Canadian academics and politicians who called upon the federal government to implement a wide range of economic nationalist policies. The justification for this intervention was particularly pronounced in the 1967 report of the federal Task Force, *Foreign Ownership and the Structure of Canadian Industry*. Prominent among its many criticisms of American branch plants were the allegations that they seriously limited Canadian sovereignty:

> ...a basic political problem... namely [the] decision-making power of the Canadian government has been reduced in regard to economic relations involving American subsidiaries. The essence of the extra-territoriality issue is not the economic costs... but rather the potential loss of control over an important segment of Canadian economic life.
>
> ...a new National Policy is required. The nation has been built, but its sovereignty must be protected and its independence mainteined (*Foreign Ownership* 1968: 72, 339).

Significantly, both sides interpreted the 1965 Auto Pact, which provided for free trade in vehicles and parts, as vindication of their position. And, indeed the statistics were impressive. By 1967 trade in auto parts had become the largest single item in Canadian-American trade. Exports to the United States increased from $ 75 million to $ 900 million, while imports from the U.S. rose from $ 600 million to $ 1.3 billion. Investment in the Canadian industry as a result of the Auto Pact was estimated at about $ 500 million, Canadian vehicle production was up by 35% and employment in the industry increased by 27%. For the continentalists, this sectoral free trade agreement showed the immense possibilities of a comprehensive free trade agreement. For the economic nationalists, it was the triumph of Canadian priorities (Bliss 1987: 493; Cameron 1986: 155 – 166).

During the 1970s the Liberal government of Pierre Elliott Trudeau experimented with a variety of policies which sought to increase Canadian participation in crucial sectors of the domestic economy. In 1973, for example, the Canadian Development Corporation (CDC) was created with a mandate "to help develop and maintain strong Canadian controlled and managed corporations in the private sector of the economy and give Canadians greater opportunities to invest and participate in the development of Canada. The establishment of the Foreign Investment Review Agency (FIRA) in 1974 as a watchdog over foreign takeovers was even more unpopular with American multinationals and the American government. Nor did the emergence of the national oil company, Petro-Canada, and its subsequent purchase of four foreign-based companies, win many friends on Wall Street or on Capitol Hill. Attempts to further Canadianize the oil industry through the 1980 National Energy Program also encountered strong opposition from both American interests and the western Canadian provinces. Not surprisingly, advocates of closer integration of the Canadian and American economies warmly applauded the election promises of the federal Conservative party to harmonize relations between the two countries. They were even more enthusiastic when Prime Minister Brian Mulroney and President Reagan agreed at their March, 1985 Shamrock Summit in Quebec City to begin tentative free trade talks (Bothwell 1981: 416–460).

2 Free Trade and Defence Integration in the 1980s

The particular circumstances associated with the free trade talks in the 1980s must be related to a number of pressing economic problems in Canada in this decade. Foremost was the apparent inability of the Canadian economy to replace the 400,000 jobs lost during the 1981–1982 "great recession," and to deal with the enormous problem of having over 2.5 million unemployed out of total work force of 13 million. The Conservative campaign slogan of "jobs, jobs, jobs" during the 1984 federal election was at least partly instrumental in one of the greatest political victories in Canadian history. Another was Mulroney's promise to restore harmonious relations with the Reagan administration, especially with reference to economic issues (Cameron 1986: xii–xv).

Ironically, it was the Trudeau Liberals who first approached Washington about free trade. However, their preferred strategy was sectoral free trade. In other words, they had hoped to duplicate the success of the Auto Pact in other areas of the economy, most notably steel products, mass transit vehicles, agricultural equipment, and computer services. Although this was a rather limited agenda – when compared with the Conservative initiatives – the fact that a Liberal government which had initiated a wide range of economic nationalist policies during the previous decade was now at the point of strengthening Canada-U.S. economic ties clearly indicated that a new era had arrived (Cameron 1986: xii–xv).

One key player in the free trade dialogue was the Business Council on National Issues (BCNI). Largely composed of the chief executive officers of Canada's largest corporations, the BCNI consistently lobbied throughout 1984 and 1985 that the only way out of Canada's economic mess was through a "trade enhancement agreement" with the United States. This viewpoint was stated rather forcefully while presenting their brief to the Joint Senate and Commons Committee on Canada's International Relations in 1986 (*Minutes ...Special Committee* 1987). It was significant that the Royal Commission on the Economic Union and Development Prospects for Canada (Macdonald Commission) had already been impressed with the BCNI-backed trade initiative. Indeed, a year before the Royal Commission had submitted its final draft, Chairman Donald Macdonald had emphatically gone on record in favor of free trade with the United States. Much was made of the fact that exports to the United States had increased from 66% of the total in the early 1970s to approximately 80% by the 1980s. The prestige of the Macdonald Commission was therefore added to the mounting pressure from Canada's "big business" sector (Cameron 1986: xiv – xxiii).

It was now time to approach the Americans. At the Shamrock Summit of March, 1985 President Reagan agreed to the Canadian request that discussions about a bilateral trade agreement be initiated. Shortly afterwards Reagan requested the United States Congress to place the free trade talks with Canada on the so-called "fast-track" agenda. Within Canada there was initial support for the principle of free trade. This was most pronounced in the Canadian west, where resource exports to the United States were judged critical to provincial prosperity. Peter Lougheed of Alberta spoke for most "westerners" when he urged his fellow premiers not to let parochial concerns prevent the country from taking advantage of this rare economic opportunity. Quite clearly Lougheed's message was primarily aimed at the two central Canadian provinces – traditional opponents of free trade. However, Quebec soon showed its willingness to consider closer economic ties with the United States, particularly after the 1985 election of Robert Bourassa and his Liberal party.

No such conversion was to occur in Ontario, the country's most industrialized and most prosperous province. Premier David Peterson's massive electoral victory (Liberal) in the fall of 1987 was, in part, a result of his public opposition to the proposed free trade agreement. Moreover, by the end of 1987 many groups had joined the Ontario premier in criticizing the Mulroney-Reagan Agreement; these included nationalist organizations, organized labor, the New Democratic Party, and in a cautious fashion, the federal Liberal party (Henderson 1987: 42 – 48).

Almost all of these critics emphasized the dire economic consequences of free trade, particularly to the industrial heartland of Quebec and Ontario. One 1985 study on the Quebec situation estimated that up to 230,000 jobs were at risk in the province. The Report also claimed that of 18 industrial sectors in the province free trade would have a positive effect on only four, and a negative impact on the remaining 14 (Cameron 1986: 121 – 123). Similar predictions emerged from a 1986 study commissioned by the Peterson government: 281,000 jobs in the province would be threatened. It was imperative, the Ontario Report argued, that the Mulroney government take a stong stance in defending unique Canadian economic and political structures in the forthcoming meetings with the Americans:

> It is vital that the U.S. negotiators recognize the significant structural difference between the U.S. and Canadian economies. These structural differences may well require the use of different policy instruments to pursue even mutually held goals. The 'level playing field' has to take into account the

> unique characteristics of industrial structure, geography, climate, population and culture of our two countries (Cameron 1986: 121 – 135).

An important issue associated with the free trade discussions was the matter of government procurement practices. In the 1985 briefing paper prepared by the United States Trade Representatives which carefully examined the range of Canadian trade policies which would be affected by free trade, particular reference was devoted to the existing pattern of procurement adopted by Ottawa and the provinces:

> Canada's federal and province-owned telecommunications agencies, utilities, and transportation agencies generally follow strong 'buy national' policies. Products affected include telecommunications, heavy electrical and transportation related products.... Canada's Department of Supply and Services maintains an informal 10 percent preference level for 'Canadian content' that benefits domestic bidders. Other agencies such as the Department of Public Works and Defence Construction Ltd. and Crown Corporations also adhere to a 'buy national' system of purchasing practices.... Canada has indicated it will give liberalizing procurement practices in both nations a high priority in bilateral trade negotiations (Cameron 1986: 54).

The links between free trade and the development of a continental system of government procurement would have special significance in the area of defence contracts. American companies such as General Dynamics, Boeing, McDonnell-Douglas, and General Motors have already enjoyed great success in selling military hardware to the Canadian Armed Forces. With the new defence policy of 1987, *Challenge and Commitment*, the possibilities of lucrative contracts were enhanced. The Department of National Defence has indicated that during the next 15 years it is prepared to spend over $ 183 billion. This includes an estimated $ 8 billion for a fleet of 10 to 12 nuclear-powered attack submarines.

> Over the past two decades with the development of nuclear power the Arctic has become an operating area for submarines.... In a period of tension or war, Soviet submarines could operate off the deep channels of the Canadian Archipelago to intercept Allied submarines entering the Arctic. Moreover, the Soviets might use these channels in war to reach the patrol areas in the North Atlantic....
>
> Submarines are essential to meet current and evolving long-range ocean surveillance and control requirements in the Atlantic and Pacific as well as in the Arctic. Nuclear-powered submarines (SSN's) are uniquely capable anti-submarine platforms.... Given the vast distances in the three ocean areas in which Canada requires maritime forces and the SSN's unlimited endurance and flexibility, the Government has decided to acquire a fleet of nuclear powered submarines to enhance the overall effectiveness of the Canadian navy (*Challenge and Commitment* 1987: 45 – 49).

Public reaction in Canada towards this dramatic elevation of the military potential of the Canadian navy, and the enormous costs associated with this undertaking, has varied. According to some observers the modernization of Canada's armed forces was long over due, and the Conservative party's initiatives were both rational and timely. One such endorsement came from Professor R. B. Byers, a respected Canadian defence analyst. While admitting that the SSN program could be criticized on economic grounds, for technological reasons, and that it "would be undermining support for the Non-Proliferation Treaty, Byers generally supported the government's contention that nuclear submarines were essential in order for Canada to meet its national and international responsibilities.

> Canada is a maritime nation with important security and sovereignty interests in three oceans, the Atlantic, the Pacific, and the Arctic.... This is a recognition that Canada's future maritime forces must have the military capabilities to cope with a high threat environment at sea. Acquisition of such capabilities would also ensure that Canadian sovereignty can be protected (Byers 1987: 13).

Not did Byers share the concerns of those critics who argued that the "SSN's would mean acceptance of, and involvement with U.S. maritime strategy" (Byers 1987: 11 – 20). There were, however, many who insisted that the implications of acquiring nuclear submarines would mean further American control over Canadian military planning. These critics became even more vociferous when the Canadian government began to explore the possibilities of purchasing the Trafalgar class nuclear submarine from Great Britain. The problem was that the Trafalgar submarines contained some technology of American origin, and that under the 1958 U.S.-U.K. Agreement on the exchange of military technology, the American government would have to agree to the purchase (*Toronto Star*: September 20, 1987: 1; *London Free Press*: November 25, 1987: 1).

In the House of Commons, both the New Democratic party and the Liberals denounced the 1987 White Paper on Defence in general, and the SSN program in particular.[3] Yet neither of the opposition parties disagreed with the current level of defence spending – about $ 10 billion – or $ 400 on a per capita basis. At this level Canada is slightly ahead of most of its NATO allies – Belgium, Denmark, Greece, Italy, Luxembourg, Portugal, the Netherlands, Spain, Turkey, and Iceland (*London Free Press*: September 11, 1987: 1).

Canadian defence contractors were, however, interested in more than the nuclear submarines. At a meeting with Defence Minister Perrin Beatty in November, 1987 Kenneth Lewis, president of the Aerospace Industries Association of Canada, called upon the federal government to demonstrate "the political will to sustain the strengthening actions described in the white paper"

Table 2. Canadian military exports, 1959 – 1985 ($ million)

Year	United States	Europe	Other	Total
1959 – 1969	2,418.8	439.8	207.0	3,065.6
1970	226.5	41.2	68.5	336.2
1975	188.5	58.6	33.7	280.5
1980	481.7	142.1	97.9	721.7
1981	826.6	149.4	174.8	1,150.8
1982	1,027.9	157.8	248.4	1,434.1
1983	1,207.4	128.6	145.2	1,481.2
1984	1,360.5	243.1	149.8	1,753.4
1985	1,644.2	154.0	104.5	1,902.7
Total for period 1959 – 1985	11,262.1	2,238.2	1,795.7	15,296.0

Source: Regehr 1987: 17

(Toronto *Globe and Mail,* November 19, 1987: 3). It was no coincidence that Lewis had already been one of the major spokesmen in favor of Canadian involvement in the American Strategic Defence Initiative during the 1985 – 1986 national debate on this issue, and a major "booster" for increased sales of military goods and services to the United States during the Reagan administration (see Table 2).

In June, 1985 a Special Joint Committee of the Senate and House of Commons was appointed to consider Canada's international relations, with particular reference to "Canada's participation in research on the Strategic Defence Initiative and on Bilateral Trade with the United States." Between October, 1985 and May, 1986 public hearings were conducted both in Ottawa and across the country with groups and individuals concerned with SDI, and free trade. Yet despite the provocative links between these two important options for Canada, most of the briefs related to either one or the other. For example, the influential Business Committee on National Issues (BCNI) initially chose only to concentrate on the free trade issue, while arguing in general terms that Canada should explore all types of bilateral arrangements with the United States. Thomas D'Acquino, chief executive officer of the BCNI, placed special emphasis on the new type of Canadian businessmen:

> Historically, those who have followed the Canada-US trade debate have recognized that a large part of the opposition to liberalized trade has come from central Canadian manufacturers. During the course of the last 18 months or two years, a considerable number of major manufacturers from central Canada have changed their minds.... [P]art of the reason is that they are so

> much more confident; they are bigger now; they feel that they can compete more effictively. That aspect of confidence, rather than fear, is one that I think we all have to be aware of (*Proceedings... Joint Committee* 1985 – 1986 Session 17: 44 – 45).

Spokesmen for the aerospace industry were much more direct: "Canada's acceptance of the U.S. invitation to participate in the research phase of the Strategic Defence Initiative is so logically correct that opposition to it, we believe, can stand only on emotional grounds." Speaking for an industry which included 156 companies with 45,000 employees, and sales of $ 3.2 billion, Kenneth Lewis radiated confidence. In part, it was because the Canadian aerospace market was primarily civil with only 25% going to the military. Of this, 10% went to the Canadian Forces, 5% to the other NATO allies, and 10% to the United States under the Defence Development and Production Sharing Agreement. Yet according to Lewis the importance of this military connection was essential: "there is no doubt that high-technology defence requirements are a major driving force behind a nation's total aerospace industry." He estimated that Canadian participation in SDI could create 50,000 additional aerospace jobs by 1992, and about 100,000 by the year 2000. Equally important was the opportunity to share in American technology:

> SDI research will create a tremendous technological surge and accelerate progress in the areas of remote sensing, computers, communications, artificial intelligence, optics, materials, robotics and many others. Some argue that there are other ways to acquire such technology, but none can be viewed as more dramatic in scope or have the same impetus as SDI (*Proceedings...* Session 6: 44 – 48).

Lewis also emphasized that unlike other industries "90% of research and technology are common to civil and military aerospace." Thus, there would be ample opportunities for Canadian companies to transfer "spin-off applications" of the research to the Canadian civil market. This opportunity, however, would depend on an official commitment on the part of the Canadian government: "it is unlikely that any Canadian company or other entity will be permitted to share in SDI work, except where we have some technology that cannot be obtained in the United States...". As a result there would likely be a brain drain of Canadian scientists and technicians to the United States: "We may be headed for another Arrow situation in terms of opportunity lost." There was also the strong possibility that a rebuff of the Reagan offer "could add difficulty of Canada retaining, let alone gaining more, access to the U.S. market, so vital to our economy."

Many of these points were highlighted in the speech of Lieutenant General R. J. Lane, spokesman for the Federation of Military and United Services Institutes of Canada. Drawing upon his experience as former Deputy Commander of NORAD, Lane emphasized that "the USA has been more than willing to share its research and development program with us but only when we were a full partner contributing financial and other resources."

> SDI participation will help us remain in the forefront by working on the state of the art technologies. We have already carried on research in several of these technologies and thus should continue to expand our knowledge, make a worthwhile contribution to the common cause and contribute to a better economic future. (*Proceedings...* Session 13: 100–110).

Despite their assertive stance, those advocating participation in SDI represented the minority point of view. Most of those who appeared before the Joint Committee strongly opposed Canada even being involved in the research side of "Star Wars." Opposition was particularly pronounced from the various peace groups. Of these, the testimony of two organizations, Initiative for the Peaceful Use of Technology (IPUT) and the Engineers for Nuclear Disarmament (END), were of special interest, since they assessed SDI from a technological, economic, and moral perspective. Representatives of IPUT devoted most of their criticism to refuting the technological viability of SDI: "Computer science may be divided by religious wars, but if there is something very close to a consensus on the SDI, and that is that its computer system is certain to be technically unreliable." They also questioned the economic advantages for Canada if participation were to occur. Spokesmen of END were even more critical of the argument that SDI would result in substantial economic and technological "spinoff":

> Such a vast expenditure on nonproductive military purposes would pose a threat to an already shaky world economy.... As engineers we view with alarm reports of the rapid deterioration of the civil works – roads, bridges, dams, water supply, sewage disposal and drainage system – that comprise infrastructure upon which our whole North American society depends. By diverting vast sums for defence we are heading for disaster in our whole economy (*Proceedings...* Session 6: 78–79).

Not surprisingly, given its past commitment to the international peace movement, the Canadian Labour Congress also denounced SDI. It was morally wrong, it would escalate the arms race, and there were minimal economic rewards for Canada:

> ...few net jobs as far as we can ascertain will be created. Indeed, with a great deal of money being spent... at complex and uncharted technologies... what moneys will be left for other programs that in fact do create jobs?
>
> Our brief commends the work of Canada's North-South Institute in showing how military research and development is not a job creator of consequence; but even if it were we would oppose it. More jobs in a world made more dangerous is not a goal of the Canadian Labour Congress and nor should it be for Canada (*Proceedings...* Session 13: 190).

The Interim Report of the Joint Committee was submitted to the House of Commons in November, 1985. It was a carefully worded document which attempted to find common ground between the supporters and opponents of Canada's involvement in SDI. On balance, the Committee tended to side with the opponents, and the majority of members endorsed the resolution "that technological and economic factors be considered subordinate to strategic and arms control concerns in the formation of the government's decision" (*Proceedings...* Session 5: 90 – 91). Part of the reason for taking this position was related to nationalist considerations that participation in SDI could "threaten Canada's independence in both domestic and foreign policy" (*Proceedings...* Session 5: 52 – 53). The Committee also had serious reservations whether "participating countries will be allowed full access to the key technological developments that will result from the research phase of SDI," particularly since the U.S. Congress had traditionally taken a strong position against "permitting other countries, even allies, access to technology that is developed with U.S. funding."[4]

But if SDI did not guarantee an opportunity for honing Canadian scientific and technological capabilities, what were the alternatives? According to the Joint Committee, one possibility for Canadian technological development was the development of a space-based warning, surveillance, and communication system for air defence. "Such a system," the Committee reasoned "would allow Canada to monitor air and naval activity in Canadian territory consistent with our NORAD role, to monitor surrounding waters that are our responsibility under NATO, and to enhance our ability to participate in arms control verification activities." What made this strategy even more attractive was that this space-based system involved key areas of technological developments and ones in which Canada had already achieved some expertise. In this regard, the Canadian aerospace industry was viewed as a critical player, and the Committee recommended that the federal government undertake "a much more aggressive effort to develop Canadian capabilities in the aerospace field" (*Proceedings...* Session 5: 65 – 66).[5]

Although the Mulroney government eventually decided not to accept the American invitation to participate in SDI research, it was a qualified rejection. Indeed, there is no barrier against specific Canadian companies accepting SDI contracts, and some have apparently taken advantage of the gigantic pool of $ 8 billion allocated by Congress for SDI research and development (Regehr 1987: 167).[6] What is even more alluring is greater access to the gigantic Pentagon budget. A number of Canadian companies, most notably those in the aerospace field, have been able to obtain American military contracts through the Defence Production Sharing Agreement and through the Canada-U.S. Defence Development Sharing Program, which provides full R & D funding. In the byzantine world of American military procurement, Canadian companies have often received substantial assistance from federal agencies such as the Canadian Commercial Corporation and the Export Development Corporation. Equally important has been financial assistance from the Defence Industry Productivity (DIP) program, with its mandate "to enhance economic growth through the promotion of viable defence-related exports" (Regehr 1987: 104 – 110).[7] In many instance, the major arms producers in Canada are subsidiaries of powerful multinationals who are often able to obtain contracts through their parent company.

There have been many critics of these stronger links between the Canadian industries and the Pentagon, as was evident during the 1985 hearings of the Special Joint Committee of the Senate and House of Commons on Canada's International Relations. Perhaps the most sweeping indictment of the broader aspects of this relationship has been provided by Ernie Regehr in his book *Arms Canada: The Deadly Business of Military Exports*:

> Canadian military production involves Canada uncritically in military doctrines and programs that are a threat to peace; the structure of the military industry leaves Canada vulnerable to political pressures from our primary customer, the United States, and thereby undermines Canada's capacity to assess and pursue independent and innovative foreign policy and defence options; Canadian military production does not deliver the economic benefits it promises (Regehr 1987: xix – xx).[8]

3 Conclusion

Between 1939 and 1988 Canada has had close military and economic relations with the United States. The exact pattern of this interaction has varied over the years, but one dominant trend emerges – the gradual fusion of Canadian and American interests. During the Second World War there was an unprecedented level of cooperation between the two countries, in part, made possible through such agreements as Ogdensburg and Hyde Park. In the immediate postwar years, defence ties were strengthened particularly during the Korean War and with the creation of NORAD. Although free trade was not established, the United States became Canada's major trading partner and within the country American direct investment reached unprecedented levels. The Auto Pact established sector free trade and the Defence Production Sharing Agreement allowed Canadian companies to compete for lucrative Pentagon contracts.

There have been, however, periods when Canadian-American relations were rather strained, most notably during the early 1960s and the 1970s. Yet even when the Diefenbaker and Kennedy administrations had serious disagreements over Cuba and nuclear weapons, there was no trade or investment disruption, and no threat that either country would withdraw from either DPSA or NORAD. Nor did the economic nationalist policies of the Trudeau government prevent Canada from becoming even more dependent on the United States market, and a more active partner in defence production.

The Canada-U.S. Free Trade Agreement has once again focused public opinion on Canada's complex military and economic relationship with the United States. And Canadian are very divided on these issues. For some, the Agreement is a great challenge, an opportunity to expand their participation in the most affluent market in the world. Canada's trade surplus of $ 14 billion in 1983, $ 19.8 billion in 1984, and $ 20.5 billion in 1985 clearly show the benefits of this economic relationship. Moreover, Canada was the only country in the world to gain a substantial share of American military contracts in 1985 over $ 1.6 billion in military goods were exported to the United States (Cameron 1986: xvii – 1). For others, free trade means economic exploitation, social disruption, and the loss of sovereignty. These critics often use the examples of joint defence production and the performance of NORAD to justify their opposition to further economic integration with the United States. In particular, they stress that the Pentagon primarily uses the integration of the defence industry "as a means towards policy integration." To what extent this means conformity with global American defence and foreign policy remains to be seen. But it is perhaps useful for Canadians to consider the words of historian Gwynne Dyer, "great powers don't have friends, they only have interests, and we're one of America's interests" (Dyer in Farlanger 1986: 16 – 18).

Notes

1 A comprehensive public opinion poll conducted by the *Toronto Star* in December, 1987 reported the following reaction of Canadians to the following aspects of the Free Trade Agreement: (a) 56% of those polled believed that Canada would lose of its sovereignty or independence; (b) 61% declared that the United States would receive more benefits than Canada; (c) 43% said that the continental energy part of the Agreement was unacceptable; (d) 38% opposed easing restrictions on U.S. companies in the financial sector; (e) 52% of those polled in Ontario claimed that there would be a substantial loss of jobs in their province (*Toronto Star*, January 10, 1988: 4).

2 Between 1981 and 1983 Litton had contracts for 327 guidance systems from the U.S. Defence Department worth approximately $ 80 million. The company also received a grant of $ 26.4 million from the Canadian government's Defence Industry Productivity Programme, and a five-year interest-free loan of $ 22.5 million.

3 The NDP position that Canada should withdraw from NATO and pull the 6,000 Canadian troops and squadrons of CF-18 fighters out of Europe, differs from both the Conservatives and Liberals.

4 The exponents of this viewpoint were greatly disturbed by evidence that large numbers of American military personnel would be required in order to install different aspects of the SDI system in Canada. This, they claimed, was completely unacceptable since it "would be a violation of Canadian sovereignty." They also argued that the long-term implications of SDI would mean "substantial military integration," and thereby "signal the end of Canada's special role as a nation particularly devoted to the resolution of international disputes, the negotiations of arms control agreements, and the maintenance of peace."

5 *Proceedings...* (1985–86: 65). It was also felt that involvement in SDI would "compete with other important military programs for limited government funding." Much better, the Committee reasoned, to continue the Canadian and American "long history of cooperation on military programs... on a cost-sharing basis."

6 John Polanyi, Nobel Prize laureate in chemistry, from the University of Toronto, has been a particularly effective critic of Canadian involvement in Star Wars. In a September 3, 1985 editorial in the Toronto *Globe and Mail* Polanyi denounced SDI as "a vast and deliberate acceleration in the pace of research into ABM technology." He also charged that the American invitation to Canada was "not because it is in need of our scientific and technical assistance," but rather that the Pentagon sought "to obtain, if possible, a political vote of confidence in SDI. That in good conscience we cannot give."

7 The Canadian Commercial Corporation is a federal coordinating agency which assists Canadian firms in dealing with foreign governments. Most of the contracts that CC administers are for military goods and services, with the majority being with the United States. During the period 1969–1985 the following aerospace and electronics companies received vast amounts of funding through DIP grants:

Company	*Amount Received ($)*
*Pratt and Whitney Canada Ltd., Quebec	333,242,094
*De Havilland Aircraft of Canada, Ontario	124,802,247
Canadair Limited, Quebec	123,101,286
*Litton Systems, Canada Ltd., Ontario	77,736,442
*McDonnell Douglas Canada, Ltd., Ontario	66,242,203
*Bell Helicopter (Textron), Quebec	56,636,566
*Canadian Marconi Co.	46,158,013
*General Motors of Canada, Ontario	29,170,169

Figures tabulated from the Public Accounts of Canada. The companies marked with an asterisk (*) are American branch plants.

8 Not surprisingly, there is no mention of SDI in the December 1987 text of the bilateral trade agreement, and little mention of military aspects of free trade.

References

Bliss, Michael (1987): *Northern Enterprise: Five Centuries of Canadian Business.* Toronto: McClelland and Stewart.

Bothwell, Robert, Ian Drummond, and John English (1981): *Canada Since 1945: Power, Politics and Provincialism*. Toronto: University of Toronto Press.

Byers, R. B. (1987): The 1987 Defence White Paper: An Analysis. *Canadian Defence Quarterly* (Autumn): 11 – 20.

Cameron, Duncan (ed.) (1986): *The Free Trade Papers*. Toronto: J. Lorimer.

Challenge and Commitment: A Defence Policy for Canadian National Defence (1987). Ottawa: Department of National Defence.

Clark, Ronald (1965): *Tizard*. London: Meuthen & Co.

Cuff, R. D. and Granatstein, J. L. (1978): *American Dollars – Canadian Prosperity: Canadian-American Economic Relations, 1945 – 1950*. Toronto: Samuel-Stevens.

Dyer, Gwynne in Shirley Farlanger (1986): Doing a Finland. *Peace Magazine*, June/July, 16 – 18.

Dziuban, Colonel Stanley (1959): *Military Relations Between the United States and Canada*. Washington: Office of the Chair of Military History.

Eggleston, Wilfrid (1950): *Scientists at War*. Toronto: Oxford University Press.

Eggleston, Wilfrid (1978): *National Research in Canada: The NRC, 1916 – 1966*. Toronto: Clarke, Irwin.

Foreign Ownership and the Structure of Canadian Industry: Report of the Task Force on the Structure of Canadian Industry (1968). Ottawa: Queen's Printer.

Francis, Dean (1970): *Negotiation and Management of Defence Contracts*. New York: Macmillan.

Free Trade Agreement Between Canada and the United States of America (1987). Ottawa: Department of External Affairs.

Goodspeed, D. J. (1958): *DRB: A History of the Defence Research Board of Canada*. Ottawa: University of Toronto Press.

Gowing, Margaret (1974): *Independence and Deterrence, 1945 – 52*. London: MacMillan.

Granatstein, J. L. (1985): The Course of Canadian-American Relations Since 1945. In Doran, Charles and John Sigler (eds.), *Canada and the United States: Enduring Friendship, Persistent Stress*. Englewood Cliffs, N.J.: Prentice-Hall.

Granatstein, J. L. (1986): *Canada 1957 – 1967: The Years of Uncertainty and Innovation*. Toronto: McClelland and Stewart.

Green, Christopher (1980): *Canadian Industrial Organization and Policy*. Toronto: McGraw-Hill-Ryerson.

Henderson, Michael (ed.) (1987): *The Future on the Table: Canada and the Free Trade Issue*. Toronto: Masterpress.

Herken, Gregg (1982): *The Winning Weapon: The Atomic Bomb in the Cold War, 1945 – 1950*. New York: Vintage Books.

Jockel, Joseph (1983): The Canada-United States Military Cooperation Committee and Continental Air Defence. *Canadian Historical Review* (September): 352 – 377.

Johnson, Harry (1963): *The Canadian Quandry: Economic Problems and Policies*. Toronto: McGraw-Hill.

Kevles, Daniel (1979): *The Physicists*. New York: Vintage Books.

London *Free Press* (Ontario) (Sept. 11, 1987; Nov. 25, 1987; Dec. 11, 1987).

Minutes of the Proceedings and Evidence of the Special Committee of the Senate and House of Commons on Canada's International Relations, Session, 33rd Parliament (1987): Ottawa: Supply and Services Canada.
Niosi, Jorge (1981): *Canadian Capitalism*. Toronto: J. Lorimer.
Owram, Doug (1986): *The Government Generation: Canadian Intellectuals and the State, 1900 – 1945*. Toronto: University of Toronto Press.
Polenberg, Richard (1972): *War and Society: The United States, 1941 – 1945*. New York: J. B. Lippincott.
Proceedings of the Special Joint Committee of the Senate and the House of Commons on Canada's International Relations, 1985 – 86. Ottawa: Supply and Services Canada.
Regehr, Ernie (1987): *Arms Canada: The Deadly Business of Military Exports*. Toronto: J. Lorimer.
Rosenblum, Simon (1985): *Misguided Missiles: Canada, the Cruise and Star Wars*. Toronto: J. Lorimer.
Sherwin, Martin (1977): *A World Destroyed: The Atomic Bomb and the Grand Alliance*. New York: Vintage Books.
Stacey, C. P. (1970): *Arms, Men and Governments: The War Policies of Canada, 1939 – 45*. Ottawa: Queen's Printer.
Toronto *Globe and Mail* (September 3, 1985; Nov. 19, 1987).
Toronto *Star* (September 20, 1987).
Villa, Brian (1981): Canada and Atomic Collaboration, 1941 – 1943. Unpublished paper in possession of author.
Willoughby, William (1979): *The Joint Organizations of Canada and the United States*. Toronto: University of Toronto Press.

Economic and Political Tensions in U.S.-Canadian Relations: The Free Trade Issue

Volkert Wiesner

1 Introduction

Trade between the United States and Canada reached a total value of U.S. $ 129 billion in 1986. This is by far the biggest exchange of goods and services between two single countries in the world. Surprisingly at first sight, the U.S.-Canadian trade relationship plays no (or at least no significant) role in the current debate over tariffs, trade barriers, and protectionism – neither in Europe nor Japan nor the United States.

But this does not mean that the matter is free of tensions. Trade as well as direct foreign investment from one single source – the U.S. – is a perennial issue in the Canadian political debate. The United States is Canada's most important customer: the U.S. share of Canadian exports has been climbing steadily from 38% at the turn of the century, to 56% in 1960, to 78% in 1987. That means that the Canadian economy depends heavily on what is happening south of the border. It is often said in Canada that if the U.S. sneezes, Canada catches a cold.

In May 1985, both countries started official negotiations over a comprehensive free trade agreement, removing all remaining tariffs, quotas, and trade barriers within the next decade. After 16 months of highly controversial talks the two governments reached agreement and a treaty was signed by President Ronald Reagan and Prime Minister Brian Mulroney on January 2, 1988, which was sent to the U.S. Congress and the Canadian House of Commons for approval. President Reagan already called the trade accord an "important model for other nations seeking to improve their trading relationships" and to Brian Mulroney the pact is simply "a good deal" (Time October 19, 1987 b: 38).

Before dealing with the most important results of the trade negotiations this chapter will describe some of the relevant historical and political conditions shaping the environment of the talks. It concentrates more on the Canadian view of the issue for a number of reasons: The debate over free trade is incomparably more intense in Canada than in the United States, and it can be expected to dominate the political discussions up to the next federal elections – in late 1988 or early 1989. And because it will be Canada which can find itself in the role of either the big winner or the big loser once the free trade pact comes into effect in 1989.

2 Canadian Trade and Investment Policies: Some Historical Aspects

2.1 Shaping the Patterns of Dependence

In the early decades of the nineteenth century, as the United States developed into an independent and steadily industrializing country, Canada remained a British colony with all the attributes of a colonial economy: producing staple goods for export (fish, furs, wheat, wood, and minerals) and importing finished goods mainly from Britain. As part of the British Empire, Canadian goods entered the British market duty-free – which, curiously enough, led to the first heavy dependence on trade with the southern neighbor, for to take advantage of the privileged Canadian position with Britain, American producers shipped their goods duty-free via Canadian harbors to England.

In 1849, when the British introduced general free trade, abolishing most of the special trade relations with their North American colony, the Canadian mercantile class (which had flourished under the former conditions) pressed the Colonial Office to negotiate a reciprocity treaty with the U.S. under which staple commodities could enter the American market duty-free. A group of most influential Montréal businessmen – representing the center of Canadian trade and commerce – went even further in signing a petition which demanded complete political union with the United States (Saywell 1983: 22).

The first U.S.-Canadian reciprocity treaty was in effect from 1854 to 1866. It guaranteed Canadian staple producers participation in the prosperity of the American economy, mainly by delivering lumber for house construction and food for the growing urban centers. When the treaty was abrogated by the U.S. in 1866 (not least to protect domestic resource producers in the border states of New England as well as in New York), it had an enormous psychological impact, not only on those Canadians earning their money with trade and resource production: "There remained… a strong belief that the future of Canada lay in some kind of formal commercial ties with the American metropole" (Appel Molot and Williams 1984: 81).

But the renewal of the free trade pact was not on the political agenda of the first Canadian national government elected in 1867, when through the British North America Act (BNA) the Dominion of Canada came into being. The policies adopted up to the end of the century by the ruling Progressive Conservatives consisted of three major elements: A high tariff wall of 35%

on all imports, erected in 1879 to protect the slowly growing manufacturing industries against the influx of American finished goods; settlement of the west; and construction of the transcontinental railway (finished in 1885) to foster the process of nation-building in this vast and sparsely settled country. The government expected that goods manufactured in Canada would be purchased by Canadians across the country, that the export of wheat by the developing prairie-province economies would generate capital needed for the consumption of domestic products as well as for the construction of the railway system, and that the railway would carry staple commodities east for export and manufactured goods west for sale.

These policies seemed essential to promoting the process of nation-building, while they strengthened the further continental integration of the economy: The high-tariff strategy produced an inflow of U.S. branch plants and subsidiary firms to guarantee their mother companies unrestricted access to the Canadian market and resources. So as early as the 1920s the present characteristic structure of the country as a typical branch-plant economy was already fully developed. American corporations were dominant in Canada's most dynamic industrial sectors, while Canadian ownership was concentrated in less capital-intensive industries such as textiles, clothing, footwear, food processing, and furniture manufacturing. These patterns of foreign ownership have not changed substantially up to the present day, as Table 1 shows (see p.148). "Canada", concludes Naylor, "was the pioneer of the process of industrialization by invitation. [While the high tariff] was generally regarded as a sort of declaration of industrial independence from the U.S...., it becomes a matter of inviting American capitalists to shift the locus of their production northward" (Naylor 1973: 44).

Not only the patterns of foreign ownership, but also the structures of Canadian-American trade were shaped in the first two decades of the twentieth century. Herbert Hoover, then Secretary of Commerce in Washington, described them in a letter to the Secretary of State in 1923:

> An analysis of the trade between the two countries reveals clearly the fact that our exports to Canada consist, to a very considerable extent, of manufactured products, many of which could be produced by the establishment of manufacturing plants in Canada or by the expansion of existing plants. Our imports from Canada, on the other hand, consist largely of raw materials, some of which could not be obtained from other sources without considerable injury to Ameican interests depending on such materials.... It is, therefore, quite obvious that under the circumstances, it would be inadvisable to take any action that might result in disturbing the existing economic relations" (quoted in Kasurak 1979: 59–60).

Hoover, by the way, also gave an interesting description of the then-common perception of American decision-makers that the (favorable) relationship with

Table 1. Foreign control of Canadian Industry, 1970 and 1980 (per cent of total)

	Assets 1970	1980	Sales 1970	1980
Food	44	29	33	27
Beverages	32	32	30	35
Tobacco products	86	100	82	100
Rubber products	93	91	91	90
Leather products	22	23	20	20
Textile mills	53	54	49	54
Knitting mills	21	15	18	14
Clothing industries	14	14	11	13
Wood industries	33	19	23	17
Furniture industries	21	12	19	11
Paper and allied industries	45	35	47	38
Printing, publishing, and allied	15	12	13	12
Primary metals	43	13	41	15
Metal fabricating	45	34	43	37
Machinery	75	52	77	59
Transport equipment	85	71	90	84
Electrical products	68	54	66	62
Non-metallic mineral products	63	70	53	60
Petroleum and coal products	100	70	99	82
Chemicals and chemical products	80	77	83	76
Miscellaneous manufacturing	51	43	50	42
Total manufacturing	59	48	56	51
Mineral fuels	82	53	91	74
Total mining	70	45	75	59

Source: Whittington and Williams 1984: 85

the northern neighbor would, after all, develop well in the American interest if it was left to "natural" economic forces. In 1927, for example, when the first American legation was established in Canada, U.S. President Calvin Coolidge originally opposed this decision because in his view there was nothing to do for an American diplomat in Ottawa. However, he was obliged to change his mind only because Canada itself had appointed a minister in Washington (Kasurak 1979: 57). Much of the irritation in the United States about protectionist measures finally taken by Canada in the 1970s and early 1980s can be traced back to this lack of awareness of what might be in the interest of the northern partner. Or, as John Holmes put it: "The major difference between Canadians and Americans on the subject of their relationship is the intensity of their perceptions" (Holmes 1976: 247).

2.2 Canadian Free-Trade Initiatives Since the 1930s

Not surprisingly initiatives concerning trade between the two countries have been mostly taken by Canadian governments. But up to the 1930s the free trade issue was "too hot for political parties to touch" (Wonnacott 1987: 15) because the debacle of the free-trade oriented Liberal party at the polls in 1911 was well remembered for a long time. In 1935 and 1938 two U.S.-Canadian reciprocity treaties were negotiated, allowing nearly three-quarters of Canadian exports to enter the American market duty-free. After another agreement in 1944, eliminating tariffs on agricultural machinery, the Canadian Prime Minister Mackenzie King started secret negotiations with the United States in 1946 to create (for the first time in North American history) a free trade area on the continent. Canada, which had come out of the Second World War as the third largest exporting nation, feared falling back into an economic depression similar to that of the 1930s because of the loss of the collapsed European markets and the lacking forces of wartime production. Export had declined in 1946 by 20% and in its trade with the U.S. Canada faced a $ 1 billion deficit (Fay 1980: 39 – 40).

The way the negotiations on both sides were handled then – starting with Canadian secretiveness, American reactions, up to the irritation in the Canadian public – reveals some striking parallels to what was going on in and on the fringe of the recent free trade talks. While the Canadian interest was simply to promote exports to the U.S., the Truman government answered with what it called the "bold and striking plan" of a comprehensive customs union: all tariffs should be removed, import quotas on particular goods should only occasionally be allowed, and each country should be free in its tariff policies towards third countries. A customs union like this, the American negotiators summarized in 1948, would strengthen the "joint economic and military potential," alter the east-west pattern of trade to a "predominantly north-south movement," and integrate the Canadian economy "much closer to that of the United States" (Fay 1980: 47). Within the U.S. State Department the benefits were seen clearly: "The present may offer a unique opportunity of promoting the most efficient utilization of the resources of the North American continent and knitting the two countries together – an objective of United States foreign policy since the founding of the Republic" (Thorp 1948, quoted in Holmes 1976: 270).

Before formal negotiations were started on this basis (to which the Canadian government had fully agreed), the plan became public in Canada in March

1948. Reactions clearly showed that those were right who had thought the proposed customs union would be "political dynamite in Canada" (Fay 1980: 47). No matter how far the economic integration of the country had already developed, the idea of a customs union did (and still does) generate strong reactions in the general public, stirring up old Canadian anxieties over political annexation by the power to the south. Thus, once discussed in public, the plan provoked obvious opposition throughout the Canadian press; a customs union "would mean the political absorption of this country" (*Globe and Mail*, or "national suicide" (*Ottawa Citizen*), while the *Saskatoon Star Phoenix* coined the slogan: "Co-operation ever, union never!" (quoted in Fay 1980: 50). The effect was that Mackenzie King, being acccused of selling out the country, broke off all negotiations immediately. For a long period free trade was again an issue better avoided in the Canadian political debate.

The policies adopted by both Liberal and Progessive Conservative governments during the following years therefore concentrated more on sectoral trade arrangements. The most important one was the so-called Auto Pact of 1965, allowing automobiles and parts to cross the border duty-free. The Auto Pact had an enormous impact on industrial production, especially in eastern Canada, as well as on trade patterns. Within the first five years, Canadian imports of U.S. cars and parts increased from only 3% to 40% of the domestic market, while exports to the U.S. increased from 7% to 60% of the total Canadian output in the automotive industries (Gibbins 1985: 185). At first sight the Auto Pact did a lot to compensate for Canada's structural trade imbalance in favor of manufactured goods. As shown in Tables 2 and 3, "motor vehicles and parts" today constitute by far the largest share of total Canadian trade.

In fact, this most important trade sector has to be seen as an "intrafirm transfer of goods between U.S. firms and their Canadian branches which incidentally pass over an international frontier" (Appel Molot and Williams 1984: 86). This becomes obvious when the large volume of foreign control in Canadian "transport equipment" industries is considered, as shown in Table 1. While Canada, thus, benefits from job creation and taxes, the domestic automobile industry rapidly developed into an integrated sector of U.S. automobile production, depending heavily on industrial and financial decisions made in Detroit or elsewhere in the United States.

3 Trudeau and the New Investment Policy

At the beginning of the 1970s, not least caused by the integration of the automobile industry, Canadians showed a significant change in their attitude towards foreign control over their economy. According to ten Gallup polls

Table 2. Exports by commodities, 1981 – 1984 (million Can $)

Commodity	1981	1982	1983	1984
Wheat	3,728	4,289	4,648	4,710
Animals and other edible products	5,714	5,933	5,761	6,108
Metal ores and concentrates	4,086	3,192	2,896	3,670
Crude petroleum	2,505	2,729	3,457	4,390
Natural gas	4,370	4,755	3,847	3,886
Other crude materials	4,250	4,108	4,073	5,404
Lumber	2,989	2,913	3,965	4,254
Wood pulp	3,819	3,221	3,049	3,908
Newsprint	4,326	4,086	3,956	4,784
Fabricated metals	8,352	7,373	7,707	9,448
Other fabricated materials	11,054	10,272	11,296	13,597
Motor vehicles and parts (partial)	13,185	16,518	21,227	29,404
Other machinery and equipment	9,969	9,953	9,718	12,403
Other domestic exports	2,990	2,483	2,556	3,578
Subtotal	81,337	81,825	88,155	109,543
Reexports	2,474	2,705	2,458	2,952
Total exports	83,811	84,530	90,613	112,495

Source: Statistics Canada, *Canada Handbook* 1986: 230

between 1964 and 1982 the number of those who viewed the amount of U.S. capital invested in Canada to be "enough now" rose from 46% in 1964 (the year prior to the Auto Pact) to a maximum 71% in 1975. Over the same period the percentage of those who wanted to see more U.S. capital fell from 33% to only 16% (Gibbins 1985: 189). Also in 1975, 58% of the public were ready to support a policy of buying back a majority control over U.S. companies in Canada, even if this might mean "a big reduction in our standard of living" (Appel Molot and Williams 1984: 93) – figures never reached in Canada before or since. The Trudeau government's answer to this growing nationalistic sentiment (and pressured by the social-democratic New Democratic Party, which tolerated the Liberal minority government) was the establishment of the Federal Investment Review Agency (FIRA) in 1974 to examine and control all new foreign investment. The expansion of foreign-owned companies already active in Canada into business "unrelated" to their usual activities also came under review. The major criteria for approval of new investment applications were those of expected substantial benefits for the

Table 3. Imports by commodities, 1981 – 1984 (million Can $)

Commodity	1981	1982	1983	1984
Meat and fish	689	678	773	925
Fruits and vegetables	1,802	1,873	1,880	2,169
Animals and other edible products	2,743	2,387	2,350	2,812
Coal	834	932	841	1,094
Crude petroleum	8,004	4,979	3,319	3,376
Other crude materials	3,469	2,780	3,080	3,525
Textiles	1,426	1,193	1,483	1,734
Chemical products	3,814	3,586	4,393	5,212
Fabricated metals	4,753	2,834	3,223	3,900
Other fabricated materials	4,554	4,182	4,917	6,366
Motor vehicles and parts (partial)	16,203	15,124	19,286	26,409
Industrial machinery	7,296	5,657	5,292	6,614
Agricultural machinery	2,386	1,688	1,514	1,769
Aircraft, aircraft engines, and parts	2,351	1,523	1,815	2,224
Electronic computers	2,327	2,647	2,886	4,242
Other machinery and equipment	8,781	7,880	9,826	12,587
Other imports	8,050	7,913	8,732	10,886
Total imports	79,482	67,856	75,608	95,842

Source: Statistics Canada, *Canada Handbook* 1986: 235

Canadian economy, such as job creation, increasing trade or research and development activities in Canada rather than in foreign company headquarters. What remained free of the review process was the expansion of existing branch plants into "related" business. Therefore, it was often criticized in Canada that FIRA was not really a strong instrument to control or even roll back the already existing degree of foreign investment (as it was perceived to be by most U.S. officials), but it kept the issue in the minds of the public, and – more important – in the media.

Tensions between the Canadian and American governments over Trudeau's investment policy arose as late as in 1980 when two events converged: The election of Ronald Reagan in Washington and the re-election of Trudeau in Ottawa (after a short Progressive Conservative interlude under Joe Clark). One of the first actions taken by the new Liberal government was to announce the National Energy Program (NEP). The essence of the NEP was to increase Canadian ownership in the critical sector of energy fuel by offering subsidies and protected exploration rights on Crown land in the Canadian north and on off-shore sites to companies with a minimum of 50% Canadian ownership. Several American companies with major interests in Canada suddenly found themselves in a less competitive position. Canadian firms, such as Dome Petroleum, Canadian Pacific, and Seagram's bought out some Canadian branches of American transnationals to make a profit out of the NEP. The Reagan administration was pressed to take action in this matter. From the spring of 1981 to the following winter Ottawa was confronted with a large number of initiatives, not only from the White House but also from Congress, including open threats of massive economic retaliation. Both FIRA and the NEP survived these attacks, but the United States successfullly prevented NEP from being extended into economic areas other than energy (Clarkson 1982: 7–13).

4 Mulroney and the Revival of Free Trade Negotiations

In December 1984, immediately after his landslide victory in the federal elections, Progressive Conservative Prime Minister Brian Mulroney chose the Economic Club of New York to declare that Canada was "open for business again," announcing major changes in the government's policies on energy, trade, and foreign investment (*Canadian News Facts*, December 19,1984). Despite the obvious fact that FIRA had never "closed" the country for business – the approval rate of investment applications had varied between 83% and 96% (Appel Molot and Williams 1984: 89) – FIRA was replaced in June 1985 by a new agency with the much more friendly name Investment Canada. The aim was to promote foreign investment rather than to review or even hinder it from crossing the border. Virtually all foreign investment and all but large foreign takeovers have since then been allowed to proceed without any scrutiny.

Under the new bill, any corporation is considered 100% Canadian-owned when a simple majority of voting shares is in Canadian hands – under FIRA it had to be two-thirds. This affected some 20 corporations with American participation which are now treated as Canadian firms without any limitation of their activities in Canada (*Canadian News Facts*, April 19 and June 19, 1985). This shift in investment policies towards "continentalism" can not sufficiently be explained by the free-enterprise ideology of the new government. The belief that a greater degree of integration into the U.S. economy is beneficial for the country has always been characteristic of crisis situations in Canada. At the turn of the century, in the 1930s and in the early postwar period, it was the Liberals who had strongly supported what one Canadian observer describes as the "Canadian ideology of mainstream economics" (Clarkson 1978: 45–65) – always connected with strong efforts to talk about free trade with the Americans.

In the early 1980s Canada experienced its severest economic crisis since the Great Depression. Within only 18 months, from the spring of 1981 to the winter 1982 the GNP fell by 6.5%, industrial production fell by 18%, and unemployment rose by 80% from 850,000 to 1,500,1000 – with nearly half a million lost jobs in the four basic industries of forestry, mining, manufacturing, and construction (Robinson 1984: 7). It is, therefore, not at all surprising that the free trade issue would come up again sooner or later. Thus, it was not only Brian Mulroney for the Conservatives, but before him the Liberal Finance Minister, Donald Macdonald, head of a Royal Commission appointed by Trudeau in late 1982, who called for a comprehensive free trade arrangement with the U.S. – in September 1985 when the Commission's Report on the Economy was released. To what extent "mainstream economics" had already captured the minds of Canadian decision-makers again becomes obvious by the fact that 12 of the 13 Macdonald commissioners agreed to the hypothesis that "free trade would ensure Canada's access to the giant U.S. market, would make Canadians richer, reduce unemployment, cut prices, attract foreign investment, ease federal-provincial strife, increase the competitiveness of the economy and boost production" (*Canadian News Facts*, September 19, 1985). That only one commissioner (the labor representative) disagreed to this delightful vision led the Prime Minister of the resource-rich province of Alberta, Peter Lougheed – one of the strongest supporters of free trade – to make the remark: "If the Macdonald Commission , which I felt was so heavily loaded with Liberals and centralists, feels the way to go is free trade, that speaks a lot for the conclusion" (*Maclean's*, September 16, 1985 a).

Initial opposition to a free trade pact was concentrated on Canadian labor unions fearing a loss of jobs in less competitive industries such as textiles (protected by a 25% tariff wall), tobacco, food, and furniture. Multinationals, so their argument, could decide to serve the Canadian market directly from the U.S. rather than produce in Canada. Unprotected competition would require job-replacing technology and workers could be pressured into making major concessions in wages and working conditions resulting in a lower standard of living for many Canadians. A union-financed report on the impact of free trade (presented in December 1985), therefore, proposed a general shift in economic policies towards "more emphasis on economic self-reliance in Canada as an alternative to free trade, with export policy playing a secondary role" (*Canadian News Facts*, December 19, 1985). In January 1986 the unions started to form a nationwide coalition against free trade, headed by the Canadian Labor Congress, and joined by a number of different interest groups, such as the National Farmer's Union, the Canadain Council of Churches, the Council of Canadians, as well as the National Action Committee on the Status of Women (*Canadian News Facts*, January 4, 1986).

The women's organizations stressed the fact that two-thirds of the workers in the most vulnerable manufacturing industries (textiles, toys, small electrical products, and leather products) are female and that even free traders admit that there could be up to 800,000 jobs lost in these sectors alone. And because women working in manufacturing industries tend to be older, with a majority of immigrant women who are less likely to speak English or French and often having less formal education than the Canadian average, it has to be feared that most of them could find themselves permanently unemployed (*Vancouver Status of Women* 1987).

In farming, free trade critics are concentrated among wine producers and grape growers, who employ some 3,200 people in small, family-owned wineries mainly in Ontario, British Columbia, and Nova Scotia, producing about Can $ 225 million worth of wine in 1986. They fear that the bigger California wineries could increase their market share in Canada from the current 10% to 50%, if no quotas or tariffs are imposed (*Mclean's*, August 10, 1987 b). Also Canadian brewers, representing a Can $ 2 billion-a-year industry, could be among the losers under a free trade pact. Squeezed by provincial laws stipulating that beer sold in a particular province has to be brewed there, the structure of the industry is dominated by a number of small plants across the country, while the large-scale American breweries are expected to have enough capacity to serve the Canadian market three times over. Following a recent study conducted for the Canadain brewers, the largest American brands such as Coors, Miller, and Budweiser could immediately increase their Canadian market shares from 15% to 40% under free trade conditions. As a result, about 8,000 of the Canadian brewing industry's 20,000 workers would lose their jobs (*Mclean's*, August 10, 1987 b).

Political support for the free trade critics came from Québec's Prime Minister Robert Bourassa and his Ontario colleague David Peterson, both Liberals, accompanied by Ed Broadbent, leader of the social-democratic New Democratic Party (NDP). Bourassa, not previously known as an economic "nationalist," expressed his fears about the possible "internal dynamics of the integration process. If we start one degree of economic integration, it will be difficult to stop the others" (*Canadian News Facts*, December 19, 1985). The experience of the EEC shows, added Bourassa, that free trade leads to a customs union between countries, which would in turn lead to common political institutions – an idea never very popular in Canada since the days of Confederation. David Peterson, who strengthened his political influence with a landslide victory in Ontario's September 1987 election (the Liberals won 95 of 130 seats – an increase of 44), made free trade the big issue in his campaign. The Prime Minister of Ontario, where both small-scale farming and heavy industries are concentrated (Ontario produces 50% of all Canadian manufactured goods, 80% of Canada's steel, 75% of its electronic products, and 90% of its automobiles and parts), set out a basic line of six conditions for his aproval to a trade deal: protection for the agricultural sector; maintaining the Canada-U.S. Auto Pact; the continued right of Canada to screen foreign investment; protection of cultural industries; the continued ability to promote regional economic development; and creation of an adequate dispute-settlling mechanism (*Maclean's*, September 21, 1987 d).

The NDP is the only Canadian party which strongly opposed any free trade negotiations from the beginning. Historically linked with the labor unions, the NDP follows their arguments of possible job losses. The political weight of the party with its traditional basis in the prairie provinces increased in 1987, not only by its winning three federal by-elections in the Yukon Territory, Ontario, and Newfoundland, but – most of all – by leading constantly in the nationwide polls. The result of a Gallup poll conducted in July 1987 showed that 41% of the decided voters favored the NDP at the federal level, compared with 35% for the Liberals, and only 23% for the governing Progressive Conservatives. Already two months earlier, NDP leader Ed Broadbent had topped the polls as Canada's most popular politician (*Maclean's*, August 3, 1987 a).

5 Trade Negotiations and the Case of the Cultural Industries

Due to intense lobbying by Canadian officials, trade talks started in May 1986. In the United States the Canadian dispute over free trade found no following. Describing the widespread ignorance towards policy matters related to Canada, Frederick Stokeld, director of international business relations for the U.S. Chamber of Commerce, declared in September 1985 that "there is no great outcry for free trade from U.S. business because its interests in Canada are never focused. I hate to say this, but they tend to treat it like U.S. business in California" (*Maclean's*, September 16, 1985 a). For a long time the only American supporter of the idea seemed to be President Reagan, who brought the matter before Congress. One reason why an increasingly protectionist Congress finally gave its approval could have been the assumption that free trade with Canada would be useful as an example to the real targets of U.S. protectionism, i. e., Japan and Europe.

However, the talks were accompanied from the beginning by a number of "unfriendly acts" on the part of the U.S. Department of Commerce. The very day when the teams met for the first time, a 35% import tariff was imposed on Canadian wooden shingles, threatening 4,000 jobs in Alberta and British Columbia (Woller 1986: 44). Another measure followed in October 1986, passing almost unnoticed in the U.S., but causing a lot of irritation in Canada: unter long-standing pressure from the U.S. forestry industry, the Department of Commerce introduced another tariff of 15% on Canadian lumber, which holds a 32% share of the American softwood market for house construction (*Time*, January 12, 1987 a). But more important for the Canadian public's opinion about risks and benefits of free trade was the early U.S. announcement that nothing was to be excluded from the talks – an "everything or nothing" approach, which very much reminded Canadians of the U.S. handling of the free trade issue in the late 1940s (which finally led to the break-off of all negotiations). Again the talks were to include everything from various government programs to foster regional development, the Auto Pact, to – most sensitive issue for Canada – the "cultural industries" such as publishing, broadcasting, and film production. Immediately after that U.S. announcement, Prime Minister Mulroney was forced to declare publicly (after changing the term "free trade" into "freer trade") that the "essence of Canada..., our political sovereignty, our system of social programs, our commitment to fight regional disparities, our unique cultural identity... [is] not at issue in these negotiations (*Canadian News Facts*, December 19, 1985).

As a matter of fact, Canadian cultural industries (key elements to safeguard and strengthen the relatively young country's cultural and national identity) can only survive under a system of government programs, quotas and subsidies, some examples of which are:

- Prior to 1976, Canada had no significant magazine publishing industry of its own. The market was occupied mainly by U.S. products such as *Time* and *Reader's Digest*. Under a tax legislation imposed in 1976 (Bill C-58), Canadian firms are no longer allowed to deduct the costs of advertising in periodicals circulating in Canada unless they are 75% Canadian-owned, have 80% Canadian content, and are printed in Canada. *Time*, which had been adding only five or six pages a week to its U.S. edition, was prompted to close its Canadian edition, clearing the way for *Maclean's* to become a weekly (and today Canada's most important) news magazine in 1978. To put Bill C-58 on the bargaining table would mean not only giving up Canadian magazine publishing, but would guarantee the free trade issue a very critical press.
- With regard to broadcasting, Bill C-58 forced a number of T.V. stations along the U.S. border, which were initially established to "milk" the Canadian advertising market, to close down. Until 1976 these T.V. stations held an estimated share of 10% of all Canadian television advertising (Bahr 1986: 9). Since its inception Bill C-58 has been discussed on the government level between the two countries several times. Democratic U.S. Senator Moynihan, for example, named it "a test of our will to protect U.S. service

industries faced by unreasonable and unfair discrimination by a U.S. trading partner" (Bahr 1986: 10). Congress answered with a law limiting tax deductions for U.S. citizens attending cultural events in Canada, causing Canada estimated revenue losses of several hundred million dollars (Bahr 1986: 10). More important in broadcasting than Bill C-58 was Canadian legislation (1968) to cut back foreign investment in this sector to a maximum of 20% only – the only initiative ever taken in Canada to lessen existing foreign ownership in a particular industry by law. In addition, the Canadian Radio-television and Telecommunications Commission imposed Canadian-content rules for both radio and television, not only to "Canadianize" media content, but also to foster the domestic film- and tv-production industry. Since 1968, 50% of all television content has to be devoted to homemade productions, the quota in radio was set at the 30% level.

- A Canadian film industry would not exist without various government programs, subsidies, and public institutions, the first of these being the National Film Board, established in 1939 to produce and distribute documentaries, and the Canadian Film Development Fund (now Telefilm Canada), which spends some Can $ 60 million a year on drama and feature-film production for both television and the cinema. The essential importance of government subsidies becomes evident when the structure of the Canadian film distribution system is considered: Since 1947, distribution is totally under the control of the Motion Picture Association of America, a subsidiary of the Hollywood majors. In addition, the two largest cinema chains in Canada (Odeon and Famous Players) are controlled by Paramount (belonging to the U.S. media conglomerate Gulf and Western). Due to these structural conditions, no Canadian government or regulating body to the present day has been able to impose screen quotas for domestic film productions (as exist, for example, in France and Great Britain). The effect is that from nearly 450 feature films produced in Canada between 1968 and 1978, only 14 reached the screens of the two major cinema chains (Pendakur 1981: 34). Today, about 80% of all Canadian box-office revenues (with only 1% earned with Canadian films) are going abroad (Fox 1984: 37). These are obviously conditions under which government subsidies can hardly be blamed as "unfair competition" (Moynihan) to U.S. service industries.

When Clayton Yeutter, White House trade representative and U.S. chief negotiator, came for his first visit to Ottawa in December 1985, he nevertheless made clear that he wanted cultural industries to be an issue in the talks. Said Yeutter: "I would be concerned if the term culture is defined in such a way that it would have a major dampening impact on the overall negotiating process" (*Canadian News Facts*, January 4, 1986). But despite the strong verbal commitment to political and cultural sovereignty made by Mulroney, it had already become evident a month earlier that the Canadian government was willing to accept these U.S. conditions, when a secret plan of how the free trade issue should be handled in public was published by *Maclean's* (November 11, 1985 b), leading to what the magazine called "shock and bewilderment in Canada's cultural community" (*Maclean's*, November 18, 1985 c).

The real test case for how far the U.S. was prepared to go was the purchase of the Canadian publisher Prentice-Hall by the U.S. company Gulf and Western in March 1986. Gulf and Western (with its already-mentioned dominant position in Canadian film distribution) also owns two other Canadian publishing houses (Globe Modern Curriculum Press and Allyn and Bacon Publishers, both educational publishers), as well as the New York based publishing house of Simon and Schuster. Gulf and Western threatened – introducing military vocabulary into an economic issue – to adopt a "scorched-earth policy in Canada" if it was to be pressured to sell a majority share of Prentice-Hall to Canadian owners (Bahr 1986:3). The Canadian government finally reached a solution forcing Gulf and Western to give up its majority in its two other Canadian branches, rather than selling a single share of Prentice-Hall to Canadians. The way in which this deal was handled did a lot to change the friendly climate in Canada towards free trade, with the public now seeing its own government under heavy pressure from the American side to pay an "entrance fee" for trade talks: "The lobby from Gulf and Western was absolutely incredible," a Canadian official was quoted in the Toronto *Globe and Mail* afterwards as saying, "It was heavy. It was directed from the White House to the Prime Minister's office" (Bahr 1986: 4).

6 Will Canada Be the Loser in the Free Trade Deal?

For more than a year the trade negotiations continued without any significant progress. In the United States there was only little attention paid to the possible creation of the world's largest free trade zone. Only a few days before the Congressional deadline of October 5, when a draft had to be submitted, the widespread ignorance was "slowly turning into quiet interest" (*Globe and Mail*, August 5, 1987). This "quiet interest" was demonstrated by some influential members of the U.S. Senate Finance Committee, in August 1987, who declared that "Congressional approval of a pact would hinge on Canada easing its stance on such items as foreign investment and a binding trade disputes mechanism" (*Globe and Mail*, August 7, 1987). A binding procedure to settle transborder trade disputes was one of the key issues in the talks, because the Canadians insisted on a body making them independent from Congressional decisions in the U.S. The Senators were accompanied by a coalition of some 50 members of the House of Representatives from 18 northeast and midwest states, who made clear that "if the United States is to seriously consider pursuing a viable dispute resolution mechanism, the foremost and clearest concern is therefore that Canada agrees to bring its subsidy programs and policies to the negotiating table" (*Globe and Mail*, August 7, 1987).

In Canada, the final stage of the negotiations was overshadowed by a dramatical shift in public opinion towards the governing Progressive Conservatives, who made free trade the key issue on their political agenda. In March 1987 the polls showed a disastrous approval rating of only 22% for the Mulroney government – the lowest for the Tories since 1942 (*Business Week*, March 19, 1987). The explanation, according to *Business Week*, is that: "Mulroney is now widely regarded as too submissive to the U.S. Voters fear that Canada will be the loser in free trade negotations with the U.S., and that Mulroney is an ineffectual defender of Canadian interests.... Those who worry about overwhelming U.S. cultural influence are concerned that Mulroney will make the nation more vulnerable by cutting subsidies to the publishing, broadcasting, and film industries.

Thus, political pressure on the Mulroney government was high. In the final stage of the talks, Canadian negotiators made the creation of an independent body to resolve any arising trade conflicts the sticking point – one of the key demands of both the Liberals and the NDP. Due to U.S. resistance, the Canadians finally agree to a vague paragraph that panels of Canadian and American experts would be empowered to "mediate" arising trade disputes (*Time*, October 19, 1987 b). What was the outcome concerning other highly controversial issues such as cultural industries, foreign investment, or farming?

- In the case of cultural industries, the Canadians reached a limited success. They are permitted to continue to take measures to promote cultural development such as T.V. and radio content quotas or government subsidies for film production. But in the Agreement, these activities are limited to publishing, film, video music, and broadcasting – and are not to be extended to other industries. The U.S.A. was unable to get Bill C-58 rescinded (no tax deduction for Canadian advertising in foreign media circulating predominantly in Canada). On the other hand, the Americans won a major concession in the case of retransmission of American satellite signals in Canada. Up to now Canadian cable-T.V. systems have distributed U.S. signals without paying any fees to the American-originating stations. Now the Canadian government has to provide copyright protection for satellite signals which could mean higher rates for Canadian cable-television subscribers (*Inside U.S. Trade*, October 9, (IUST) 1987: 10).

- With regard to farming, Canadian wine producers are expected to be the losers in the deal. The Canadians agreed to eliminate their pricing system for American wine, which had kept prices artificially high, within the next seven years. Over the same period American wine producers are guaranteed increased access to the Canadian distribution and marketing networks (IUST 1987: 15).
- The Auto Pact remains unchanged, which could be regarded as a Canadian (and, first of all, Ontarian) success. But Canada had to agree that no other car manufacturers are permitted to receive Pact or Pact-like benefits. That means that the U.S.-Canadian auto trade will remain a business between the big American car manufacturers and their Canadian branches (IUST 1987: 14).
- In the most sensitive sector – energy – both sides agreed to prohibit any restriction of import and export. Canada additionally agreed not to return to the restricive investment policy in this sector existing from 1980 to 1984 under the legislation of Trudeau's NEP (IUST 1987: 15). This has to be regarded as a very far-reaching Canadinan concession concerning not only the future of this most important Canadian industry, but also in its limitation of political decision-making in general.
- Finally, in the issue of foreign direct investment, it was the explicit American objective not to harm the already far-reaching liberalization of the investment climate as installed by the Mulroney government. Thus, a "freeze" of these standards could be seen as an American success. But the Canadians were ready to make major concessions in this area too: under the trade agreement no foreign firm with assets of less than Can $ 150 million will be screened in its investment policy in Canada. This reduces the possible total number of foreign firms to be reviewed under the Investment Canada Act from the present 7,500 to only 500. For Canadian firms which are affected indirectly due to changing ownership of their parent companies in the U.S., Canada also agreed to stop all review activities (IUST 1987: 18).

From this outline of only the most important aspects of the Free Trade Agreement between Canada and the United States, it appears to be more than unlikely that free trade will not dominate the Canadian political debate at the federal and provincial levels before the Agreement comes into effect in January 1989. The resource-rich and export-oriented western provinces will certainly agree and Ontario's doubts might be weakened by the further extension of the Auto Pact. The opposition parties have already announced their strong resistance. Liberal leader John Turner summarized the critical views on the very day the pact became public: "When he was elected, our

Prime Minister said that Canada was open for business. Today the Prime Minister has put Canada up for sale" (*Time*, October 19, 1987 b). The United States, in its turn, is already preparing the next step: its negotiators are now looking for further trade liberalization with its southern neighbors, Mexico and in the Caribbean, to create the world's largest free trade area – North and Middle America (*Economist*, February 6, 1988).

References

Appel Molot, Maureen and Glen Williams (1984): The Political Economy of Continentalism. In Michael S. Whittington and Glen Williams (eds.), *Canadian Politics in the 1980s*. Toronto: Methuen, 81 – 104.

Bahr, Frank M. (1986): Cultural Babies and the Buyout Bathwater – a European view of what may go down the trade negotiations drain. Marburg, unpublished paper.

Business Week (1987): How the Free Trade Talks are Clobbering Canada's Tories. March 19: 31.

Canadian News Facts (1984): Mulroney Sells Canada in New York. 18(22), Dec. 19.

Canadian News Facts (1985): Investment Bill to be Changed. 19(7), April 19.

Canadian News Facts (1985): Foreign Investment Bill Passed. 19(11), June 19.

Canadian News Facts (1985): Macdonald Report on the Economy. 19(16), Sept. 19.

Canadian News Facts (1985): Bourassa Warns About Free Trade/PM Stresses Cultural Sovereignty/Report Rejects Freer Trade. 19(22), Dec. 19.

Canadian News Facts (1986): Free Trade Movement is Formed/U.S. Wants Full Trade Talks. 20(1), Jan. 4.

Clarkson, Stephen (1978): Anti-Nationalism in Canada – The Ideology of Mainstream-Economics. *Canadian Review of Studies in Nationalism* 5(1): 45 – 65.

Clarkson, Stephen (1982): Canada and the Reagan Challenge. *Canadian Forum* 62(723): 7 – 13 and 35.

Economist (1988): The Yukon to the Usumacinto. February 5: 68 – 69.

Fay, Terrence (1980): The Proposed Canadian-United States Customs Union, 1947 – 1948 – A Bold and Striking Plan. *Bulletin of Canadian Studies* 4(1): 39 – 53.

Fox, Francis (1984): *The National Film and Video Policy*. Ottawa: Minister of Supply and Services Canada.

Gibbins, Roger (1985): *Conflict and Unity – An Introduction to Canadian Political Life*. Toronto: Butterworths.

Globe and Mail (1987): Canada-Watchers Sceptical on Trade. Aug. 5: A1.

Globe and Mail (1987): U.S.-Congressmen Give Advice on Canadian Concessions. Aug. 7: A2.

Holmes, John W. (1976): *Canada – A Middle-Aged Power*. Toronto: MacClelland and Stewart.

Inside U.S. Trade (1987): Confidential Appraisal of U.S.-Canada Pact Weighs Benefits, Shortfalls. Oct. 9 (Special): 14 – 20.

Kasurak, Peter (1979): American "Dollar Diplomats" in Canada, 1927 – 1941 – A Study of Bureaucratic Politics. *American Review of Canadian Studies* 9(2): 57 – 71.

Maclean's (1985 a): Free Trade/MacDonald's Masterplan. Sept. 16: 24 – 38 and 12.

Maclean's (1985 b). A Secret Plan for Free Trade and Sovereignty. Nov. 11: 14 – 21.

Maclean's (1985 c): The Battle over the Cultural Border. Nov. 18: 69.

Maclean's (1987 a): On the March/Not Just Another Nice Guy/Now the NDP Would Govern. Aug. 3: 8 – 11, 12 – 13; and 14 – 15.

Maclean's (1987 b): Potential Victims of a Trade Pact. Aug. 10: 22 – 23.

Maclean's (1987 c): Hard Lines on Trade. Aug. 17: 34.

Maclean's (1987 d): The Big Red Wave. Sept. 21: 12 – 16.

Naylor, Tom (1973): The History of Domestic and Foreign Capital in Canada. In Robert Laxer (ed.), *Canada Ltd. – The Political Economy of Dependency*. Toronto: MacClelland and Stewart, 42 – 56.

Pendakur, Manjunath (1981): Cultural Dependency in Canada's Film Industry. *Journal of Communiction* 31(3): 34.

Robinson, Lukin (1984): Recovery or Stagnation? *Canadian Forum* 63(735): 7.

Saywell, John (1983): *Kanada einst und heute*. Toronto: Clarke Irwin.

Time (1987a): Eye for Eye, Tooth for Tooth – The U.S. uses Brinkmanship to Handle a Trade Dispute. Jan. 12: 36.

Time (1987b): Big Hug from Uncle Sam. Oct. 19: 38.

Vancouver Status of Women (1987): *What Women Should Know About Free Trade*. Vancouver: Vancouver Status of Women.

Whittington, Michael S. and Isten Williams (1984): Canadian Politics in the 1980s. Toronto: Methuen.

Woller, Rudolf (1986): Handelskrieg zwischen USA und Kanada? *Canada Journal* 4(7 – 8): 44.

Wonnacott, Paul (1987): The United States and Canada: The Quest For Free Trade – An Examination of Selected Issues. *Policy Analysis in International Economics*. March, No. 16. Washington D.C.: Institute for International Economics.

Part IV
Security Policy

NATO Costs and U.S. Economic Imbalances

David P. Calleo

One way or another, the American economy has been in deficit to the world economy nearly every year since the end of the Second World War. Most years throughout the entire postwar period, for example, the so-called basic balance – designed to measure the external relations of the "real economy" (current account plus long-term capital flows) – has been negative. Since the early 1970s, the U.S. has also generally run a trade deficit and, since the 1980s, a current account deficit as well (Table 1).

Table 1. U.S. basic balance of payments 1950–1984 (current account plus long-term capital flows; in millions of dollars)

	Basic balance	Trade balance[d]	Current account[d]
1950	–3,432[a]	1,122	–1,840
1955	–1,461[a]	2,897	430
1960	–1,138[b]	4,892	2,824
1965	–1,923[b]	4,951	5,431
1970	–3,891[b]	2,603	2,331
1975	666[b]	8,903	18,116
1980	–6,612[c]	–25,480	1,873
1984	–75,204[c]	–112,522	–106,466

Sources:
[a] Organization for Economic Cooperation and Development (1964: 16, 18).
[b] Organization for Economic Cooperation and Development (1979: 10–11).
[c] International Monetary Fund (1986a: 23).
[d] Economic Report of the President 1987 (358).

In the early postwar years, America's external deficit helped pay for European and Japanese reconstruction and defense and was therefore a major boon for the rest of the world. Since the mid-1960s, it has been an increasingly serious problem, both reflecting and exacerbating America's growing difficulty in fitting its economy within a liberal international economic regime. The American imbalances have greatly strained that regime. The U.S. payments deficit broke down the Bretton Woods international monetary system in August of 1971; an unsteady dollar has meant increasingly chaotic international monetary conditions thereafter. By now, in the last years of the 1980s, America's monetary and trade problems with the international economy have led to widespread fears of a gradual or perhaps catastrophic breakdown of the postwar economic order.

Creating and sustaining a global liberal economy has ostensibly been among the fundamental goals of postwar American geopolitical strategy. Why has the United States been perpetually out of equilibrium with such an economy? Why has it, in other words, been so unable to live within the rules of international economic conduct laid down by itself?

There are several approaches to answering the question. Economists regularly come forward with ad hoc, short-term explanations. Either U.S. macroeconomic policy is said to be expanding too rapidly or European and Japanese too slowly (see McCulloch's and Destler's contributions to this volume). Longer-term explanations blame protectionist and mercantilist tendencies in Europe and Japan, insufficiently flexible mechanisms for adjusting inappropriate exchange rates, or cultural changes bringing a decline in America's work ethic, thriftiness, or entrepreneurship. Europeans tend to blame American policies and institutions, Americans to blame European policies and structures. Both unite to blame the Japanese.

Broad geopolitical explanations have also had considerable appeal. The American deficit can be seen as the result of overextended American military commitments. Such a view seemed only natural in the late 1960s and early 1970s, when the acute problems of the dollar and the demise of the Bretton Woods system coincided with the Vietnam War.

In recent years, this geopolitical explanation has gained credibility from the widely perceived link betwen America's internal fiscal deficit and its external balance of payments deficit. An American fiscal deficit, of course, is hardly a new phenomenon. Since 1960, the United States has run such a fiscal deficit every year but one (Economic Report of the President 1987: 331). In the Reagan era, however, these fiscal deficits have reached astonishing dimensions; their coincidence with similarly gargantuan payments deficits makes a connection seem highly plausible. That these Reagan fiscal deficits are themselves closely tied to an extraordinary increase in the U.S. military budget during the Reagan years helps complete the chain of cause and effect that links the payments deficit to geopolitical causes. Finally, the very large proportion of U.S. military spending that can be attributed to forces for NATO (roughly half the annual total according to some estimates from the Department of Defense itself) suggests that America's economic imbalances – its fiscal and payments deficits – are particularly tied to its preponderant role in the defense of Europe.

While present circumstances give a certain plausibility to geopolitical explanations for the economic imbalances, how well do these explanations stand up to a more rigorous economic and political analysis?

The direct effect of NATO spending on the balance of payments is minimal. The net exchange costs of NATO forces are generally reckoned at not more than a few billion dollars each year – not very significant against a current account deficit that exceeded $ 40 billion in 1983 and has been well over $ 100 billion annually in the years following.[1] Instead, whatever serious effect the NATO commitment has on U.S. external economic imbalances passes through a chain of cause and effect that starts with NATO's place in the military budget and extends to the effects of that budget on U.S. fiscal policy, to the relationship in the U.S. political economy between fiscal and monetary policy, and finally to the consequences of monetary policy for the balance of payments. In other words, assessing the geopolitical link to economic imbalances requires a systemic analysis of the connections between the NATO commitment, U.S. macroeconomic policy, and the behavior of the American political economy in the world political economy. Such a systemic analysis involves all sorts of complex methodological issues as well as a wide range of political judgments. Any model is likely to be extremely untidy. The rest of this chapter will try to sketch the main elements and issues to be addresseed by such a model.

1 NATO and U.S. Fiscal Policy

For a start, how does NATO spending affect U.S. fiscal policy? Getting some grasp on this question requires considering its two constituent elements:

- The weight of NATO expenditures in the U.S. military budget
- The weight of the military budget in America's fiscal deficit

1.1 NATO and the U.S. Military Budget

Experts differ over the proportion of U.S. military spending that can be attributed to NATO forces. The Pentagon during the Reagan administration has estimated the needs of NATO forces in fiscal 1985 at roughly 58% of the military budget – some $ 177 billion of the $ 306 billion requested.[2] Earl Ravenal, a well-known private analyst with extensive Pentagon experience, estimated the 1985 request for NATO at $ 129 billion (40% of the total request), as contrasted with $ 47 billion for the forces for Asia and $ 59 billion for the "global" Rapid Deployment Force. Ravenal's estimate for the NATO portion of the fiscal 1986 budget rose to $ 134 billion, or 42.5% of the $ 314 billion requested.[3]

Whatever the precise figure, it is very large and a very substantial proportion of the defense budget. Every year, Ravenal estimates, NATO's proportion has been from 40% to 50% of the total defense budget. The reason is not difficult to understand. Conventional forces are far more expensive than strategic nuclear forces. Ravenal estimates the requests for strategic forces in fiscal 1985 at only 23% of the total, as opposed to corresponding figures of 40% for conventional European forces. A large part of U.S. conventional forces are tied to the European commitment. Of its 18 standing army divisions, for example, the United States earmarks ten for European defense. Five are stationed in Europe and five remain ready in the U.S. for quick deployment to Europe.[4]

America's NATO force requirements are not only very large, but also unusually costly. American conventional forces are in general expensive. Manpower must be hired at economically competitive wages since the United States does not have conscription.[5] Continental Europeans may find this peculiar but traditionally the United States never had conscription or a large standing army in peacetime. The nearly 30 years of the draft army after World War II was a great exception in American history. By 1973, the reaction to Vietnam combined with the absence of any convincing territorial threat brought a return to the normal historical pattern. A reversion to conscription seems unlikely without some sharp new sense of threat.

Since the NATO theater is an ocean away, American NATO forces have exceptionally heavy and expensive logistical requirements. Geopraphy also denies the United States the possibility of relying heavily on being able to deploy expeditiously a cheap army of reserves. In short, in contrast to the Soviets or other European powers, the U.S. has a substantial comparative disadvantage in deploying ground forces in Europe. Hence the great expense of the conventional forces it does deploy or earmark for Europe.

If the United States no longer committed ten standing divisions for NATO, what would it do with them? If they were needed for other purposes, the budgetary savings might be minimal. But if any substantial part of the forces were disbanded, the savings could be very large. Ravenal proposes allocating three divisions to an "Atlantic" force (as opposed to the current ten for NATO) – along with seven tactical air wing equivalents and three carrier battle groups. As he reckoned it in 1986, his new force structure, if adopted, would, by 1995, mean that instead of having spent a cumulative $ 2.2 trillion on NATO, the U.S. would have spent only $ 900 billion. Ultimately, with his reorganization, only 26% of U.S. defense spending would be absorbed by NATO, as opposed to his current estimate of 42%. Ravenal's NATO proposals are part of his general plan for reorganizing U.S. forces. He has proposed overall land forces of eight divisions (six army and two marine), in contrast to the eighteen army and three marine requested by the Reagan administration for 1986. By 1995, his overall force structure would be costing, as he reckoned it, only $ 158 billion in annual expenditures (in 1986 dollars), as opposed to the Reagan request in 1986 for $ 314 billion, which he estimated would lead to an annual defense budget of close to $ 750 billion by 1995. This latter figure highlights another feature of current American defense spending: its rapid rise in projected annual expenditures, the reasons for which will be discussed in a later section (Ravenal 1985b: 69; see also Ravenal 1985a: 1032).

Our aim here is not to debate the merits of alternative estimates and force structures. Rather it is to show that U.S. NATO forces are a substantial portion of the U.S. military budget. Whatever may be thought of Ravenal's more radical proposals, cutting and disbanding U.S. NATO forces even by half could, for example, easily save in due course, from 10% to 20% annually on the military budget, i. e., from $ 30 billion to $ 60 billion in current annual expenditures and substantially more in the projected annual expenditures for the next decade.[6]

1.2 The Military Budget and the Fiscal Deficit

To put these NATO costs in macroeconomic perspective requires considering, first of all, the role of the military budget in the federal fiscal situation. In 1984, for example, military spending accounted for some 27% of the overall federal budget and 16.6% of overall government spending in the U.S. (U.S. Department of Commerce 1987: 317; International Monetary Fund 1986b: 934). The American budget deficit for fiscal 1986 was $ 220.7 billion, with total spending at $ 989.8 billion. The current estimates for fiscal 1987 are $ 173.2 billion for the deficit and $ 1,015.6 billion for total federal outlays (Economic Report of the President 1987: 331). A NATO saving of $ 30 billion to $ 60 billion would, on the face of it, have a substantial fiscal impact although it would hardly, by itself, be a panacea for America's fiscal difficulties.

Logically there is no intrinsic reason to attribute a fiscal deficit to one sort of spending rather than to another. Major European states, for example, spend in proportion to GNP substantially less on defense than the U.S. (Table 2). Despite lower defense spending, European states also frequently have fiscal difficulties (Table 3).

European fiscal problems are often blamed on what are seen to be the excessive claims of the welfare system on the public purse. Why not blame American deficits on civilian overspending? For that matter, why not attribute the American deficit to undertaxing rather than overspending? American levels of taxation, for example, are markedly lower than European (Table 4).

Table 2. 1984 Defense spending as percent of GNP and in $ per capita

	% GNP	$ per capita
FRG	3.3	328
France	4.1	370
Italy	2.7	161
U.K.	5.5	416
U.S.	6.4	1001

Source: International Institute for Strategic Studies (1987: 212).

Table 3 . General government financial balances
(in percentage of GNP or GDP)

	1975 – 84[a]	1985	1986[b]	1987[c]	1988[c]
FRG	– 3.1	– 1.1	– 1.0	– 1.0	– 1.1
France	– 1.6	– 2.6	– 2.8	– 2.8	– 2.6
U.S.	– 1.9	– 3.5	– 3.2	– 2.9	– 2.5

[a] Average
[b] Preliminary
[c] Projected
Source: International Monetary Fund (1987: 14).

Table 4. Tax revenues as percent of GDP (all levels of government, social security contributions included)

	1980	1984
FRG	38.0	37.7
France	42.5	45.5
Italy	33.2	41.2
Netherlands	45.8	45.5
U.K.	35.3	38.5
U.S.	30.4	29.0

Source: U.S. Department of Commerce (1987: 828).

In effect, any practical judgment on the role of one fiscal element or another in causing the American deficit must presuppose some model for what is a *normal* balance between levels and types of expenditure and the levels and types of taxation in an advanced industrial society like the United States. Obviously judgments of this sort involve a high degree of conjecture.

2 U.S. and European "Fiscal Profiles"

The analyst can hope to give some objectivity to his judgment through a comparative study – both among similar countries or, over time, within the same country. Statistical comparisons between countries, of course, always have questionable elements. Nevertheless, if it can be demonstrated that the contemporary U.S.A. has a distinctive "fiscal profile," a pattern of taxation and expenditure different from other countries or from itself at another time, the differences may give some insight into the causes for the heavy fiscal deficits of recent years. For a comparative study to have plausibility, the countries and circumstances must be similar enough to justify a comparison. Comparisons between proportions of military spending in the United States and in Denmark, for instance, or contrasts between American military spending in 1935 and 1955, are not likely to yield any convincing general norms.

In trying to develop some norm for American behavior perhaps the most appropriate cross-country comparisons are with France and Germany. While these European states may not be global superpowers, they are major states with military establishments ranking in size and modernity among the world's half-dozen greatest. Both are also rich capitalist democracies with highly developed standards of public welfare.

In their fiscal profiles, France and Germany resemble each other more closely than either resembles the United States, although all three have run substantial fiscal deficits during one period or another. The most striking European/American fiscal contrast lies, first of all, in the level of spending and taxation: per-capita rates of both are much higher in the two European states than in the U.S.A. Secondly, the balance between civilian and military spending is different: the civilian spending of European governments is much larger proportionately than the American (Table 5).

2.1 Why are U.S. Taxes Lower?

Perhaps the most interesting practical question raised by these fiscal comparisons is why Europeans tolerate so much higher levels of taxation than do Americans. If Americans paid the same proportion of their GDP in taxes as

Table 5. 1983 Central government expenditures (and revenues)

	FRG	France	U.S.A.
Expenditures as % of GDP	31.5	44.8	26.2
Revenues as % of GDP	29.4	41.9	19.9
Social security and welfare as % of central govt. spending	50.0	44.0	34.0
Defense:			
as % of GDP	2.9	3.3	6.1
as % of central govt. spending	9.3	7.4	23.7

Source: International Monetary Fund (1986b: 52, 74, 80 and 82).

the French and Germans do, the American fiscal deficit would vanish. If Europeans paid only the same proportion of their national incomes in taxes as the Americans, European fiscal deficits would presumably be enormous.

Why are American taxes so low? Various answers can be imagined. America is, after all, the land of the Boston Tea Party. The Slogan of the American Revolution was, "No taxation without representation," an interesting contrast with the "Liberty, equality, and fraternity" of the French, or the "Peace, bread, and land" of the Soviets.

While such anthropological explanations may have their place, a link between objects of spending and taxation levels seems at least equally plausible. In effect, the European taxpayer receives a great deal back from his taxes. To a degree never approached in America, the European welfare state is a welfare state for the middle class. Higher education and medical care are mostly financed by the state rather than the individual consumer. Public spending provides safe and well-kept cities, good public transport and highways, along with amenities particularly dear to the middle class, like theater and opera. Publicly funded pensions are much more generous and much more geared to previous income. It is perhaps then not so surprising that there is a constituency for taxation in Europe that does not exist in America. Whether a European sort of welfare state could produce tolerance for European-scale taxes in America is an interesting question. The experiment has never been tried. It is also worth noting that U.S. taxes are much more direct than European, which means that they fall more heavily and obviously on middle-class incomes and real property.

In short, comparing the direction of spending and the incidence of taxation across the Atlantic seems to help explain why U.S. tax levels are substantially lower. The comparison also suggests that hoping to balance the present fiscal deficit by seeking European tax levels is rather unrealistic politically. Heavy civilian spending is the other side of Europe's high taxes. To expect one without the other seems improbable in a democracy. Common sense therefore suggests that raising taxes is not likely to be the simple solution to America's fiscal imbalance that some analysts and politicians have suggested. Changing the tax/GNP ratio would very probably require changing the civilian/military mix.

2.2 Fiscal Balance and Economic Growth

What about the possibility for achieving fiscal balance through more rapid economic growth? Politically, it is usually easier to raise tax rates at a time of rapid growth and rising incomes than of slow growth or declining incomes. In any event, since greater economic growth generally means disproportionately increased state revenues, a fiscal deficit can logically be blamed on the failure of an economy to grow sufficiently.

This relationship between general growth and fiscal balance confronts fiscal policy with a basic paradox: policies that seek to balance a budget may lower growth and thereby make fiscal balance unachievable. Conversely, a "full-employment budget" that plans a deficit may result in growth that eliminates the deficit. This theoretical debate has often dominated practical politics. The "Reagan revolution," for example, was based on the so-called Laffer curve which presumed that radical tax cuts would generate enough growth and new income to compensate.[7] Fiscally, the experiment has not been a great success in the 1980s, although proponents often argue that it did succeed in the mid-1960s.

Noting the connection between fiscal balance and general economic growth raises another elusive connection: between America's economic growth and its high rate of military spending. Does high military spending stimulate or retard growth? The evidence is unclear.[8] Heavy U.S. military spending has had a high technological spinoff, but does public support for technology need the military rationale? Would direct subsidies to civilian technology be a more efficient wax to promote growth? How much does the military emphasis in U.S. technology inhibit its commercial application? Despite the technological spinoff from high military spending, average U.S. growth has been slower than Japanese or West European, for whatever reason, throughout much of the postwar period (Table 6). The comparatively rapid growth during the Reagan era may seem an exception, but this recent U.S. growth has been linked to a presumably unsustainable level of foreign borrowing (Table 7). Over the years, the most rapid growth has, in fact, been enjoyed by the Japanese, who have had, by far, the lowest military spending. To add insult to injury, they seem particularly competitive in products requiring the commercial application of high technology.

Table 6. Growth rates in real GDP

	1953 – 1972[a]	1973 – 1979[b]	1979 – 1982[b]
FRG	5.2	2.4	1.0
France	5.5	3.1	0.2
Italy	5.3	2.6	1.2
Japan	9.7	3.6	4.1
U.S.	3.7	2.6	0.1

Sources:
[a] Boltho (1975: 9).
[b] Organization for Economic Cooperation and Development (1984: 44).

Table 7. U.S. current account, net foreign claims, fiscal and savings-investment balances (1985 – 1988) in percentage of GNP/GDP

	actual		projected	
	1985	1986	1987	1988
Current account balance	– 2.9	– 3.3	– 3.1	– 2.7
Net foreign claims	– 2.2	– 5.3	– 8.2	– 10.4
General government financial balance	– 2.9	– 3.3	– 3.1	– 2.7
Private saving	17.0	16.2	16.3	16.8
Gross private investment	16.5	16.3	16.5	17.0

Sources:
International Monetary Fund (IMF) 1987: Tables 3 and 5, pp. 14, 18).
According to an IMF projection, assuming that real exchange rates remain unchanged, and cumulating the consequences of their resulting current account projections, the U.S. net debtor position was 8.2% of GNP in 1987 and should reach 17% of GNP in 1991 and still be increasing (IMF 1987: 18).

In summary, the international comparison of fiscal practices does demonstrate that the U.S. has a distinctive fiscal profile, one with proportionately lower civilian spending and taxation and a markedly greater emphasis on military spending. If anything, international comparison suggests that a high proportion of military spending limits the relative capacity to tax, but does not induce enough general economic growth to compensate adequately.

3 U.S. Military Budgets over Time

If comparative international analysis suggests the difficulty of raising U.S. taxes to cover higher military costs, comparing American military budgets from one postwar decade to another seems to point to a different conclusion. It is commonly noted that the U.S. was able to sustain a much heavier defense burden in proportion to GNP in the earlier postwar period; and it is often implied that only the pusillanimity of its leaders, or the decline of political consensus, prevents the U.S. from doing so now. Broadly speaking, since 1960 the civilian sector of the American budget has grown dramatically in relative terms, while the military sector has shrunk in relative but not absolute terms. The exaggerated fiscal imbalance of the 1980s results from restoring the military sector of the budget, at least in part, but without raising the overall tax burden[9] or shrinking the civilian sector. These trends suggest two fundamental explanations for the current fiscal imbalance:

1. The U.S. civilian sector has grown too large for fiscal stability.
2. The Reagan military budget is unnecessarily large.

As can be seen in Table 8, the United States entered the 1960s with a very high percentage of GNP devoted to military outlays (9.5%). National defense was 56.4% of the total federal budget. By 1965, the military spending as a percentage of GNP had fallen to 7.5%, and as a percentage of federal outlays had fallen to 45.9%. By 1970, despite the Vietnam War, the proportions remained roughly the same, although the absolute amount of military spending, in constant dollars, had jumped from $ 181.4 billion to $ 225.6 billion. Starting in 1971, the defense proportion of federal spending began to decline rather sharply – from 44.3% of outlays in 1970 to 23.8% in 1978. As a percentage of GNP, military spending fell from 8.2% to GNP in 1970 to 4.8% in 1978. Meanwhile, civilian expenditures grew, from 11.6% of GNP in 1970 to 16.3% in 1978. In effect, the United States had gradually acquired a welfare state, although still not on anything like the scale of France and Germany.

3.1 Can American Civilian Expenditures Be Cut?

What about achieving balance by cutting U.S. civilian spending? To argue that the U.S. should reduce its comparatively low level of civilian spending seems implausible in international terms. It presupposes that Americans will be permanently more willing to do without the state services common in comparably rich countries, or that these services can be provided more efficiently and cheaply in the U.S. Neither proposition is convincing. It is significant, moreover, that even the most conservative European governments have been unable, and indeed unwilling, to do anything other than slow the growth of civilian spending. Among the Europeans, moreover, relatively high civilian spending has been combined with relatively higher revenues than in the U.S.; in the German case, at least, the combination achieves a substantially better fiscal performance than in the U.S.

Table 8. Federal budget and defense spending in billions of 1982 dollars

	Total Outlays	Defense	Def. as % Outlays	Outlays as % GNP	Defense as % GNP	Nondef. as % GNP
1950[a]	42.6	12.4	29.1	15.9	5.1	10.8
1955[a]	66.5	39.9	60.0	17.7	11.0	6.7
1960	340.4	192.1	56.4	18.2	9.5	8.7
1965	394.9	181.4	45.9	17.6	7.5	10.1
1970	509.4	225.6	44.3	19.8	8.2	11.6
1975	586.0	159.8	27.3	21.8	5.7	16.1
1976	609.8	153.6	25.2	21.9	5.3	16.6
1977	622.6	154.3	24.8	21.1	5.0	16.1
1978	652.2	155.0	23.8	21.1	4.8	16.3
1979	660.2	159.1	24.1	20.5	4.7	15.8
1980	699.1	164.0	23.5	22.2	5.0	17.2
1981	726.5	171.4	23.6	22.7	5.3	17.4
1982	745.7	185.3	24.8	23.7	5.9	17.8
1983	776.5	200.8	25.9	24.3	6.3	18.0
1984	788.8	210.4	26.7	23.1	6.2	16.9
1985	846.1	226.7	26.8	24.0	6.4	17.6
1986[b]	850.0	232.0	27.3	23.4	6.3	17.1

[a] U.S. Department of Commerce (1975: 314). Figures are in current rather than 1982 dollars

[b] Estimated

Source:

U.S. Department of Commerce (1987: Tables 479, 481, and 521; pp. 292, 295, and 317).

3.2 Are Reagan's Defense Costs Too High?

What of the second proposition, i.e., that the Reagan defense budget has been much higher than needed? Defenders of the Reagan increases can observe how defense spending had declined sharply as a proportion of GNP. But defense outlays (in constant 1982 dollars) did not decline nearly as precipitously in absolute terms. Defense outlays in 1960 were $ 192.1 billion (9.5% of GNP and 56.4% of federal outlays). In 1965 outlays were $ 181.4 billion, or 7.5% of GNP and 45.9% of federal outlays. By 1976, their lowest year, defense outlays were $ 153.6 billion (5.3% of GNP and 25.2% of federal outlays). By 1980, the last year of the Carter administration, the absolute defense outlay had risen to $ 164.0 billion. Not until 1982 was absolute defense spending at the pre-Vietnam level of 1965. By 1983, absolute spending ($ 200.8 billion) had surpassed the 1960 level. In other words, the decline of U.S. defense spending in the 1970s was sharper when considered as a percentage of GNP or federal outlays than when measured in absolute or constant dollars.

The relative constancy of these absolute figures, however, understates the real decline in America's military position, a deterioration brought about by both internal and external developments. Internally, since America's comparative advantage over the Soviets lies in advanced technology, the increasing complexity of American weapons probably means that to maintain the traditional lead, real U.S. defense costs must, if anything, increase regularly in absolute terms. Unless defense costs rise less rapidly than other costs in the economy – an improbable assumption – defense is thus likely to want a progressively greater rather than lesser share of U.S. national income. In short, over time, if U.S. defense spending is remaining constant in real terms, military preparedness is probably declining.

Aside from this general point about the trend to more expensive weapons, the end of conscription and the switch to an all-volunteer professional army also raised American defense costs sharply, above all for manpower – a development of particular significance for the NATO commitment. In short, with manpower costs having risen much more than the general price level, constant defense spending, even when adjusted for general inflation, probably means real military decline.

Along with this internally driven decline has come an additional deterioration of the U.S. balance with the Soviets caused by a quantum leap in Soviet strategic technology. Ever since Sputnik presaged the end of U.S. continental invulnerability, experts have anticipated a radical decline in the U.S. strategic position. Throughout the 1960s, however, these consequences were mitigated by the still-overwhelming U.S. superiority in the number of strategic missiles and bombers. Even after the Soviets had achieved parity in the number of launchers, adding MIRVed warheads to U.S. missiles prolonged American superiority several more years. By the mid-1970s, however, the Soviets had themselves acquired the MIRV technology, which permitted them a dramatic increase in warheads. U.S. strategic superiority suddenly began to diminish radically (see Table 9).

Growing awareness of the shifting strategic balance alarmed both Europe and the U.S.A. Without strategic superiority, America would seem dangerously overextended – in both Europe and the Middle East. The most notable fiscal result was the Carter administration's reversal of the long decline in defense spending. Carter called for a strategic buildup around a large but mobile MX missile. The United States began emphasizing new technologies in conventional defense. New "smart weapons" (precision-guided conventional missiles) were

Table 9. Growth of U.S. and Soviet strategic arsenals[a]

	1964	1971	1976	1980	1984
	(Number of ICBMs/Total)				
U.S.					
Launchers	925/2035	1054/2070	1054/2163	1054/2026	1037/1803
Warheads	925/2665	1254/4230	2154/9406	2154/8708	2137/9509
U.S.S.R.					
Launchers	200/330	1510/2090	1527/2817	1398/2557	1398/2522
Warheads	200/330	1510/2510	2339/4036	3154/5530	7460/9345

[a] As defined unter Salt 1, e. g., ICBMs, SLBMs, long-range bombers

Source: International Institute for Strategic Studies (1964, 1976, 1980, 1984).

to be used in the NATO theater to overcome Soviet superiority in manpower. Building conventional forces and tactics around these weapons promised major new increases in costs for such forces.[10]

The Reagan administration greatly augmented the Carter arms buildup. Reagan's increases emphasized technology still further, not only for conventional forces, but for "Star Wars," an anti-missile defense that could, if successful, restore the traditional American strategic lead or even the relative invulnerability of the 1950s. At the same time, the administration very substantially increased the navy.[11]

The fantasies of SDI aside, Reagan's force goals could reasonably be seen not as a wanton escalation of the arms race, but as an heroic effort to redress the long-deferred military requirements of U.S. commitments. The cost of filling these needs adequately had inevitably risen, at least in absolute terms, as U.S. strategic superiority had declined and manpower costs had soared. The declining strategic margin undermined extended deterrence and indicated the need for more adequate conventional forces, particularly in Europe, but also in the Persian Gulf.

In short, the Reagan military buildup, even if exaggerated and wasteful in execution, was probably a truer approximation of the real cost of adequately maintaining the traditional postwar military commitments than the relatively lower defense budgets of most of the 1970s. If so, substantial cuts in the Reagan military budget are not easy to reconcile with continuing all the traditional postwar commitments. Instead, the trend is that these commitments will grow steadily more expensive in the face of strategic parity, high manpower costs and high-technology weaponry for conventional as well as strategic forces.

This rising military trend, moreover, has a parallel rising civilian trend. Just as the Nixon, Ford, and early Carter years deferred military costs, and resulted in a subsequent explosion, the Reagan years have similarly built up a backlog of deferred civilian costs. Pressure is beginning to build up for a major overhaul of the American educational system, for example. In any event, an aging population implies major upward pressure on welfare costs.[12]

Consciousness of such trends in both military and civilian spending suggests that the American fiscal crisis will, if anything, grow more rather than less acute in future years. If so, one tendency is likely to be a more and more serious reconsideration of traditional entitlements, including geopolitical commitments that mandate such a large defense budget. Already there is a more urgent American interest in arms control deals with the Soviets – above all in the NATO theater – as well as a growing resentment of America's NATO commitment in circles that include many of the administration's neoconservative supporters and some of the military (e. g. Krauss 1986; Kristol 1981, 1982, 1986).

3.3 Lessons of the Reagan Buildup for U.S. Fiscal Policy

Despite its determination to reverse the decline in U.S. military capabilities, the Reagan administration was unwilling to confront the electorate with the real cost. Instead, responding to powerful popular forces, the administration sponsored a substantial cut in income taxes – even though concurrent rises in Social Security taxes meant that the overall tax burden remained roughly the same. The administration claimed it would recoup the inevitable deficit through "supply-side" growth and cuts in the civilian budget. Although a Reagan boom eventually did follow, government revenues never caught up. And while the administration did succeed in slowing the growth of civilian spending, it did not even seriously try to reverse the 1970s growth of the civilian sector. The unprecedented fiscal deficits of the 1980s were the result.[13]

Reagan's combined fiscal and military policies suggest three general hypotheses:

1. Since the Reagan administration, despite its profound determination to restore U.S. military power, was unwilling to take on the task of convincing the public to pay for the buildup through tax increases, any probable successor is unlikely to achieve (or attempt) tax increases linked to military spending.
2. While its defense buildup and reluctance to increase taxes, as well as its ideological predilections against the welfare state, logically drove the Reagan administration toward cutting civilian spending, it did not succeed

in doing so, according to some observers did not seriously try. Any probable successor is therefore unlikely to do better at cutting civilian spending.

3. Given current geopolitical commitments, cuts in military spending that would have substantial impact on the fiscal deficit would also be hazardous militarily and are therefore unlikely. Even with the Reagan buildup, the pressure of rising costs will make America's ability to continue its traditional commitments less and less secure. This hypothesis helps explain why a Democratic Congress, although highly critical of Reagan's management of the Pentagon, nevertheless has been unwilling to return to anything like the pre-Reagan levels of defense spending.

When these three propositions are taken together, they explain why the present huge American fiscal deficit is unlikely to disappear, at least as long as it can be financed without provoking any sharp cutback in American living standards.

4 Fiscal Policy and Monetary Policy

So far we have been talking primarily about the relationship between NATO spending and the U.S. fiscal imbalance. To affect the external balance, there must be a link between the fiscal imbalance and monetary conditions that affect the external balance. Although the link is widely perceived, the precise connections are complex and contentious in theory and often baffling in practice, particularly with floating exchange rates and with the dollar still the world's principal reserve and transactions currency. Probably the simplest case to analyze is where a large fiscal deficit is financed by a generous monetary policy sponsored by the central bank. Where fiscal laxness and monetary ease reinforce each other, the most natural result is some combination of capital outflow, domestic inflation and depreciating currency. If the currency depreciates fast enough, and the domestic economy is large and self-sufficient enough, the trade and current account balances can remain strong. Eventually, this formula leads to accumulating inflationary consequences with increasingly violent reactions in currency and domestic capital markets.

Such was the general American picture throughout most of the 1970s, when easy money and a declining dollar – what might be called the Nixon formula – finished off the Bretton Woods system and lasted until the currency and credit market crises of 1978 and 1979.

More complicated is a case where a country's central bank tries to maintain tight monetary conditions in the face of a large fiscal deficit. As the Federal Republic of Germany has sometimes illustrated, it is possible with such a policy to have a substantial fiscal deficit without a current account deficit (Table 10).

Table 10. Federal Republic of Germany, Fiscal and External Balances (as percent of GNP/GDP)

	Actual			Projected	
	1975–1984	1985	1986	1987	1988
General government financial balance	–3.1	–1.1	–1.0	–1.0	–1.1
Current account	0.3	2.1	4.0	3.1	2.4

Source: International Monetary Fund (1987: 13).

Tight money means that a government's fiscal deficit is financed by crowding out other borrowers in the capital market or, for a time at least, by attracting foreign capital through relatively high interest rates resulting from the tight monetary policy. With floating exchange rates, the latter course can rather quickly become self-defeating insofar as it causes the currency to appreciate and thereby lowers competitiveness and employment in domestic industry. If such trends continue, domestically produced goods are crowded out at home and abroad by cheaper foreign goods and trade and current account balances deteriorate. Even if domestic demand remains strong, domestic industry does not flourish correspondingly. Industrial profits, investment, and employment all deteriorate. Meanwhile, the rapidly growing foreign and domestically held debt begins to raise fears about the economy's long-term prospects.

In Germany, these developments ultimately produced a determined move toward fiscal balance.[14] With the borrowing needs of the government sector sharply curtailed, monetary conditions grew easier. Upward pressure on the currency lessened and Germany's trade and current account balances improved.

By 1979 the United States Federal Reserve, with Paul Volcker as its chairman, had seemingly embarked resolutely on a German-style tight money policy. Starting in 1979, the Federal Reserve succeeded in restricting monetary conditions to a degree seldom if ever before experienced in postwar U.S. capital markets. In 1981, however, the incoming Reagan administration pressed forward with its arms buildup and tax cuts, with the huge fiscal imbalance that was the natural consequence. The results were an exaggerated version of the initial German experience. Thanks to an unprecedented inflow of foreign capital, the dollar appreciated strongly. Trade and current account balances began to deteriorate sharply, which ultimately depressed the domestic economy, particularly those parts affected by the price of internationally traded goods and services (Table 11).

Table 11. U.S. Indicators 1979–1985 (% of GNP)

	Trade balance[a]	Current account[b]	Basic balance[c]	Gross fixed capital formation[b]
1979	−1.1	−0.03	−0.6	+2.4
1980	−1.1	+0.07	−0.02	+2.6
1981	−0.9	+0.21	+0.6	+2.4
1982	−1.2	−0.24	+0.1	+2.3
1983	−2.0	−1.3	−0.9	+1.8
1984	−3.1	−2.8	−1.7	+1.9
1985	−3.2	−3.0	−1.4	+2.4

Sources:
[a] Economic Report of the President (1987: 358).
[b] International Monetary Fund (1986b: 691).
[c] Organization for Economic Cooperation and Development (1986: 113).
+, surplus; −, deficit

In the United States, neither the Reagan administration nor the Congress could bring down the fiscal deficit sufficiently for a German-style solution. The gap between combined domestic entitlements and foreign goals, on the one hand, and the revenue available to the federal government, on the other, has remained too large to permit a return to monetary ease through fiscal balance. Instead, as early as 1982, the depressing consequences of tight money in the face of the fiscal deficit were apparently forcing the Federal Reserve back to printing money. A Reagan boom was the result (Table 12).

Table 12. Percent Change in Money Supply[15]

	1979	1980	1981	1982	1983	1984	1985	1986[a]
M1	7.2	6.7	6.5	8.8	9.8	6.0	12.2	11.6
M2	17.4	0.0	10.0	8.9	12.0	8.6	8.2	6.6
M3	9.6	10.3	12.4	9.4	10.4	10.7	7.2	7.0
L	10.8	9.9	11.7	9.9	11.0	11.7	8.6	7.4

[a] Change from March 1985 to March 1986

Source: U.S. Department of Commerce (1987: 491).

The dollar fell sharply, the Reagan boom faltered, credit markets grew nervous, and fears of a simultaneous return to inflation and recession arose once more. The American economy's next turning cannot be easily predicted. Perhaps the most likely longer-term evolution will be a gradual return to the pattern of the 1970s. Easy money will finance the fiscal deficit, spur domestic recovery, perhaps encourage a capital outflow, and regularly depreciate the dollar. Trade and current account balances will improve. With luck, the Volcker interlude of genuinely tight money will keep inflationary expectations within acceptable limits for some time to come.

Such a scenario would not be at all atypical for the United States. Traditionally, easy money is the American way out of a fiscal deficit. The Federal Reserve, unlike the Bundesbank, has seldom been able to sustain a tight monetary policy long enough to force the rest of the government to adopt a balanced fiscal policy. Hence, the customary U.S. monetary ease and weak dollar since the 1960s – with interludes of restriction as at the end of the 1960s or the early 1980s.[15]

Why is the United States so "addicted" to easy money? Three broad explanations are common: cultural, institutional, and geopolitical. Culturally, it is said, the Americans have never had the traumatic experience with inflation suffered by Germany, and partly as a result, monetary stability does not rank high among American priorities. Institutionally, the American political system does not give its central bank the same autonomy to influence macroeconomic policy as does the Federal Republic. Finally, the huge size of its economy, and the special "hegemonic" international role of the dollar, together exempt the United States from many of the international sanctions that force other countries to discipline their monetary policy. America's lack of internal and external monetary restraints, combined with its civilian/military fiscal dilemma, thus seem to explain the long external imbalance.

5 Systemic Justice

From a geopolitical perspective, America's external imbalance represents rough justice within our "Trilateral" system. Europeans and Japanese are unwilling or unable to bear the burden of their own defense. To do so, the U.S. typically maintains a military force too great for the fiscal resources that the American political system can generate. And the U.S. typically finances this fiscal deficit by easy money. This results, in turn, in America's perpetual external imbalances, the costs of which are visited heavily upon America's affluent military protectorates. Thus, they pay for the American military services they consume.

Ideally, this arrangement might continue indefinitely, as indeed, it has continued well enough since the 1960s. Unfortunately, however, these economic practices have certain high and accumulating long-range costs – as the present malaise in the international economy suggests. Whether these costs have now reached the point where they exceed the risks of a change in military roles will certainly be among the most serious issues that will confront political leaders in the Western alliance over the coming decade.

Notes

1 Until the breakdown of the Bretton Woods system, American policymakers often emphasized the direct balance of payments aspects of "burden sharing" – or its lack. See, for example, Connally (1971). For the accompanying calculations, see *Survey of Current Business*, June 1971, Table 1.

2 See Holloran (1984). The Pentagon estimates are reported to be derived from the fiscal year 1985 defense budget. For a recent discussion, see Krauss (1986: 25). For a detailed discussion of the methodology, see Ravenal (1984).

3 Ravenal (1985a: 1026), as well as Ravenal (1984: 16 – 17) which contains "A Note on Methodology," pp. 18 – 21. See also Ravenal (1985b: 69 – 70).

4 See International Institute for Strategic Studies (1987: 28). For recent reorganizations and their significance, see U.S. Department of Defense (1986: 133 – 136).

5 Ending conscription in 1973 resulted in a cut of 600,000 in standing forces, a further 20% cut in the selected reserves, and 60% in the standby reserves. For the budgetary and military significance, see Coffey (1980: 51 ff.).

6 By their nature, these estimates are based on very complex assumptions and can never be very precise. Ravenal's proposed cuts, which would leave only three "Atlantic" divisions, result, he has reckoned, in lowering NATO's share of the defense budget from 42% to 26% (based on the 1986 budget request). I have used (1982: 257) a rather conservative estimate arrived at with Congressional analysts, which, in the spring of 1981, saw rough savings within three years of $ 4.56 billion for each NATO division disbanded without any cuts in U.S.-NATO naval or tactical air forces. (U.S. military spending in fiscal 1982 was $ 185.3 billion.) As Ravenal and many others note, the present defense budget has a built-in rise in expenditures – because of commitments to weapons systems, etc. – that make achieving its projected size highly improbable within the context of the American political system or economy. It is with this in mind that a fundamental reexamination of geopolitical commitments and tasks seems not only desirable, but indeed inevitable.

7 For a critique of the Reagan administration's understanding and application of the Laffer curve see Stockman (1986), especially pp. 10 – 11 and 272 – 273.

8 For a critical view of the long-range economic benefits of Reagan's high defense spending, see Rothschild (1981: 15).

9 Reagan's cuts in direct income taxes were roughly balanced by sharp increases in social security taxes.

10 Not all agree on this. Although it flies in the face of both common sense and historical experience, McNamara (1986: 119 – 121) argues that the costs of smart weapons would be modest.

11 The Navy grew from 479 ships in 1980 to 567 in 1987 and was to reach a target of 600 ships by 1989. Expenditures, in constant 1987 dollars rose from $ 73 billion

in 1981 to $ 104 billion in 1987. The other branches of the service received similar funding increases (U.S. Department of Defense 1986: 178 – 179, 314).

12 For a recent analysis of these problems, see Peterson (1987: 96 ff).

13 For a critical discussion of the Reagan administration's macroeconomic policies by an insider, see Stockman (1986).

14 The West German federal budget deficit amounted to 6.1% of GNP in 1975. By 1984 it had been reduced to 1.4% of GNP. For an analysis of German fiscal and monetary policies in the late 1970s, including the vital role played by the Bundesbank in achieving a reduction in the federal deficit without succumbing to inflationary pressure, see Wilson (1985: 77 – 102).

15 M1 is currency plus demand deposits plus travelers checks of nonbank issuers plus other checkable deposits at banks and thrift institutions; M2 is M1 plus overnight RP's and Eurodollars, balances of general purpose and broker/dealer money market mutual fund shares, money market deposits accounts, and savings and small time deposits at commercial banks and thrift institutions; M3 is M2 plus large time deposits and term RP's at commercial banks and thrift institutions, term Eurodollars, and balance of institutions – only money market mutual funds; and L is M3 plus other liquid assets such as savings bonds, short-term Treasury securities, bankers' acceptances, and commercial paper.

16 Between Eisenhower and Volcker, the Federal Reserve tightened monetary conditions sharply but briefly in 1966 and more determinedly from 1968 to 1970 – a restraint discarded by Chairman Arthur Burns under strong pressure from the Nixon administration for reflation. For my extended effort to track and explain U.S. economic policy through the 1960s and 1970s, see Calleo (1982) and, more recently, Calleo (1987), chap. 6. The latter assesses the arguments for and against a European-directed NATO.

References

Boltho, Andrea (1975): *Japan: An Economic Survey, 1953 – 1973*. London: Oxford University Press.

Calleo, David P. (1982): *The Imperious Economy*. Cambridge, Mass.: Harvard University Press.

Calleo, David P. (1987): *Beyond American Hegemony*. New York: Basic Books.

Coffey, Kenneth (1980): *The Strategic Implications of the All-Volunteer Forces*. Chapel Hill: University of North Carolina Press.

Connally, John B. (1971): Remarks of the Hon. Secretary of the Treasury, at the International Banking Conference of the American Bankers Association, Munich, Germany. *U.S. Department of the Treasury News*. Washington, D.C.: Government Printing Office, May 18.

Economic Report of the President 1987. Washington, D.C.: Government Printing Office.

Holloran, Richard (1984): Europe Called Main U.S. Arms Cost. *New York Times*, July 20: 2.

International Institute for Strategic Studies (1964): *The Military Balance 1964–72*. London.

International Institute for Strategic Studies (1976): *The Military Balance 1976–77*. London.

International Institute for Strategic Studies (1980): *The Military Balance 1980–81*. London.

International Institute for Strategic Studies (1984): *The Military Balance 1984–85*. London.

International Institute for Strategic Studies (1987): *The Military Balance 1986–87*. London.

International Monetary Fund (1986a): *Balance of Payments Statistics*, vol. 37, no. 2. Washington, D.C.

International Monetary Fund (1986b): *Government Finance Statistics Yearbook 1986*. Washington, D.C.

International Monetary Fund (1987): *World Economic Outlook*, April 1987. Washington, D.C.

Krauss, Melvyn (1986): *How NATO Weakens the West*. New York: Simon and Schuster.

Kristol, Irving (1981): NATO at a Dead End. *Wall Street Journal*, July 15: 26.

Kristol, Irving (1982): Reconstructing NATO: A New Role for Europe. *Wall Street Journal*, August 12: 18.

Kristol, Irving (1986): Global Unilateralism and "Entangling Alliances." *Wall Street Journal*, February 3: 20.

McNamara, Robert (1986): *Blundering into Disaster. Surviving the First Century of the Nuclear Age*. New York: Pantheon Books.

Organization for Economic Cooperation and Development (OECD) (1964): *Statistics of Balance of Payments 1950–1961*. Paris.

Organization for Economic Cooperation and Development (OECD) (1979): *Balance of Payments of OECD Countries 1960–1977*. Paris.

Organization for Economic Cooperation and Development (OECD) (1984): *OECD Historical Statistics 1960–1982*. Paris.

Organization for Economic Cooperation and Development (OECD) (1986): *OECD Economic Surveys 1986/1987, United States*. Paris.

Peterson, Peter (1987): The Morning After. *The Atlantic* 260 (4): 43–69.

Ravenal, Earl C. (1984): *Defining Defense: The 1985 Military Budget*. Washington, D.C.: Cato Institute.

Ravenal Earl C. (1985): Europe Without America: The Erosion of NATO. *Foreign Affairs* 63(5): 1020–1035.

Ravenal, Earl C. (1985): NATO: The Tides of Discontent. *Policy Papers in International Affairs* 23. Berkeley: Institute of International Studies.

Rothschild, Emma (1981): Reagan and the Real America. *New York Review of Books*, February 5, 1981.

Stockman, David Alan (1986): *The Triumph of Politics: How the Reagan Revolution Failed*. New York: Harper and Row.

Survey of Current Business, June 1971.

U.S. Department of Commerce (1975): *Statistical Abstract of the U.S. 1975*. Washington, D.C.: Government Printing Office.

U.S. Department of Commerce (1987): *Statistical Abstract of the U.S. 1987*. Washington, D.C.: Government Printing Office.

U.S. Department of Defense (1986): Caspar W. Weinberger, *Annual Report to the Congress, Fiscal Year 1986*. Washington, D.C.: Government Printing Office.

Wilson, John Oliver (1985): *The Power Economy: Building an Economy that Works*. Boston: Little, Brown.

Security Implications of High Technology Cooperation Between the U.S.A. and the Other Industrialized Countries

Hanns-D. Jacobsen

1 International Economic Interdependencies as a Source of Conflict and Cooperation

Already for some time the awareness of increasing international economic interdependencies has been growing. To a much higher degree than twenty or even ten years ago national societies are permeable to international influences. This is particularly true with regard to high-technology sectors. Reasons for this are high R & D expenditures which cannot be absorbed by the smaller industrialized economies alone, the necessity to have large markets and to employ economies of scale, and the increasing mobility of economic agents, particularly companies and firms which have improved their international communication considerably.

These developments have proven to be new sources for cooperation and conflict between the countries concerned. Cooperation between governments has been intensified in a variety of areas in order to overcome the erosion of national policy measures which result from greater mobility of firms and funds. There have been many attempts made such as informal agreements, guidelines, and other efforts to cope with the technical, political, and security implications of high-technology developments, such as the establishment of internationally agreed standards, the inclusion of high-tech trade in international organizations (e.g., GATT), and the agreement on criteria for export controls.

But there have also been new sources of conflict which may even have more effects on the international environment than all the initiatives that are taken to make the system work more smoothly. Joan Robinson once pointed out that the democratic nation state tends to act nationalistically because, above all, the elected politicians feel a primary responsibility toward their own constituency. Thus, if a country's economic performance is lacking relative to that of other countries, the responses will be, in all likelihood, nationalistic. In fact, this kind of reaction has been the case during recent years with regard to creating favorable conditions to improve international economic "competitiveness" – a catchword which has characterized the increasing conflict potential between the industrialized nations for some time now.

At the end of World War II the United States was the only intact economic power; its economic competitiveness was virtually unmatched. Due to its huge production potential, its high productivity, and as a result of the nearly unlimited absorption capacity of the other major industrialized countries in Europe and the Far East, the United States was able to increase its foreign trade dramatically. Domestically, however, it turned out that the Americans spent much more of their income on consumption than, for instance, the Europeans and the Japanese, so that the result was a comparatively lower rate of savings and investment. High consumption expenditures also influenced the import structure: high-quality consumer goods were mostly imported. The countries exporting them were quite satisfied with this situation. For them the U.S. market was very attractive. The high demand of the American consumers fitted together with the relatively low wages and the undervalued currencies of these countries. Thus, it was not surprising when at the beginning of the 1970s the U.S. trade balance finally turned negative and an increasing deficit began to entrench itself. High consumption in the United States also had another adverse effect. It meant that for research and development, for the creation of advanced technology, and, finally, for the modernization of plants and equipment there were far less investment funds available than in other Western countries.

This development was accompanied by a worldwide internationalization of economic interactions which created adverse effects for the U.S. economy. Ironically, these internationalization processes took place with the massive participation of transnational companies of U.S. origin, which not only initiated the exodus of labor-intensive production to low-wage countries but also contributed to the flooding of the U.S. market with relatively inexpensive consumer goods. A similar effect – on a higher technological level – originated from the rapid growth of Japanese exports to the United States, which were not balanced by a corresponding access of U.S. products to the Japanese market.

2 The Issue of International Economic Competitiveness

During the 1970s increasing foreign economic pressure made it clear that the United States, with the exception of some growth industries, was on the verge of losing its international economic competitiveness, which once had been so outstanding. A variety of indicators show that the U.S. economy – compared with those of other industrialized nations – experienced a secular decline since the mid-1960s. For example, since then there has been an erosion of U.S. shares in world markets for manufactured goods, including high-technology goods. Since the early 1970s there has also been an erosion of U.S. shares of world exports of productive services as opposed to service flows representing earnings on overseas investment. Furthermore, there has been evidence that the U.S. technological capability compared with that of Japan or West Germany has been in relative decline for quite some time (President's Commission on Industrial Competitiveness 1985; Scott 1985; Jacobsen 1986). Most striking has been the U.S. productivity performance: Since the end of the 1960s there was a substantial decline in productivity growth rates throughout most sectors of the U.S. economy lagging behind such major competitors as West Germany and Japan.[1]

Slower productivity growth in the U.S. economy was the major reason for the United States' fading ability to compete internationally. In several sectors, such as steel, autos, machine tools, and also semiconductors, productivity levels in other industrialized countries equal or exceed U.S. levels. The greatest challenge did not come from the traditional rivals in Europe, but from East Asian countries – from the newly industrialized countries such as South Korea, Taiwan, Singapore, Hong Kong, and above all from Japan. Their competitive pressure is not primarily based on a favorable endowment of natural resources, but on coherent national strategies which mobilize their productive capacities in order to create comparative advantages by government policies to generate economic growth and to improve international competitiveness. Japan and the other countries mentioned have industrial policies which are motivated by the goal of guiding or influencing the structure or composition of the economy in specific directions. These strategies which represent a mix of trade policy, tax and subsidy policy, financial and interest-rate policy, research and development policy, and antitrust policy, focus on sectors which promise more than average growth or rapid technological change.

In contrast to this the United States, as well as most European countries, have been practicing strategies which primarily aim at high consumption or, particularly in Europe, at secure and just distribution of income, instead of addressing the major causes of the underlying sources of the decline of its competitive edge. Thus, the level of net capital formation in the U.S. decreased, and the U.S. savings rate fell to record lows. Furthermore, the overall quality of the U.S. labor force in terms of literacy, mathematics and science training, and school drop-out rates got worse.

The international economic competitiveness of the United States has decreased especially in the traditional industries (National Academy of Engineering 1982, 1983, 1985a). But also in high-technology sectors there have been dramatic changes (National Research Council 1983; National Academy of Engineering 1984, 1985b; Office of Technology Assessment 1983). The U.S. trade surplus in high-tech products shrank steadily from $ 26.6 billion in 1981 to $ 3.3 billion in 1985; with Japan alone the U.S. had to bear a $ 18.6 billion high-tech trade deficit in 1985 (U.S. Department of Commerce 1986: 16). And in the longer run the competitive pressure from the East Asian countries is likely to rise.

There have already been a variety of measures and initiatives in the United States, made by Congress and the administration as well, against increasing competition on the domestic and on third markets. There was action in the monetary field: In 1985 the dollar started to decline sharply against the currencies of Japan and Western European countries; the Plaza and Louvre meetings of the major Western countries in 1985 and 1987 succeeded in stabilizing the dollar at a level which improved the opportunities for U.S. exports. Another result of the huge U.S. trade deficit was the call for "fair trade" practices and for protectionist measures against "unfair" trade partners. The public discussion in the United States is building up and creating an atmosphere which puts additional pressure on both houses of Congress and on the administration; the "Gephardt Amendment' to the Trade Bill, which calls for retaliatory measures against surplus countries, is a case in point.

3 Strategic Implications of the United States' Economic Decline

The deterioration of the U.S. economic competitiveness, however, is the result of several factors which have to be analyzed in their complexity. Certainly, the overvalued dollar made U.S. products too expensive on many world markets. This high dollar was the result of macroeconomic policies which had been caused by the huge budget deficit, by restrictive monetary policies, and interest rates which exceeded those in most other countries of the world. Thus, the high value of the dollar alone cannot be viewed as the major reason for lacking competitiveness, because its symptoms (low productivity growth, trade deficit, etc.) were apparent also during 1977 through 1979, when the dollar was undoubtedly undervalued. And although the dollar has gone down since early 1985, at the end of 1987 there was no indication that the trade deficit would decrease remarkably. This allows the conclusion that the competitiveness problem of the U.S. is not just a trade or a dollar problem, but a deep-rooted structural problem which has its origins in the lack of a strategic policy for national competitiveness. The U.S. has not been able to match the successful industrial policy strategies of its major competitors.

To a certain extent the United States' loss of competitiveness in recent decades can be interpreted as a natural and not reversible process when one takes into account the unique situation of the U.S. after World War II, when it dominated world production and world trade. The successful postwar reconstruction and the increasing prosperity of the other industrialized countries inevitably diminished the relative global position of the U.S. and led to a decline in its hegemony (Olsen 1982; Krasner 1983; Keohane 1984). From an economic viewpoint this might be a process of necessary structural adjustment because many of those sectors which contributed to the dominant economic position of the U.S., including steel, textiles, and agriculture, had to witness increasing comparative disadvantages. After all, other hegemons such as Great Britain during the late nineteenth and early twentieth centuries had to bear similar experiences.

From a strategic and not just economic standpoint, however, these developments pose a much more serious problem for the United States, particularly with regard to high technologies. The reason for this has been the perceived dual role of the United States, "both as the principal guarantor of Western security and as a leading defender of the economic system of the free world. In this context, U.S. technological preeminence and high technology industries take on strategic importance, and the maintenance and protection of a broad U.S. technological base is a vital element of national security policy" (U. S. Department of Commerce 1983: 4). Failure on the part of the United States to maintain technological leadership could lead to adverse consequences for the United States and for the balance of power between the Soviet bloc and the Western nations. Thus, the American effort to regain technological superiority proves to be not only an economic initiative to assist central sectors of the economy and to aim at more employment, productivity, and growth – but it also obviously serves national security considerations.

As has been pointed out, there is much doubt whether the impact of monetary and trade measures is sufficient to cope with the complex phenomenon of lacking U.S. competitiveness. A more favorable dollar exchange rate and a greater demand of other countries for U.S. goods are certainly of much help in solving the balance of trade problem and improve the U.S. position on the world markets. Such measures appear to be necessary but are by no means sufficient. Therefore, it is not surprising that increasing discussion is taking place about the formulation and implementation of broader economic strategies by the United States, strategies fit to meet the international challenges.

Many of the proposals thus far presented stress the importance of further promotion of high technology and industrial policy measures. This has to be pointed out, because the term industrial policy as a bundle of government measures, which directly or indirectly influence the performance of either sunset industries or sectors which promise economic take-offs, is not very popular in the United States (Foster 1985). And indeed, if one has a close look at the government activities of the United States during recent years one has to accept the conclusion that a consistent and offensive industrial policy – in contrast to Japan and other industrialized countries – does not exist.

However, there is a major and important difference. In the United States the Department of Defense (DOD) has already for a long time supported R & D systematically, thus pursuing a quasi-industrial policy. In 1985 the Pentagon's share of federal R & D expenditures accounted for 72.7% (National Science Board 1986: Table 2.12). The Reagan administration's emphasis on strategic modernization through research and development has resulted in an 18% increment (in constant dollars) in defense R & D between 1985 and 1986. This increase represents the continuation of an acceleration in defense R & D funding which began in 1980. Between 1980 and 1985, federal funds for defense R & D grew at an estimated average annual rate of 11.7% in constant-dollar terms. With these funds, the Department of Defense (DOD) is supporting virtually all major areas of high-tech developments in the United States, the Strategic Defense Initiative (SDI) being only one, though important, area. The DOD has been funding such sophisticated technologies as lasers, artificial intelligence, and advanced materials. It also supported the development of fuel-efficient jumbo jet engines, superspeed computers, high-density semiconductors, vision-equipped robots, and computer-aided manufacturing systems. There are even further initiatives, including those to bolster the nation's leading research universities and to provide high-risk venture capital for innovative high-tech entrepreneurs (Reich 1985). Whether intentional or not, die DOD remains a powerful instrument in ensuring America's competitiveness in advanced technologies by conducting its quasi-industrial policy.

However, there are many doubts as to whether such close meshing of civilian and military R & D in the United States will finally result in the intended outcomes and enable high-tech firms to compete internationally (Stowsky 1986: 46). After all, the Pentagon's involvement modifies the firm's strategies and thus its structure, which under normal conditions is dictated by industrial efficiency, profit maximization, and its institutional and political setting. Practices which might otherwise be expected to promote competitiveness, such as state-of-the-art procurement, direct subsidies for R & D, diffusion through personnel, volume production, price premiums, and "buy American" provisions, can shade easily into threats to the competitive performance of contracting firms – technical over-sophistication, applied R & D, over-specialized personnel, sole-sourcing, cost-plus contracts, damaging insulation from competitive pressures to innovate, and restrictions on diffusion in the name of national security (Brueckner and Borrus 1984).[2]

4 Defense-Oriented Industrial Policy of the United States and International Technological Cooperation

This, however, leads to some fundamental political problems which affect technological cooperation between Western countries. In order to prevent the diversion of U.S. high technology to the Soviet Union and other Communist countries, the United States took a variety of initiatives to protect and to control the outflow of high technology. There have been new secrecy rules, a new export control legislation and, finally, specific contracts between the DOD and research institutions dealing with advanced technology limiting the availability of the results. The regulations implementing the national security export control regime are extensive and complex. Many federal departments such as the Department of Commerce, the Department of State, the Department of Defense, the Department of Energy, the Central Intelligence Agency, and the Customs Service share adminsitrative responsibility for their implementation and participate in the export control policymaking process.

The DOD has been most active in strengthening the control system and in improving what it calls "technological security" (U.S. Department of Defense 1986) in order to stop Soviet acquisition of advanced Western technology, which supposedly was helping the USSR to overtake the West militarily. The DOD has automated its review of license applications and its procedures for tracking diversions. Beginning in 1983, it has published an annual report to Congress on technology security. Early in the Reagan administration the DOD became a driving force within a new Senior Interdepartmental Group on Transfer of Strategic Technology. The DOD also transferred $ 30 million from its budget to help the Customs Service's new program of Operation Exodus, designed to stop illegal exports of high technology. Furthermore, the Pentagon has established a Defense Security Administration which formalized the cooperation between the political officers of the DOD and the technical specialists from the office of the Under-Secretary for Research and Engineering. In conflict with the Commerce Department, the Defense Department won authority to review proposed exports in several fields of high technology, not just to COCOM (Hardt and Tomlinson 1983; Jacobsen 1988)[3] nations but also to 15 non-COCOM nations. These include neutral European nations such as Austria, Sweden, and Switzerland, but also industrializing nations in Asia such as Singapore, South Korea, Taiwan, and the Philippines, and selected Middle Eastern nations with ties to the Soviet bloc.

In recent years, the DOD has used its increased influence within the U.S. government to press successfully for several major shifts in international control of technology. DOD technical experts, for example, provided the key arguments in the U.S. effort to bring COCOM to grips with the high-technology advances of the 1970s. In June 1984, COCOM members agreed to control such technologies as computer software, telecommunications switching equipment, industrial robots, electronic grade silicon, and advanced computers. The DOD also tried to bring about greater participation by allied defense ministries in export control policy which in almost all COCOM countries is under the supervision of the economics ministries. To further this trend, Defense Department officials have exchanged visits with their counterparts in several allied defense ministries to discuss common technical and administrative problems. The DOD also has initiated and led the U.S. effort to expand the use of defense experts at COCOM meetings and to establish a permanent advisory group of such experts at COCOM headquarters in Paris.

Of particular concern to American and also foreign companies using American technology are reexport controls which are required under the current export administration regulations of the United States. Since they are extraterritorial, reexport controls affect American companies, in that they could prompt foreign customers to seek products from other nations rather than become entangled in the reexport obligations attached exclusively to U.S. goods and technology. No other nation imposes reexport limitations on its own products in any way comparable to those the United States imposes on U.S.-controlled products. The business community in paticular claims that the underlying idea stems from a simplistic model of international trade. The sophistication of international economic relations particularly with regard to advanced technology goods which has taken place in recent years is undoubtedly very difficult to be administered successfully by such regulations.[4]

In effect, these regulations and the increased defense-initiated efforts not only impede economic cooperation and scientific exchange within the United States, jeopardizing the success of all these costly undertakings, but they also contribute to hindering economic cooperation with companies or governments of other Western and friendly countries.

For non-American firms it has become much more difficult to cooperate with American companies in the areas of advanced technology. This defense-initiated factual high-tech protectionism of the United States bears the danger that non-American firms are excluded from the development of advanced technologies because there might be the possibility of security risks.[5] There have been cases of excluding non-American students from courses at certain universities, of DOD-initiated bans to present papers at international conferences, of scientific conferences closed to "non-U.S. citizens," of withdrawing the common practice of offering foreign scholars office space in research institutions. Furthermore, there have been delays or even rejections of licensing of technologies for non-American companies, of limitations of access to scientific journals of U.S. firms, of increased security injunctions in connection with supercomputer deliveries to public institutions of friendly nations, of curbs concerning the access to technical data banks in the United States. Some American affiliates of Western European companies are even suspicious of being excluded from potential defense contracts.

It is true that this kind of discrimination and its effects on West-West cooperation in the field of high technology are very difficult to evaluate. Companies concerned shy at the public discussion of such problems, particularly when such a huge market as the United States is affected or when it concerns major economic and technological cooperation partners. And taking into consideration that a great part of industrial trade takes place without any difficulty, it would certainly be overstated to conclude a fundamental change in the political-psychological climate in non-American companies or to assume a general perception change toward non-cooperation. Nevertheless, there has been greater caution in non-American companies, particularly in Western Europe including the Federal Republic of Germany, with regard to using advanced technology of U.S. origin. After all, they have to take into consideration that access to the U.S. market or to U.S. high technologies has to be traded with the acceptance of U.S. export control regulations. And this limits the economic and political ranges of choice for companies and governments concerned not just with respect to their trade with the East but also with other parts of the world which might pose a danger to the U.S. national security – but not necessarily to that of other countries.

Advanced technology – and this is mostly technology which can have both civilian and military applications – plays a more and more increasing role in the foreign economic relations of the industrialized countries and has already become a decisive factor in their international competitiveness. The U.S. habit, however, to view international economic interactions in high technology primarily from a security point of view has induced foreign companies and governments to check their technological cooperation with the United States, to not increase it, or even to reduce their technological dependence on the United States by creating comprehensive technology programs of their own. EUREKA is a case in point.

For most West European companies such action proves to be very costly or even impossible, because in many cases they are too closely connected with U.S. firms technologically. Nevertheless, there can be no doubt that the companies concerned only reluctantly accept U.S. control efforts.

5 The Need for Cooperation in the Alliance

Also in the United States the pressure from companies which fear long-term damage to their foreign economic interests has risen. This became evident after the U.S. Department of Commerce finally, at the end of 1986, decided to loosen its grip on U.S. companies with regard to licensing procedures and to shorten the control list for some products. This became even more clear after the publication of a report by the National Academy of Sciences (Panel on the Impact of National Security Controls 1987)[6] on the link between export controls for security reasons and global economic competition. This report took up all the criticism which had been previously voiced by companies, government agencies, and the allies with regard to security-related export controls. It was pointed out that the potential costs of an unchanged national security export control system are likely to rise in an international environment which economically and technologically is dramatically different from that of most of the postwar period. Changes in the international marketplace are making the diffusion of technology "rapid and global in scope," and the global market for dual use technology is growing, as commercial developments using advanced technology are now often ahead of military deployments. Furthermore, "U.S. dominance over advanced technology is declining." For these reasons, a "fully multilateral approach" to controls would be necessary. The panel also points out that the scope of current U.S. national security controls undermines their effectiveness, impedes the export sales of U.S. companies, and their extraterritorial aspects engender allied mistrust and weaken allied unity. While potential benefits of export controls appear to be greatest for a narrow range of items, the potential costs "are spread across an enormous volume of transactions representing a large share of U.S. trade." The panel estimates that 40% or approximately $ 62 billion worth of all U.S. exports of non-military manufactured goods were shipped under licenses requiring prior approval; 90% of individual license applications are for exports to Free World countries; and only 13% of all applications are for very sensitive items requiring the most stringent review. All in all the panel calls for a strengthening of the COCOM mechanism and suggests that the administration should give greater importance to maintaining U.S. technological strength, economic vitality, and allied unity. At the same time the panel recommends some basic changes in U.S. policy:

1. The control only of COCOM-proscribed items
2. Within COCOM, negotiations with member countries about controls on exports to third countries
3. Negotiations with third countries
4. The removal of items whose control is no longer feasible
5. The maintenance of unilateral controls only on a temporary basis
6. The elimination of reexport authorization requirements between COCOM members
7. The maintenance of current control procedures on the transfer within COCOM of sensitive information, technical data, and know-how

8. The reduction of the scope of the COCOM list and modification of the COCOM decision-making policies and procedures
9. The maintenance of a clear separation between national security and foreign policy export controls

It is certainly not surprising that the Department of Defense rejected most of these recommendations (Auerbach 1987). And there are many reasons to believe that a fundamental change of policies is unlikely to occur. After all, the United States much more than its allies views its foreign economic policies as a tool of its foreign and security policies. Examples are the targeted granting of economic aid and the imposition of sanctions. Thus, a political function of U.S. foreign economic relations is their contribution to foreign policy and security goals. Measures such as the grain embargo against the Soviet Union in January 1980, the embargo of equipment for the Siberian gas pipeline to Western Europe in December 1981 and June 1982, and the economic sanctions against Libya in Januar 1986 had led to priority conflicts in the administration, caused disputes between social groups domestically, and, finally, created conflicts with the allies.

6 Conclusions

On the assumption that a major change in U.S. policies is unlikely to occur for some time, the following conclusions seem plausible:

- There are incentives for the Western industrialized countries to develop their own technological base not just for economic but also for political reasons because in the United States there is a deep involvement of the military in the development of advanced technologies which are likely to increase and not decrease. This involvement might cause short-term innovation in certain high-tech sectors, but the spillover effects to civilian production in the national economy are likely to be limited and technological cooperation with allied countries impeded.
- With regard to the massive U.S. efforts in certain high-tech sectors which are funded or supported by the DOD and as a result of the limited availability of their results, other countries or groups of countries have hardly any choice but to develop their own programs for the advancement of science and technology and to conduct their own industrial policies. Thus, the competition between the major industrial powers on their domestic markets and on third markets is likely to increase.
- The future role of the United States within this increasing competition is not easy to determine. On the one hand, there have been dramatic successes with regard to the development of new technologies in the United States,

and on the other, there is no doubt that the relative position of the United States in international high technology trade has deteriorated. Although the U.S. trade balance shows slight signs of recovery this is not the result of increased measures to improve U.S. competitiveness (as, for instance, recommended by the President's Commission on Industrial Competitiveness in January 1985) but simply the effect of exchange rate manipulation in favor of the U.S. dollar.

- Thus, there is an increasing call for political action to deal with the problems involved. High investment in R & D by the industrialized countries leads to more technological competition on the world markets because the domestic markets are too small to guarantee sufficient rates of return. There is a pressing need to provide access to these markets, and cooperation is necessary in these fields to bear the enormous costs involved and also to prevent disruptions. But at the same time there are tendencies which point in the opposite direction, some of them have been mentioned above. Failure to cope with these developments may lead to further frictions and disruptions in the world economy. It may even lead to a growing conflict between the worldwide trend towards increasing international interdependencies, on the one hand, and national security oriented considerations, on the other. This cannot be in the interests of the major industrial countries and certainly also not in the interests of the United States.

Notes

1 Some U.S. authors have argued that the loss competitiveness has been relatively small and is insignificant at best. They suggest that a simple decline of the dollar's value and a growing comparative advantage in services will restore the competitiveness of U.S. producers and reverse recent declines in U.S. shares of world markets (Lawrence 1984: 49–50; Krugman 1987). Other economists, however, argue that as a result of the size and persistence of the dollar's overevaluation there have been adverse long-term effects which cannot easily be reversed. Thus, many U.S. producers have abandoned markets altogether or have moved production offshore, while many foreign firms have entered markets that were previously dominated by U.S. producers. And with regard to the service sector one has to acknowledge that most of the new jobs have been low-skill and low-paying with high turnover and poor training (Tyson 1987: 10–16).

2 They conclude the existence of a catch-22: "Although the DOD relies upon a sound industrial base for the maintenance of American military "high-tech" superiority, defense policies can no longer effectively promote the competitive position of U.S. semiconductor firms in international markets" (Brueckner and Borrus 1984: 81).

3 COCOM is the acronym for Coordinating Committee on Multilateral Export Controls, an organization which was founded in 1949 and is located in Paris. Its members

are Japan and all NATO members except Iceland. COCOM is working on an informal basis, its decisions are not published, and unanimity of all members present is the decision-making rule. COCOM controls apply to the USSR, the People's Republic of China, Eastern Europe (except Yugoslavia), and Asian communist countries. Cuba is not subject to COCOM controls. (Hardt and Tomlinson 1983; Jacobsen 1988)

4 A business representative has put it this way: "For example, a semiconductor produced by one manufacturer is incorporated into a microprocessor by another manufacturer. That microprocessor is then programmed or reprogrammed and incorporated, let us say, into an electronic testing device. That device is then integrated into a large, automated machine tool system. Very often, the ultimate product itself is subject to export controls that simply duplicate reexport requirements on its components. This process often criss-crosses national boundaries, during which products and technology lose their national identity. Multiply the process by millions of components and scores of technologically sophisticated countries, and the conclusion is unavoidable: full compliance with U.S. reexport controls is virtually impossible without totally hamstringing the modern global trading system" (Majak 1986: 4). As a comprehensive analysis of this issue area cf. Rosenthal and Knighton (1982).

5 This concern has been the subject of a study published in the United Kingdom (MacDonald 1986). Initially, this report was to be published by the OECD in Paris. The United States reportedly refused to accept the manuscript. See also MacDonald (1988); Hein (1984); Schulte-Hillen and Wietersheim (1986).

6 See Panel on the Impact of National Security Controls on International Technology Transfer (1987). The panel comprised 21 individuals, including a number of former high-level U.S. defense and intelligence officials as well as business executives and academics, and was chaired by General Lew Allen, former U.S. Air Force Chief of Staff.

References

Auerbach, Stuart (1987): High-Tech Export Panel Defended by Chairman. *Washington Post*, 15 January 1987: E1, E10.

Brueckner, Leslie with Michael Borrus (1984): *Assessing the Commercial Impact of the VHSIC (Very High Speed Integrated Circuit) Program.* BRIE Working Paper 5. Berkeley: Berkeley Roundtable on the International Economy.

Foster, Charles R. (1985): Warum gibt es in den USA keine koordinierte Industriepolitik? *Politische Vierteljahresschrift* 26(2): 149 – 159.

Hardt, Hohn P. and Kate S. Tomlinson (1983): COCOM's Operating Procedures and an Assessment of Its Effectiveness. In A. S. Becker (ed.), *Economic Relations with the USSR – Issue for the Western Alliance.* Lexington and Toronto: D. C. Heath, 111 – 127.

Hein, Werner (1984): *Beschränkung des internationalen Technologietransfers durch die USA. Studie im Auftrag des Bundesminnisteriums für Forschung und Technologie.* Washington, D.C.: Bundesministerium für Forschung und Technologie.

Jacobsen, Hanns-D. (1986): *Internationale Wettbewerbsfähigkeit und nationale Sicherheit der USA.* Ebenhausen: Stiftung Wissenschaft und Politik.

Jacobsen, Hanns-D. (1988): The COCOM Policy of the United States. In H. Haftendorn and J. Schissler (eds.) *The Reagan Administration – Towards a Reconstruction of American Strength.* Berlin-New York: de Gruyter (in press).

Keohane, Robert O. (1984): *After Hegemony. Cooperation and Discord in the World Political Economy.* Princeton: Princeton University Press.

Krasner, Stephen D. (ed.) (1983): *International Regimes.* Ithaca and London: Cornell University Press.

Krugman, Paul. R. (1986): Introduction: New Thinking about Trade Policy. In Paul R. Krugman (ed.), *Strategic Trade Policy and the New International Economics.* Cambridge, Mass. and London: MIT Press, 1–22.

Lawrence, Robert Z. (1984): *Can America Compete?* Washington, D.C.: Brookings Institution.

MacDonald, Stuart (1986): Controlling the Flow of High-Technology Information from the United States to the Soviet Union: A Labour of Sisyphus? *Minerva* 24(1): 39–73.

MacDonald, Stuart (1988): *Benefits Beyond Belief – Assessing the Cost of United States Export Controls.* London: Centre for Economic Policy Research.

Majak, Richard R. and American Electronics Association (1986): *Testimony Before the Export Control Policy Forum on Reexport Controls of the Department of Commerce* on June 23, 1986. Washington, D.C.: Department of Commerce.

National Academy of Engineering/National Research Council (1982): *The Competitive Status of the U.S. Auto Industry.* Washington, D.C.: National Academy Press.

National Academy of Engineering/National Research Council (1983): *The Competitive Status of the U.S. Fibers, Textiles, and Apparel Complex.* Washington, D.C.: National Academy Press.

National Academy of Engineering/National Research Council (1984): *The Competitive Status of the U.S. Electronics Industry.* Washington, D.C.: National Academy Press.

National Academy of Engineering/National Research Council (1985a): *The Competitive Status of the U.S. Steel Industry.* Washington, D.C.: National Academy Press.

National Academy of Engineering/National Research Council (1985b): *The Competitive Status of the U.S. Civil Aviation Manufacturing Industry.* Washington, D.C.: National Academy Press.

National Research Council (1983): *International Competition in Advanced Technology: Decisions for America.* Washington, D.C.: National Academy Press.

National Science Board (1986): *Science Indicators – The 1985 Report.* Washington, D.C.: Government Printing Office.

Office of Technology Assessment (1983): *International Competitiveness in Electronics.* Washington, D.C.: Government Printing Office.

Olsen, Mancur (1982): *The Rise and Decline of Nations.* New Haven and London: Yale University Press.

Panel on the Impact of National Security Controls on International Technology Transfer of the Committee on Science, Engineering, and Public Policy of the National

Academy of Sciences, the National Academy of Engineering and the Institute of Medicine (1987): *Balancing the National Interest. U.S. National Security Export Controls and Global Economic Competition ("Allen-Report")*. Washington, D.C.: National Academy Press.

President's Commission on Industrial Competitiveness (1985): *Global Competition – The New Reality*, 2 vols. Washington, D.C.: Government Printing Office.

Reich, Robert B. (1985): High Tech, a Subsidiary of Pentagon, Inc. *New York Times*, 29 May, 16.

Rosenthal, Douglas E. and William M. Knighton (1982): *National Laws and International Commerce: The Problem of Extraterritoriality*. Chatham House Papers 17. London, Boston and Henley: Routledge and Kegan Paul.

Schulte-Hillen, H. and B. v. Wietersheim (1986): *Analyse von Beschränkungen des Zugangs zu außergemeinschaftlichen Informationsquellen – Abschlußbericht*. Köln: Commission of the European Communities.

Scott, Bruce R. (1985): U.S. Competitiveness: Concepts, Performance, and Implications. In B. R. Scott and G. C. Lodge (eds.), *U.S. Competitiveness in the World Economy*. Boston: Harvard Business School Press, 13–70.

Stowsky, Jay (1986): *Beating our Plowshares into Double-Edge Swords: The Impact of Pentagon Policies on the Comercialization of Advanced Technologies*. BRIE Working Paper 17. Berkeley: Berleley Roundtable on the International Economy.

Tyson, Laura d'Andrea (1987): *Creating Advantage: Strategic Policy for National Competitiveness*. BRIE Working Paper 23. Berkeley: Berkeley Roundtable on the International Economy.

U.S. Department of Commerce (1983): *An Assessment of U.S. Competitiveness in High Technology Industries*. Washington, D.C.: Government Printing Office.

U.S. Department of Commmerce, International Trade Administration (1986): *United States Trade – Performance in 1985 and Outlook*. Washington, D.C.: Government Printing Office.

U.S. Department of Defense (1986): *The Technology Security Program*. A Report to the 99th Congress, Second Session. Washington, D.C.: The Department of Defense.

Toward a Reconstruction of American Leadership? An Evaluation of the Reagan Administration's National Security Strategy

Helga Haftendorn

An Overview

The fortieth President of the United States came into office with a promise to make America strong again, and to restore confidence in American leadership worldwide. Based on a strong economy and a credible defense posture, Ronald Reagan's security strategy had three declared goals:

1. Contain the Soviet Union and restrain its actions
2. Reinvigorate American alliances and restore relationships with friends in order to have them support U.S. interests and goals
3. Work toward progress in the developing countries

Has the Reagan administration achieved what it had set out to do? Has it provided credible leadership, both at home and abroad? What kind of leadership did it want to reconstruct?

At home, a strong presidency was to reunite the American people, to reconstitute its self-respect after the humiliations of Vietnam, Watergate, and the Iran hostage crisis, and to fill it with confidence about America's mission in the world. Thus, domestic support for its international role was to be provided.

Abroad, leadership implied a reactivation of the hegemonic position the United States had enjoyed in the first decades after World War II. Hegemony is defined as a situation in which "one state is powerful enough to maintain the essential rules governing interstate relations, and willing to do so" (Keohane and Nye 1977: 44). For exercising leadership, the U.S. had to rebuild its economic and military resources, and make them preponderant again. It criticized previous administrations for having permitted these resources to decline, and for lacking the determination to make and enforce international rules. Instead of shaping international events, they had let America become the victim of events. The restoration of America's power was to give the United States the capability and the will to control international outcomes.

1 A Vision of America's Destiny

The Reagan administration did not come into office with an elaborated foreign policy concept, but rather with the vision of, and belief in, a strong America, and a set of assumptions and policy guidelines on how to realize it.

Its most striking feature, at least from a European perspective, was the reassertion of U.S. exceptionalism. Reagan saw America as "a nation of destiny," as a "shining city on a hill," the "exemplar of freedom and a beacon of hope for those who did not now have freedom." After the humiliations of the 1970s, the "American dream" was to be resurrected, and the American people consoled with itself.

For America to play its proper role in the world, it had to set its own house in order. The two highest priorities were restoring a sound economic base at home, and rebuilding military strength. To this had to be added a realistic view about the nature of the world and the challenges the United States was facing.

In the view of the Reagan administration the most significant threat to American security and national interests was the global challenge posed by the Soviet Union. The U.S. was not yet ready to acknowledge the existence of a second superpower, but wanted to contain Soviet hegemonic aspirations. During the period of détente, Moscow had undertaken an unprecedented military buildup while the U.S. had let its defense efforts slip. It had also expanded the reach of its foreign policy; had supported so-called wars of national liberation, exploited regional instabilities, and conducted an aggressive and illegal war in Afghanistan. On top of it, the Soviets had directed a massive propaganda campaign at the United States and its allies.

The strategy of containment with which the Reagan administration wanted to meet the Soviet threat, was to balance strength and negotiation. By creating new realities in the military equation, Washington wanted to establish a new relationship with the Soviet Union based upon restraint and reciprocity.

In the struggle for freedom, peace, and prosperity, the United States wanted to rely on allies and friends. Thus, it had to reinvigorate the traditional alliances and to establish closer levels of consultation with those who shared common values with America; its policies were to reflect a greater understanding and sensitivity to its friends' needs. This also necessitated the elimination of a number of contemporary aggravations.

The third challenge was to establish a just and responsible relationship with the developing world. The United States was to provide active assistance to those who were struggling for their own self-determination, freedom, and a reasonable standard of living and development.

This perception of the challenges facing the United States, and the strategies to cope with them, did not change much through the two administrations. The goals remained constant, though the rhetoric mellowed.

The implementation, however, was much less ideological than the rhetoric suggested. Basically, the Reagan administration reacted in a pragmatic way to domestic and international demands. It needed more time to issue policy directives on major foreign policy questions than most previous administrations. Also, its output was more "muddling through" than the results of a "grand strategy."

2 Economic and Military Strength as the Foundation of Worldwide Leadership

On top of the Reagan administration's political agenda was strengthening the economic and military capabilities of the United States to match its greatly increased security interests.

In his economic program, which President Reagan submitted to Congress three weeks after his inauguration, he called for deregulation, and the reduction of government spending. He also proposed to lower taxes, and to work toward a balanced budget. Tight monetary policy should bring down the inflation rate. This supply-side economics was to stimulate investment and to provide for steady economic growth.

It took about two years before the economy picked up and the U.S. was on its way out of the recession. However, neither the structural problems of its economy were solved nor a balanced budget achieved. Reduced tax rates and greatly increased defense expenditures combined to produce the worst budget deficit the U.S. has seen. With the Gramm-Rudman-Hollings budget law it was Congress that took the initiative to put a cap on government spending. The budget squeeze also significantly circumscribed further increases in defense expenditures, while the trade deficit strengthened the trend toward more protectionism.

It had been a campaign promise "to halt the decline in America's military strength and restore that margin of safety needed for the protection of the American people and the maintenance of peace" (President Reagan at a press conference on October 2, 1981). Besides significantly increasing the defense outlays (from 4% – 5% of the last Carter budget to 9% – 10% in real terms during the first Reagan years), Secretary of Defense Caspar Weinberger and the Pentagon continued on the course staked out by the previous administration:

- The B-1 bomber program, canceled by Carter, was resumed, and a new advanced airplane with "stealth" characteristics was to be developed.
- The navy was to be strengthened and expanded to have 600 ships afloat; new Trident submarines were to be constructed, and various new missiles were to be ordered.
- The MX missile was to be built and deployed in hardened silos.
- The communications and control system (C^3I) was to be strengthened and rebuilt, the air defenses were to be improved.

Except on the MX issue, this program was initially supported by a defense-minded Congress and a public ready to make sacrifices for strengthening defense.

The problems the Reagan administration encountered in implementing this policy, however, were threefold. One was the opposition by both legislators and a grassroots nuclear freeze movement toward deployment of the MX which the administration sought to cope with, first, by changes in the basing mode, and then by mandating an expert commission (the Scowcroft Commission) to reappraise the issue of strategic weapons and to come up with specific recommendations on how to deal with them. The second problem was living up to the campaign slogan that a "window of vulnerability" was jeopardizing the strategic forces of the U.S.A. Reagan's proposal for a Strategic Defense Initiative (SDI) was a radical solution to both problems, promising in the long term to eliminate the threat of strategic nuclear missiles altogether. Third, on the "guns vs. butter" issue, support for guns began to slip already in 1982/1983, when the constituency felt that the administration was doing its share on defense, and when the impending budget deficit cast forth its shadow.

Military doctrine continued to be based on "PD 59," developed by the Carter administration, but was made more explicit. The military options proposed ranged from a "demonstration shot," to the capabilities for limited nuclear war, and to the capacity of the U.S. strategic forces "to prevail and to be able to force the Soviet Union to seek earliest termination of hostilities on terms favorable to the United States... even under the condition of a prolonged war" (Kaplan 1983: 387, citing the 1982 Weinberger Defense Guidance). The use of nuclear weapons could but be a last resort if the security and the vital interests of the United States could not otherwise be safeguarded.

The trend continued to de-emphasize the role of nuclear weapons. To escape the dilemma of either risking defeat or destruction, the nuclear threshold had to be raised, and the conventional defense strengthened. Unwilling to reintroduce the draft, Washington instead urged its NATO allies and Japan to assume a larger share of the burden, increase their defense expenditures, and follow through with the 1978 Long-Term Defense Program. By the same logic, the Reagan administration, with the support of a public otherwise weary of American military entanglements abroad, continued to maintain sizable military forces in Western Europe.

The Carter doctrine, which stated that the United States would intervene in the Persian Gulf if the Western supply of crude oil were cut off, was reaffirmed. More impressive than the Rapid Deployment Force (another Carter legacy) was the creation of a 600-ship navy as an instrument for projecting U.S. military power to distant but vital regions. At the same time the United States prepared to cope with conflicts in more than one region at a time.

> Handling such contingencies simultaneously could stretch our military resources thin. But we will not restrict ourselves to meeting aggression on its immediate front. If we are forced to war, we must be prepared to launch counter offensives in other regions and try to exploit the aggressor's weaknesses wherever they exist. If aggression by superior forces cannot be reversed where it occurs, we should not be confined to that particular arena (Weinberger in his Council on Foreign Relation's Address, June 17, 1981).

But would commitments be commensurate to capabilities? Initially, arms control did not occupy a prominent place on the Reagan agenda. The emphasis was on arms, not arms control, the latter being regarded as an instrument of security policy, not a goal. Only from a position of strength would negotiations with the Soviet Union yield results that were in the interests of the United States.

The administration would have liked to have its strategic arms modernization program passed by Congress before returning to the negotiating table. However, a combination of domestic and foreign pressures combined to change this timing. To meet congressional opposition to the MX deployment, and the urging of the NATO allies to keep the 1979 NATO Two-Track Decision intact, in November 1981 the President announced in a National Press Club speech the resumption of negotiations on intermediate-range forces (INF). In his Eureka College commencement speech in May 1982 he proposed new talks on strategic arms reductions (START) to succeed the old negotiations on the limitation of strategic weapons (SALT).

Given the reluctance of both sides to put forward realistic arms control proposals, the U.S.-Soviet negotiations had an unpromising start. They came to a full stop after deployment of Pershing II and cruise missiles in Western Europe started in the fall of 1983. Their resumption was further complicated by the SDI program, and the President's unwillingness to negotiate on it. However, in the second Reagan administration a number of domestic and international factors converged to improve the prospects for an American-Soviet arms control agreement. It was seen as an alternative means to achieve the administration's security policy goals, given Mr. Gorbachev's aggressive negotiation policy and the mounting domestic political and financial constraints within the United States.

Both the economic recovery and the efforts to strengthen the military posture – which in reality were less impressive than in rhetoric – produced a significant change in the political climate of the United States. A majority polled in 1986 was convinced that the U.S.A. was militarily superior – or at least equal – to the Soviet Union, while in a poll in 1982 similar majorities felt that the U.S. was inferior. This changed attitude was reinforced in the campaign slogan of 1984: "American leadership is back!"

3 Neo-Containment of the Soviet Union

The Reagan administration's policy regarding the Soviet Union had two dimensions. On the rhetorical level it was a conflict against an "evil empire" and justified on moral grounds. On the policy level the Soviet Union had to be contained for political and geopolitical reasons. A wide range of opinions existed within the administration on how the confrontation should be managed, and under what circumstances cooperation was advantageous. There was consensus that a strong military posture was needed to manage the U.S.-Soviet relationship.

It took the administration until December 1982 to chart out a compromise course. NSC directive no. 75 established three long-term objectives:

> (1) to contain Soviet expansion and to moderate Soviet international behavior;
> (2) to encourage, by the limited means at the disposal of the United States, change in the Soviet system toward greater liberalism over time; and
> (3) to negotiate agreements that were in the interests of the United States (Garthoff 1985: 1012).

As negotiations could only be successful from a position of strength, U.S. military power had to be rebuilt before Washington would return to the negotiating table.

The military force posture served two functions. One was to make nuclear deterrence credible, either to prevent war, or, should war break out, contain it, and win it. The other was to provide for a political instrument to control the American-Soviet arms competition by either threatening further armaments or offering mutual reductions.

Other instruments for containment were export controls and economic sanctions. The prime target were technologically advanced products with military applications. In order to follow through with its policy of denial, Washington risked serious conflicts with its European allies (as in the case of the Urengoy pipeline embargo). As the quick lifting of the grain embargo inherited from Carter indicated, this administration was quite sensitive to the economic interests of its own domestic constituents.

Just as there was no uniform attitude concerning policy vis-à-vis the Soviet Union within the Reagan administration, it changed over time from an attitude shaped by ideological convictions to a more pragmatic approach. One reason was personal, and went along with the change from Haig to Shultz, and the latter's increasing influence compared to hardliners like Allen and Perle. Another was the inability to gain congressional support for a continued confrontation, and, above all, to beef it up with commensurate defense programs. A third factor was changes in the Soviet Union: with a new and dynamic general-secretary at the helm in Moscow, Washington risked being pushed onto the defensive if it did not vigorously respond to the various Soviet initiatives. Rhetorically the President justified the turn toward a more cooperative policy with the very success of his "policy of strength":

> "America has repaired its strength. We have invigorated our alliances and friendships. We are ready for constructive negotiations with the Soviet Union." (Reagan in his September 24, 1984 speech to the United Nations).

A series of summit meetings contributed to a mellowing of the frost between the two antagonists, but the road to an arms control agreement remained thorny. Progress was only made when domestic pressures increased. As the Iran-Contra scandal unfolded in Washington, the negotiations gained in substance and picked up in speed. By the end of 1987 an INF agreement was at hand. It provided for the removal and destruction of all land-based intermediate-range nuclear weapons (American Pershing II and cruise missiles, Soviet SS-20 as well as systems ranging from 500 to 5500 kilometers), to be verified by mutual on-site inspections. There were other agreements as well as a declaration of intent to achieve drastic reductions in strategic nuclear weapons. Thus an administration highly critical and suspicious of the Soviet Union achieved the first major breakthrough on the road to disarmament in postwar history: an agreement to abolish two categories of weapons systems already deployed.

4 Leader of the Free World

Also high on the Reagan agenda was the revitalization of alliances and the strengthening of the relationships with friends around the world. The administration believed that its allies expected the United States to assume a leadership role; it attributed many past problems to the absence of such leadership. America's alliances were simultaneously a basis for its claim to leadership as well as a precondition for any successful competition with the Soviet Union.

In alliance policy special attention was given to strengthening the common defense. Washington urged its NATO partners to implement the 1978 NATO Long Term Defense Program and the 1979 Two-Track Decision, and emphasized the modernization of conventional forces. At Washington's prodding, NATO in 1984 committed itself to a Conceptional Military Framework in which measures to improve the readinesss, mobility, survivability, and endurance of conventional forces were spelled out. There was also increased emphasis on burden-sharing with Western Europe and Japan. In spite of the financial squeeze and recurrent suggestions from members of Congress, the Reagan administration strongly opposed any reduction of its overseas forces.

The Federal Republic of Germany is a cornerstone in Washington's alliance strategy because of its geopolitical position, and its economic and political weight. The activities of the peace movement in West Germany were thus anxiously watched, and the consent to the deployment of Pershing IIs and Cruise Missiles was considered a test case of Bonn's alliance solidarity.

Relations with the United States' European allies were troubled by three bundles of problems: by the differing perceptions and policies vis-à-vis the Soviet Union, by security concerns, and by economic conflicts. In the latter case Japan was in the same boat with Western Europe.

While the United States favored a policy of neo-containment and, if possible, punishment of the Soviet Union for its invasion of Afghanistan, a number of West European allies, notably the Federal Republic of Germany, wished to continue with the policy of détente initiated with the 1967 Harmel doctrine. In their view the policy of détente had been quite successful in improving the situation in divided Europe, although it had not fulfilled all hopes. The United States expected its partners to support its policy of demarcation and denial, while the Europeans urged it to take a more accommodating position. However, in this process of conflicting interests they had to recognize that their influence amounted to but a veto power, though Washington had to change at least its tactics and to assimilate some of its partners' demands. The implementation of the NATO Two-Track Decision had been contingent on the resumption of arms control negotiations by Washington, and a few years later its willingness to negotiate on battlefield nuclear weapons and on conventional forces served to get allied endorsement for the Double-Zero solution in an INF agreement.

Another issue of European concern has been the changes in the U.S. military posture and in its military doctrine. Some allies objected strongly to the concept of deterrence by punishment, and to any notion that a nuclear war could be fought and won. For them, the only acceptable doctrine was that of deterrence by denial. Raising the nuclear threshold was no solution either as the Europeans neither had the capacity for significant conventional increases nor the will to endure a large conventional war on their territory given the risk of their own annihilation. SDI aroused further suspicions that the U.S. was risking the stability of deterrence and was willing to create zones of unequal security. Offering the allies the chance to cooperate in the technical development of the SDI program served neither to satisfy their economic interests nor to dispel their doubts.

Economic problems were caused by the huge trade deficit and the resulting protectionist tendencies in the United States (which corresponded to similar tendencies in Japan and in the European Community, notably its CAP). Another source of friction was imbalances in monetary affairs. But the most acute conflict resulted when Washington embargoed all deliveries for the Urengoy pipeline, applying these restrictions both ex post and extra-territorially to all parts of U.S. origin or patent. The U.S.A. only gave in and settled for a face-saving device (stricter COCOM controls and restrictions on credits) when its own industry joined in the protest of the West Europeans.

Alliance leadership was thus an asset as well as a liability – for all partners. As indicated by the pipeline conflict, the Reagan administration tended to proceed without its allies' consent if consultations did not yield quick results. Multilateral cooperation was not to impair its ability to lead forcefully, as was stated by Vice-President Bush in 1983: "I am sorry. The United States is the leader of the free world and under this administration we are beginning once again to act like it" (Watt 1984: 529). Washington did not apparently recognize that with its unilateralism it was impairing the very foundations on which its leadership rested.

5 The Reagan Doctrine and the Quest for Worldwide Leadership

In the view of the Reagan administration the countries of the Third World were figures in the global balance of power system. In order to advance its interests worldwide, the United States had to exert greater influence on these states, to win them as allies in the struggle against international communism, and to integrate them into the world economic system dominated by the West.

In an address before the Philadelphia World Affairs Council, President Reagan (October 15, 1981) outlined the basic premises of U.S. policy regarding the developing countries:

> The need to revitalize the United States and the world economy as a basis for the social and economic progress of our own and other nations, and the need to provide adequate defenses to remain strong, safe, in a precarious

> period of world history. In this context, U.S. relations with developing countries play a critical role. These countries are important partners in the world economy and in the quest for peace.

The most effective means for promoting a higher level of growth and development in these countries was to liberalize trade and open up markets, and to improve the climate for private capital flows. Instead of grand new programs, regulations should be rescinded to strengthen the private sector and thus stimulate steady growth. One of the most serious problems, the debt crisis, was likewise to be resolved through the existing monetary facilities. This was the gist of the Baker Plan, a call by Secretary of the Treasury Baker in October 1985 on the World Bank as well as on private finance institutions to reschedule the defaulting credits of the 15 most severely affected countries if they were prepared to undertake far-reaching reforms and to liberalize their economies.

In foreign aid new priorities were set. Increased emphasis was given to military assistance and related programs, the volumes of which were significantly increased. They were to provide for military stabilization in Third World countries as a precondition of their economic development. The Economic Support Fund was upgraded to serve as a flexible instrument giving aid to those countries which were of critical importance to the U.S. politically or militarily, like Israel, Egypt, Pakistan, El Salvador, and Turkey. Economic assistance programs were revised; their emphasis shifted from multilateral to bilateral projects. Additional regional programs were initiated like the Caribbean Basin Initiative and the Econommic Policy Initiative for Africa.

Special attention was focused on Central America. Support for the "Contras" in Nicaragua had been initiated by the Carter administration when the Sandinistas seemed to veer off their democratic course. The Reagan administration stepped it up, both by beefing up the Duarte regime in El Salvador with military aid and advisers, and by launching a massive propaganda campaign against "Cuban proxies" in Central America. The CIA initiated a number of large-scale clandestine operations which in the summer of 1984 culminated in the mining of Nicaraguan harbors to shut off Soviet reinforcements for the Sandinistas.

Though there was considerable concern both in the American public and in Congress that the United States could be drawn into a military conflict in Central America – a new "Vietnam" – this resulted in only half-hearted efforts to efffectively control the U.S. involvement. Though Congress circumscribed appropriations for counter-insurgency operations and even cut off all funds for fiscal year 1985, covert actions continued under the direction of the NSC and with funds diverted from other purposes. Only later, in the Iran-Contra scandal, were the dimensions of U.S. entanglement in Central America to bring down the Sandinista regime in Managua revealed.

In spite of its strong commitment to the causes of freedom and democracy, the Reagan administration was quite reluctant to use military force in furthering its interests. The U.S. 1983/1984 engagement in Lebanon was in line with previous commitments to peace-keeping forces; it was withdrawn after a disastrous attack against the Marine headquarters with the loss of 241 lives disintegrating its domestic support. The invasion of Grenada was in a different category; it was seen as a largely successful "surgical strike" to reaffirm American control of developments in the Caribbean. Another issue was the combat of terrorism (and its most obvious villain, Colonel Ghadafi of Libya), which after the La Belle incident in West Berlin led to the air raids in Tripoli and Bengazi. The Reagan administration emphasized that it would support its allies and friends with military and economic assistance, but not military means unless the security of the United States and its vital interests were threatened.

The shift from the retrenchment of U.S. power in response to the Vietnam War, to a cautious though noticeable expansion, occurred during the last year of the Carter administration. It was basically a response to the deterioration of East-West relations. In publicly announcing its support for anti-communist rebel forces in various parts of the world – Afghanistan, Angola, Cambodia, Ethiopia, and Nicaragua – the Reagan administration went a step further. Besides providing military and humanitarian aid for "freedom fighters" as the President liked to call those rebels he saw as "good guys," it lent them political and moral support. Their cause was declared legitimate and legal, as they were fighting for freedom and democracy, and in accordance with international law as an act of self-defense.

The formulation of these maxims in early 1985 that became known as the Reagan doctrine served three purposes. The most immediate was to lend support to the administration's request for funds in support of the Contras which was heavily resisted by Congress for fear of a military involvement in Central America. The Reagan doctrine was to give a moral justification to their cause, and also to make a distinction between indirect and direct U.S. involvement. With the Iran-Contra scandal unfolding, the doctrine's messianism was blemished when the gap between its high moral aspirations and the illegal or immoral means of its implementation became evident.

In a more general sense the purpose of the Reagan doctrine was to send a message to the Soviets on the limits of intervention in Third World areas. The Reagan administration challenged the status quo and reinforced its claim for peaceful, international change. With the support of anti-communist rebels, the U.S. tried to solve the dilemma that under the conditions of the nuclear age it had to balance its conflicting goals to fight for freedom and to preserve peace. The downfall of the authoritarian regimes in Haiti and the Philippines was interpreted as a vindication of this strategy. Above all, the Reagan doctrine served to substantiate the administration's claim that American leadership was back. To no small degree it was also addressed to the American public.

6 An Assessment

Has the Reagan administration achieved what with so much fanfare it had set out to do? Has it succeeded, with its economy revitalized and its military force posture strengthened, to shape international events according to its interests? And has it demonstrated effective global leadership?

If taken at face value, the Reagan agenda amounted to a sweeping change in the global correlation of forces – to make America number one in world affairs. In a multipolar world, however, changes can no longer be brought about unilaterally, nor can a so much more interdependent United States disentangle itself from infractions of its freedom of action. The Reagan administration's commitment to far-reaching international changes thus remained a vision, or a long-term goal, not a program for action.

Only incremental change was possible by utilizing the military, economic, and diplomatic potential of the United States. The central correlation of forces with regard to the Soviet Union, measured in military potential and options, was not dramatically altered. The increases in the U.S. defense budget which had already been initiated by the Carter administration, and which kept leveling off in the second Reagan administration after their dramatic surge in the first, prevented a further decline to the disadvantage of the United States, but no realignment. The three most significant initiatives were the launching of the SDI program, the modification of the role of nuclear weapons, and the return to serious arms control negotiations with the Soviets. Taken together, these changes can be considered a "revolutionary evolution" in security policy. SDI was a progam for the third millennium, which if realized would invalidate nuclear deterrence and significantly change power relations worldwide. While it tended to undermine the credibility of the U.S. security guarantee with respect to its allies, in the short run it exercised some leverage on the Soviets, challenging them to request the inclusion of SDI in an arms control framework. On the part of the U.S.A., a more promising attitude to arms control negotiations resulted from a combination of international and domestic demands which produced a situation in which an agreement was more in the American interest than an uncompromising posture vis-à-vis resourceful Soviet initiatives and financial constraints on the U.S. defense budget.

The East-West conflict had its impact on alliance relations as well. In order to keep its leadership position intact, the United States had not only to keep the nuclear guarantee credible, but at the same time to demonstrate its willingness to preserve the fruits of détente in Europe. The intrinsic problem of American leadership was the different conceptions the Reagan administration and America's allies in Europe had of both. The United States interpreted leadership above all as forceful, if unilateral action, while its partners asked for concerted policies based on extensive consultation. Given the differing priorities on various issues, consultations were bound to result in frustration, either because of demonstrated lack of understanding, or of too cumbersome and time-consuming procedures.

The recovery of the U.S. economy was much more limited than the Reagan administration had aimed for, but it did serve as a valuable stimulus to worldwide trade and output. The upswing was largely financed with foreign funds attracted to the U.S.A. by a strong dollar and high interest rates. In this process the United States was transformed from a leading creditor nation to the largest debtor. It is difficult to see how the Reagan administration will balance its fiscal and currency deficit while refusing to raise tax revenues or to significantly lower government spending. Another negative result was significant asymmetries in the balance of current accounts.

In September 1985 the Reagan adminstration departed from its previous claim that the U.S. economy could outgrow the deficit crisis and in doing so also enhance the currencies and the trading position of its partners. In a concerted effort, the five leading nations took measures to bring the dollar down in order to make the U.S. economy more competitive, and to ward off protectionism.

On balance, the United States has not regained its economic leadership. Its economic capabilities have further declined vis-à-vis its major competitors, the European Community and Japan. In spite of the low dollar, the trade deficit still looms large. The 1988 Trade Act will not improve access to markets for American products, but might invite further protectionism.

With the Reagan administration in office, the U.S.A. has become more dependent on the international economy than less. The percentage of its import trade in comparison to its GNP has risen to 15%; foreign investments amounted to more than $ 150 billion. American banks also carried the largest share in providing credits to major debtors in the Third World. However, the U.S.A. continued to advocate the practice of laissez-faire economics, while its partners emphasized the need for collective action. The economic summits deteriorated into great media events. Contrary to the assumption that the breakdown of hegemonic regimes will invite post-hegemonic patterns of multilateral action (Keohane 1984: 49), the U.S.A., the E.C. countries, and Japan each followed their own national strategies, only balanced by valiant though largely unsuccessful efforts to ward off protectionism.

The Reagan doctrine was most successful in its domestic application. In the Third World, the material and moral support for rebel forces was in most cases just enough to achieve stalemate, not victory. The democratic changes in Haiti and the Philippines were the result of indigenous developments which the United States started to support just in time to claim a role in bringing about change. The doctrine was further blemished by the gap between its moral justification and the illegal means it was implemented with.

It remains open to debate whether it was the result of sending the right signals to the Soviets which Moscow respected, or just plain luck, but so far the Reagan administration has been spared a major international crisis. The Beirut disaster was offset by the quick success in Grenada, the terrorist attacks on U.S. citizens by the strike on Libya. But neither was the United States prepared to support or to initiate a negotiated solution for one of the conflicts in Central America or in Southwest Asia. It repudiated the Contadora peace plan, and it lacked imagination to devise a solution to the Iran-Iraq conflict, beyond supporting the U.N. Security Council resolution. In both cases Washington came dangerously close to military involvements for which the American public was not prepared.

Crisis broke at home with the Iran-Contra affair. This consisted of a mixture of international entanglements and domestic wrongdoings, which undermined the credibility and the moral integrity of the Reagan administration.

In questioning the moral foundation on which the Reagan agenda was built, the Iran-Contra scandal undermined the very basis on which the Reagan administration's claim of worldwide leadership rested: the assumption of U.S. uniqueness and moral superiority. Much more than inadequate economic and military resources this affair unveiled the hollowness of its assertion of worldwide leadership. From its start the Reagan rhetoric had been contested abroad by friend and foe alike, but for a limited time it had been successful at home enough to remarshall confidence and self-respect in the American people humiliated by Vietnam, Watergate, and the Iran hostage crisis. Over time, however, it became evident that the United States was not able to exercise moral leadership. The Reagan administration's foreign policy neither followed a grand design, nor was it based on superior moral principles; its achievements were largely due to a pragmatic adaptation to domestic and international challenges.

References

Bode, William R. (1986): The Reagan Doctrine. *Strategic Review* (Winter): 21–29.

Brown, Seyom (1983): *The Faces of Power: Constancy and Change in United States Foreign Policy from Truman to Reagan*. New York: Columbia University Press.

Copson, Raymond W. and Richard P. Cronin (1987): The Reagan Doctrine and its prospects. *Survival* (Jan./Feb.): 40 – 55.

Davis, Tami R. and Sean M. Lynn-Jones (1987): Citty Upon A Hill. *Foreign Policy* 66 (Spring): 20 – 38.

Garthoff, Raymond L. (1985): *Détente and Confrontation: American Soviet Relations from Nixon to Reagan.* Washington, DC: Brookings Institution.

Goldstein, Walter (ed.) (1986): *Reagan's Leadership and the Atlantic Alliance. Views from Europe and America.* Elmsford, N.Y.: Pergamon.

Hacke, Christian (1986): Außenpolitische Grundlinien der Regierung Reagan. *Aus Politik und Zeitgeschichte. Beilage zur Wochenzeitung Das Parlament,* B 37 – 38/86 (13 September): 3 – 16.

Haig, Alexander M., Jr. (1981): Eine strategische amerikanische Außenpolitik. *NATO Brief* (December): 3 – 9.

Haig, Alexander M., Jr. (1984): *Caveat. Realism, Reagan, and Foreign Policy.* New York: Macmillan.

Kaplan, Fred (1983): *The Wizzards of Armageddon.* New York: Simon and Schuster.

Kegley, Charles W. Jr., and Eugene R. Wittkopf (1987): The Two Faces of the Reagan Administration's Foreign Policy Approach. *USA Today* (January): 10 – 15.

Kirkpatrick, Jeane J. (1982): Dictatorships and Double Standards. *Commentary* 65: 34 – 45.

Kirkpatrick, Jeane J. (1985): *The Reagan Doctrine and U.S. Foreign Policy.* Washington: Heritage Foundation.

Keohane, Robert O. (1984): *After Hegemony. Cooperation and Discord in the World Political Economy.* Princeton, N.J.: Princeton University Press.

Keohane, Robert O. and Joseph S. Nye (1977): *Power and Interdependence. World Politics in Transition.* Boston and Toronto: Little Brown.

Krauthammer, Charles (1986): Morality and the Reagan Doctrine. *New Republic,* September 8: 17 – 24.

May, Bernhard (1987): *Reagan und die Entwicklungsländer. Die Auslandshilfepolitik im amerikanischen Regierungssystem.* München: Oldenbourg.

Nye, Joseph S. (1982): U.S. Power and Reagan Policy. *Orbis* (Summer): 391 – 411.

Osgood, Robert E. (1981): The Revitalization Of Containment. *Foreign Affairs* 60(3): 465 – 502.

Osgood, Robert E. (1986): Continuity and Change in U.S. Foreign Policy: Reagan's Foreign Policy in a Postwar Perspective. In Walter F. Goldstein (ed.), *Reagan's Leadership and the Atlantic Alliance. Views from Europe and America.* Elmsford, N.Y.: Pergamon, 12 – 33.

Oye, Kenneth A., Jobert J. Lieber, and Donald Rothchild (1987): *Eagle Resurgent? The Reagan Era in American Foreign Policy.* Boston, Toronto: Little Brown.

Pranger, Robert J. (ed.) (1984): *Dimensions of U.S. Foreign Policy in the 1980s.* Washington, D.C.: American Enterprise Institute.

Reagan, Ronald: Address before the Philadelphia World Affairs Council. October 15, 1981. *American Foreign Policy: Current Documents,* vol. 1981. U.S. Department of State, Washington, D.C.: Government Printing Office: 63 – 69.

Reagan, Ronald: Press conference, October 2, 1981. *American Foreign Policy: Current Documents*, vol. 1981. U.S. Department of State, Washington, D.C.: Government Printing Office: 136–138.

Reagan, Ronald: Address to the United Nations General Assembly in New York, September 24, 1984. *American Foreign Policy: Current Documents*, vol. 1984, U.S. Department of State, Washington, D.C.: 221–227.

Reilly, John E. (ed.) (1987): *American Public Opinion and U.S. Foreign Policy.* Chicago: Chicago Council on Foreign Relations.

The Tower Commission Report (1987): The Full Text of the President's Special Review Board. New York: Random House (A New York Times Special).

Thompson, W. Scott (ed.) (1980): *National Security in the 1980s: From Weakness to Strength.* San Francisco: Institute for Contemporary Studies.

U.S. Department of State, Bureau of Public Affairs (1984): *Realism, Strength, Negotiation: Key Foreign Policy Statements of the Reagan Administration.* Washington, D.C.: Government Printing Office.

U.S. Department of State (1984 ff.): *American Foreign Policy: Current Documents*, vols. 1981, 1982, 1983. Washington, D.C.: Government Printing Office.

Watt, David (1984): The Conduct of American Foreign Policy: As a European Saw It. *Foreign Affairs* 62(3): 521–532.

Weinberger, Caspar: Address to the Council on Foreign Relations, June 17, 1981. *American Foreign Policy: Current Documents*, vol. 1981. U.S. Department of State, Washington, D.C.: Government Printing Office: 45–49.

White House (1987): *National Security Strategy of the United States*, January. Washington, D.C.: Government Printing Office.

Wieseltier, Leon (1986): What Went Wrong? An Appraisal of Reagan's Foreign Policy. *New York Times Magazine*, December 7: 43–49, 137, 148.

Part V
Postwar Policy Options: Case Studies

Left-Wing New Dealers, Moderate Communists, and Enlightened Bourgeois: Progressive Capitalism as a Program for the Postwar U.S.A.

Malcolm Sylvers

In a period when one hears talk of the decline of American economic hegemony and when even the International Monetary Fund indicates a new world financial order to be a primary objective, it may be of interest to take another look at one part of the debate in the United States towards the end of World War II on how the world was to be put back together after the defeat of the fascist powers. This chapter examines the ideas put forward in 1944 and 1945 by the left-wing New Dealer Henry Wallace, the Communist leader Earl Browder, and the enlightened businessman Eric Johnston. In three influential books, they essentially proposed that America, acting as a progressive capitalist power, participate in the moral and material reconstruction of the world in friendship with the Soviet Union and in harmony with the rights of all peoples to self-determination. Although such a program, victim of the Cold War and perhaps of the actual needs of monopoly capitalism, did not become reality, it deserves somewhat more attention than it has received to date.

The object of this essay, therefore, is to consider neither the reality of U.S. foreign policy nor the question of the objective origins of the Cold War; an attempt rather is made to illuminate the thinking behind what might have been an alternative policy.[1]

Far from the wartime battlefields and destruction, Americans had more time, material resources, and physical security than other peoples to carry on a vast national discussion on public policy. The positions developed by Wallace, Browder, and Johnston represent one tendency in a debate which took as its starting points the development of relations between the Big Three and the functioning and needs of the U.S. economy.

1 The Political Setting

The Atlantic Charter agreed to by Roosevelt and Churchill in August of 1941 – before the attack on Pearl Harbor – based "hopes for a better future for the world" on opposition to territorial changes not in accord with the peoples concerned, respect of all peoples to choose their own form of government, international collaboration to secure improved labor standards, economic advancement and social security, and abandonment of the use of force "for realistic as well as spiritual reasons." Freedom of the seas and "the enjoyment of all states, great or small, victor or vanquished, of access, on equal terms, to the trade and to the raw materials of the world which are needed for their economic prosperity" were also affirmed (Burns 1956: 130–131).

In the January 1942 joint "Declaration of the United Nations," after the United States and the Soviet Union had entered the war, a pledge was made for a complete victory "to defend life, liberty, independence and religious freedom, and to preserve human rights and justice in [the Allies'] own lands as well as in other lands" (Dallek 1979: 320). Although the Teheran Conference, in which the United States, Great Britain, and the Soviet Union took part in November 1943, dealt primarily with military coordination – including the firm commitment of the U.S.A. and Great Britain to open the "second front" the following spring –, questions relating to France, Indo-China, Poland, and the future status of a defeated Germany were discussed, as were ideas for a new international organization. The Teheran declaration of the Big Three "recognize[d] fully the supreme responsibility resting upon us and all the nations to make a peace which will command good-will from the overwhelming masses of the peoples of the world" (Sherwood 1948: 776–799; Churchill 1951: 342–407; Burns 1956: 406–414; Dallek 1979: 431–440).[2]

The final words of the Declaration stated that "We came here with hope and determination. We leave here friends in fact, in spirit, and in purpose." Roosevelt commented that "I got along fine with [Stalin]; and I believe that we are going to get along very well with him and the Russian people – very well indeed."[3] In the autumn of 1944 delegates from the Big Three began discussions in the Harvard residence "Dumbarton Oaks" on how to model a postwar security organization. The United States indeed had come far from its traditional antisovietism, which had only in part been dissipated by recognition in 1933 in one of the New Deal's first diplomatic measures (Dallek 1979: 439).[4]

The domestic economic situation was the other essential element in the American debate on the postwar world: the question in short was what was going to happen with the overwhelming increase in U.S. productivity which had developed during the war. In 1944 "the country was producing for the military effort alone at a rate nearly as high as the gross national product in

1929" (Brody 1975: 267). In terms of capital investment, job opportunities, and consumption, what would substitute, once the war was over, for the 300,000 aircraft, 100,000 tanks, and 70,000 landing craft produced in that year? The answer given by many – including Wallace, Browder, and Johnston – was intimately linked to the question of international relations and postwar reconstruction.

The ideas of these three were shared by many others. Sumner Welles in his *The Time for Decision* – a 1944 Book-of-the-Month Club selection which sold almost half a million copies – argued against an exclusively military approach and for a United Nations organization which would go beyond Britain, the Soviet Union, and the United States. Even more significant was the success of Wendell Wilkie's 1943 *One World* – it sold a million copies in eight weeks – which saw the war as part of a process of liberation for the world's peoples and called not only for U.N. cooperation, but also an end to "racial imperialism at home and abroad" (Dallek 1979: 267; Burns 1956: 357–358, 515).

Plans for future cooperation between the government and functional groups within the economy and for the coexistence of public, private, and semi-private enterprises in the development of a welfare state were also frequently discussed. Moreover, the foundation for a permanent mixed economy was considered necessary for the often-stated "postwar federal commitment to full employment." Based on New Deal and war experiences like the National Resources Planning Board as well as the more business-oriented Committee for Economic Development, such plans accepted governmental fiscal and monetary policies as legitimate devices to prevent either postwar depression or inflation (Markowitz 1973: 57–64).[5]

There was still strong isolationist sentiment, especially in Congress. But among many conservatives – far from the ideas of Wallace, Browder, and Johnston, and even among those who looked with suspicion on a future international organization – a consensus was growing at least on the point that the United States would be present as a leading power in world affairs and that such a presence would be expressly economic as well as political. Representative of the conservative "internationalist" perspective were the ideas of a Henry Luce who, in opposition to a reforming presence of the U.S.A. in the world, proclaimed instead a clearly hegemonic American presence which would institute the beginning of an "American century."

On these broad questions of principle, Roosevelt mediated and maneuvered somewhat less than usual. In his State of the Union message at the beginning of 1943 he spoke again of "freedom from want" – one of the Four Freedoms (together with freedom of speech, freedom of religion, and freedom from fear) articulated in his 1941 message – and how people at home and at the front were expecting full employment and assurance against the evils of all major hazards "that will extend from the cradle to the grave." And if in December of that year he made his famous comment that Dr. New Deal had been substituted by Dr. Win-the-War, the State of the Union message in early 1944 – considered by Burns to have been Roosevelt's most radical speech – reaffirmed the values of American liberalism as he struck out against the "pests who swarm through the lobbies of Congress and the cocktail bars of Washington" and the "selfish pressure groups who seek to feather their nests while young Americans are dying." Work stoppages were also criticized – Roosevelt proposed a national service law to prevent them – but it was clear to all that such groups were primarily identified in the realm of business.

In this address, the President called for increased taxes on profits, legislation to prevent "exorbitant profits and assure fair prices to the Government," and price controls on food. Most striking was his reference to a "second Bill of Rights," which would assure "equality in the pursuit of happiness" since "true individual freedom cannot exist without economic security and independence": the right to a job, to a good education, to housing and medical care, to extensive social security and unemployment provisions, to fair prices for farmers, as well as the right of businessmen not to be dominated by the monopolies at home or abroad were all included. Though Roosevelt obtained little success with his Congress, such ideas were often repeated until his death 15 months later.

On all occasions the winning of the war and the achievement of such objectives were coupled to the founding of an international organization which would make another armed conflict impossible. Despite Roosevelt's concern about how certain East European immigrant groups, important to the Democratic party, would react to the Soviet presence in their former homelands, Roosevelt nonetheless placed himself squarely among those who believed that cooperation with the Russians and trust in Russia were essential (Burns 1956: 361, 424–426, 507, 515, 528).[6]

Together with a review of the military situation, the Yalta conference in February 1945 brought increased though not final agreement on a number of points: the structure and representation in the future U.N. organization, the role of France, the dismemberment of Germany, the composition of the Polish government and its holding of elections, and the claims of the Soviet Union in the Far East together with the Soviet pledge to enter the war against Japan shortly after the defeat of Germany. A sort of framework for many of these questions was provided by a Declaration on Liberated Europe which committed the Big Three to assist liberated peoples in the complete destruction of nazism and fascism; political and economic problems were to be solved by democratic means and these peoples were to be helped in the establishment of internal peace and democratic governments through free elections.

Criticism of the Yalta conference would soon become an essential part of the Cold War polemic against the Soviet Union and often against Roosevelt himself. The general view of the participants, however, was expressed by Hopkins, who wrote that "The Russians had proved that they could be reasonable and farseeing and there wasn't any doubt in the minds of the President or any of us that we could live with them and get along with them peacefully for as far into the future as any of us could imagine." The President did in fact judge the atmosphere at the concluding dinner at Yalta to be "that of a family" and to a cabinet member he asserted that he had gotten the best deal possible (Sherwood 1948: 850 – 870; Dallek 1979: 508 – 521; Churchill 1951: 346 – 394; Ragionieri 1965; Clemens 1970).

Roosevelt has frequently been seen as a pragmatist, an improviser, or even an opportunist; at the very least he has been judged the creator of the Broker State which chaotically and continually adjusts conflicting interests. His biographer James Burns nonetheless considers his foreign policy and plans for the postwar world to have been consistent and coherent (Burns 1956: 547). The application of the Four Freedoms as well as the goals of the Atlantic Charter could for the President only be achieved through big power unity and cooperation, the complete eradication of nazism, general disarmament, and a United Nations with power to enforce the peace.

Such publicly declared concepts by Roosevelt on America's future role in the postwar world constituted a political and intellectual framework for the works of Henry A. Wallace, Earl Browder, and Eric Johnston. Although Wallace's *Sixty Million Jobs* appeared last of the three – in 1945 after the death of the President, while the other two had been published in the preceding year – his analysis is the proper starting point, in that he spoke from within the government, the organ which was central to the carrying out of postwar plans.

2 Henry A. Wallace

Henry A. Wallace had, of course, been a part of the New Deal since its inception and in varying ways had always been identified with the progressive forces within the administration. His dedication to the President as the main representative of his own ideas did not waver even after Roosevelt refused him, for internal party reasons, decisive support for reconfirmation as the vice-presidential candidate in 1944. After the election, free to choose whichever cabinet position he desired, he became Secretary of Commerce, indicative of the essential role he gave to this sector in postwar plans.

In May of 1942, Wallace delivered a famous speech which contrasted Henry Luce's "American century" with what he called "the century of the common man."[7] The historian Norman Markowitz has given an apt contrast of the ideas of the two men. Luce saw the New Deal policies as having weakened the United States by demagogy about "economic abundance." For him the postwar peace was to be "based consciously on opposition to any social change inconsistent with American free enterprise and on the expansion of the American private enterprise system and its benefits throughout the world." The speech of Wallace, instead, reflected "a combination of the radical democratic and evolutionary positivist views of social progress, of linear development in history, punctuated by revolutionary epochs (the American and Russian revolutions and the Second World War) in which the people triumph over the forces of demagogy and exploitation that seek to keep them in bondage" (Markowitz 1973: 48, 50, 51).

For Luce, writing even before the United States' entry into the war, the postwar world would necessarily be divided into hostile blocks; for Wallace the free world, as he called it, would include the Soviet Union because of, again to quote Markowitz, "that state's adherence to the ideals of equality, justice, and security." Wallace had been a supporter of Wilson and the League of Nations and as a convinced internationalist he believed that good relations between the Soviet Union and the United States were to be the cornerstone of the postwar world. It was, in fact, on this essential issue that he broke with Truman in 1946. Wallace felt that raising living standards and maintaining world peace together, "the two Allies would gradually become more alike, developing one system that would combine the best of political and economic democracy." He did not deny the use of political terror in the Soviet Union, but underlined that its ideology had never advocated racial supremacy or glorified war as the fascists had; it was, moreover, fear of Germany which had provoked the purges, the pact with Hitler, and the Finnish war (Markowitz 1973: 165–166). Wallace admitted in *Sixty Million Jobs* that "the Russian system of government is not for us"; but the fact that "the Russian government will not, for a number of years, permit its citizens certain basic freedoms that we prize so dearly" did not eliminate its wanting to make a secure peace. Moreover, the United States had "nothing to fear from Communism... if our free-enterprise system lives up to its opportunities."

For Wallace 60 million jobs – a slogan used by Roosevelt in the 1944 campaign – was synonymous with the peacetime requirements of full employment. Such an objective would assure the doubling of the standard of living of the poorest "and that as a result of this doubling process, the rest of us will have our own incomes made more certain, and we all will have the satisfaction of living in a broadly based democracy for the first time." Areas of "governmental responsibility" in the transition from war to peace were necessary and although governmental control of the economy such as existed during the war was not the objective, the cry of the danger of losing our freedom through planning was judged to be "the deliberate claptrap of confusionists." Unemployment was costly due to the loss of productive capacity and had to be eliminated; central to the employment problem was finding markets for the products of the 18 million (of the 60) who would be at work in manufacturing, mining, and construction.

The three million businessmen – a category which for Wallace was part of the 60 million jobs and went from "the proprietor of the corner drugstore" to the chairman of the United States Steel Corporation – must be both visionary and practical. The markets they would find would be both domestic and foreign. "There are still plenty of undeveloped frontiers at home.... We must conquer the slums; we must rid ourselves of undernourishment; we must raise the general level of health; and we must make it possible for everyone to develop his or her latent capacities for work and profitable recreation."

And yet, "Beyond our physical borders lie new horizons abroad" since the United States has assumed "a long-awaited leadership in world cooperation." Wallace's vision was truly global: "we look east to Europe for the opportunity to assist in restoring war-torn countries; we look west across the Pacific to aid in the industrialization of Asia; and we look south to fruitful cooperation with the Latin American republics where a total population somewhat larger than that of the United States is eager to use our industries, our skill and technical know-how, in raising its living standards."

Technology, development of those areas outside the U.S.A. still undeveloped, and expansion of the American economy were intimately combined in the vision of Henry Wallace: "Modern science and modern tools and equipment can increase the productivity and raise the wages and standards of living of men of all races – white and yellow, brown and black –, of all languages, and of all countries." Such a process of industrial and agricultural development throughout the world "will open up an unlimited new frontier of opportunities for the investment of American funds and the work of American hands and brains." Wallace calculated that repairing the war devastation, plus the initial steps toward industrialization in backward countries, would require from 55 to 65 billion dollars worth of plant and equipment in the few years immediately after the war. According to him "approximately half of this could easily come from the United States if suitable arrangements for its financing were worked out." The desire for collaboration with the Soviet Union could not overlook the fact that – as he stated in an article in the same year that this book was published – only the United States had the wealth and the skill to lead in world reconstruction (Markowitz 1973: 173).

The global outlook of Wallace was evident from his suggestion – for which he was often ridiculed – of TVAs along the Danube and the Ganges, along China's Yellow River and the Yangtze, the Jordan, the Tigris, and the Euphrates. Foreign trade, moreover, had to be conceived of as a two-way street: "we must realize that the real prosperity of nations depends not on what we all sell, but upon what we all consume." Nor was it only a question of raw materials: businessmen should also seek out "the varied goods and speciality products of the craftsmen of other countries." In this light Wallace supported in *Sixty Million Jobs* the creation of what would become the International Monetary Fund and the World Bank as means to help nations in meeting their foreign exchange requirements and in finding investment funds. The United Nations had an important role to play in reducing trade barriers and ending "private and irresponsible monopoly" in international commerce. In no sense, however, was such a vigorous development of trade to mean a struggle for supremacy between the nations since "economic warfare is as destructive of prosperity as military warfare."

Wallace did not consider his program of a government-aided expanding economy to be in contrast with the free-enterprise system. The Secretary of Commerce indicated the American system of profit making – greater production at lower prices, more efficiency, and higher wages for a huge mass market – as being most in harmony with the object of increasing living standards. The enemy of this dynamic capitalism was for him monopoly and he called on government to aid, for example, small businesses in scientific research, since they could not support the costly large laboratories which were necessary.

Wallace examined the needs and desires of the various groups in American society. The worker desired security in his job and purchasing power for himself and his family. He expected new dislocations and uprootings, but looked to government and industry to cooperate with labor to make the transition as short as possible. This hypothetical worker also justly looked forward to the elimination of discrimination against Catholics, Jews, and Negroes, as well as labor-management cooperation. The farmer had an equal interest in full employment, as this would assure a higher level of farm income due to increased consumption; he would also benefit from social programs such as school-lunches. Businessmen, too, needed government assistance and orientation.

The people expected these groups to cooperate among themselves and with the government "to arrive at the maximum in unified policy." The role of government was in fact crucial and a proper balance between absolute liberty and absolute control had to be found "at the point where the minimum measure of control will give us the maximum of liberty."

Wallace was against a planned economy, which was his definition of socialism; he was, however, insistent on government guidelines for the economy, which he outlined in detail through the mechanism of a national full employment budget to be submitted to Congress annually by the President. Such a budget would cover not only the expenditures and receipts of the federal government, but everything that would be bought and consumed each year by all segments of the nation. The government would make estimates of economic behavior and then employ incentives to influence it: tax and credit devices would stimulate both consumers and businessmen to spend more and therefore create more jobs while also being used to control inflation. Government funds for public works and direct investment in the development of national resources (river valley projects, land conservation, reforestation, and rural electrification) were additional instruments to be utilized as a stimulus of private initiative in order to achieve full employment.

Planning guidelines were ideally also to be drawn up on the local level and this form of activity seems to have met his desire to link a dynamic capitalism with grassroots democracy. He was, he relates, impressed by the many booklets he had received from cities and towns on their expected future growth; they showed that "Main Street was not waiting for either Wall Street or Pennsylvania Avenue." Industries, moreover, should also be encouraged to do their own planning and keep the government informed. The citizens' job was to decide "what part we want business to play, and what part we want government to play" in order to arrive at full employment.

Henry Wallace concluded his book with a homage to the spirit of America – a country "that has produced more than any other people who have ever lived on this earth" and where "all things are possible" – together with an appeal for an understanding of "the fatherhood of God and the fundamental decency of man."

3 Earl Browder

Wallace was no longer vice-president when he wrote *Sixty Million Jobs*, but he nonetheless remained an important political leader. The influence of Earl Browder, the leader of the Communist Party of the United States (CPUSA), was exercised in a much more indirect way. With less than 100,000 members in a country of 140 million the CP, due to capable militants operating at the base of the society, was, however, able to play a leading role in certain sectors of the new trade-union movement, the CIO; it achieved, moreover, a notable presence in the cultural world. On the local level – especially in northern metropolitan areas and cities of the industrial midwest – the CP was important as a support for left-leaning candidates of the Democratic party. The CIO Political Action Committees, in which the Communists were often the driving force, were perhaps decisive for the President's reelection in 1944.[8] Browder's book *Teheran. Our Path in War and Peace* may not have been a Book-of-the-Month selection, but nonetheless it was published in 1944 in 100,000 copies.

Browder was arrested during the period of the German-Soviet Pact when the U.S. Communists opposed Roosevelt's support of Britain. After the Nazi invasion of the Soviet Union, the CP's position evidently changed, and once the U.S. entered the war after Pearl Harbor the basis had been laid for a full integration of the Communists into the war effort; in 1942 the CP leader received a presidential pardon.

Browder made national unity and the unity of the United Nations forces the cornerstones of CP policy and, based on this, developed a coherent vision as to how the country's economy should be run during the war and what the postwar world would be like. Although such positions were most fully developed in *Teheran*, written in early 1944 shortly after the conclusion of the historic Big Three conference, the main lines of such ideas can be found in his writings in the preceding two years (Browder 1942, 1943).[9]

Browder, like Wallace, liked to think globally and he obviously enjoyed the idea that his small movement could have influence beyond its numerical strength. He was not, in short, content with simply being a minor pressure group on the left of the broad Roosevelt coalition. Despite his constant affirmation that the CPUSA was an American party which made its own decisions, he often put himself forward as an unofficial representative of a world movement even after the dissolution of the Comintern in 1943. He frequently warned American political leaders that the persecution of a small group of American Communists (there were still many in Congress who were intent on juridically limiting the role of the Communists denying them their rights as a political group) would render more difficult the country's relations with those parts of the emerging new world – Europe and Asia – where the Communists seemed destined to play an important role. According to Browder (but this was in part wishful thinking) one could not be an ally of the Soviet Union and fight against nazifascism while at the same time suppressing Communists at home.

The CP during the war became less and less anticapitalist in its immediate and middle-term perspective. Browder noted bluntly that the U.S. Communists were few and that "no ruling class had ever been overthrown by revolution unless and until it had brought disaster upon that nation by false policies, greed and incompetence." Hoover had brought the country to the brink of revolution, but Roosevelt in fact had reduced tensions, since "he gave people reasonable hope of remedying their intolerable condition." The U.S. would remain capitalist but, posing the theme of coexistence, he considered that this system was not in any case "so fragile that it can't exist in the presence of socialism."

American capitalism was the most advanced technologically, but lagged in "self-understanding and self-consciousness." If therefore Browder accepted capitalism in general, he displayed an impatience with the ignorance of the

U.S. capitalist class. Needlessly inciting the workers to strike and opposing all sorts of necessary planning and streamlining of production, it had showed itself incapable of understanding its own interest in a quick victory over nazifascism. He was equally critical of the government for its inability to design policies for the objectives it wished to reach (e.g., a plan to control inflation in order to avoid strikes). It is hard not to qualify his attitude as a strange mixture of arrogance and naiveté: "In the U.S. we have to win this war under the capitalist system. Therefore we have to find out how to make the capitalist system work. And since the capitalists themselves, who are in charge of that, are not doing a job that satisfies us, we have to help the capitalists to learn how to run their own system under war conditions."

Browder considered government intervention in the economy, in the form of planning, a requirement for the war effort; such planning was not socialism nor even a step towards socialism but only state capitalism, a necessity imposed by the war. Wages had to be seen as a part of this planning and as a way of aiding production: "equality of sacrifice" between capitalists and workers was rejected as a confused slogan. Towards the end of 1943 Browder made the controversial recommendation of wage incentives linked to productivity, a position which may have cost the Communists some support in the factories.[10]

The starting point for discussion in *Teheran* was the great changes brought to the world by the violence of Hitlerism and that of the movement to destroy it. The Teheran agreement meant for Browder that the Soviet Union had finally been accepted by the West. Therefore the two sides were to adapt themselves to each other seeking "a program and perspective not out of their own desires and ideologies, but from the possibilities of agreement between them which would preserve the most vital interests of each and thus create the possibility to reconstruct the whole world order of nations."

Towards the end of his book, Browder dealt with the American political scene and how the Communists could influence it. It was here that he launched his proposal for the dissolution of the party and its substitution by a Communist political association which would permit the Communists to spread their ideas more efficiently, acting as independent voters rather than having their own party and competing on the electoral level. In May 1944 he managed to put through such a transformation which in mid-1945 was the main reason for his dismissal from party leadership.

Much more interesting than this proposal – however important it was in the development of American Communism – was the fundamental analysis Browder made of what he considered to be the "vital interests" of American capitalism and how they could be met. Since there was not in America even a potential majority for a socialist perspective, the majority in this country in support of "Teheran" not only was "to accept the existing economic system as its... starting point," but national unity had to include "a decisive part of the big capitalists." Such men must bring the system to a "maximum of self-limitation to meet a minimum of governmentally imposed regulation that will effectively curb the anti-social and anti-national tendencies of big capital."

The main economic problem facing the country, according to Browder, was how after the defeat of nazifascism one could find an immediate substitute for the war market of 90 billion dollars in terms of peacetime goods. The Communist leader proposed that half be found in the foreign market and the rest in the domestic one. The former was primary given the need of feeding and rehabilitating the war-ruined peoples and reconstructing their shattered economies. Such an economic task was evidently in keeping with the Teheran vision of peaceful collaboration after the war. Browder made a suggestion that Wallace's world TVA program would resemble strikingly: "our government can create a series of giant industrial development corporations, each in partnership with some other government or group of governments, and set them to work upon large-scale plans of railroad and highway building, agricultural and industrial development, and all-round modernization in all the devastated and underdeveloped areas of the world."

Increasing the domestic market meant raising the conditions of the producing population, since there was no room for a huge program of capital investment within the United States. This could be done either through large-scale governmental programs in educational, health and general environmental improvement, or through a doubling of the purchasing power of those who habitually spent all their income. Such an increase in purchasing power could not be accomplished through the accumulated decisions of individual private enterprises; in order to avoid disadvantages to single firms it had to be a public policy with the power of government behind it. The domestic market, in reality, would have to be increased even more, given that the United States would be receiving imports from abroad in payment for its expanded exports.

After this description of what was no less than a national and international relaunching of the New Deal on a scale to which it had never existed, Browder then proceeded to analyze how future developments in the rest of the world would relate to the needs of American capitalism. In all cases he found no incompatibility but rather points of contact between these needs and those of the democratic development of the area in question. Most of Europe west of the Soviet Union, he declared in a December 1943 speech shortly after the Teheran meeting, was to be reconstructed on a capitalist bourgeois democratic basis; it would neither remain fascist nor become socialist. The cartel system would not, however, be abolished as an economic structure, since the nature of the capitalist system was monopolistic. Nevertheless, far-reaching reforms would take place and they were in the interests of the United States, since "Only the new democratic Europe is capable of buying and selling on the world market, *and paying its bills*, in a fashion and on a scale necessary to fit, with America, into a single world order."

With regard to the underdeveloped world the perspective was no different. A new Asia would arise after the defeat of Japan and this could not be similar to the old prewar colonial empire system which, if resurrected, "will not and cannot operate to the benefit of America, not even to the benefit of American monopoly capitalism." A stable Asia required "the rise of free and independent national states comprising all the principal peoples of the continent, and their inclusion into the mainstream of world development, politically and economically." In Africa the old imperial system would meet a similar fate: the continent "would be industrialized with its native populations drawn into participation in the process and in its benefits." Such a development "would open another of those huge markets for America and England, which are essential at once when the war ends if the world is not to plunge into another devastating economic crisis like that of 1929–33." As to Latin America, where, moreover, the ideas of Browder had their most direct influence in the world Communist movement, the United States had to give evidence of the permanence of its Good Neighbor policy in taking "the lead in proposing a common program of economic development... on a huge scale in some degree commensurate with Latin America's great reserves of land, raw materials, and manpower, and with the Anglo-American ability to furnish capital and create markets for heavy industry products."

In all of these areas the United States had to support democratic forces not only because they were the ones actually fighting nazifascism (as in Yugoslavia and China), but because they represented the demands of developing democracy which directly intersected with the needs of U.S. capitalism. Once the political framework of dependency was eliminated – and Browder did call for the independence of Puerto Rico – capitalism in the underdeveloped world, according to the American Communist leader, could draw profits behaving in a non-imperialist manner, developing these areas rather than operating in a way so as to keep them necessarily in a state of dependence and misery.

Within the United States and certainly linked with his proposal to dissolve the party, Browder foresaw a continuation of the Teheran spirit of national unity. The Communists were to aim at labor-management collaboration and avoid, if possible, strikes. Raising wages – part of the expanding market scenario – was to be accomplished as "a *national aim* to be pursued by all classes and institutions with the same determination with which we now conduct the war."

This was the Teheran spirit and collaboration along these lines would continue because, in Browder's view, it was in the national interests of Britain and the United States as generally conceived by the ruling classes. The ruling classes might, however, because of insufficient political acumen or backward ideological traditions, not always understand their real interests. In the United States, for Browder, it was the special task of the Communists, "a small but influential part of the national war consensus" to explain, through the use of Marxism, the new world realities to the capitalist class and encourage those elments within it which had already arrived at such an understanding. Browder, in short, proposed for his movement the role of Communist counselor to the capitalist prince, the prince being at times the President, at times the actual holders of economic power.

4 Eric Johnston

Wallace and Browder were political leaders who sought to guide American capitalism in the postwar world; Eric Johnston was himself an American capitalist who in *America Unlimited*, published in 1944, sought the same objective. Johnston put himself forward as a fairly typical middle-sized American businessman whose Horatio Alger life had included selling newspapers as a youth in Spokane, Washington and then working on Seattle's docks while a college student. He rapidly achieved success in the field of electrical contracting and retail supply and in the early years of the Great Depression was president of his hometown Chamber of Commerce. Elected president of the United States Chamber of Commerce in 1942, he occupied an influential position from which to discuss the role of business and the United States in the postwar world. If his book contains much specific advice on this subject, it is also a tract of his philosophy on what is America and why it – "a nation without precedent in human history for the spread of knowledge, for standards of living and of decency, for the prevalence of political and spiritual freedoms" – is for him, no less than for the early Puritans, the "city on the hill," an example for the rest of the world.

He sees the spiritual values of the United States – freedom, self-respect, democratic justice – as resulting from a mixture of competition and self-interest with cooperation. Such competition did not necessarily mean the ruin of some, since (in contrast with Europe) wealth in American was not fixed, but rather "an ever-expanding, snowballing element, so that the enrichment of one implies some measure of enrichment of all."

The idea of opportunity as the key to the American experience is linked to his view of American capitalism. For Johnston there are three main capitalisms in the world: that of the bureaucrats (e.g., the Soviet Union and Nazi Germany), which he firmly rejects as inimical to freedom; that of private monopoly and special privilege, which he combats since they limit opportunities; and lastly, that which he prefers and which exists in America, although threatened: "people's capitalism." As a champion of small and middle-sized business, he insisted that monopoly practices be curbed by government. Monopoly is, nevertheless, distinguished from mere bigness, which can coexist with open competition: his own prosperous activity in the electrical manufacturing field despite the presence of General Electric and Westinghouse is cited as proof.

"People's capitalism" was in America, according to Johnston, a reality since almost all participated in the system. If he is not very convincing on this – included as capitalists are all those "who own insurance policies, a few shares of stock in some business, whose savings on deposit in the banks are invested in business ventures" – what is significant is his sense that the system functioned through interdependence: labor, management, and agriculture were firmly intertwined and the prosperity of one was linked to the others; the one could not go ahead at the expense of the others.

Capitalism for Johnston "has no need of apologetics," since "it glows with the colors of perfection when compared with other known and tried economic systems." And yet Johnston is a reformer and willing to admit to "the faults and inequities of our way of life" such as hunger and unemployment and he is critical of those spokesmen of American capitalism who "have thought it necessary to deny, explain away, or even praise aspects of American life which no normal, decent-minded, warm-hearted human being can possibly approve."

In this light, his evaluation of the New Deal is substantially positive despite his complaint that in the government there had been many – socialists, communists, collectivists, superplanners – who operated with a spirit of vendetta and class warfare and who considered capitalism parasitic and the Depression an opportunity to deliver the *coup de grâce* to it. Roosevelt is judged to be "a real democrat... with a genuine sympathy for the underdog," "as fine a specimen as our country has produced", although he had sought to confer unconstitutionally exceptional powers on the government.

Johnston approved of relief for farmers and for all Americans in distress and considers the slogan "Let them starve" to be one of savagery, and out of place in a civilized society. He supports the Security and Exchange Commission which, purged of bureaucratic accretions, could be "a spur to investment in job-making enterprises." The Wagner Act and Social Security are also considered positively, as is the right to collective bargaining; with regard to unions, they are judged here to stay, although he is critical of undemocratic practices in some of them. He considered it unfortunate that "management-labor relations have... been frozen into patterns of mutual distrust and hostility"; such a situation was not warranted by the facts since "upon their relationship there is no shadow of the feudal memories of master and serf which still darken management-labor dealings in some other parts of the world." Both sides must maintain the right of expression of intelligent self-interest, facing issues squarely, analyzing problems honestly, and reaching equitable solutions.

For Johnston, no less than for Wallace and Browder, the United States was slated to play a leading role in the postwar world. "There is no imaginable road to global peace and economic improvement which does not pass through our country. Whether we like it or not, whether we approve it or not, it is our destiny to play the lead role in the great drama of postwar economic reconstruction.... We have attained that role by virtue of the American system of enterprise that made us strong." He speaks proudly of the lend-lease contributions which have "tipped the scales of victory"; in this success government had played a dominant part, but while he admits to "isolated instances of war profiteering," he insists that "credit for the most astounding production job in all human history must go primarily to American capitalism."

Johnston enumerated the main features of the postwar economic situation: the United States would be in possession of the greatest plant capacity, sources of raw material, natural and synthetic, and skilled mechanics and technicians than ever before in its history; there would be a tremendous backlog of accumulated demand for all types of commodities in the United States, and the people would have unprecedentedly large savings with which to satisfy these deferred demands; "an economic vacuum will exist in most of the nations of the world, and it is an immutable law of nature that a vacuum must be filled." Given this, the postwar period would contain both problems and opportunities.

The "elephantine government directed economic structure" could not be dismantled overnight: "the liquidation of our swollen government-in-business must be planned [and] intelligently paced." The transition was to be accomplished as a cooperative effort without class warfare and no specific element in the complex American society – capital, labor, agriculture – could expect to take advantage of the situation. He gave his approval to "full employment," understood as the maximum possible (rather than 100%, which he judges impossible due to the dynamic nature of the U.S. economy).

For someone who has defined free private business as a motorcycle – "It must move. If it stops, for lack of gasoline, it topples over" – his preoccupation with expansion is not surprising. Johnston denounced as defeatist those who had asserted that there was no more room for growth and that the United States had achieved "maturity" and must henceforth decline.

In which direction would this expansion go? Where would the "frontiers of expansion" – a chapter title in his *America Unlimited* – be found? Like Wallace and Browder, he did not reject expansion of the domestic market in that poverty is one of the frontiers to be conquered: "slums, substandard homes and diets, children deprived of the minimal conditions of civilized living, a thousand-and-one proofs that there is unlimited room for economic improvement." Despite this it is clear for him that an important part of this postwar expansion would be directed abroad.

Johnston stated openly that his 1943 trip to Latin America as the chairman of the United States Commission on Inter-American Development was also made as a businessman looking for postwar opportunities for "American capital, brains, and brawn." Everywhere he saw these possibilities from the first-class hotels which did not yet have modern dry cleaning equipment, to a small village in Brazil where the people raised cattle chiefly for hides since the riverboats lacked refrigeration. His comment on the latter was typical: "An opportunity, I made a mental note, for the American refrigeration industries."

American businessmen had much to offer. They were needed and wanted, but, Johnston warned, as partners, and not "exploiters" (his quotation marks). They had to adapt to local situations and avoid patronizing attitudes. Yet South American businessmen were judged by him to be often backward, seeking to make a large profit on a small turnover, while "our philosophy of small profit on large sales is still alien to him." Johnston pointed with pride to a jointly owned factory in Argentina where the workers were employed at double what they had previously been paid. Now, however, "for the first time these workers are able to purchase luxuries as well as necessities. They can now think of buying radios, cosmetics, and other products normally imported from the United States." According to Johnston, industrialization in Latin America was not to be seen as a threat to U.S. exports. If every person in South America could buy one cotton garment, he hypothesized, there would be an enormous increase in the local textile industry "and this would mean that South America would be in the market for looms and many other kinds of textile machinery manufactured in the United States."

The country had to continue with the Roosevelt Good Neighbor policy in opposition to political imperialism. The economic relations that Johnston wished with the underdeveloped world were, however, meant to be the opposite of philanthropy. "I do not want to make those peoples into wards of the great nations.... The underdeveloped regions of the world want our American and British capital; but they want to mingle it with capital and representation of their own."

When he visited Britain he refused to be discouraged by the assumptions found there in favor of government participation and monopoly. Here, too, cooperation was necessary and possible. "We have more capital," he noted, but "Britain has more knowledge of the intricate mazes of international credits, exchanges, and finance. We have the greater wealth; they have the greater experience. Let us pool them!" Once again the accent was on the link between nations' economies: "British prosperity is essential to American prosperity."

In his conclusion he insisted on the theme of the U.S.A. as part of a world community. "Despite our colossal weight in world affairs, we are far from outbalancing the rest of the nations. The voice of America is listened to, but it is not a solo; it must be harmonized with the chorus of nations." Help in postwar reconstruction was not only humanitarian, but in the self-interest of the United States: "Countries sunk in chaos and poverty are the breeding places of Mussolinis and Hitlers and new world wars." Domestic prosperity rather than handouts and charity was the key to a stable society; America was interested in world stability since "no country is self-sufficient in this complex technological era." He naturally spoke out against trade barriers and emphasized that since America was a creditor nation she had to welcome imports in order to permit the servicing of the debt.

Johnston says little in this book on the Soviet Union: its system denied political freedom and limited economic opportunity, but he evidently did not place it on the same level as the Axis powers. Stalin's remark at Teheran that U.S. production was essential for the Allied victory was noted with special pleasure, since it came from "the ruler of a nation that had contributed many millions of lives to the common victory." (Equally pleasing to the president of the U.S. Chamber of Commerce was that Earl Browder had declared a "truce with the capitalist order." Whatever his motives, stated Johnston, "it was grudging confirmation, from the extreme Left, that our people's capitalism had regained its old health and vigor.") After "the magnificent showing of the Russian people in the war," they can be expected to compete with the United States for world leadership and world markets. Such an "inevitable competition between "the greatest democratic capitalist society and the greatest collectivist society ever known... will have... something truly titanic." But such rivalry did not necessarily mean conflict, especially armed conflict.

His sparse comments on the Soviet Union can be best understood within the framework of his overall program in international relations: acceptance of a multilateral organization in the maintaining of peace; effective military preparedness as insurance against the possible failure of such world organization; tolerance for the political and economic systems of other nations and non-intervention in their internal affairs; the maximum encouragement of world trade consistent with American interests. Relations here with the U.S.S.R. seem to be understood more in terms of peaceful coexistence than anything else and his conclusion – alongside a hymn to the American values of freedom of opportunity and active optimism and the statement that man's capacity for greatness was being tested in America – spoke of the horror of war and the inacceptability of group and race hatreds. The president of the United States Chamber of Commerce had no doubts that the superiority of the American system would be easily and peacefully demonstrated.

5 A Comparative View

The books by Wallace, Browder, and Johnston have much in common as they state and search to revolve the central question of the diplomatic and economic postwar position of the United States. All three make a notable effort to reflect on the functioning of the sytem as a whole as opposed to its single parts. With differing emphasis they all underline, at times indirectly, several elements: the importance of continuing the Teheran spirit and that conflicts between the Big Three are to be avoided (and to this Wallace added that the socio-economic systems of the Soviet Union and the United States were somewhat less differnt than often imagined); the development of the war-torn areas and the colonial world is a necessary path; such a development can and will be non-exploitative in that the areas will take the path of development and not dependency; this development is, moreover, no threat for U.S. capitalism; the capitalism of increased production at lower prices – the American form – is the most "social" way that the system can operate; political imperialism is considered something of the past, a political choice and not a necessary outcome of the system; foreign areas of investment and the free flow of imports and exports are an absolute necessary for the economy, although the internal market also has room for expansion; without such foreign areas the enormous problem of reconversion cannot be faced by the economy; planning and government intervention in some form are necessary; industrial conflicts within the United States must be avoided and labor-management cooperation is to be fostered; a strong patriotism is tempered somewhat by the need that America make a search for common values.

The three authors were, of course, aware of their holding similar positions. Browder, the least important of the three, had commented favorably in *The Communist* on Wallace and Johnston. Johnston's en passant ironic remark on Browder supporting capitalism probably masked the feeling – also present in Wallace – that the CP, because of its position in important trade unions, was a key factor in the avoidance of industrial conflict. Moreover the Secretary of Commerce certainly considered the CP an influential factor in Democratic party politics. Undoubtedly to the annoyance of the CP's leader, however, neither considered him the necessary path for communicating with the Soviet Union.

There were certainly differences: Browder saw more of a role for the state in the economy, while for Johnston and Wallace government was to play only a subsidiary role. Moreover, the Communist leader had no objection to monopoly, while the other two maintained an antimonopoly position and rhetoric. It is no surprise that the businessman Johnston exalted the capitalist class, while the other two were rather suspicious of this group of citizens: Browder, after all, was still a communist despite his notable revisions of traditional Marxism and Leninism, while Wallace had consistently fought against "the interests" during the New Deal. And if Wallace thought in terms of combining the best in the United States and the Soviet Union, the Communist leader and the president of the Chamber of Commerce naturally had different views as to which social system better met the interests of the people.

The ideas put forward in their books were in 1944 and 1945 within the boundaries of the general political discussion even if not accepted by all who discussed postwar plans. In addition a claim could be made that more than others they represented the ideas of the President. All this was to change with the development of the Cold War under Truman. The transformation in American attitudes was perceptible almost immediately after the death of Roosevelt, certainly by Potsdam. On a series of crucial questions – the handling of the atom bomb, the organization of the U.N., the reconstruction loan to the Soviet Union, as well as the latter's claim to German reparations – the new President, a man of limited vision from the provinces, backed by nuclear weapons and pressed by the increasing displeasure of East European immigrant groups, showed no desire to continue in the pursuit of collaboration with that power that had given most and suffered most for the common victory.

As early as October of 1945, Truman – as if anticipating the comments of a President of the 1980s – spoke of how "we shall not give our approval to any compromise with evil." By the spring of 1947 positions had further hardened with the Truman Doctrine meant to construct a bastion of anticommunism and the Marshall Plan which sought to keep Western Europe anchored to the United States and if possible to wean Eastern Europe away from the Soviet Union; the Soviets for their part did everything possible to strengthen their control over that part of Europe they had liberated and which they justly considered a zone of vital national security.

The increasingly harsh Cold War atmosphere reduced space for dissent and Truman's foreign policy was necessarily accompanied by a witch hunt begun long before the arrival on the political scene of the junior senator from Wisconsin. The positions developed in the three books under consideration came to be considered subversive and it may be of interest to sketch out briefly the ideological and political destiny of the authors during the immediate postwar period.

Those who have given major weight to the U.S.S.R. for the breakdown of wartime collaboration with the United States have often indicated the removal of the U.S. Communist leader Earl Browder to be one of Stalin's opening moves in the Cold War. In the same month as Roosevelt's death, an article appeared in a French Communist periodical strongly criticizing Browder for having dissolved the CPUSA in the spring of 1944 (Duclos: 1945). Such an action was judged incorrect given the task of combating the fascist tendencies of American monopolies. Shortly after the publication of this article – considered the authentic voice of the Soviet leadership although written by a PCF leader – Browder was removed from office and replaced by William Z. Foster. What is interesting is that Foster's more militant class struggle outlook did not mean a fading of the Communist emphasis on the general Popular Front outlook developed by the party from the mid-1930s. The reconstituted Communist party under Foster certainly became more sectarian, especially as the Cold War took root; in its general political outlook it did not, however, become extremist and it not only considered valid the line followed during the war under Browder but criticized Truman above all for having deviated from the Roosevelt policies. Browder was faulted for having thought that the capitalist class would *naturally* have followed the path of collaboration and for having taken away that instrument – the party – which alone would have been able to coerce the capitalists into following a line of peace with the Soviet Union. Although Browder's "Keynesianism" was attacked, nowhere was it assumed that the scenario he had laid down for U.S. capitalism was an impossible one.[11]

Wallace, on the other hand, remained on the political scene a few years longer, going down to defeat for his policy of friendship with the Soviet Union. Like many other New Dealers, Wallace was also distraught over how the new President departed from the domestic policies of Roosevelt. Truman rapidly showed himself to be a solid friend of special-interest monopoly capitalists – Ickes broke with him over the question of oil concessions – and he only half-heartedly pushed the full employment bill which was central to Wallace's reasoning in *Sixty Million Jobs*. The Secretary of Commerce, however, split with Truman primarily on the question of foreign policy. Most of those in Congress who would oppose the Truman Doctrine did so from an old-fashioned isolationist position; Wallace, instead, from the time of his Madison Square Garden speech of September 1946, emerged as a symbol for all those who wished for a continuation of what they felt was the essential Roosevelt policy – collaboration with the Soviet Union for an active reconstruction of the postwar world along peaceful lines.

The forces which supported such policies dwindled as the majority of liberals came to accept the Cold War.[12] Wallace, leading those liberals who stayed together with the political left in a new edition of the Popular Front coalition, ran in the 1948 elections for President as a third-party alternative. Despite the Cold War legend, which has the Soviet Union, Cominform decisions, and the CPUSA behind the formation of this party, American Communists were initially far from enthusiastic about the newly formed Progressive party (PP); for them it lacked the necessary labor support, since most of the CIO was in the Truman camp. The development of big power tensions and perhaps suggestions by the international communist movement did move the CP to an all-out support of Wallace; by that time, however, his campaign and the formation of the Progressive party was well on its way. The usual Communist organizational abilities and the notable qualities of many party representatives, together with the scarce presence of other organized groups, did allow the CPUSA to assume an extensive if not determining influence in the campaign.

The 1948 elections were probably the last moment when the line of friendship with the Soviet Union as a central aspect of United States foreign policy would be raised as an issue by a group with something of a national audience. The Progressive party platform proposed a form of world government – this was incidentally a position quite distant from the Communist approach; an end to "the tragic prospect of war" was considered a "joint responsibility of the Soviet Union and the United States"; peace was indicated as "the prerequisite to survival" and the "anti-Soviet hysteria" sweeping America was denounced "as a mask of monopoly, militarism and reaction." Despite a vigorous campaign and a dramatic challenge by Wallace to segregation in the South, the electoral results were considered disastrous. The PP polled only slightly over 1 million votes – less than 2.5% of the popular suffrage, even slightly less than that received by the white-supremacist candidate who had bolted the Democratic party.[13]

Unlike Browder and Wallace, Eric Johnston, the progressive businessman, shifted his political positions a great deal in a short time. Although he was somewhat less extreme than others, he rapidly became an integral and even important part of the Cold War consensus. Towards the end of his presidency of the U.S. Chamber of Commerce he had assumed leadership of the Motion Picture Association of America, the self-regulating policymaker for the film industry. In this capacity, after a very timid opposition to the House Un-American Activities Committee which was investigating Hollywood, he instituted in the fall of 1947 the blacklist, suggesting to the major studios that they agree not to employ "proven Communists."[14]

In 1948 Johnston published *We're All in It*, a sort of sequel to *America Unlimited*. He naturally restated his belief in American partnership capitalism – a new name for "people's capitalism" – so different from that of other lands; again found U.S. productive supremacy in its high level of technology and management and worker skills; and reaffirmed that America needed reforms and that social legislation was not socialism.

The role of the United States as a world power was emphasized once more and Johnston underlined that this was not a temporary situation; world industrialization was still considered beneficial to American capitalism and he repeated here that the U.S.A. must buy and invest ever more abroad. Aid was still envisualized as "a springboard" as opposed to "a wheelchair." And he was naturally enthusiastic about European economic integration.

Towards the Soviet Union he took what by 1948 was the traditional line stating that one could not rely on friendship and cooperation with it; that one must be wary of "appeasement"; that the difference in ideals between the two countries was total. ("In Russia, a man is counted. In America, he counts.") Johnston refused, however, to link this with a blanket hatred for everything Russian as was common at that time; there is, in fact, in this book far less antisovietism than one might expect. He showed even more interest in the country than was evident in his previous book and spoke with sympathy of the "Russian character" and of the country's bigness similar to that of the United States. He reminisced fondly about his trip to the U.S.S.R. in 1944 during the "grand alliance" and especially the time spent in Novosibirsk with the energetic party chief, a "Russian edition of a big city ward boss," "a slavic Jimmy Cagney... who knows everyone in his area and everything about them." Even Stalin, now seen as a mixture of Ghengis Kahn and Dali Lama, is remembered as an intelligent leader in that he understood the importance of U.S. productivity.

If Johnston was different from others in the Cold War consensus, it was essentially that for him world leadership was to be exercised primarily through the economy as opposed to military alliances. He considered it in the American interest to have a politically independent – but evidently pro-Western – Europe which could operate as a buffer between the two major powers. The concentration on U.S. economic might is the real constant in Johnston's outlook.

Placed together, the ideas of Wallace, Browder, and Johnston in 1944–1945 seem to have the flavor of what might be called a popular front placed under bourgeois hegemony. Considering the attention given to the dependent workers as a category and the recognition of the need for social legislation and the elimination of discrimination, perhaps one could also describe it as a reformist social-democratic vision devoid of any hope of a major transformation of the society. Democratization was, in fact, openly seen as a process which would further strengthen the bases and legitimacy of the prevailing capitalist system.

The views they exposed came from the standpoint of the interests of the system, however much the emphasis on friendship with the Soviet Union and a general pluralistic approach to world affairs gave them a radical coloring in the eyes of many. In their concentration on the economic needs of the system – the question of foreign markets and the expansion of the U.S. capitalist economy – they differed little from others with less progressive ideas. All three seem to have seen the creation of the United Nations as a way of maintaining the peace *and* protecting the interests of the country.

And yet it does not seem correct to view them as simply proponents of a variant of "open door imperialism"; their desire for a strong United States participation in world reconstruction was not meant to render this reconstructed world subordinate to the United States either economically or politically.[15] Wallace, Browder, and Johnston believed that their country possessed a leading – or even the leading – role in world affairs; but this did not for them mean that it had a right to dominate the others. Although the Communist leader was naturally the one who spoke up most directly for the Soviet Union, all agreed that the U.S.S.R. also had rights and needs which were to be respected. As an idea, then, the progressive capitalism wished by these three in 1944–1945 is far afield from the "American century" advocates.

More pertinent, but more difficult to answer, is whether such a design was politically and theoretically a genuine option. Had Soviet security interests in Eastern Europe been met, would Stalin have been willing to accept that the U.S.A. was not only the leading power economically, but that its influence extend all over the globe?[16] The Soviet system did not have the same need for continual economic expansion abroad and in any case for a long time it necessarily would have concentrated on domestic reconstruction. Stalin seems to have been quite eager for fruitful economic relations with the U.S.A. in the postwar period and he had raised the question at the first meeting of the Big Three in Teheran.

It is possible that even had a unified political will in favor of progressive capitalism in the United States been expressed, it might not have worked. Perhaps the health of American capitalism and its thirst for expansion demanded, objectively, the political and economic subordination of as much of the world as possible, as opposed simply to an extension of influence; perhaps the existence itself of the Soviet Union, no matter how damaged, represented an unacceptable threat to the United States.

The comments of Markowitz on the ideology of Wallace might well be extended to Browder and Johnston: the Secretary of Commerce's dream of a "Keynesian cooperative commonwealth... the One World coming after the war with black and white and Russia and America together, with jobs, peace, and freedom for all" was laced with internally unresolvable contradictions. "Defining the cooperative commonwealth as a middle path between capitalism and socialism, Wallace accepted capitalism in the present in the belief that the development of science and technology would modify its competitive and debasing aspects and thereby give rise to a new and more humane society in the future." He could thus "spend a lifetime denouncing imperialism while advocating trade expansion and condemning a materialist culture while making social relationships dependent upon economic relationships between the groups within the economy and between the nation and the world" (Markowitz 1973: 325, 1–2, 52).

Wallace and Johnston, moreover, certainly appear naive in their criticism of monopoly and their feeling that mature capitalism could exist without it. It is, however, striking that none of the authors foresaw that the alternative to progressive capitalism would prove to be neither war nor depression, but rather the successful construction of U.S. economic hegemony abroad with the armaments sector playing domestically a decisive and permanent role.

If theoretically it is not clear that American free enterprise could have prospered in association with world social revolution, the project of progressive capitalism was never politically tried: quite simply those who supported it lacked sufficient importance or representativeness. Within the United States there were even commentators who, already by 1945, were convinced that the "American century" concept had been victorious.[17]

Browder's ideas may well have been accepted by the vast majority of American Communists and left-wing political activists, but the CPUSA and its immediate supporters were never really a central factor of American politics; the influence they had from the mid-1930s derived from their connection to the New Deal forces. Aş to Wallace, he certainly was not alone within government circles.[18] One should not, however, underestimate the hostility to him within the Democratic party; he was not, afer all, reconfirmed as the vice-presidential candidate in 1944, a fact which had enormous consequences. And even many of those close to Wallace – like Frances Perkins and Harold Ickes – would not support him in 1948. Eric Johnston in his *America Unlimited* phase seems still more unrepresentative. Although it is hard to calculate, one wonders how many small and medium-sized businessmen considered a project of friendship with the Soviet Union as well as U.S. aid for world development, which would allow foreign countries to maintain their independence, to be in their interests.

An attempt to formulate public policy along such lines probably depended to a great extent on support by Roosevelt. If the President often gave general approval for such concepts, he died at the crucial moment when he would have been called upon to fight for them on the domestic front. How deeply he was attached to these ideas is therefore an open question. It would appear that only the President had the prestige and the popular appeal to put them through, although by no means is it certain that he would have been able to. The Communists, as mentioned, were weak; the Progressive party was an organization put together at the last moment. Neither had any real roots among the possessors of economic power. The theoretical ideas of a progressive monopoly-dominated capitalism could not, therefore, be tested.

The idea of a progressive U.S. capitalism which, operating abroad, would reform backward societies and render them similar to the United States has, of course, been a sub-theme in postwar American foreign policy, particularly present during the Democratic administrations of Kennedy and Johnson. Whatever the strength of such ideas and desires among individual diplomats and capitalists, Third World reality certainly can not be taken as proof that American economic influence has worked in this way.

The antisoviet and anticommunist objectives of the Marshall Plan prevent evaluating it as an example of progressive capitalism, at least as intended by the three authors under consideration. It did certainly help Western European societies resemble the United States; moreover, despite the latter's decisive economic and political influence for the first two decades after the war, such societies were not locked into a state of permanent dependency. The point obviously is that previous to the Marshall Plan they had not been colonial areas, but rather already developed capitalist countries. On the other hand, one could ask paradoxically whether the vibrant success of the Western European economies, together with that of Japan, in challenging United States economic hegemony, does not indicate that the Marshall Plan itself may actually have been, in the final analysis, at odds with the best interests of American monopoly capitalism.

In any case the formulations of Wallace, Browder, and Johnston should not be taken only as a minor chapter in the intellectual history of postwar America or a missing chapter in the political history of the country's economy. Given the difficulties and contradictions of present-day American economic policy towards the rest of the world, one can wonder if such ideas might not be useful today as a stimulus in discussing alternatives open to the U.S. political leadership.

Notes

1 With regard to the origins of the Cold War, suffice it here to say that, despite recent attempts at a "post-revisionist synthesis" (Gaddis 1983), this author remains in general agreement with the revisionist school of William A. Williams (1959), Lloyd Gardner (1964), and Joyce and Gabriel Kolko (1972), although the "continuity" aspect of this position has tended to eliminate all distinctions between Roosevelt and Truman, while the view of anticommunism as merely a technique of mass manipulation has oversimplified domestic politics. This tendency has, however, not only correctly placed the responsibility for increased tension with the Soviet Union on the Truman policy of containment, but has indicated as the kernel of this policy the desire to maintain a world Open Door for U.S. economic expansion and domination, even at the cost of denying the legitimate right of the Soviet Union to security in Eastern Europe. (It should be clear that such a historiographical view does not necessarily imply a positive appraisal of the regimes instituted by the Soviet Union to meet its security needs.) The work of the revisionists is especially helpful as a corrective to studies such as Dallek (1979) which greatly underestimate the intensity with which U.S. policymakers related to broad economic issues.

2 The minutes of the conferences of Teheran and Yalta have been published in the *Foreign Relations of the United States* series (1961, 1955). The Soviet minutes of

the same as well as the official communiqués and protocols are printed in Ragionieri (1965).

3 The spirit of good will which prevailed even reduced the friction between Churchill and Stalin: the former not only presented to the Soviet leader a specially forged "Sword of Stalingrad" on behalf of George VI, but even toasted him as worthy to stand with the mightiest figures of Russian history and as meriting the title of "Stalin the Great" (Sherwood 1948: 793). Churchill's extremely detailed six volumes of war memoirs curiously omit the "Stalin the Great" toast.

4 On the background of U.S.-U.S.S.R. relations, see Maddux (1980) and Bennett (1985). See also the dispatches and diaries of the first two U.S. ambassadors to the Soviet Union in Bullitt (1972) and Davies (1943).

5 This excellent work is useful for the study not only of Wallace, but of the foreign policy debate and American liberalism in general during the war and after.

6 For the limits of reform during the war see Brody (1975).

7 For Wallace's public speeches from the inauguration of the New Deal through the Second World War see Wallace (1943, 1944).

8 On the CPUSA during the war see Isserman (1982).

9 For Browder's positions from the time of his prison release to the publication of this book see, aside from his many articles in the CP theoretical monthly *The Communist*, Browder (1942, 1943).

10 Of the literature on the Communist party and the working class during the war see especially Keeran (1980: 226–249), Lichtenstein (1982) and Schatz (1983: 105–164).

11 For the history of the CPUSA in the postwar period, see Shannon (1959) and Starobin (1972). For the "Teheran" ideas of Browder, seen in the context of a fundamental conflict with Foster and within the international Communist movement, see Sylvers (1986). After his expulsion Browder criticized Foster's leadership of the party, but continued to support the ideas he had previously put forth.

12 For the collapse of popular front liberalism see Markowitz (1973) and McAuliffe (1978).

13 On the 1948 Wallace campaign see especially MacDougall (1965). Wallace later broke with the Progressive party over the Korean War and supported the U.S. government; he gradually, but steadily, grew more hostile to the Soviet Union, and finally came to judge his 1948 campaign as having been manipulated by the Communists.

14 For a short sketch of the entire career of Johnston, see Schoenebaum (1978). For his role in the Hollywood witch hunt and blacklists see Ceplair and Englund (1980).

15 The view of Wallace as an "open door imperialist" is expounded in Radosh and Liggio (1971).

16 In this regard perhaps the truly sophisticated "open door imperialists" were those in the State Department, analyzed by Mark (1981), who favored a "diplomacy of accommodation" with the Soviet Union hoping that the latter's "natural" sphere of influence in Eastern Europe could nonetheless remain open to American economic penetration.

17 Gardner (1964: 264) mentions the views of Rexford Tugwell, Bruce Catton, and Archibald MacLeish, who, among others, were convinced that by the end of the

war the businessmen were in control and that the enemies of progress had occupied all strategic places of power. According to MacLeish, "the peace we will make... will be a peace of oil, a peace of gold, a peace of shipping... a peace in brief... without moral purpose or human interest."

18 Despite their continual administrative conflict within Roosevelt's cabinet, Ickes and Wallace had very similar ideas during the war and immediately thereafter. See Ickes (1943: 342–343) where he calls for a "people's peace," which would not only be antifascist, but also against "the power-statesmen of Europe" who "will want to revive the old international racket." It comes as no surprise that his militancy for racial equality and against the monopolies was combined with an insistency that trade barriers be removed so that countries could freely exchange their resources. With regard to the question of friendship with the Soviet Union and the idea that the U.S.S.R. and the U.S.A. had lessons to exchange, perhaps the most influential text of this period was Davies (1943).

References

Bennett, Edward M. (1985): *Franklin D. Roosevelt and the Search for Security. American-Soviet Relations, 1933–1939*. Wilmington, Del.: Scholarly Resources.

Brody, David (1975): The New Deal and World War II. In John Braeman, Robert H. Bremner, and David Brody (eds.), *The New Deal. vol 1: The National Level*. Columbus, Ohio: Ohio State University Press, 267–309.

Browder, Earl (1942): *Victory – and After*. New York: International Press.

Browder, Earl (1943): *Wage Policy in War Production*. New York: International Press.

Browder, Earl (1944): *Teheran. Our Path in War and Peace*. New York: International Press.

Bullitt, Orville H. (ed.) (1972): *For the President. Personal and Secret. Correspondence Between FDR and William C. Bullitt*. Boston: Houghton Mifflin.

Burns, James MacGregor (1956): *Roosevelt: The Lion and the Fox 1882–1940*. New York: Harcourt Brace.

Ceplair, Larry and Steven Englund (1980): *The Inquisition in Hollywood. Politics in the Film Community 1930–1960*. Garden City, N.Y.: Doubleday.

Churchill, Winston (1951): *The Second World World. vol. 5: Closing the Ring*. Boston: Houghton Mifflin.

Clemens, Diane Shaver (1970): *Yalta*. New York: Oxford University Press.

Dallek, Robert (1979): *Franklin D. Roosevelt and American Foreign Policy, 1932–1945*. Oxford: Oxford University Press.

Davies, Joseph E. (1943): *Mission to Moscow*. New York: Pocket Books.

Duclos, Jacques (1945): A Propos de la Dissolution du Parti Communiste Americain. *Cahiers du Communisme* (April): 21–38.

Foreign Relations of the United States. The Conferences at Malta and Yalta 1945 (1955): Washintgon, D.C.: Government Printing Office.

Foreign Relations of the United States. The Conferences at Cairo and Teheran 1943 (1961): Washington, D.C.: Government Printing Office.

Gaddis, John Lewis (1983): The Emerging Post-Revisionist Synthesis on the Origins of the Cold War. *Diplomatic History* 7: 171 – 190.

Gardner, Lloyd (1964). *Economic Aspects of New Deal Diplomacy*. Madison, Wis.: University of Winconsin Press.

Ickes, Harold (1943): *The Autobiography of a Curmudgeon*. New York: Reynal and Hitchcock.

Isserman, Maurice (1982): *Which Side Were You On? The American Communist Party During the Second World War*. Middletown, Conn.: Wesleyan University Press.

Johnston, Eric (1944): *America Unlimited*. New York: Doubleday.

Johnston, Eric (1948): *We're All in It*. New York: Dutton.

Keeran, Roger (1980): *The Communist Party and the Auto Workers Unions*. Bloomington, Ind.: Indiana University Press.

Kolko, Joyce and Gabriel Kolko (1972): *The Limits of Power. The World and United States Foreign Policy. 1945 – 1954*. New York: Harper and Row.

Lichtenstein, Nelson (1982): *Labor's War at Home. The CIO in World War II*. Cambridge, Eng.: Cambridge University Press.

McAuliffe, Mary Sperling (1978): *Crisis on the Left. Cold War Politics and American Liberals. 1947 – 1954*. Amherst, Mass.: University of Massachusetts.

MacDougall, Curtis D. (1965): *Gideon's Army*. New York: Marzani and Munsell.

Maddux, Thomas R. (1980): *Years of Estrangement. American Relations with the Soviet Union. 1933 – 1941*. Tallahassee, Fla.: University Presses of Florida.

Mark, Eduard (1981): American Policy toward Eastern Europe and the Origins of the Cold War, 1941 – 1946: An Alternative Interpretation. *Journal of American History* 68(2): 313 – 336.

Markowitz, Norman D. (1973): *The Rise and Fall of the People's Century. Henry C. Wallace and American Liberalism. 1941 – 1948*. New York: Free Press.

Radosh, Ronald and Leonard Liggio (1971): Henry A. Wallace and the Open Door. In Thomas G. Paterson (ed.), *Cold War Critics*. Chicago: Quadrangle, 76 – 113.

Ragionieri, Ernesto (1965): *Da Teheran a Yalta. Verbali delle conferenze dei capi di governo della Gran Bretagna, degli Stati Uniti e dell'Unione Sovietica durante la seconda guerra mondiale*. Rome: Editori Riuniti.

Schatz, Ronald W. (1983): *The Electrical Workers. A History of Labor at General Electric and Westinghouse 1923 – 60*. Urbana, Ill.: University of Illinois Press.

Schoenebaum, Eleanora W. (ed.) (1978): *Political Profiles. The Truman Years*. New York: Facts on File, 264 – 266.

Shannon, David A. (1959): *The Decline of American Communism. A History of the Communist Party of the United States since 1945*. New York: Harcourt Brace.

Sherwood, Robert (1948): *Roosevelt and Hopkins. An Intimate History*. New York: Harper.

Starobin, Joseph R. (1972): *American Communism in Crisis, 1943 – 1957*. Cambridge, Mass.: Harvard University Press.

Sylvers, Malcolm (1986): The 1944 – 45 Upheaval in American Communism: Earl Browder and William Z. Foster on the Postwar Perspectives for the United States. *Internationale Tagung der Historiker der Arbeiterbewegung. 21. Linzer Konferenz 1985*. Wien: Europaverlag, 256 – 279.

Wallace, Henry A. (1943): *The Century of the Common Man*. New York: Reynal and Hitchcock.
Wallace, Henry A. (1944): *Democracy Reborn*. New York: Reynal and Hitchcock.
Wallace, Henry A. (1945): *Sixty Million Jobs*. New York: Reynal and Hitchcock.
Williams, William A. (1959): *The Tragedy of American Diplomacy*. Cleveland: World.

The Changing Role of the U.S.A. in Financing Yugoslav Economic Development Since 1945*

Novak Janković

In 1981, the centennial of American-Yugoslav relations,[1] the governments of both countries could be satisfied with the mutual benefits of their relationship. This may seem strange at first sight, because these two countries have not shared the same, or even a similar, economic and social system for the past 40 years. Quite to the contrary, they follow fundamentally different political and social philosophies. Still, politics are not based on attraction but, as George Allen, the U.S. ambassador to Yugoslavia in the early 1950s, remarked, on "cool-blooded calculation of the interests of both sides" (Štrbac 1987: 19). Apparently, the postwar governments of both the U.S.A. and Yugoslavia discovered corresponding interests that served as the basis for their rather successful mutual relations.

What was the substance of these interests? From the American point of view, the Yugoslav regime, although socialist (communist), represented an obvious exception in Eastern Europe after its complete break with the Soviet Union in 1948. Yugoslav military and political independence, together with signs of market orientation and a relatively open economy, were seen as a weak point in Soviet strategy, and, hopefully, even as a possibly positive example for other Eastern European countries. Thus, the Yugoslav case enabled the U.S.A. to play a more refined and influential role in a region that would otherwise have been completely out of reach.

On the other hand, U.S. determination to support Yugoslav economic development financially was of crucial importance to the new government of a less-developed country further impoverished by the war. In addition, the country desperately needed help to overcome the consequences of the total economic and political blockade imposed by its former ideological allies in

* I would like to acknowledge the contributions of Dragana Gnjatović who provided me with valuable commentary, Slobodan Blagojević who supplied important data, and Milena Lopušina who helped with the word processing. Also, the substantial editorial help of Peter Jaschner must be mentioned.

Eastern Europe in 1948. In other words, U.S. support was of vital importance to the domestic legitimacy of the Yugoslav government. This constellation of interests has served as the common ground for their mutual cooperation since 1948.

In this chapter, after a brief review of American-Yugoslav economic relations, the data on U.S. financial assistance to Yugoslavia will be compared with those for other countries. The structure of U.S. assistance in the 1950s and 1960s as well as its significance for the Yugoslav economy will then be analyzed in greater detail, followed by a discussion of the recently developed Yugoslav debt to the U.S.A. Finally, a few conclusions will be drawn on U.S. policy options towards Yugoslavia during the entire period under discussion.

1 A Brief Review of American-Yugoslav Economic Relations

Prewar economic relations between the United States and Yugoslavia were characterized by modest trade and low U.S. capital investment. The share of exports to the U.S.A. varied from 0.3% in 1920 to 5% of total Yugoslav exports in 1939. During the same period the share of imports from the U.S.A. was always lower than 6% of total Yugoslav imports (Statistički godišnjak 1940: 38). While modest trade could be explained by historical and geographical reasons, as well as high transportation costs, low American direct investments were influenced more by political factors. Before the war the leading role of the U.S.A. among capital-exporting countries was not reflected in the Yugoslav economy, which itself was characterized by huge imports of foreign capital. Nearly half of all capital in prewar Yugoslavia was foreign, mostly British, French, Austrian, and German. Of 520 foreign firms only 40 were American, a majority of which were engaged in the extraction of oil (Dimitrijević 1958: 160). Prewar Yugoslavia, then, was obviously considered a strategically uninteresting country for the U.S.A. Only a few years later, however, it was to become a country of extreme strategic importance for the U.S.A. – which set off a rather generous flow of capital and goods to Yugoslavia.

Economic aid started as early as 1946 in the form of indirect aid through the United Nations. Between 1945 and 1947 Yugoslavia received from the UNRRA $ 415 million, 300 million (or 72%) of which was American.[2] In 1947 Yugoslavia was offered participation in the Marshall Plan, but it refused the offer as did all other Eastern European countries. All of them, including Yugoslavia, decided to rely completely upon the Soviet Union. Only a year later, however, Stalin and the Cominform were accusing the Yugoslav communist leadership of "revisionism" and betrayal of "socialist internationalism." Trade with Yugoslavia was immediately terminated, which resulted in an almost total economic blockade of that country. In addition, its eastern border was threatened by a strong military build-up. The following years, from 1948 to 1950, during which this underdeveloped country was isolated from both East and West, represented the greatest challenge to the new regime. The deal with the U.S.A. and Western countries in general, however, was struck almost overnight. Already in 1949 a broadening of trade and small, yet psychologically important, credits were provided by the International Monetary Fund, the Bank for Reconstruction and Development, as well as the Export-Import Bank. In 1950, finally, a rather generous flow of all kinds of economic aid started to pour into Yugoslavia continuing throughout the whole period of now almost 40 years.

The decisions concerning economic aid were not easy for either of the two governments. The U.S. government was going to thereby support a communist country financially, thus contributing to its further success and domestic legitimacy. The Yugoslav government, on the other hand, had to explain to the public why such help was being requested from the country's fiercest ideological enemies of only a short time ago. Still, "Realpolitik" prevailed on both sides and the conditions necessary for cooperation were met by the partners involved. On the American side, and the West in general, these conditions included the belief that Tito's split with the Soviet Union was not temporary and that Yugoslav-Soviet relations had reached such a critical stage that Soviet military action might be imminent. In a letter to his Foreign Secretary, Charles Peak, Britain's ambassador to Yugoslavia, wrote in January 1951 that there could be no doubt that developments during the previous year had made the split "between the Soviets and Tito's regime irreparable.... Goliath is looking with anger at David over the chasm and David, with increasing haste, is looking to the West for the sling and stone. The outcome which could still show to be fatal for the adversary lies in the future." The ambassador then reminds the minister of his statement that British policy should aim at "keeping Tito above water" and states that Tito's regime had stayed in power until the end of 1950 only because of British and other Western economic aid (Štrbac 1987: 21).

Another problem contributing to the rather quick decision on aid to Yugoslavia was the extreme drought devastating the wheat harvest of 1950. Without any shipments of imports a large portion of the population would have been seriously threatened with food shortages in the winter of 1950/1951. The U.S. government became aware that Yugoslav defense capabilities would also be threatened by such s situation. As a result, wheat shipments valued at $ 16 million were sent to Yugoslavia already in November 1950. It is important to note that this happened under the Mutual Defense Assistance

Act. President Truman announced that a drought and hunger could seriously threaten Yugoslav military strength and the independence of that geostrategically important country. Incidentally, this country, at the time, possessed the strongest military force in Europe outside the U.S.S.R.! George Perkins, Assistant Secretary of State for European Affairs, pointed out clearly that Yugoslavia should be supported, because it showed to the whole world how Stalin's domination and exploitation of small nations worked. However, Perkins underlined the fact that Yugoslavia was a communist country and that the U.S. government had made it clear that "diplomatic and trade relations as well as financiel aid do not by any chance mean approving the internal policy of the government of Yugoslavia" (Štrbac 1987: 19). But, as not all possible consequences of particular policy measures can be completely separated one from another, Mr. Perkins' words have to be taken with a grain of salt. For, on the contrary, given the benefit of historical hindsight it seems quite obvious that the U.S. government, with different and higher political reasons in mind, contributed to the improvement of the position and domestic legitimacy of the Yugoslav government at the time. The U.S. Senate and the House of Representatives approved aid to Yugoslavia (voting 60:21 and 225:142, respectively) and on December 29, 1950, President Truman signed the Yugoslav Emergency Relief Act, the official beginning of aid that continued throughout the 1950s and 1960s. Technically, it was a tripartite program of aid as agreed on by the U.S.A., Great Britain, and France at the London Conference in 1951. Quantitatively, however, almost all the aid was American. From 1950 to 1965, Yugoslavia received a total of approximately $ 1.9 billion in tripartite aid and other forms of financial assistance (credits, etc.). Of this amount, $ 1.8 billion (or 95%) was American aid.

It is important to note that from the beginning both sides agreed that U.S. financial assistance would not be hinged on any political preconditions. On the U.S. side, the mere existence of an independent country in Eastern Europe, even if communist, was considered to be of great political interest. Despite occasional American resistance to U.S. government policy towards Yugoslavia, economic, and consequently political, relations gradually improved during the 1950s. Immediately after Khrushchev had signed the guarantees of independence in Belgrade in 1956, U.S. Secretary of State, John Foster Dulles, came to Yugoslavia on the first official visit by a member of the administration. In 1960 Tito visited Eisenhower in Washington, although American reactions to the establishment of the movement of nonaligned countries that year in Belgrade were far from positive and mutual relations deteriorated over the following years. In 1962 Yugoslavia was deprived of its most-favored-nation status. Moreover, it suffered a temporary suspension of financial aid due to its trade with Cuba. Mainly because of this, Tito again went to the U.S.A. in 1963 to sign an agreement with President Kennedy that put mutual relations on a new basis, namely, "the principle of equality and benefits to both sides." Congress approved the agreement and reinstated Yugoslavia's most-favored-nation status on 1964. Despite many differences and serious disputes in the late 1960s (on the issue of Vietnam), American-Yugoslav relations continued on a high and steady level. Nixon's 1970 visit to Yugoslavia, the first by a U.S. President, and Tito's return visit to Washington in 1971 resulted in a declaration of "long-term relations between the two countries with different social systems" (Štrbac 1987: 19). In 1973 the Yugoslav government agreed to guarantee the security of American private investment in Yugoslavia with regard to "noncommercial risks," thus settling a question of particular importance to the American side. Mutual visits on the highest level continued in the following years when Gerald Ford came to Yugoslavia in 1975 and Tito met President Carter in Washington in 1978. Even a delegation of the Yugoslav Communist party (the League of Communists of Yugoslavia) was invited by both the Democratic and Republican parties in 1979.

Immediately after Tito's death in 1980, President Carter visited Yugoslavia and expressed the deep American concern for Yugoslav independence and territorial integrity. On the occasion of the centenary of American-Yugoslav relations in 1981, Secretary of State, Alexander Haig, stated:

> We can be very satisfied with our current relations which are firmly built on mutual trust and understanding, relations which are enabling us to communicate on all levels with mutual respect and openness.... Our countries showed that cooperation in different areas can exist between two different social systems (Sjedinjene države 1981: 20).

These words were confirmed later when the Yugoslav President, Mika Špiljak, visited the U.S.A. in 1984, the only communist leader before Gorbachev to have met President Ronald Reagan in Washington.

The entire postwar period of American aid to Yugoslavia can be divided into two parts. The first started in 1950 soon after the break in Yugoslav-Soviet relations and ended in the mid-1960s. During that period aid consisted mainly of grain and arms representing an important contribution to the economy (sometimes more than 10% of GNP) and was provided mainly in the form of grants. Towards the end of this period, as Yugoslavia came to be considered a nearly self-sustaining country, assistance began to be provided almost exclusively as credits. While during the first period the U.S. administration and its agencies were almost the only source of assistance, the second period, from the late 1960s through the 1980s has been characterized by other OECD governments, international financial organizations, and commercial banks participating in financial assistance to Yugoslavia as well. Nonetheless, the data indicate that American sources were still dominant in the second period, albeit not to the same degree as earlier.

Table 1. Summary of Major U.S. Government Foreign Assistance, Military and Other, f[or] Selected Areas and Countries in the Postwar Period, July 1, 1945 to December 31, 1984 (millio[ns] of dollars and equivalents)

	Total (net)	Total (net) per capita[c] ($)	Grants (net)	
			Total (net)	Total per capita ($)
Total, all areas	263,256	87.49	181,778	60.41
Total, Europe[a]	61,921	92.56	51,517	77.01
Total, Western Europe[b]	59,109	341.67	50,210	290.23
Greece	4,742	557.22	4,062	477.32
Portugal	1,414	155.28	926	101.69
Spain	3,009	96.01	1,351	43.11
Turkey	10,302	331.06	6,531	209.88
Total, Eastern Europe	2,812	6.91	1,308	3.21
Czechoslovakia	186	13.23	186	13.23
East Germany	17	1.06	17	1.06
Hungary	21	2.07	17	1.68
Poland	1,851	59.40	630	20.22
Romania	112	5.92	11	0.58
Yugoslavia	2,862	148.45	1.777	92.17

[a] Including U.S.S.R. [b] Including Yugoslavia [c] According to the 1964 population

Source: *Annual Report to the President and to the Congress for Fiscal Year 1985*, National Advisory Council on International Monetary and Financial Policies, Washington (1985: 214–219).

Credits accepted in the mid-1970s were not used efficiently, leaving Yugoslavia unable to meet its debt obligations in the early 1980s. The Yugoslav debt had to be refinanced in a process managed by the IMF, Western governments, and a group of 600 commercial banks. So far, this has meant paying interest on earlier credits, while postponing the repayment of principal. According to official sources, Yugoslavia at present owes $ 20 billion to its creditors, including an American share of $ 2.3 billion.

It should be noted that the credits used for purchasing food in the 1950s and 1960s were largely repayable in Yugoslav currency (similar to the cases of Poland, Israel, Tunisia, etc.). This meant that the U.S. government paid dollars to American firms exporting to Yugoslavia, while its dinar account with the central bank in Belgrade kept growing. In 1967 this practice was discontinued (mainly due to Yugoslav trade with Cuba). From now on, almost all credits had to be repaid in dollars. Part of the U.S. government's account

	Credits (net)		Other assistance (foreign currency)		
Military grants	Total (net)	Total per capita ($)	Total (net)	Currency claims acquired	Less currencies used
79,060	66,578	22.13	1,760	20,330	18,569
27,331	9,835	14.70	569	4,348	3,780
27,331	8,588	49.64	311	3,725	3,415
2,605	680	79.91	...	279	280
656	488	53.59	...	27	26
879	1,574	50.22	84	818	733
4,606	3,708	119.16	63	702	638
...	1,247	3.06	258	622	364
...	...	...	...	...	...
...	...	...	...	...	...
...	4	0.39	...	...	...
...	963	30.90	258	622	364
...	101	5.34	...	...	...
722	930	48.24	154	865	711

with the Yugoslav central bank was used by the U.S. embassy in Belgrade, Fulbright programs, or deliveries of Yugoslav merchandise to the U.S. army in Europe (!). The remainder was even offered as new credit to the Yugoslav government.

American financial assistance to Yugoslavia represents an economically and politically significant fact of postwar U.S.-European relations. In the next section of this chapter, the relative importance of this assistance will be considered by comparing financial aid to Yugoslavia with that to other Eastern or Southern European countries.

2 The Relative Importance of U.S. Government Financial Assistance to Yugoslavia

The significance of total U.S. financial assistance to Yugoslavia from the standpoint of American interests and policy options can be appraised by comparing it with the aid given to other countries in the region (see Table 1 for the data). Since Yugoslavia geographically is part of both Eastern and Southern Europe, countries from these regions have been chosen for the

Table 2. Summary of Major U.S. Government Net Foreign Assistance, July 1, 1945 to Decembe 31, 1984 for Selected Years, Areas, and Countries (millions of dollars)

	Total (39 years)	Calendar	
		1984	1983
Total, all areas[a]	250,116	12,569	10,273
Total Europe[b]	61,921	673	761
Total, Western Europe[c]	59,109	693	707
Greece	4,742	− 14	44
Portugal	1,414	122	64
Spain	3,009	220	101
Turkey	10,302	443	491
Total, Eastern Europe	2,812	− 20	54
Czechoslovakia	186	− 3	− 2
East Germany	17	...	...
Hungary	21	− 2	− 2
Poland	1,851	42	74
Romania	112	− 18	5
Yugoslavia	2,862	16	20

[a] Does not include # 13,140 million investment in international financial institutions
[b] Including U.S.S.R. [c] Including Yugoslavia

Source: *Annual Report to the President and to the Congress for Fiscal Year 1985*, National Advisory Council on International Monetary and Financial Policies, Washington (1985: 220 – 223).

comparison. Politically, Yugoslavia represents a special case, a fact also evident in Western ambivalence and hesitation regarding the classification of Yugoslavia. The Annual Report to the President of the U.S.A. for 1985, the main source for data provided in Table 1, classifies Yugoslavia as a Western European country. Still, a comparison with Southern European countries, politically more connected to the U.S.A., and Eastern European countries, with a similar type of government, seems appropriate from a political point of view.

Total American financial assistance to Europe has, for obvious political reasons, been distributed quite unevenly. Through the Marshall Plan it was concentrated on Western Europe, with a per capita average of $ 340 of American aid during the whole postwar period. In Southern Europe all countries except Greece received less per capita help. Except for Poland, assistance was very small in Eastern Europe. Yugoslavia, on the other hand, received as much aid as all other Eastern European countries together. On average, a Yugoslav received more aid than a Spaniard, although Turks and

years				July 1, 1945 to Dec. 31, 1978
1982	1981	1980	1979	
10,893	9,416	10,279	7,190	189,495
513	669	892	627	57,786
458	495	1,176	421	55,158
– 52	– 49	– 18	36	4,794
– 2	– 100	– 81	105	1,307
14	79	173	138	2,285
696	393	587	352	7,340
55	174	– 285	206	2,628
...	...	...	...	191
...	...	...	...	17
– 4	3	– 4	8	22
86	236	– 243	129	1,525
– 16	– 49	– 23	76	138
– 31	12	22	– 25	2,847

Greeks, especially, were American "favorites" in Europe. The small amount of aid to Eastern Europe was provided mainly in the form of grants immediately after the war (except for Poland). The share of grants in total assistance was fairly equal for all other countries. A majority of military grants went to Greece and Turkey. Yugoslavia was awarded the same amount of military grants as Portugal and Spain. The data on credits show that only Spain and Poland received more credits than grants, which can be explained by the fact that grants were the dominant form of assistence immediately after the war and during the 1950s. Other forms of assistance were made available largely as sales of farm products for local currencies. The amounts of local currencies were mostly acquired and used by the U.S. government except in the case of Poland and Yugoslavia.

It should be kept in mind that Table 1 provides only data on U.S. government aid, excluding assistance from other U.S. sources. Still, the data are very important and relevant for at least three reasons. First, U.S. government assistance represents American economic and political interests. Second, during the 1950s and early 1960s, it was almost the only kind of assistance. Third, for their own security, commercial banks and other private creditors mainly followed U.S. government directions later. To elucidate the dynamics of U.S. government assistance in the past several years, pertinent data are presented in Table 2.

Although the U.S. government provided more than $ 60 billion in financial assistance from 1979 to 1984, the bulk of this amount was concentrated outside Europe. Turkey was the single largest recipient of assistance in this period, followed, on a much smaller scale, by Spain. Eastern Europe in general slowly repaid its credits with the exception of Poland. Yugoslavia has maintained the status quo during the past six years. It is important to note that during this period there has been a growing overall trend to increase loans from the U.S. government in areas outside Eastern Europe. Also, the relative importance of borrowing from the U.S. government has diminished, since financial assistance to developing countries now comes from different countries and sources as compared with the case in the 1950s. Therefore, the relations between creditors and debtors unable to repay their debt obligations is today's crucial international problem, and not just a bilateral one.

The comparative data on U.S. government financial assistance suggest the conclusion that postwar U.S. administrations obviously considered Yugoslavia a rather important country for promoting American interests. The possible damage to Russian interests in the region was apparently ranked higher than purely academic reasoning in political philosophy.

3 U.S. Government Financial Assistance to Yugoslavia from 1950 to 1965

The period from 1950 to 1965 represents the most interesting and significant period in the American-Yugoslav economic relations. Therefore, it deserves to be analyzed in more detail. In this period, the U.S. government was the dominant, in fact almost the only, external financier of Yugoslav economic development. In the 1970s the role of the U.S. government declined relative to other countries as Yugoslav borrowing abroad, although still large, became diversified and internationalized. As mentioned above, total U.S. government assistance to Yugoslavia between 1950 and 1965 amounted to $ 1.8 billion. Detailed and structured data necessary for a more profound analysis of this assistance are provided in Table 3.

The assistance was provided in the form of grants, agricultural surpluses, and credits repayable in dollars. Agricultural surpluses present a certain problem for analysis, because they were granted or sold on credit repayable either in dollars or local currency. Therefore, total aid in food is divided into four columns, as suggested by Public Law 480 of 1954, which regulated the sale of U.S. agricultural surpluses to foreign countries. Under Title I of that law, food was sold on credit repayable in the local currency of the receiving country. Quantitatively, this was the largest single kind of aid to Yugoslavia in the entire period. Under Titles II and III, food was granted because of

Table 3. U.S. Economic Assistance to Yugoslavia, 1950 to 1965 (in millions of dollars)

Fiscal year	Grants	Credits	Agricultural surpluses			Total
			Title I	Titles II and III	Title IV and GSM-3, GSM-4	
1950	...	40.0	...	...	...	40.0
1951	92.9	15.0	...	...	...	107.9
1952	81.5	...	...	24.8	...	106.3
1953	122.4	...	...	0.2	...	122.6
1954	66.5	...	...	1.1	...	67.6
1955	42.7	...	52.0	61.9	...	156.6
Total	406.0	55.0	52.0	88.0	...	601.0
1956	15.0	15.0	71.2	8.7	...	109.9
1957	1.5	13.5	90.3	32.8	...	138.1
1958	3.4	8.0	71.9	28.8	...	112.1
1959	3.9	59.2	94.8	27.9	...	185.8
1960	3.8	40.8	19.2	14.2	...	78.0
Total	27.6	136.5	347.4	112.4	...	623.9
1961	3.3	102.7	30.4	14.1	...	150.5
1962	0,5	...	93.1	15.1	17.3	126.0
1963	−0.2	−0.8	92.1	14.3	16.2	121.6
1964	−0.4	...	18.2	13.4	46.1	77.3
1965	−0.1	−0.3	...	3.6	94.1	97.3
Total	3.1	101.6	233.8	60.5	173.7	572.7
Total 1950–1965	436.7	293.1	633.2	260.9	173.7	1797.6

Sources: *Foreign Aid Program*, Compilation of studies and surveys, Special committee to study the foreign aid program, United States Senate, Washington (1957: 1541–1556); *U.S. Foreign Assistance and Assistance from International Organizations*, July 1, 1945 to June 30, 1965, Agency for International Development, Washington (1966: 228).

natural catastrophes or for other humanitarian reasons. Unter Title IV and paragraphs GSM-3 and GSM-4 of that law, food was sold on credit repayable in dollars.

The data on total aid (last column of Table 3) show that the amounts varied over the period, but without any recognizable statistical tencency.[3]

Even a brief look at the structure of Table 3, however, shows a gradual movement from grants to credits during the period. In the first five years aid was provided mainly in grants consisting of military equipment, whereas

Table 4. Share of Total and U.S. Foreign Assistance in Yugoslav GNP and Net Investments, 1950 and 1965 (%)

Year	Ratio of total foreign financial assistance to Yugoslav GNP	Ratio of U.S. financial assistance to Yugoslav GNP	Share of total foreign assistance in Yugoslav net investments	Share of U.S. financial assistance in Yugoslav net investments
1950	20.1	6.8	91.3	30.9
1951	31.4	14.3	155.4	70.8
1952	15.3	12.3	72.9	58.5
1953	28.2	14.2	127.3	64.2
1954	10.2	6.1	44.2	26.6
1955	8.3	7.0	44.5	37.4
Total	18.9	10.1	89.3	48.1
1956	5.6	5.0	28.8	25.8
1957	7.6	4.2	40.1	22.2
1958	6.7	4.1	30.6	18.7
1959	6.0	6.0	28.1	28.1
1960	6.4	2.3	25.7	9.2
Total	6.5	4.3	30.7	20.8
1961	7.3	3.8	27.8	14.5
1962	6.2	6.2	23.0	23.0
1963	6.0	5.1	23.3	19.7
1964	5.9	1.7	21.8	6.2
1965	3.8	3.0	16.9	13.2
Total	5.8	4.0	22.6	15.3
Total 1950–1965	10.4	6.1	47.5	28.1

Sources: As in Table 3 and Dragana Gnjatović: *Uloga inostranih sredstava u privrednom razvoju Jugoslavije* (The Role of Foreign Resources in Yugoslav Economic Development), Ekonomski institut, Beograd (1985: 47–48).

wheat made up the dominant form of aid in the late 1950s. About one-third of this wheat was granted, while the remaining two-thirds were sold on credit repayable in Yugoslav currency. As mentioned earlier, part of the Yugoslav dinars thus earned were either spent by the American embassy in Yugoslavia, kept in its dinar account with the central bank in Belgrade, or even offered as new credit to the Yugoslav government. In the early 1960s, however, credits repayable in dollars were introduced. Later, they became the only method for Yugoslavia to obtain American wheat.

In order to estimate the real impact of U.S. government financial assistance on the Yugoslav economy, it is necessary to compare the data on assistance with some major indicators of the Yugoslav economy at the time. The gross national product (GNP) and net investments in the economy have been selected as relevant indicators. The relation of foreign aid to these indicators is presented in Table 4.

Total foreign aid to Yugoslavia (including war reparations and restitutions, private transfers, etc.) hovered around 10% of GNP in the whole period, although there were years when this share reached up to 30%. Column 4 of Table 4 shows that in those years foreigners financed not only net investments but even the viability, or simple reproduction, of the economy. American sources accounted for the dominant part of the assistance, which varied at around 6% of GNP and 30% of net investments, sometimes reaching nearly 15% of GNP and 70% of net investments! In fact, the first four years of extremely large U.S. assistance were followed by a fairly steady flow of financial resources not significantly disturbed by political events and cycles in American-Yugoslav relations. It should also be remembered that the bulk of U.S. assistance in this period consisted of food and arms.

4 U.S. Financial Assistance Through the 1970s and the Current State of Yugoslav Indebtedness to the U.S.A.

An outstanding feature of the topic of this chapter is the greater availability of precise data on financial assistance for the early 1950s and 1960s than for the more recent period. This can be explained by two different sets of facts. First, American aid in the 1950s and 1960s was managed mainly through governmental agencies and therefore well documented by statistical data. Later, however, other institutions like American commercial banks and international financial institutions with mostly American resources entered the process of financing. This led to many methodological problems in collecting, comparing, and presenting statistical data. Second, Yugoslav borrowing abroad was exclusively managed by the Yugoslav central bank in the 1950s and 1960s, whereas regional central banks, commercial banks, and even independent firms joined in the borrowing later, when they were considered reliable partners. When the debt crisis culminated in the early 1980s, even the Yugoslav central bank was unable to calculate the total amount of loans taken out in various forms and by various institutions of the Yugoslav economy. Because of this, international financial institutions, with the approval of the Yugoslav authorities, have asked a private English accounting firm to audit Yugoslav central bank papers in order to estimate the total amount of debt! Under these circumstances, any individual effort to collect precise data from official Yugoslav sources seems not very promising. Moreover, some of the data have been classified so that a certain confusion exists in Yugoslav publications concerning amounts, types, and sources of borrowing from abroad in the past two decades. Due to these difficulties the role of the U.S.A. in financing Yugoslav economic development in the past 20 years will be estimated on the basis of less comprehensive and less precise data than in the previous section.

Shipments of American wheat to Yugoslavia continued through the late 1960s. Between 1966 and 1970 wheat valued at $ 235.4 million was sold to Yugoslavia in credit (Godišnji izveštaj 1972: 128). From 1950 to 1970 wheat deliveries amounted to $ 1.3 billion representing the single most significant item of assistance. Yet, the single most significant institution of assistance was the American Export-Import Bank (Eximbank). The flow of credits from this bank began as early as 1949 and, by the end of 1983, had reached the total amount of $ 1.5 billion in credits to Yugoslavia (Export-Import Bank 1983: 34) making Yugoslavia one of the ten biggest users of Eximbank credits. The most important event in Yugoslav relations with the Eximbank occurred in 1970 when the first official operational agreement on mutual relations was signed. After that, credits steadily increased to ever larger proportions. According to Yugoslav sources, the amount of credits reached $ 853 million between 1972 and 1975. In 1975 alone, credits amounted to $ 503.4 million (Godišnji izveštaj 1975: 123)! According to the agreement of 1970, the Eximbank credited Yugoslav commercial banks and firms directly, but asked for guarantees of the Yugoslav central bank. From 1978 on, these guarantees became unnecessary, since Yugoslav commercial banks were considered reliable partners. Yet, at that time the Yugoslav economy was already in deep, albeit invisible, trouble. The foreign debt kept rapidly growing, while Yugoslav exports did not. The period of confidence in Yugoslav commercial banks lasted only five years until 1982, when the illiquidity of the Yugoslav economy and its inability to repay its debt became obvious. Now, all foreign financiers, including the Eximbank, have asked for guarantees of the Yugoslav government, such as mortgages on ships, airplanes, property abroad, for every single dollar of new credit. In the past five years Yugoslavia has succeeded in paying interest on credits taken out earlier, but it has remained largely unable to repay principal. Therefore, new loans contracted during the past five years have been just sufficient to repay previous ones. The credits were taken from the International Monetary Fund, Western governments, and a group of 600 Western commercial banks acting in complete coordination. According to American sources, U.S. government credits currently owed by Yugoslavia amount to $ 629 million, $ 593 million of which are carried by the Eximbank alone (National Advisory Council 1985: 250; see Table 5).

It has been argued that the U.S. government is no longer the single most important creditor of developing countries. However, it is not easy to estimate the total debt owed to the U.S.A., including commercial banks and the U.S. share in international financial organizations. According to Yugoslav sources,

Table 5. Outstanding Indebtedness of Foreign Countries on U.S. Government Credits, as of December 31, 1984, for Selected Areas and Countries (millions of dollars)

	Total	Repayable in U.S. dollars	Repayable in other than U.S. dollars	Due and not paid 90 days or more	
				Principal	Interest
Total, all areas	69,040	67,255	1,785	1,158	790
Total, Europe[a]	12,496	12,249	247	522	184
Total, Western Europe[b]	10,408	10,161	247	75	2
Greece	668	622	46	...	...
Portugal	487	486	1	...	...
Spain	1,550	1,453	98	...	...
Turkey	3,559	3,502	57	1	1
Total, Eastern Europe	2,088	2,088	...	...	...
Czechoslovakia	...	...	...	...	...
East Germany	...	...	...	...	...
Hungary	4	4	...	...	...
Poland	966	966	...	...	...
Romania	101	101	...	...	...
Yugoslavia	629	602	27	74	1

[a] Including U.S.S.R.

[b] Including Yugoslavia

Source: Annual Report to the President and to the Congress for Fiscal Year 1985, National Advisory Council on International Monetary and Financial Policies, Washington (1985: 250–259).

the present total debt to all U.S. institutions amounts to $ 2.3 billion. The ratio of debt repayments to exports to the U.S.A. is represented in Table 6.

The U.S.A. is still the single biggest creditor of the Yugoslav economy, although the share of U.S. government credits is not as high as earlier (12%; see Table 5). More than $ 2 billion debt to the U.S.A. is neither a small nor too high an amount for an economy exporting goods valued at more than $ 10 million annually. Yet, the debt in U.S. credits is extremely high compared with the exports to this country. Because of this, great efforts have been made lately to broaden and enlarge mutual trade. Besides ham, furniture, textiles, leather, and raw materials, the traditional Yugoslav exports to the U.S.A., products on a more advanced technological level, such as cars, have been exported to the U.S.A. recently. On the other hand, the Yugoslav government has tried hard to attract foreign, especially American, capital either directly or through joint ventures. Although a certain influx of American capital has occurred in the past two or three years, especially to less-developed southern and eastern regions, it is still far below the desired level.

Table 6. Yugoslav Indebtedness Towards the U.S.A., 1978 to 1984 (millions of dollars)

Year	Total	Debt repayments	Exports to U.S.A.	Repayments to exports ratio (%)
1978	1,905	210	371	56.6
1979	1,608	258	373	69.1
1980	1,883	319	393	81.2
1981	1,899	249	385	64.6
1982	1,577	...	311	...
1983	1,794	305	346	88.1
1984	2,350	304	432	70.4

Source: Bilten Narodne banke Jugoslavije (Bulletin of the Yugoslav National Bank), No. 12, (December 1985); *Statistički godišnjak Jugoslavije* (Statistical Yearbook of Yugoslavia), Beograd (1985: 152).

5 Conclusion

Postwar U.S. financial assistance to Yugoslavia began after the break in Soviet-Yugoslav relations in 1948 and has continued up to the present time. The U.S. government alone has provided a total of $ 2.8 billion in grants and credits during the entire postwar period. Thus, Yugoslavia ranks with all of Eastern Europe or somewhere between Portugal and Spain (Table 2). In the 1950s and early 1960s U.S. assistance represented about 6% of Yugoslav GNP and 30% on net investments in the economy (Table 5). The aid program was conducted almost exclusively by the U.S. government and consisted mostly of food and arms (Table 4). Later on, in the 1970s and 1980s both the sources and the substance of assistance became more diversified. International financial organizations, commercial banks, and other foreign governments participated in lending to Yugoslavia. Their credits were mainly used for the purchase of industrial technology and various semifinished or intermediate products. It is important to note that the rather steady flow of U.S. financial assistance to Yugoslavia throughout the whole period from 1948 to 1984 was hardly disturbed by political events or changes in the White House. Currently, Yugoslavia's entire indebtedness is $ 20 billion, including $ 2.3 billion to American creditors and $ 629 million to the U.S. government alone.

There can be no doubt that U.S. financial assistance has been an important contribution to Yugoslav postwar economic development. The question of the significance and success of that help for Yugoslavia, as well as for some other economically less-developed countries, has not been dealt with here. There remains the question of whether the assistance was worthwhile from the point of view of American interests. Were there any better policy options for the U.S.A.? Unfortunately, the answer to this crucial question depends on knowledge not readily available, namely, of the original intentions and hopes of the administrations that established assistance to Yugolavia. If they hoped for gradual changes in the Yugoslav economic and social system towards a Western-style democracy, or, that Yugoslavia might become a model for other Eastern European countries, these hopes have not been fulfilled so far. However, there is not much evidence that this was considered realistic on the U.S. side. It must be remembered that, according to the gentlemen's agreement at Yalta in 1945, Yugoslavia was predestined to be under the equal influence of both sides and this has apparently been respected. Let us then assume that U.S. hopes connected with the assistance to Yugoslavia were more realistic with regard to the following three points:

1. The need to strengthen Yugoslav defense capabilities and to protect its independence
2. The need for presence and a more refined role in a region that might otherwise have remained without any American influence
3. The need to show that a relatively open economy and society, even if communist and less developed, can provide its citizens with a better perspective than the majority of Eastern European countries

If so, we may conclude that the American hopes have been fulfilled.

Without American aid Yugoslavia might easily have become a full-fledged member of the Eastern bloc, since it would have hardly been able to defend and feed itself in the early 1950s. With this aid, however, the Yugoslav government was able to increase not only its military strength and political independence, but also its domestic legitimacy and popularity. All U.S. administrations since the war seem to have tried to contribute to the former rather than to the latter, although at any given time the one could have hardly been achieved without the other.

Notes

1 Diplomatic relations were established in 1881 between the U.S.A. and the Principality of Serbia, the only independent state in the region at the time. The documents were signed in Belgrade by the Special Deputy of the Secretary of State, Eugene Schuyler, and the Minister of Foreign Affairs, Cedomilj Mijatović.

2 The United Nations Relief and Rehabilitation Administration (UNRRA), a temporary international agency for providing economic help to countries impoverished by the Second World War, provided a total of $ 3.6 billion for help during its existence from 1943 to 1947.

3 The respective value for a sign test is $z = 0.2582$, which is within a confidence interval limit of 99%.

References

Agency for International Development (1966): *U.S. Foreign Assistance and Assistance from International Organizations, July 1, 1945 to June 30, 1965*. Washington, D.C.

Bilten Narodne banke Jugoslavije (Bulletin of the Yugoslav National Bank) (1985) December, no. 12.

Dimitrijević, S. (1958): *Strani kapital u privredi bivše Jugoslavije* (Foreign Capital in the Economy of Former Yugoslavia). Beograd: Nolit.

Export-Import Bank (1983): *Annual Report*. Washington, D.C.

Gnjatović, D. (1985): *Uloga inostranih sredstava u privrednom razvoju Jugoslavije* (The Role of Foreign Resources in Yugoslav Economic Development). Beograd: Ekonomski institut.

Narodna banka Jugoslavije (1972): *Godišnji izveštaj* (Annual Report). Beograd.

National Advisory Council on International Monetary and Financial Policies (1985): *Annual Report to the President and to the Congress for Fiscal Year 1985*. Washington, D.C.

Sjedinjene države i Jugoslavija – sto godina saradnje (US and Yugoslavia – A Hundred Years of Cooperation) (1981): A supplement to *Pregled*, no. 216.

Special Committee to Study the Foreign Aid Program. United States Senate (1957): *Foreign Aid Program. Compilation of Studies and Surveys*. Washington, D.C.

Statistički godišnjak (Statistical Yearbook) (1940): Opšta državna statistika kraljevine Jugoslavije, Beograd.

Statistički godišnjak Jugoslavije (Statistical Yearbook of Yugoslavia) (1985): Beograd.

Štrbac, Č. (1987): Jugoslavija posle 1948, iz britanskih arhiva (Yugoslavia after 1948, from British archives). *Politika*, March, 5 – 14.

Stability and Change in U.S. Foreign Economic Policy Towards the Comecon Countries During the Past Twenty Years*

Adam Gwiazda

1 Introduction

Throughout the postwar period the United States has regarded economic relations with the socialist countries of Eastern Europe as a political rather than an economic problem. Therefore, U.S. foreign economic policy towards those countries has been subordinated to political goals and security considerations instead of economic aims and motivations. However, in the mid-1950s a fundamental change in international relations occurred with considerable influence on U.S. foreign economic policy towards the Comecon countries.

First of all, it was the deep transformation of the Western world that brought about some improvement in U.S. economic relations with Eastern Europe. At that time, Western Europe became more independent from the United States. Already in the mid-1950s the value of East-West trade was higher for Western Europe than the value of U.S. economic and military aid.

At the end of the 1950s the United States also ceased to treat all socialist countries as parts of a monolithic bloc. Instead, it tried to make use of existing differences between individual socialist countries in promoting its political and economic interests in that area. Nevertheless, the basic nature of U.S. foreign economic policy has not changed. Not only the Soviet Union but all Comecon countries as a group have been – and still are – treated by the U.S. administration, Congressmen, and various agencies and organizations as potential enemies rather than partners in trade. This explains why basic principles and methods of the policy towards the Comecon countries has remained relatively stable despite the lack of consensus within the U.S. administration, Congress, various committees, and other bodies involved in the shaping of foreign economic policy.

---

* Acknowledgment. The author wishes to acknowledge Peter Jaschner's editorial contributions to this paper.

The stability of American trade policy towards the socialist countries was also the result of the consequent implementation of U.S. policy against "world communism." According to U.S. government officials, trade with the communist world ought to be properly adapted to and used within the existing political, military, and economic realities (Rusk 1964). Many American experts have shared the same opinion and insisted that U.S. economic policy towards the socialist countries could not be conducted according to economic criteria, because political and military considerations were much more important (Kennan 1964). Similar statements concerning the basic assumptions and rules of U.S. foreign economic policy can be found in numerous publications, official ones as well as others (Report to the President 1971; Ahearn 1982).

There has also been a clearly visible interdependence between U.S. foreign trade policy towards the Comecon and consecutive American political and strategic doctrines from the Truman doctrine of "containment of communism," the Kennedy doctrine of "peaceful coexistence," through the Nixon doctrine of "selective coexistence," the Ford and Carter doctrines of "transition from confrontation to negotiation," to the present "new" anticommunist crusade of the Reagan administration, which considers the socialist countries, especially the Soviet Union, to be an "empire of evil" (Crabb 1982).

It should be noted that the U.S.A. has always regarded trade and economic cooperation with the Comecon countries as well as other socialist countries to be an instrument of its political and strategic goals. In other words, trade has always been, and is likely to remain, "a hostage of politics." This attitude of the U.S. administration on economic relations with the Comecon countries has greatly determined both the methods of U.S. foreign economic policy and the highly selective approach to individual Comecon countries.

2 Main Methods and Approaches of U.S. Foreign Economic Policy Towards the Comecon Countries

During the period under consideration the United States used alternately at least three approaches in its foreign economic policy towards Comecon and other socialist countries. First, total boycott of trade and economic cooperation, second, export controls, the method used most commonly during the past 20 years, and third, moderate promotion of trade as well as economic, scientific, and cultural cooperation with individual Comecon countries.

The policy of total economic boycott in the form of an economic blockade was conducted by the United States against the Soviet Union in the early 1920s. After the Second World War this policy was not implemented against any Comecon country. However, in the 1960s and the first half of the 1980s the U.S.A. pursued a policy of partial boycott towards individual Comecon countries in the form of economic sanctions and credit restrictions, as well as grain and technology embargoes.

Export controls, however, were the most frequently used method designed to confine economic cooperation and trade with those countries to the lowest possible level. Within the system of export controls, national security and political goals were given absolute priority over economic advantages. This approach to U.S. foreign economic policy was already developed in the 1940s when COCOM was founded in 1949 in order to coordinate Western export policy and to control the export of strategic goods to the East. It must be stressed that the U.S.A. was the main driving force in setting up COCOM, a non-formal agreement of fifteen Western countries and Japan (including all NATO members except Iceland). Two other countries, Sweden and Switzerland, cooperate closely with the committee observing the common list of strategic goods excluded from exports to socialist countries (McIntyre and Culpitt 1980).

It is important to note that the whole, rather complicated, system of American foreign economic policy has been shaped to serve the main purpose of export controls, i. e., to limit rather than expand trade with Comecon countries. This can be seen in U.S. trade legislation, institutional arrangements, and credit and financial relations with the Comecon countries, as well as the whole system of decentralized export controls. Some experts describe the way in which the U.S. formulates and conducts its trade policy as a "decentralized mess" (Cohen 1977: 58).

It is conceivable then how under such conditions the U.S.A. could not formulate, implement, and maintain a coherent foreign economic policy towards the Comecon countries. To some extent, this was also due to the American political system with its dispersion of power, institutional cross-checks, and massive legislative intrusions upon executive prerogatives. These factors make the formulation of a coherent trade policy all the more difficult.

Decisive influence on the shaping of U.S. foreign economic policy towards the Comecon countries is exerted by the Department of State, the Department of Defense, and sometimes the National Security Council. Paradoxically, the relatively weakest position in the decision-making process is held by the Department of Commerce, which – ex officio – should be responsible for carving trade policy.

Other reasons also help to explain the problems connected with shaping a coherent foreign policy in general, not just trade policy. Some opinions hold that in the U.S. there are

> 535 putative secretaries of state and secretaries of defense. Each congressman and senator has at least one advisor on foreign policy on a full-time basis,

> who can only justify his living by trying to make his boss into a would-be secretary of state. Some legislators have now appointed assistants to carry the titles of national security advisers.... The result is that it is very difficult for the president and his team to shape a policy and to sustain it (Brzezinski 1986: 34).

On the other hand, the existing relative stability of organizational structures and administrative procedures concerning the division of functions and roles between the Departments of State, Commerce, and Defense, as well as other federal agencies has secured the continuity and stability of export controls as a basic method of U.S. economic policy towards the Comecon countries. American export controls have been frequently criticized for their inefficiency and the bureaucratic procedures involved in granting the export licenses every exporter had to obtain for shipments to socialist countries. The fact is, however, that these export controls, despite their inefficiency, have proven to be powerful instruments in the pursuit of the main strategic goals of U.S. foreign policy, namely, the curbing of high-technology sales to Comecon countries. They also have helped to inflict heavy losses upon the economies and societies of those countries by limiting or stopping exports of grain, foodstuffs, credits, and other goods.

The third approach, the promotion of trade and economic cooperation with the socialist countries, was already formulated at the beginning of the 1960s in connection with the doctrines of "peaceful coexistence" and "building bridges." This policy was put into practice during the period of détente (Campbell 1965; Garthoff 1985; George 1983). It consisted mainly in the liberalization of export controls. A similar process had been initiated already in the mid-1960s as part of President Johnson's plan to build bridges between East and West, and later under Nixon. At the time, the U.S. loosened its controls by allowing a greater number of goods to be exported to Comecon countries without a specific license or without hindering the process of licensing.

There were many reasons for such a shift in U.S. policy. One of them was the idea prevailing in the Nixon and Carter adminstrations that the expansion of trade, especially with the Soviet Union, would contribute to a more peaceful coexistence. Other factors were of an economic nature, namely, the relatively minor effects of export controls as compared with their costs. Also, in the beginning of the 1970s American businesses grew more reluctant to comply with the strict regulations. They simply did not want to lose business opportunities in Eastern Europe, where other Western countries and firms were already substantially involved.

The change in U.S. policy also resulted from the transformation of American foreign policy under the Nixon administration. At that time a visible shift from vertical to horizontal relationships occurred. This means, relations between the U.S.A. and its allies and clients were supplanted by those between the superpowers, the United States and the Soviet Union. This shift in the direction of American foreign policy was predicated on two important assumptions. Both President Nixon and his Secretary of State, Kissinger, believed that the relationship between the U.S.A. and the Soviet Union was pivotal in world politics and that local conflicts were best approached through the superpowers linked directly or indirectly to the conflicting parties.

In order to improve U.S. relations to the Soviets Kissinger supported the concept of linkage, the idea that issues at stake for the two countries were interrelated, making it possible for the Americans to obtain Soviet agreement on certain questions by holding back on issues particularly dear to the Soviets. For instance, progress in arms limitation and human rights was to be linked to economic and technological cooperation (Nixon 1972; Stanley and Whitt 1970).

3 Dilemmas of U.S. Foreign Economic Policy Towards Comecon Countries in the 1970s

At the end of the 1960s the United States started to ease the export embargo directed at the Soviet Union. However, the Nixon administration was reluctant at that time to liberalize significantly the hitherto prevailing trade policy towards the Soviet Union and the other Comecon countries (Kissinger 1979: 1524). As mentioned above, American businessmen continued to lobby in Congress for a liberalization of existing law, in particular, the Export Control Act of 1949. Owing to these pressures Congress passed the Export Administration Act in December 1969. This act created conditions more favorable to the development of trade with the East, especially in non-military goods. It contained far less restrictions than the earlier act of 1949 and empowered the President to make the necessary changes on the list of strategic goods in accordance with changes in the international environment and the political situation (Committee on Foreign Affairs 1969: 1223).

The act of 1969 also allowed for a different treatment of individual socialist countries. Poland and Romania were the most privileged countries subject to the least restrictions of U.S. trade policy. In the second place followed the Soviet Union and the other European Comecon countries. The third place was left for other socialist countries like China, Vietnam, and North Korea, with which the U.S. did not maintain any trade relations at the time. Within the group of all socialist countries Yugoslavia enjoyed a special status in U.S. foreign policy (see the Janković paper).

Visible improvement in U.S.-Soviet economic relations occurred after May 22, 1972, i. e., after the Nixon-Brezhnev summit in Moscow and later after the signing of a U.S.-Soviet Trade and Economic Agreement on October 18, 1972. This agreement projected that total trade between 1972 and 1974 would triple compared with the situation three years before (U.S. Department of Commerce 1972: 75). In reality, the U.S. exports alone rose eightfold and total trade rose sixfold in that period. Much of this increase was due to the growth of American grain shipments to the Soviet Union rather than to U.S. imports from that country.

In fact, however, as a result of the widening policy of détente, the U.S. and the U.S.S.R. signed a trade agreement that gave most-favored-nation (MFN) tariff treatment to the Soviet Union. Yet, Congress did not consent to the agreement obliging the Nixon administration to try for a more substantial legislative change regarding East-West trade relations. Therefore, in 1973 the administration submitted to Congress a Trade Reform Act, the adoption of which was hoped to bring about congressional approval of the 1972 Trade Agreement with the Soviets. Throughout the long and difficult debate, the emphasis turned out to be not on national security but on human rights, including the right of Jews to emigrate from their respective socialist countries to Israel or other countries (Bertsch 1985: 247 – 248). While the Nixon administration wanted to link the MFN status to Soviet foreign policy, Senator Jackson and other members of Congress linked the MFN status explicitly to Soviet domestic policy.

In other words, the Nixon administration wanted to use trade to facilitate political relations with the Soviets and other socialist countries, while the advocates of East-West trade in the business community wanted the government to stay out of trade and leave it to market forces. Other groups, like the strong Jewish lobby, opted for the intervention of government in order to facilitate Jewish emigration from the Soviet Union and other Comecon countries.

The Trade Act was passed by Congress in its final version on December 20, 1974 providing that, with the exception of Poland and Yugoslavia,

> products of the nonmarket country are ineligible for nondiscriminatory treatment during any period in which the President determines that the country denies its citizens the right of opportunity to emigrate or imposes more than nominal charges on emigration (Grzybowski 1977: 508 – 509).

The act also stipulates that even if such a determination was made by the President, the final decision in this matter belonged to Congress, which must approve commercial agreements granting MFN status to the country that has properly adjusted its emigration policies.

Furthermore, the Trade Act specified that all bilateral agreements with nonmarket countries should include the following conditions: the duration of the agreement should not exceed three years with the possibility of a renewal for three additional years provided that the balance of mutual advantage is maintained; provisions should be made for the termination of the agreement for security reasons as well as immediate consultations in the case of market disruptions due to imports; the parties should be authorized to adopt any restrictions necessary to prevent such disruptions (Grzybowski 1977: 511).

This act was a typical example of "positive linkage," the central concept of U.S. economic policy towards the Comecon countries. However, there was disagreement among the administration, members of Congress, and other groups over the "rationality" of U.S.-Soviet trade policies and the use of "linkage" in order to gain substantial concessions from the Soviets and other socialist countries either in foreign or domestic policy. This conflict of interests and the lack of a uniform economic policy explain – to some extent – the relative stability of U.S. trade policy towards the Comecon. There were no fundamental changes in that policy except for a temporary short-term improvement in commercial relations between the U.S. and the Comecon countries.

A detailed discussion of all aspects and results of the policy of linkage is beyond the scope of this paper (see, for example, Jacobsen 1980; Nye 1984; Rode 1986). The passage of the Trade Act of 1974 (including the Jackson-Vanik Amendment), however, must be considered a step backwards on the road towards a more liberal U.S. foreign economic policy and improved trade relations with the Comecon countries. In fact, some progress has been made since then, including the 1975 long-term agreement on grain purchases and an agreement on scientific exchange between the United States and the Soviet Union. Yet, in the mid-1970s both sides, the U.S. and the Comecon countries, were disappointed with the results of détente (Huntington 1978: 67 – 70).

At that time pressure on Congress increased visibly in order to make it more lenient to conservative forces in American society. These circles favored further export restrictions and the introduction of controls into U.S. trade policy. In the second half of the 1970s these pressures led to the next shift in U.S. economic policy, the adoption of "negative linkage" as a method to contain the expansion of the Soviet Union and other socialist countries (Ross 1978; Kaiser 1980). The efforts of the administration and Congress were designed to prevent exports to Comecon countries, especially the Soviet Union, of any technologies likely to enhance both the military and civilian sectors of those economies. The "Bucy Report," published unter the auspices of the Defense Department (Defense Science Board 1976) contained an analysis of U.S. export controls policy to date and recommendations for the further improvement of that policy demanding strict controls of technology transfers and strategic trade regardless of the state of U.S.-Soviet relations and Soviet domestic policy.

In August 1977 the Secretary of Defense stated that the main objective of the Pentagon in the field of export controls and national security was to maintain U.S. technological superiority over its potential enemies (Department of Defense 1977). In order to achieve this goal strict controls had to be imposed on the transfer of "critical technologies" both to Comecon countries and Western countries, thus preventing the "re-export" of such technologies to socialist countries.

Conservative tendencies in U.S. foreign economic policy were also reinforced by personnel changes in the adminstration. After Watergate and Nixon's resignation this policy was shaped in accordance with the conservative views of the Defense Department with ideological arguments outweighing economic ones.

In addition, the views in the administration on economic policy towards the East were at that time not as divergent as in the mid-1960s and early 1970s. There were, for instance, no serious differences between the Department of Defense and the Department of Commerce. The "ideologization" of U.S. economic policy was also due to the radicalization of attitudes in various Western countries, the increasing popularity of Communist parties in some countries, and the growing economic and military potential of socialist countries, as well as other external and internal factors.

During the Carter years the most commonly used method in U.S. foreign economic policy was the so-called economic or lightswitch diplomacy, which consisted in turning trade on and off in order to influence Soviet behavior (Shultz 1978; Bertsch 1980). In July 1978 a practical example of that diplomacy was provided by the denial of an export license for a Sperry Univac computer ordered by TASS for the 1980 Olympics. Next, in August 1978 the U.S.A. imposed export controls on Soviet purchases of oil and gas equipment with the argument that such controls were necessary as flexible instruments of foreign policy. On August 31, 1978, Carter called for a review of a license issued earlier to Dresser Industries for the export of a drill bit plant to the U.S.S.R. A month later, the license was reapproved, but withdrawn again in November 1980.

The result of this "lightswitch diplomacy" was a growing uncertainty in U.S. trade with the Soviets and other Comecon countries. This uncertainty was mainly due to the lack of a unified foreign economic policy, which – according to some U.S. government officials – "changed almost daily" (Bertsch 1985: 253). In such a situation, the Export Administration Act of 1969, which had already liberalized U.S. foreign economic policy somewhat, was replaced by the Export Administration Act of 1979 in September. This act constituted an effort to reconcile the interests of national security with economic losses and adverse effects on the balance of payments caused by export restrictions. The act explicitly stated that "export trade must be given a high priority."

While the Export Administration Act of 1979 liberalized U.S. trade policy, some fundamental objectives underlying the 1949 Export Control Act were maintained. The 1949 act had stated that the U.S. could prohibit any exports of "potential military significance." In the Export Administration Acts of 1969 and 1979 this was slightly modified to exports making a "significant contribution to the military potential" of any nation that might prove detrimental to the national security of the United States. It should also be stressed that, in addition to the objective of U.S. national security and the protection of scarce materials from depletion, the use of export embargoes in U.S. foreign policy was stated in all trade legislation after 1949 as well as 1979.

It can be concluded that U.S. foreign economic policy towards the Comecon in the 1970s reflected both the lack of a national consensus on that policy and a conflict of interests between the Executive and Congress. Under President Carter the U.S. policy of "differentiation" manifested itself in the desire to develop good and possibly stable relations with selected Comecon countries like Poland, Romania, and, since 1978, Hungary. At the same time, bilateral relations with other Comecon countries were still characterized by mutual reserve, distrust, and caution. During this phase of East – West trade relations Romania was granted MFN status by presidential decision in June 1975. Later, on March 17, 1978, Hungary was granted MFN status on a mutual basis by a bilateral trade agreement, while Poland had enjoyed this status in 1931 – 1951 and 1960 – 1982.

During the period under consideration, the U.S.A. followed the concept of "active globalism" as opposed to the former Republican concept of "passive globalism." In Europe, it tried to improve and stabilize relations with its NATO allies, while, on the other hand, trying to "incorporate" individual European socialist countries in an all-European participation in the process of defining the "new situation" – according to its own understanding of détente. Such an approach of individual Comecon countries was also based on the expectation that expanding trade with the East would facilitate better political relations.

During the 1970s the U.S.A. also undertook many efforts to use the process of détente for the improvement of economic relations with the Comecon, i. e., to improve political relations first and then expand trade and economic cooperation. This dilemma of U.S. foreign economic policy concerning the question of what to improve first – trade or political relations or the other way round – was not resolved during the 1970s.

4 A New Phase in U.S. Foreign Economic Policy Towards Comecon Countries

The "new era" in U.S. foreign economic policy towards the Comecon began already before the Reagan years early in 1980. On January 4, 1980, in response to the Soviet invasion of Afghanistan, President Carter ordered the embargo of all U.S. grain sales to the Soviet Union in excess of the eight million metric tons guaranteed in the 1975 bilateral agreement. Invoking authority granted under the Export Administration Act of 1979 Carter thus stopped the probable sale of 17 million metric tons of grain. In addition, the export of high-technology products to the Soviet Union was also restricted and 700 export licenses were suspended by the Commerce Department. Carter also ordered the complete suspension of exports intended for the 1980 Olympic Games in Moscow. The stated purpose of the embargo was to punish the Soviet Union for its military intervention in Afghanistan in late December 1979 (Paarlberg 1980; Gwiazda 1984).

Under the Reagan administration economic relations between the U.S.A. and the Comecon countries deteriorated further. In the first half of the 1980s U.S. policy towards those countries was determined mainly by those forces in the administration and in Congress that emphasized U.S. geopolitical interests at the expense of American business and labor. Moreover, Reagan's globalist policy reasserted the rationale underlying the Truman doctrine, the cornerstone of America's postwar approach to international affairs. Globalism in U.S. foreign policy can be characterized as a desire to manage world affairs and reshape the globe in the American image. This approach was advocated by many of Reagan's top national security advisers during the early 1980s maintaining that "no area of the world is beyond the scope of American interests" (Kegley and Wittkopf 1987: 112).

This "new" U.S. foreign policy towards the world outside had, of course, been influenced by various sources and factors. One of the main reasons for such a shift in foreign policy was President Reagan's innate anticommunism. According to some analysts

> Reagan's foreign policy is less a response to the outside world than another expression of his struggle to defeat values and trends that challenge conservative truths. The enemy or problem everywhere abroad is Soviet Russia or left-wing totalitarianism opposing conventional American ideals (Dallek 1984).

The global contest with the Soviet Union was the main factor exerting decisive influence on U.S. foreign policy, including economic policy towards the Comecon.

As mentioned above, the Reagan administrations's foreign policy was characterized by so-called global activism. This concept held that no corner of the globe lay outside American interests and no issue on the global agenda should be left unattended if it touched American security concerns in any way whatsoever. Some experts rightly point out that

> the Reagan philosophy... represented a radical departure from the foreign policies of the previous decade. Presidents Nixon, Ford and Carter had consistently, albeit in different ways, conducted foreign policies that were adjusting to the changed world. Each pursued an active diplomacy to compensate for the diffusion of international power that had become so evident by the late 1960s. Ronald Reagan reversed the logic: Washington's policies should not have to adjust to the world – a strong reassertive America could make the world adjust to Washington (Gelb and Lake 1985: 466).

In practice, the foreign policy of "active globalism" no longer consisted in merely defending countries threatened by communist invasion or insurgency, but in actively and overtly assisting anticommunist "freedom fighters" everywhere, including some Comecon countries. This explains U.S. interest in maintaining the process of change in Poland in 1980/1981, i.e., within the Soviet sphere of interests. This can be supported by the response of the Reagan administration to the imposition of martial law and the crackdown on "Solidarity," the independent labor union in Poland. On December 23 and 30, 1981, Poland the and Soviet Union, respectively, became targets of U.S. economic sanctions. The administration halted the renewal of the Export-Import Bank's export credit insurance for U.S. firms selling goods to Poland, and suspended permission for Polish fishing vessels operating in American waters, as well as the right of the Polish national airline to fly to and from the United States.

The Soviet Union was also subject to economic sanctions, because it "bore a heavy and direct responsibility for the repression of Poland." Economic sanctions included seven measures, two of which were relevant to the application of the Export Administration Act. Among other goods, an extended list of oil and gas equipment was embargoed, including piledrivers as well as high-technology products such as electronic equipment and computers (Hufbauer and Schott 1985; Marantz 1986).

The sanctions against Poland, on the other hand, served two distinct but closely related functions:

> They were a political signal of condemnation addresed to government circles, and of support for the population; they also served as a tool of economic pressure on the communist establishment and its sponsors (Wasowski 1986: 167).

After all labor unions had been abolished in Poland, President Reagan imposed a new sanction on October 9, 1982, proclaiming the suspension of the MFN status of Poland. Officially, the legal basis for the suspension of the MFN status was Poland's failure to raise imports from GATT members by 7%, an obligation formally accepted in the previous trade agreement.

The sanctions directed at Poland were subsequently removed in the course of the so-called political normalization in Poland from 1983 to February 1987. The removal of these sanctions, however, did not change the nature of U.S. economic policy towards Poland and other Comecon countries. Under the conditions of "neither cold war nor détente" in the first half of the 1980s and the general state of Soviet-American relations, this removal was a gesture of good will rather than a sign of radical liberalization of U.S. economic policy towards the East.

5 Some Concluding Remarks

When trade and economic cooperation with socialist countries, defined as "potential enemies" in the West, were regarded an instrument of foreign policy by the U.S.A., very few options existed for the shaping of a foreign economic policy appropriate to the needs of American business and labor. As sketched out briefly in this chapter, U.S. trade policy towards Comecon countries has always been determined by political and security considerations rather than by economic motives, factors, and interests. In the 1960s trade policy served as a powerful instrument in U.S. warfare against individual socialist countries and "world communism" in general. In the first half of the 1970s this policy was part of détente and a tool for the improvement of American-Soviet political relations. In the first half of the 1980s, however, trade and economic cooperation were again used by the Reagan administration as instruments to put pressure on both international and domestic behavior of the Soviet Union and other Comecon countries.

Taking into account various priorities of U.S. foreign policy and the fact that it has been stable with regard to the Comecon countries the basic pattern of American economic policy towards those countries is unlikely to be disturbed. In fact, there is no favorable environment for the formulation and implementation of an economic policy conducive to the expansion of trade with those countries. Nor could such a policy be formulated and maintained in the long run because of the dispersion of political power in the American system of checks and balances.

The continuing debate on U.S. trade policy towards Western developed and developing countries as well as Comecon countries confirms the dilemmas facing the formulation and implementation of an "appropriate" foreign economic policy (Stern 1987; Krugman 1986; Caldwell 1985). Indeed, in the case of economic relations between the U.S.A., Western Europe, and Japan, trade remains a hostage of U.S. monetary and industrial policy, or economic policy in general, whereas in the case of U.S.-Comecon economic relations trade has always been a hostage of political considerations.

Therefore, we cannot expect radical changes in current U.S. economic policy towards the Comecon countries, unless there is an appropriate change in U.S. and Soviet foreign policies. For both superpowers, East-West economic relations constitute a special field of and a framework for the realization of their "global strategies." Experience confirms that trade and economic cooperation are used as weapons in the global contest of different foreign policies rather than as factors contributing to economic welfare and the stable peaceful coexistence of all Western (capitalist) and Eastern (socialist) countries.

References

Ahearn, R. J. (1982): Political Determinants of U.S. trade policy. *Orbis* 26(2): 413 – 429.

Ailes, C. P., and A. E. Pardee (1986): *Cooperation in Science and Technology. An Evaluation of the U.S.-Soviet Agreement.* Boulder: Westview Press.

Ayubi, S. et al. (1982): *Economic Sanctions in U.S. Foreign Policy.* Philadelphia: Foreign Policy Research Institute.

Baldwin, R. (1976): *The Political Economy of Postwar U.S. Trade Policy.* New York: New York University Press.

Bertsch, G. K. (1980): U.S.-Soviet Trade: the question of leverage. *Survey* 2: 66 – 80.

Bertsch, G. K. (1981): US export controls: the 1970s and beyond. *Journal of World Trade Law* 1: 67 – 82.

Bertsch, G. K. (1985): American Politics and Trade with the USSR. In B. Parrot (ed.), *Trade, Technology and Soviet-American Relations.* Bloomington: Indiana University Press.

Brzezinski, Z. (1986): *Game Plan: A Geostrategic Framework for the Conduct of the U.S.-Soviet Contest.* Boston: Atlantic Monthly Press.

Brzezinski, Z. (1986): A Conversation with Zbigniew Brzezinski. *The National Interest* 5: 28 – 35.

Caldwell, D. (ed.) (1985): *Soviet International Behavior and US Policy Options.* Lexington, Mass.: Lexington Books.

Campbell, J. (1965): *American Policy Toward Communist Eastern Europe: the Choices Ahead.* Minneapolis: University of Minnesota Press.

Cohen, S. D. (1977): *The Making of United States International Economic Policy.* New York: Praeger.

Cohen, S. D. and R. J. Meltzer (1982): *United States International Economic Policy in Action. Diversity of Decision Making.* New York: Praeger.

Committee on Foreign Affairs, U.S. House of Representatives (1969): *Legislation on Foreign Affairs*. Washington, D.C.

Crabb, C. V., jr. (1982): *The Doctrines of American Foreign Policy*. Baton Rouge: Louisiana State University Press.

Dallek, R. (1984): *Ronald Reagan: The Politics of Symbolism*. Cambridge, Mass.: Harvard University Press.

Daoudi, M. S. and M. S. Dajani (1983): *Economic Sanctions: Ideals and Experience*. Henley: Routlege and Kegan Paul.

Defense Science Board Task Force on Export of Technology (1976): *An Analysis of Export Control of U.S. Technology. A D.O.D. Perspective*. Washington, D.C.: Government Printing Office.

Department of Defense (1977): *Interim D.O.D. Policy Statement on Export Control of United States Technology*. Press Release, September 2. Washington, D.C.

Destler, I. M. (1980): *Making Foreign Economic Policy*. Washington, D.C.: Brookings Institution.

Ellings, R. (1985): *Embargoes and World Power. Lessons from American Foreign Policy*. Boulder: Westview Press.

Garthoff, R. L. (1985): *Détente and Confrontation: American-Soviet Relations from Nixon to Reagan*. Washington, D.C.: Brookings Institution.

Gelb, L. H. and A. Lake (1985): Four More Years: Diplomacy Restored. *Foreign Affairs*. Special issue: "America and the World 1984" 63(3): 465–489.

George, A. L. (ed.) (1983): *Managing U.S.-Soviet Rivalry*. Boulder: Westview Press.

Grzybowski, K. (1977): East-West Trade Regulations in the United States: The 1974 U.S. Trade Act. *Journal of World Trade Law* 6: 503–521.

Gwiazda, A. (1984): Restrictions in U.S. Grain Exports to the USSR. *Sprawy Międzynarodowe* 2: 59–68.

Gwiazda, A. (1986): The Western Alliance Trade Policy toward the Comecon countries. *West-Ost-Journal* 3/4: 21–22.

Hardt, J. P. (1979): United States-Soviet Trade Policy. In *Issues in East-West Commercial Relations. A Compendium of Papers Submitted to the Joint Economic Committee*. Washington, D.C.: Congress of the United States.

Hatibović, D. (1987): U.S. Foreign Trade Policy. *Review of International Affairs* 888: 4–7.

Hoffman, S. (1983): *Dead Ends, American Foreign Policy in the New Cold War*. Cambridge, Mass.: Ballinger.

Hufbauer, G. C. and J. J. Schott (1985): *Economic Sanctions Reconsidered: History and Current Policy*. Washington, D.C.: Institute for International Economics.

Huntington, S. (1978): Trade, Technology and Leverage: Economic Diplomacy. *Foreign Policy* 32: 63–80.

Jacobsen, H. D. (1980): *Die Ostwirtschaftspolitik der USA. Möglichkeiten und Grenzen einer "linkage"-Politik*. Ebenhausen: Stiftung Wissenschaft und Politik.

Kaiser, R. G. (1980): U.S.-Soviet Relations: Goodbye to Détente. *Foreign Affairs* 3: 500–521.

Kegley, C. W., jr., and E. R. Wittkopf (1987): Beyond Reagan: The Future of American Foreign Policy. *Korean Journal of International Studies* 38(2): 107–150.

Kennan, G. P. (1964): Statement. In Committee on Foreign Relations, U.S. Senate, *East-West Trade. A Compilation of Views of Businessmen, Bankers and Academic Experts*, November, Washintgon, D.C.

Kissinger, H. (1979): *The White House Years*. Boston: Atlantic Monthly Press.

Krugman, P. (ed.) (1986): *Strategic Trade Policy and the New International Economics*. Cambridge, Mass.: MIT Press.

Marantz, P. (1986): Economic Sanctions in the Polish Crisis. In L. Brown (ed.), *The Utility of Economic Sanctions*. London: Croom Helm.

McIntyre, J. and R. Culpitt (1980): Multilateral Strategic Trade Controls Within the Western Alliance. *Survey* 2: 81–108.

Melanson, R. A. (ed.) (1982): *Neither Cold War nor Détente? Soviet American Relations in the 1980s*. Charlottesville: University of Virginia Press.

Nixon, R. (1972): *US Foreign Policy for the 1970s. The Emerging Structure of Peace*. A report to the Congress, February 9. Washington, D.C.

Nye, J. S., jr. (ed.) (1984): *The Making of America's Soviet Policy*. New Haven: Yale University Press.

Paarlberg, R. L. (1980): Lessons of the Grain Embargo. *Foreign Affairs* 59(1): 144–162.

Rode, R. (1986): *Sicherheit versus Geschäft: die Osthandelspolitik der USA von Nixon bis Carter*. Frankfurt: Campus.

Rusk, D. (1964): Statement. In U.S. Senate, *East-West Trade. Hearings before the Committeee on Foreign Relations*. Washington, D.C.: U.S. Government Printing Office.

Ross, A. (1978): Credits – only for détente. *Washington Quarterly* 4: 72–78.

Schnitzer, M. (1980): *U.S. Business Involvement in Eastern Europe*. New York: Praeger.

Shultz, G. P. (1978): Lightswitch Diplomacy. *Business Week*, May 29: 32.

Skurski, R. (1979): U.S. Economic Relations with the Soviet Union and East Europe. *Co-existence* 1: 20–32.

Special Committee on U.S. Trade Relations with East European Countries and the Soviet Union (1971): *Report to the President*. Washington, D.C.: U.S. Government Printing Office.

Stanley, T. W. and D. M. Whitt (1970): *Détente Diplomacy: United States and European Security in the 1970s*. New York: Praeger.

Stern, R. M. (ed.) (1987): *U.S. Trade Policies in a Changing World Economy*. Cambridge, Mass.: MIT Press.

U.S. Department of Commerce (1972): *U.S.-Soviet Commercial Agreements. Summaries and Supporting Papers*. Washington, D.C.

U.S. Government Committee on Foreign Affairs (1979): *U.S. Relations with the countries of Central and Eastern Europe*. A Report Prepared for the Subcommittee on Europe and the Middle East. Washington, D.C.

Wasowski, S. S. (1986): U.S. Sanctions against Poland. *Washington Quarterly* 2: 167–184.

Conference Participants

Professor Donald Avery
University of Western Ontario
Department of History
London / Canada

Petra Beckmann, Hamburg
Former research fellow of the John F. Kennedy-Institut für Nordamerika-studien

Professor David P. Calleo
Johns Hopkins University
School of Advanced International Studies
Washington D.C. / USA

Professor I. Mac Destler
Institute for International Economics
Washington D.C. / USA

Herbert Dittgen, Freiburg
Former research fellow of the John F. Kennedy-Institut für Nordamerika-studien

Andreas Fürst, Munich
Former research fellow of the John F. Kennedy-Institut für Nordamerika-studien

Professor Adam Gwiazda, Gdańsk, Poland
Former research fellow of the John F. Kennedy-Institut für Nordamerika-studien

Prof. Dr. Helga Haftendorn
Freie Universität Berlin
Institut für Internationale Politik und Regionalstudien

Prof. Dr. Carl-Ludwig Holtfrerich
Freie Universität Berlin
John F. Kennedy-Institut für Nordamerikastudien

Prof. Dr. Hanns-Dieter Jacobsen
Freie Universität Berlin
Fachbereich Politische Wissenschaft

Dr. Novak Janković, Beograd / Yugoslavia
Former research fellow of the John F. Kennedy-Institut für Nordamerikastudien

Dr. Helga Junkers
Stiftung Volkswagenwerk
Hannover

Prof. Dr. Michael Kreile
Universität Konstanz
Sozialwissenschaftliche Fakultät

Dr. Bernd Kubbig
Hessische Stiftung für Friedens- und Konfliktforschung
Frankfurt/M.

Prof. Dr. Werner Link
Universität Trier
Fachbereich III – Politikwissenschaften

Prof. Dr. Detlef Lorenz
Freie Universität Berlin
Institut für Volks- und Weltwirtschaft

Professor Rachel McCulloch
Brandeis University
Department of Economics
Waltham, Massachusetts / USA

Dr. Monika Medick-Krakau
Freie Universität Berlin
John F. Kennedy-Institut für Nordamerikastudien

Michael Minkenberg, Heidelberg
Former research fellow of the John F. Kennedy-Institut für Nordamerikastudien

Andreas Quint
Freie Universität Berlin
John F. Kennedy-Institut für Nordamerikastudien

Dr. Reinhard Rode
Hessische Stiftung für Friedens- und Konfliktforschung
Frankfurt/M.

Christoph Scherrer, Berlin
Former research fellow of the John F. Kennedy-Institut für Nordamerikastudien

Professor Malcolm Sylvers, Venice / Italy
Former research fellow of the John F. Kennedy-Institut für Nordamerikastudien

Professor Giuseppe Tattara
University of Venice
Department of Economics
Venice / Italy

Dr. Frank Unger
Freie Universität Berlin
John F. Kennedy-Institut für Nordamerikastudien

Volkert Wiesner, Hamburg
Former research fellow of the John F. Kennedy-Institut für Nordamerika-studien

Authors' Biographic Notes

Donald Avery is associate professor of history at the University of Western Ontario, London, Ontario, Canada. He has published extensively on the subject of Canadian immigration, ethnic and labour history including the book *'Dangerous Foreigners': European Immigrant Workers and Labour Radicalism in Canada* (Toronto: McClelland & Stewart, 1979). In recent years his scholarly activity has focused on the involvement of Canadian scientists in military related research, with particular emphasis on the period 1939 – 1960.

Petra Beckmann, born in 1957, studied political science and English and American literature at the University of Hamburg where she earned a degree in political science in 1983. Being a doctoral candidate at the Free University of Berlin since 1985, she became a Naumann fellow in 1986. She was a research fellow at the John F. Kennedy-Institute of the Free University of Berlin (1985) and a visiting scholar of the German Academic Exchange Service in Washington, D.C. (1986). She will complete her doctoral dissertation about New Right political action committees and the U.S. Senate in 1988/89.

David P. Calleo, born in Binghamton, New York, in 1934, received his undergraduate and doctoral degrees from Yale University. He has taught at Brown University and at Yale, and served, in 1967 – 68, as consultant to the U.S. Undersecretary of State for Political Affairs. In 1968 he joined the faculty at the Johns Hopkins University School of Advanced International Studies where he is professor and director of the European Studies Program. Mr. Calleo has written numerous books. The most recent are: *America and the World Political Economy*, with Benjamin Rowland, (1973), *The German Problem Reconsidered: Germany in the World System, 1870 to the Present*, (1978), *The Imperious Economy*, (1982), and *American Hegemony: The Future of the Western Alliance*, (1987). Among Mr. Calleo's recent articles are: "SDI, Europe, and the American Strategic Dilemma" in Robert W. Tucker, George Liska, Robert E. Osgood, and David P. Calleo, *SDI and U.S. Foreign Policy*; "Money and World Politics" with Susan Strange, in Susan Strange (ed.), *Paths to International Political Economy*; "American Domestic Politics and the Demands of Alliance", POLITICAL SCIENCE QUARTERLY, Spring 1983; "NATO's Middle Course", FOREIGN POLICY 69, Winter 1987 – 88; "The

Dollar and the Defense of the West" with Leonard Silk and Harold van B. Cleveland, FOREIGN AFFAIRS, Spring 1988.

I. M. Destler, born in 1939, is professor of public affairs at the University of Maryland and visiting fellow at the Institute for International Economics. His previous positions include senior fellow at the above Institute (1983–87), the Carnegie Endowment for International Peace (1977–83), and the Brookings Institution. He received his B.A. in 1961 from Harvard College and his Ph.D. in 1971 from the Woodrow Wilson School, Princeton University, and has taught at Princeton, the University of Nigeria, and the International University of Japan. Dr. Destler is author or co-author of eight books about U.S. foreign policymaking and U.S.-Japan relations, including *Our Own Worst Enemy: The Unmaking of American Foreign Policy*, and *American Trade Politics: System Under Stress*, which won the American Political Science Association's 1987 Gladys M. Kammerer Award for the best publication in the field of U.S. national policy.

Andreas Fürst, born in Augsburg in 1957, studied German and English literature, North American cultural history, economics, and political science in St. Louis, Mo. (M.A. 1980), Munich (M.A. 1985) and West Berlin. In 1986/87 he held a Congressional fellowship with Senator Carl Levin, and he is currently working on a doctoral dissertation on U.S. Congress and NATO-policy at the Free University, Berlin.

Adam Gwiazda, born in 1946, was educated at the University of Jagiellonian, Cracow and the Poznan School of Economics where in 1968 he received an M.A. in history and in 1974 a Ph.D. in economics. From 1973–78 he was a lecturer of political economy at the N. Copernicus University in Torun, and from 1978–1984 a senior lecturer of political economy at Gdańsk University. He was visiting lecturer at the Department of Political Economy, University of Aberdeen, in 1981 and at the Inter-University Centre of Postgraduate Studies in Dubrovnik. Since 1985 he is associate professor of economics at Gdańsk University and, since 1977, has engaged in research for the Polish Institute of International Affairs in Warsaw. His principal areas of interest are East-West economic relations and foreign economic policy of Western and Eastern countries. He has published two books (both in Polish): *International Economic Interdependence in the Contemporary World* (1982 and 1985) and *Problems of Contemporary Western Economics* (1987), and 80 articles in Polish, British, Dutch, American, and West German journals.

Helga Haftendorn is professor of political science at the Free University of Berlin and acting director of its Institute of International Relations. In the 1960s she was a research fellow of the Deutsche Gesellschaft für Auswärtige Politik in Bonn and in the 1970s a professor at the Armed Forces University in Hamburg. Dr. Haftendorn has published widely in the areas of foreign policy, international relations, and problems of security. Among her publications in English is *Security and Détente: Conflicting Priorities in German Foreign Policy* (Praeger, 1985).

Carl-Ludwig Holtfrerich, born in 1942, is professor of economics and economic history at the Department of Economics and at the John F. Kennedy-Institute of the Free University of Berlin. After having received his doctorate at the University of Münster in 1971, he worked for three years in business. He then taught at the Free University of Berlin (1974–80) and held a chair for economic history at the University of Frankfurt (1980–83). He was a visiting professor in Oxford in 1982 and has done research on issues in international financial and trade relations several times in the United States, especially in 1976/76 as a J. F. Kennedy Memorial fellow at Harvard University and in 1982/83 as a fellow of the W. Wilson International Center for Scholars in Washington, D.C. Among his publications are *The German Inflation 1914–1923. Causes and Effects in International Perspective* (Berlin/New York: de Gruyter, 1986) and (with H. O. Schötz) *Vom Weltgläubiger zum Weltschuldner: Erklärungsansätze zur historischen Entwicklung und Struktur der internationalen Vermögensposition der USA* (Frankfurt/M.: Knapp, 1988).

Hanns-D. Jacobsen, born in 1944, is professor for international relations at the Department of Political Science of the Free University of Berlin. From 1974 to 1987 he was a senior research fellow with the Stiftung Wissenschaft und Politik in Ebenhausen near Munich. In 1978/79 he was a German Kennedy fellow at Harvard University, and in 1984 he was a visiting fellow at the American Institute for Contemporary German Studies of the Johns Hopkins University and the Center for Strategic and International Studies of Georgetown University. In 1986 he was a fellow at the Woodrow Wilson International Center for Scholars in Washington, D.C. Dr. Jacobsen has published extensively on East-West and on transatlantic economic relations. His recent publications include *Economic Warfare or Detente* (Boulder and London: Westview Press, 1985), which he co-edited with Reinhard Rode, and *Ost-West-Wirtschaftsbeziehungen als deutsch-amerikanisches Problem* (Baden-Baden: Nomos Verlagsgesellschaft, 1986).

Novak Janković, born in Belgrade in 1951, received his university education at Belgrade University, Faculty of Economics, where he graduated in 1973 and obtained a Ph.D. in 1981 with a doctoral dissertation on theoretical welfare economics and international comparisons of economic wellbeing. Dr. Janković currently teaches political economy and comparative economic systems at the Department of Sociology, Belgrade University, and is also a part-time fellow at the Economic Institute, Belgrade. He has published on the

Yugoslav economic system and, lately, on the relevance of Post-Keynesian economic theory for socialist economies.

Rachel McCulloch is professor of international finance at Brandeis University and research associate of the National Bureau of Economic Research, Inc., Cambridge, Mass. A consultant and advisor to several government agencies and foundations, Dr. McCulloch is currently a member of the Technology Assessment Advisory Council of the Congressional Office of Technology Assessment, of the Advisory Committee of the Institute for International Economics, Washington, D.C., and of the Committee on International Relations Studies with the People's Republic of China. She was a member of the President's Commission on Industrial Competitiveness (Young Commission) and served as director of the American Economic Association Summer Program for Minority Students from 1981 until 1984. Born in Brooklyn, New York, in 1942, Dr. McCulloch was educated at the University of Pennsylvania (A.B., mathematics, 1962), the Massachusetts Institute of Technology, and the University of Chicago (M.A.T., mathematics, 1965; M.A., economics, 1971; Ph.D., economics, 1973). Prior to joining the Brandeis faculty in 1987, she taught at the Graduate School of Business of the University of Chicago, at Harvard University, and at the University of Wisconsin-Madison. She has also been a visiting scholar at the Board of Governors of the Federal Reserve System (1973), UCLA (1977), and the Hoover Institution (1984–5). Dr. McCulloch is author of numerous articles and monographs on international trade, investment, and technology transfer. Her recent publications include "Unexpected Real Consequences of Floating Exchange Rates," *Essays in International Economics No. 153* (Princeton, 1983), "Trade Deficits, Industrial Competitiveness and the Japanese," *California Management Review*, Winter 1985, and "U.S. Trade and the Dollar" (with J. David Richardson), in R. Baldwin and J. Richardson, eds., *Current U.S. Trade Policy: Analysis, Agenda, and Administration* (NBER, 1986).
Dr. McCulloch is married to Gary Chamberlain and has two children.

Michael Minkenberg, born in 1959, received his M.A. in American government from Georgetown University, Washington, D.C., in 1984. He has studied political science at the universities of Heidelberg, Freiburg, Bonn, and Cologne before leaving to Georgetown University with a Fulbright scholarship. He is a doctoral candidate at Heidelberg University, and his research interests include political culture and political parties as well as classical and modern political theory.

Christoph Scherrer, born in 1956, received degrees both in economics and in political science. He was a research fellow at the John F. Kennedy-Institute of the Free University of Berlin where he published two working papers on

"Mini-Mills – A new growth path for the U.S. steel industry?" and "The U.S. autoindustry: Can it adapt to global competition?". He is currently working on his doctoral dissertation about industrial restructuring in the United States at the University of Frankfurt.

Malcolm Sylvers, born in New York in 1941, studied at Brooklyn College and the University of Wisconsin. Presently associate professor of the history of the United States at the University of Venice, Italy, he previously taught at the University of Trieste, Italy, and in the California and Wisconsin State University systems. He has been a visiting scholar at the University of Warwick, England, a research fellow at the John F. Kennedy-Institute of the Free University of Berlin and at the Reuther Library at Wayne State University. In 1987 he was a fellow of the Salzburg Seminar on the U.S. constitution. He has published articles in various European and American journals primarily in the field of Marxism, U.S. labor and twentieth-century history. His book *Sinistra politica e movimento operaio negli Stati Uniti. Dal primo dopoguerra alla repressione liberal-maccartista* was published in 1984.

Volkert Wiesner, born in 1953, studied political science, journalism, and history at the University of Hamburg where he earned a degree in political science. In 1986 he was a research fellow at the John F. Kennedy-Institute of the Free University of Berlin. A political editor for the Hamburg weekly newspaper "Hamburger Rundschau", he is currently also a member of the research team "Non-commercial local radio stations" of the University of Hamburg where he is working on community radio experiences in Canada.

www.ingramcontent.com/pod-product-compliance
Lightning Source LLC
LaVergne TN
LVHW010550300926
849162LV00002B/292